PSYCHOLOGY OF ADJUSTMENT
An Applied Approach

Thomas L. Creer
Ohio University

Prentice Hall
Upper Saddle River, New Jersey 07458

Library of Congress Cataloging-in-Publication Data

Creer, Thomas L.
  Psychology of adjustment : an applied approach / Thomas L. Creer.
    p.   cm.
  Includes bibliographical references and index.
  ISBN 0-13-254863-1
   1. Adjustment (Psychology)   2. Adaptability (Psychology)   3. Self
-management (Psychology)   4. Change (Psychology)   I. Title.
BF335.C68   1997
155.24—dc20   96-1655
                                                              CIP

Dedicated to my wife, Pat

Acquisitions editor: Heidi Freund
Editor-in-chief: Peter Janzow
Editorial/ production supervision: Patty Sawyer (Pine Tree Composition)
Buyer: Tricia Kenny
Cover designer: Bruce Kenselaar

This book was set in 10/12 Bookman light by Pine Tree Composition, Inc.
and was printed and bound by R. R. Donnelley & Sons Company.
The cover was printed by Phoenix.

 © 1997 by Prentice-Hall, Inc.
Simon & Schuster/A Viacom Company
Upper Saddle River, New Jersey 07458

All rights reserved. No part of this book may be
reproduced, in any form or by any means,
without permission in writing from the publisher.

Printed in the United States of America
10 9 8 7 6 5 4 3 2 1

ISBN:0-13-254863-1

Prentice-Hall International (UK) Limited, *London*
Prentice-Hall of Australia Pty. Limited, *Sydney*
Prentice-Hall Canada, Inc., *Toronto*
Prentice-Hall Hispanoamericana, S.A., *Mexico*
Prentice-Hall of India Private Limited, *New Delhi*
Prentice-Hall of Japan, Inc., *Tokyo*
Simon & Schuster Asia Pte. Ltd., *Singapore*
Editora Prentice-Hall do Brasil, Ltda., *Rio de Janeiro*

CONTENTS

Preface   v
Acknowledgments   x

CHAPTER	1	Adjustment and Self-management	1
CHAPTER	2	Components of Self-management	9
CHAPTER	3	Additional Components of Self-management	18
CHAPTER	4	Selecting a Problem: Decision Making and Problem Solving	28
CHAPTER	5	Assessment and Behavior Change	36
CHAPTER	6	Behavioral Change Procedures	52
CHAPTER	7	Social Learning and Cognitive Procedures	60
CHAPTER	8	Maladaptive and Dysfunctional Thoughts	75
CHAPTER	9	Emotional Reactions	87
CHAPTER	10	Coping with Stress	101
CHAPTER	11	Time Management	113
CHAPTER	12	Effective Studying	122
CHAPTER	13	Health and Wellness	134
CHAPTER	14	Exercise	145
CHAPTER	15	Diet and Weight Control	161
CHAPTER	16	Tobacco Use	178
CHAPTER	17	Alcohol Abuse	189
CHAPTER	18	Sexual Behavior	198
CHAPTER	19	Sexual Violence	210
CHAPTER	20	Sexual Harrassment	220
CHAPTER	21	Shyness and Assertiveness	227
CHAPTER	22	Friends	237
CHAPTER	23	Dating	249
CHAPTER	24	Planning a Career	257
CHAPTER	25	Obtaining Employment	270

CHAPTER 26	The Workplace	278
CHAPTER 27	Changing Jobs	287
CHAPTER 28	Directing Others	295
CHAPTER 29	Marriage	304
CHAPTER 30	Raising Children	316
CHAPTER 31	Aging and Death	324
CHAPTER 32	Self-Efficacy	332
CHAPTER 33	Why Self-management Fails	337
CHAPTER 34	Relapse Prevention and Management	348
CHAPTER 35	Self-management Redux	356
	References	363
	Index	371

PREFACE

The preface in most textbooks consists of a few comments concerning the organization of the book, and acknowledgments to those who assisted in the book's preparation. This preface differs somewhat from this format. Rather than suggest how to use the book, it provides a brief history of the evolution of the text. The history recapitulates the increasing use of self-management techniques by people in their attempt to adjust to various aspects of their lives. It offers the context for considering the relevance of the techniques that are described, and provides the basis both for the use of the self-management skills for personal adjustment and for the current text. Four stages mark this evolution.

STAGE 1: THE CHILDREN'S ASTHMA RESEARCH INSTITUTE AND HOSPITAL

Three decades ago, a facility in Denver, the Children's Asthma Research Institute and Hospital (CARIH), later a division of the National Asthma Center, was considered the premier research and treatment facility for pediatric asthma in the world. Not only were a number of major scientific discoveries made at CARIH (most notably the isolation of IgE, the immunoglobulin that underlies allergic reactions), but the facility provided superb medical and behavioral treatment to any child with asthma who applied. Children from around the world could remain in residence for up to two years to learn how to control their asthma. Since all services were free—CARIH was sustained through voluntary contributions—the facility was, in the words of many people who look back upon CARIH, a Camelot for children with asthma and their families. It truly was a remarkable scientific and treatment center.

CARIH existed as a treatment and research facility for pediatric asthma for forty years. In the last decade of its existence, the 1970s, a change took place in the makeup of residents who came to CARIH. More and more children were admitted from minority groups in large urban areas. The population of residents at CARIH from a minority background rose from 7 percent to 31 percent over the course of a decade in which minority groups comprised 12.3 percent of the U.S. population (Creer,

Ipacs, and Creer, 1983). There were two major ramifications to this trend. First, it indicated that members of minority groups, particularly children living in urban areas, are more apt to experience asthma. This has since been reflected both in governmental surveys (e.g., Gergen and Weiss, 1990) and reports in the popular press (e.g., Nossiter, 1995). There are a number of reasons for this finding, but many center around the deterioration of the environment in urban America (e.g., Pope, Patterson, & Burge, 1993). The second ramification was that almost all the children would, after their discharge from CARIH, return to the same urban environment. As many came from homes with single, working parents and limited access to medical care, it was jointly decided by the behavioral and medical science staff to teach children self-management skills they could use to adjust to asthma-related problems and to help control their asthma.

A number of imaginative strategies emerged from this approach to the management of asthma; some, including making children solely responsible for control of their asthma medications, remain innovative twenty years after their introduction. In short, the children demonstrated they could acquire and perform self-management skills in order to adjust to most of the problems they face because of asthma (Creer, 1979).

STAGE 2: THE NATIONAL HEART, LUNG, AND BLOOD INSTITUTE

In 1977, the National Heart, Lung, and Blood Institute (NHLBI) announced a request for applications for proposals related to the self-management of childhood asthma. The NHLBI was prompted both by the large number of children with asthma and by the expense of the disorder. Approximately 15 million Americans have asthma; half of these patients are children. Asthma has been the number one cause of pediatric hospitalizations for a number of years (Reed, 1986); it is also responsible for more school absenteeism than any other chronic disease or disorder (Weiss, Gergen, & Hodgson, 1992). A program called Living with Asthma was developed based upon the research conducted at CARIH. Participation in the program resulted in significant changes in morbidity indices of asthma, including school absenteeism and health care costs (Creer et al., 1988). These findings were obtained despite the fact that CARIH merged with another facility in 1978 and literally disappeared in 1981 (the facility was bulldozed for a condo development). What was impressive was that at a five-year follow-up, many of the participants in Living with Asthma were performing the basic self-management skills they had acquired in asthma self-management to adjust to the problems they were facing as adolescents and young adults.

STAGE 3: UNDERGRADUATES AT OHIO UNIVERSITY

When CARIH closed, I moved on to Ohio University and assigned myself to teaching a course on the psychology of adjustment a year or so later. After teaching the course in the traditional manner for a quarter, it became apparent that learning self-management skills would be an effective way for students to adjust to and manage the variety of problems they encountered in college. Teaching self-management skills thus became the focus of the course. It has undergone considerable change and refinement over the past fourteen years, but the emphasis has always been on attaining two goals: teaching self-management skills and insuring that the skills are applied. The latter goal, easily the more difficult of the two, has involved close tracking of students as they attempted to apply self-management techniques to change a problem of their choice. The results of their efforts, illustrated by figures throughout the book, show that some students are successful at applying self-management techniques and others are not. This paints a realistic picture of the application of self-management to adjustment by college students.

STAGE 4: SELF-MANAGEMENT FOR ADULT ASTHMA

Concurrent with teaching college students to use self-management techniques, the NHLBI funded an award to develop and evaluate a self-management program for adult asthma. The study was unique in that the asthma of the patients was generally under good medical control at the outset of the study. Thus, for the first time, self-management and excellent medical care were not introduced into an asthma self-management study at the same time. The award resulted in conclusive evidence that adults with asthma could perform the self-management skills they were taught to help control their asthma. Findings showed significant long-term reduction in attack frequency, reduced medication use, improvement in cognitive measures, and increased use of self-management skills (Kotses et al., 1995). A cost-benefit analysis of the data by Taital, Kotses, Bernstein, Bernstein, and Creer (1995) showed that the performance of self-management by asthma patients in the study reduced their hospitalization costs from $18,488 to $1,538, and reduced income lost as a result of asthma from $11,593 to $4,589. The program was considered a success.

MODEL OF SELF-MANAGEMENT

The general model of self-management that emerged from the two threads of research is presented in this book (Creer and Holroyd, in press). It relies upon behavioral and cognitive-behavioral techniques used by both students and asthma patients. The model was based upon empirical findings by both authors. It should not be considered as cast in cement. Anyone using self-management skills should always feel free to change and adapt whatever techniques they are using to different problems and situations. This, after all, is the gist of self-management.

With respect to the structure of the book itself, chapters were written according to topics selected by students for change via self-management. Occasionally, a student will select budget management as a topic. Because the specific economic problems they chose are diverse—the most common is the goal of using long-distance telephone service less—no chapter was written specifically on this topic. The text did go through four separate editions of testing in the classroom. Wherever appropriate, feedback from the students was incorporated into the text. Other suggestions, such as where to put the chapter on self-efficacy and relapse prevention and management, were added as more experience was gained with application of self-management techniques. In addition, important concepts and techniques of self-management are repeated throughout the book. This was done in response to the reactions of both students and asthma patients.

A number of questions have been asked about self-management, including some excellent queries raised by reviewers of an earlier edition of the text. Following are some of these questions.

Does self-management work for everyone? No. A number of asthma patients ask to participate in asthma self-management when they are experiencing symptoms of asthma. When they become asymptomatic, they lose interest. Students are no different. Some students withdraw from a psychology of adjustment course when they find they will be required to conduct a self-management program on a problem of their choice; others drop out within the first few weeks of taking the course. The idea of attempting to change their behavior by themselves through self-management seems repugnant to many people, who apparently want someone to change their behavior for them. For many other asthma patients and students, however, self-management is the first opportunity they have had to take control of some aspect of their life. Nothing is more rewarding than having someone thank you for having taught them self-management skills twenty or twenty-five years earlier.

Do all people remain committed to a self-management program once they have designed and started to execute it? No. A number of students have praised the use of self-management skills in adjusting to the problems they encounter in college. They not only return, often years later, to explain their latest self-management project, but to suggest that the course be required for all college students (an idea that, fortunately, never goes beyond the author's office). To these people, self-management skills have been invaluable in their lives. However, this is a far cry from what often happens. Basically, self-management passes through three successive stages. *Stage 1 is the acquisition of knowledge about self-*

management skills. This is the easiest stage; almost anyone can learn how to help control a problem through self-management. *Stage 2 is the performance of the self-management skills.* Illustrations of self-management projects are liberally sprinkled throughout the book. Many of these reflect the success students attained in performing self-management. Other figures show that some students were not successful in achieving the goals they set for themselves. Nevertheless, they made more progress than students and patients who do not even attempt to use self-management skills. *Stage 3 is the maintenance of self-management performance.* This is by far the most difficult stage to attain. It is true that many asthma patients assert that they still use these skills to help manage their asthma years after they were taught self-management. There is no reason to doubt the veracity of their statements. Other individuals who use self-management are like those described by Schachter (1982), in that they use a variety of strategies for long-term change of addictive behaviors such as smoking and excessive eating. However, these individuals are more the exception than the rule. Research from a number of sources, including the work of Marlatt and Gordon (1980), Marlatt (1982), Kirschenbaum and Tomarken (1982), Kirschenbaum (1987), and Baumeister, Heatherton, and Tice (1994), described difficulties in attaining long-term maintenance of self-management. Based upon almost three decades of research, particularly with medical patients, the author concurs with the latter group: it is difficult to maintain gains and prevent relapse in many patients. The area is one in which more research must be conducted.

Can we trust everything an individual tells us about the results of self-management? Not unless you are exceedingly gullible. Even though it is their own problem they are trying to change, people do not always tell the truth. A major problem with a chronic physical disorder is the lack of compliance to a medical regimen (Haynes, Taylor, and Sackett, 1979). Yet a high proportion of patients with a chronic disorder refuse to reveal the truth about what they do to adhere to their treatment plans. This includes the body's rejection of kidneys by adolescents who, once they have waited for varying periods for a transplant, do not take the medications needed to prevent rejection of their new organ. Students are sometimes no better, although they don't necessarily have their lives riding on the outcome of their efforts. The only thing to say to a student reading these words is at least to be honest with himself or herself.

Finally, what about the future of self-management? Hopefully, it is very bright. There is no doubt that in an era of budgetary concerns, individuals are going to be asked to take more responsibility for their own behavior. This message is coming from all sides of the political spectrum. We certainly can't continue building more and more prisons to incarcerate those who break the law. Self-management is slowly moving toward the center of whatever managed health-care system evolves in the United States (Fries et al., 1993); it will just as surely be incorporated into other components of our social system.

Thomas L. Creer

ACKNOWLEDGMENTS

As noted, the book is based upon research conducted with asthma patients and students over the past three decades. With asthma, the results have been the development and dissemination of programs for children and adults currently used throughout the world to teach patients how to manage their condition. The basic self-management skills taught are the same as those described throughout the book. The students were those who have been taught self-management skills in the Psychology of Adjustment course taught at Ohio University over the past fourteen years. Data gathered from these students are presented throughout the text. Both students and asthma patients have not only demonstrated they can apply self-management skills in an appropriate manner, but they have used them to solve a wide range of problems. In many instances, their ideas and labor have been ingenious; in all instances, their efforts have been appreciated. They have served as inspirational teachers.

I would also like to thank the reviewers of the book, Thomas E. Billimek, San Antonio College; Juris G. Draguns, Pennsylvania State University; Mark N. Hatala, Northeast Missouri State University; Robert Hoff, Mercyhurst College; Gerard A. Jacobs, University of South Dakota; Richard Kandus, College of the Redwoods; Kenneth E. Lloyd, Central Washington University; Charles E. Majuri, Mount Hood Community College; and John O. Towler, Renison College. All of there comments were carefully considered. As much as possible, their advice was followed.

The text could not have been completed without the dedication of my coworker Kathleen Steiner. She not only developed all the graphs scattered throughout the book, but she applied her considerable talents on the computer in developing the manuscript. I am extremely indebted to Kathleen for her efforts; they go far beyond the call of duty. I am also indebted to Deirdre Levstek, who read and reread each chapter and whose comments greatly improved the final text. I would also like to thank Nicole Bryant, who, along with Deirdre, served as the co-instructor of several sections of the Psychology of Adjustment course at Ohio University. Their comments were extremely helpful.

I would be remiss if I did not thank people at Prentice-Hall who provided their considerable talents to improving the book. Heidi Freud served as the overall editor. Her comments and advice were greatly appreciated. Patty Sawyer from Pine Tree Composition was impeccable in her role as the production editor of the text. Finally, Bob Thoresen, the regional editor of Prentice-Hall, discovered an earlier version of the book and passed it along to his publisher. Without his contribution, the current text would not have seen the light of day.

CHAPTER 1

Adjustment and Self-Management

"There's only one corner of the universe you can be certain of improving, and that's your own self."
—Aldous Huxley, *Time Must Have a Stop*

"I don't know how Joan does it. She's always up on her classwork, she works part-time, and she still has time to go to movies and to do other things. She's just lucky."
—Joan's roommate, Lisa

Adjustment refers to the processes by which we change or cope with the demands and challenges of everyday life. Cognitive and emotional processes are involved in adjustment, but we rely upon behavioral changes and coping strategies in adapting to our environment. Behavior can be defined as anything we do or say. Synonyms of the term include action, activity, performance, reaction, responding, response, and skill. Behavior permits us to adjust to the ever-changing panorama of our lives. All of us had to adjust not only to the problems of childhood, but to adolescence and adulthood. We all have memories of what was required of us to move from home and adjust to college. To many, the transition from high school to college went smoothly; others may wish that they had done things differently.

Except for the extremes of age—when we are either very young or very old—we adjust to most situations through managing or regulating our own behavior. Parents and teachers direct much of our behavior when we are young, and, if we live long enough, much our action may be directed by personnel at a hospital or nursing home. The period between these extremes is when we have the opportunity to apply self-management skills. At an informal level, self-management is any action we perform by ourselves, whether getting dressed or eating a meal. You have used self-management to direct most of the behaviors you have already performed today. More formally, self-management refers to those processes, internal or transactional with the environment, that enable us to guide our activities over time and across settings. As pointed out by Karoly (1993), self-management involves regulation of thought, affect, behavior, or attention through our application of specific mechanisms and skills. We all use self-management procedures in almost everything we do. Sometimes we are successful; other times we are not. It doesn't take long for us to learn, however, that some people are more skillful than others at managing their lives. Like Joan, they demonstrate their skills at using self-management procedures.

The goal of this text is to teach you skills required to apply self-management procedures in a systematic manner to any problem you encounter. To do so, you will need to develop skills in self-management. These skills are enumerated in Table 1–1. As noted, a self-management skill is our ability to do something well. We all have skills we can perform; at the same time, there are skills we would like either to perform or to perform better. A skill is acquired through knowledge and honed through practice. Usually, a skill consists of a behavior that we adapt to fit a particular situation or event; this requires that we learn a wide array of specific skills to perform across an equally wide array of situations. There is a general skill—self-monitoring—that we can apply across a variety of situations. The goals of self-management are defined in terms of specific behaviors in specific situations. This usually requires that we either stop or start behaving in particular ways. Ultimately, we hope to learn to master self-management skills so that we can use them in any setting.

A term related to skill is competency. As described by Mischel (1986): "The concept of 'competencies' refers to the individual's abilities to transform and use information actively and to create thoughts and actions (as in problem-solving), rather than to store static cognitions and responses that one 'has' in some mechanical storehouse. Each individual acquires the capacity to actively construct a multitude of potential behaviors with the knowledge and skills available to him or her. Great differences between persons exist in the range and quality of the cognitive and

TABLE 1–1 Self-Management Skills

A self-management skill is the ability to do something well. It is developed through knowledge and practice. Following are particular aspects of self-management skills.

1. A skill is a behavior that we adapt to fit a particular event or situation.
2. We often do not learn general skills that can be applied across a wide range of situations, but specific skills that apply to specific tasks. Examples might be the skills that are required either for studying or taking examinations. However, there is a general self-management skill—self-monitoring—that we can apply across situations.
3. Since self-management is comprised of a number of skills, we must think about both the behaviors we need to perform and the situations where we need to perform them. Successfully passing an essay examination, for example, is a specific situation that requires a specific set of behavioral skills.
4. Goals for self-management are defined in terms of specific behaviors in specific situations. Sometimes, our goal is to stop behaving in a particular way; sometimes our goal is to start behaving in a particular way.
5. An aim in performing self-management skills is to master them. When we can perform these skills in a variety of settings, we have achieved mastery criteria for self-management.

behavioral patterns that they can generate. That becomes obvious from even casual comparisons of the different competencies, for example, of a professional weight lifter, a chemist, a retardate, an opera star, or a convicted forger" (p. 308). By the time you complete this text, you should be well versed in being able to perform specific self-management skills. You should also be able to use and transform the knowledge you have acquired about these skills to better regulate your behavior. These competencies will be unique to you in permitting you to solve the problems you face.

IMPORTANCE OF SELF-MANAGEMENT

Table 1-2 enumerates reasons why self-management skills are important. Several of these reasons were adapted from suggestions by Fred Kanfer, a pioneer in self-management, and Bruce Schefft (1988).

1. *Only you know all the behaviors you can perform.* While others can perform particular behaviors, only you know the behaviors you can perform in a given situation. In addition, you are the only one with knowledge that you actually performed a given behavior. Thus, while you can tell a professor that you don't know how you could have done poorly on an examination (a comment he or she may believe), you are the only one who knows that you did not study but blew off the night before the examination by going to a movie.

2. *Only you know what and when you should perform in a given way.* In any given situation, only you know what actions you should take. Many of you have driven a car for several years. You generally know what the posted speed limits are on a given stretch of highway. It thus becomes your decision as to whether you want to abide by whatever speed limit is posted.

3. *Only you can reward the behaviors you perform.* It is nice to receive rewards from others, such as a paycheck or a high grade on an

TABLE 1-2 Reasons for Using Self-Management Techniques

1. Only you know all the behaviors you can perform.
2. Only you know what and when you should perform in a given way.
3. Only you can reward many of the behaviors you perform.
4. You are more motivated when you perceive that you have some personal control over a situation.
5. You are more apt to comply to a change plan that you have helped develop.
6. Pursuing and attaining the goals you set acts as a strong source of motivation.
7. Self-attributions following self-management reinforce your independent actions.
8. Self-management is ethically and socially valued more than passive approaches.
9. Self-management facilitates generalization.
10. Only you can control your own behaviors and achieve self-selected goals.

exam. These are referred to as *extrinsic reinforcers*. We are motivated to perform given tasks in order to obtain such reinforcers, although we may not enjoy the tasks themselves. Intrinsic reinforcers also guide and maintain our behavior. These reinforcers are inherent in the tasks we perform. Intrinsic reinforcers that motivate our behavior include curiosity, challenge, and the pleasure of performing a task. Intrinsic reinforcement not only encourages us to perform in specific ways, but it often maintains our behavior during periods that transpire between external rewards.

4. *You are more motivated when you perceive that you have some control over a situation.* You may be asked to design and conduct a self-management project to change a behavior. Your participation in setting goals for yourself makes them attractive, and leads to a greater investment of energy and effort on your part (Kanfer and Schefft, 1988).

5. *You are more apt to comply to a change plan that you have helped develop.* Changing some behaviors is not always an easy task; think of trying to lose weight or to quit smoking. If you have developed the change plan, however, you are generally more adherent to the stipulations of the proposal than would be the case if the plan was imposed upon you.

6. *Pursuing and attaining goals you set acts as a source of motivation.* When you believe that you are in the driver's seat with respect to setting goals, you generally are more motivated to attempt to achieve the goals.

7. *Self-attributions following self-management reinforce your independent actions.* Kanfer and Schefft (1988) point out that whenever you perceive yourself as the source of behavioral change, this increases your self-confidence. Greater self-confidence, in turn, leads to greater risk taking and willingness to act autonomously.

8. *Self-management is ethically and socially valued more than passive approaches.* We are often hesitant to surrender control over our behavior to someone else. When we are asked to do so, we may question the motives of the others, as well as question the value of such action. For this reason, we view self-management as more ethical; from a social perspective, we also perceive it as more valued.

9. *Self-management facilitates generalization.* Generalization is the occurrence of the same behavior across settings or over time. When you successfully control some aspect of your behavior in one environment, such as at college, you become more likely to control the same behavior in another environment, such as at work. Being able to perform this same behavior (such as eating less) across settings can be a significant outcome of successful self-management.

10. *Only you can control your own behaviors and achieve self-selected goals.* When it comes down to it, we decide what we are going to do from the moment we awaken in the morning until we go to sleep at night. How well you accomplish the daily goals you set is determined, to a great extent, by your own decisions and behavior. Systematic application

TABLE 1-3 Examples of Behavioral Deficits or Excesses That Have Been Changed

Behavioral Deficits	Behavioral Excesses
Poor study habits	Being overweight
Lack of assertiveness	Smoking cigarettes
Poor time management	Substance abuse (e.g., alcohol)
Poor eating habits	Use of bad language
Lack of exercise	Negative thoughts
Lack of public speaking skills	Jealousy
Lack of appropriate social skills	Overuse of caffeine
Inability to relax	Procrastination
Lack of positive thoughts	Too much stress
	Test anxiety
	Poor budget management

of self-management skills can enhance your daily performance in any setting.

EXAMPLES OF SELF-MANAGEMENT PROJECTS

There may be a number of behaviors that you may wish to change. These usually fall into two categories: *behavioral deficits* and *behavioral excesses*. Behavioral deficits are characterized by too little of a given behavior being performed in a given situation. Examples might be lack of physical exercise or work skills. Behavioral excesses, on the other hand, are too much of a given behavior in a given situation. Examples might include anxiety or smoking cigarettes. Illustrations of behavioral deficits and excesses selected for change by students who have previously taken the course are listed in Table 1-3. It must be emphasized that these are merely illustrations. Only you can decide what behavior you think is important for you to change. This decision, in the long run, becomes an ultimate test of self-management.

LIMITATIONS OF SELF-MANAGEMENT

There are boundaries that dictate how successful you may be in applying self-management techniques. Several were suggested by Ford (1987).

Organismic Boundaries

We have certain genetic characteristics that, through interaction with environmental factors, create the basic matrix of capabilities we each possess. These conditions may constrain, although they do not necessarily determine, the success of self-management procedures (Ford, 1987). For example, despite your best efforts, you may find that you lack the ability to become an engineer. You simply lack the potential for learning engineering skills. Or, to take a more extreme example, you may find that although you are a very competent basketball player, you lack the physical talent to do all the things with a basketball that Michael Jordan can do. No matter their prowess in the game, all players eventually encounter organismic boundaries in trying to imitate Michael Jordan.

Environmental Boundaries

Self-management procedures may be constrained or facilitated by the kind and the organization of environmental conditions within which we live. As Ford (1987) noted, the environment provides and limits options for each of us. As will be described in Chapter 2, the context within which behavior occurs may interact with and change our behavior. In addition, there are events over which we simply have no control. For example, while we may make every attempt to promote our health and prevent disease, we all lack the ability to prevent occasional infections such as common colds.

Selective Action

It is impossible to deal simultaneously with all the conditions within and around us. Therefore, we are able to attend to only the conditions that we perceive are relevant to what we are trying to do and how we are trying to do it (Ford, 1987). *Situation specificity* indicates that the resolution of specific problems or situations require certain behaviors. However, these behaviors may not be in our behavioral repertoires. For example, while you may be able to answer a question adequately in class, would you be able to engage in conversation if you were on a televised network talk program? To be competent in the latter situation may require that you develop and refine conversational skills.

Individual Differences

Differences exist among people from the moment life begins; these individual differences continue to evolve throughout life. Individual differences are not fixed, but are dynamic patterns that themselves vary and change (Ford, 1987). This is of importance in self-management. The aim for you is to maximize your own abilities in performing a given task in a particular context.

Performance Variability

We rarely behave exactly the same way twice, even in similar circumstances. At any moment, however, all the performance possibilities of which we each are capable is in our behavioral repertoire (Ford, 1987). Each of you will acquire self-management skills. Performance variability will be exhibited in how you later perform these skills in given situations. However, you can enhance your ability to perform self-management techniques: (a) by increasing the performance of these procedures; (b) by obtaining similar results through a broader range of self-management skills; and (c) by using the same skills in different circumstances to produce different results. If self-management techniques prove useful in improving your grades, for example, they might be applied to enhance your ability to speak in public or to manage your time more efficiently.

Unpredictability of Behavior

Behavior is highly complex. As a result, we may or may not be able to predict the results of our performance. We can often predict how we will behave on any given day. In the morning, unless we are ill or incapacitated, we are likely to predict that we will arise and start another day. Our prediction is likely to be fulfilled. However, we are often unable to predict many of the major events that occur in life. It is difficult, if not impossible, to predict major events, such as whom we will marry, where we will live, how successful we will be, or how long we will live. We simply lack the knowledge to make precise predictions regarding most significant events that occur over the course of a lifetime. For example, a couple may marry after knowing each other a day, a student may pick a major because he liked the professor in the first course he took in college, or a college graduate may accept her first job offer without considering other options.

We may quickly make such decisions and then exhilarate in or suffer the consequences. The irony is that there are so many small and irrelevant events—such as becoming angry at a roommate or remaining attached to a romantic relationship after it is over—that occupy our time and thoughts. We accumulate an increasingly large satchel of what we perceive as the bad decisions we have made in our lives. Many times we say, "What if . . ." or "If I had only . . ." The weight of the baggage dictates what we do with our lives, as well as how much joy and happiness we experience.

It is imperative that we concentrate on the probabilistic nature of behavior and the consequences that are apt to result from behaving in a certain way. If you perform in a certain manner, a particular outcome is likely, but not certain, to occur. Studying for an examination is apt to result in a passing grade. However, there is always a degree of uncertainty because you may be asked questions on material that you did not review or may have forgotten. All you can do is hope that the scores on the tests you studied for and those you did not study for balance out according to some sort of probability equation.

SUMMARY

Adjustment requires that we change or cope with the challenges and demands of everyday life. Arguments were made for the development and application of self-management skills by each of you, to enable you to adjust most effectively to events as they occur. These behaviors—specific behaviors that you can perform in specific situations—will be acquired in the course of the class. Once you have acquired them, they can be strengthened through their performance throughout the remainder of your life.

EXERCISE

In the space below, list potential behavioral deficits or excesses that you would like to change. Eventually, you might use these lists in deciding the exact behavior you want to change while taking the course.

Potential Behavioral Deficits
Potential Behavioral Excesses

REVIEW TERMS

Adjustment
Behavior
Competency

Intrinsic reinforcement
Self-management

QUESTIONS

List ten reasons why self-management skills are important.
Discuss six limitations to self-management.

CHAPTER 2

Components of Self-Management

"He is most powerful who has power over himself."
—Seneca, *Epistulai ad Lucilium*

"It's not that I'm lucky or anything like that. At the beginning of each term, I sit down and set my goals. I attempt to set up a schedule that will help me attain these goals. Occasionally, I review my progress. I decide if I need to do something different, like study more for one course than another. This way, I control my study time as much as I can."

—Joan

Joan's life did not naturally evolve in an orderly manner; unless there are severe restraints upon our behavior, as may exist in a totalitarian society, no one's life is naturally arranged. We all face a certain amount of ambiguity and chaos in daily living. In addition, as described in Chapter 1, there are limitations that determine our ability to regulate our behavior. We attempt to impose a pattern upon our lives that will permit us to survive and, hopefully, develop according to the demands we face daily. Joan made a conscious effort to create order in her life. Based upon her knowledge of how she had managed her past actions, she established a pattern that permitted her to manage her studies effectively.

If we analyze how we regulate our behavior, we will discover that there are several components to successful self-management. A model of self-management is depicted in Figure 2–1. The model serves as the structure for the book; for this reason, you may wish occasionally to review Chapters 2 and 3. The components of the model form an empirically based framework that can benefit anyone who wants to regulate his or her behavior in an effective and efficient manner. The model offers several advantages over other paradigms proposed for self-management in that it (a) permits a refined analysis of behavior; (b) is anchored by the self-monitoring of behavior; (c) acknowledges the interactive role played by context in dictating the behaviors we perform; (d) ties self-management to current approaches to decision-making; and (e) allows you to tailor a self-management program precisely to fit your individual goals.

The model depicted in Figure 2–1 has six components: (a) goal selection, (b) information collection, (c) information processing and evaluation,

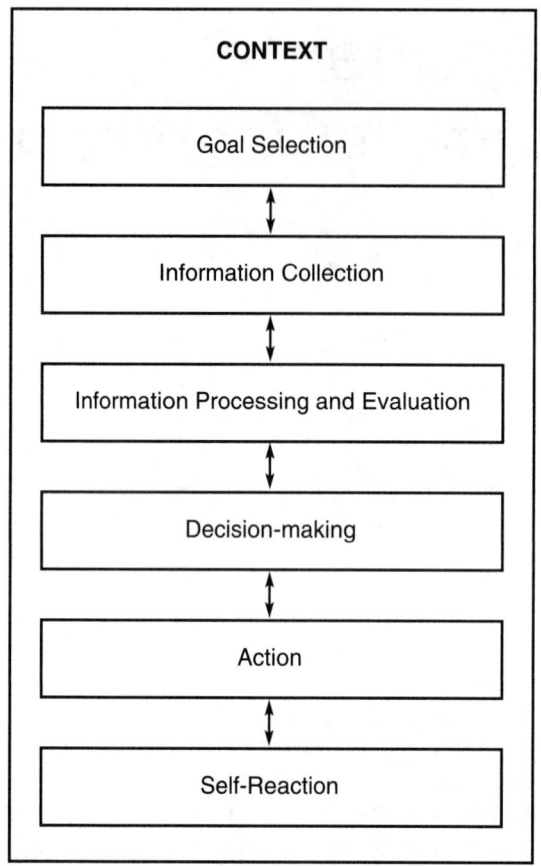

FIGURE 2–1
A model of self-management.

(d) decision making, (e) action, and (f) self-reaction. Three components—goal selection, information collection, and information processing and evaluation—will be discussed in this chapter. The remaining components—decision making, action, and self-reaction—will be the focus of Chapter 3. There is constant interaction among the components. Based upon self-reaction, for example, we may decide that we need to select different goals to pursue. All components are, however, embedded within context.

CONTEXT

Context refers to the setting where a particular behavior or set of behaviors occurs. It includes the environment or setting, prior events, and accompanying events. Context influences how specific variables affect our behavior at any moment in time (Sulzer-Azaroff and Mayer, 1991). Consider how you behave at home versus at school. At home, your behavior is governed in large part by discriminative stimuli in your environment, and by your experiences and expectations of how you should behave. When around friends in a dorm or apartment, you likely behave in a different manner. The *discriminative stimuli* that compose this context prompt different behaviors. (Stimuli reliably present when a response has been reinforced are called discriminative stimuli.) When subsequently present, discriminative stimuli signal that a response will probably have a favorable outcome. The presence or absence of discriminative stimuli systematically alters the probability of your responding (Sulzer-Azaroll and Mayer, 1991). An example of a discriminative stimulus is the starter's pistol in a race. When you hear it fire, it is a signal for you to start running immediately.

Context interacts with all the behaviors we perform. Against this backdrop, the other components of self-management can be described. Before doing so, however, three types of contextual variables will be described: setting events, establishing operations, and establishing stimulus.

Setting Events

Setting events are stimuli or contexts that can exert general control over your behavior. They may alter the discriminative stimuli that govern your performance. If you wish to study, for example, a number of stimuli—including a desk, a good light, and a low level of noise—may become discriminative stimuli that promote study behaviors. If there are a number of friends in the room making a lot of noise, these setting events fail to promote your ability to study. When your friends leave, the discriminative stimuli will again serve to prompt studying behaviors.

Establishing Operations

Establishing operations are specific events that can influence the reinforcing or punishing function of both the stimulus and the behavior that leads to it. Sulzer-Azaroff and Mayer (1991) offer the illustration of establishing operations where a person is invited to dinner. The person declines, which is very much out of his character. Why? Because the individual had just indulged himself in an ice cream sundae, and food was not reinforcing to him at that moment. Or perhaps you would like to go to a movie tonight, but your instructor informed you that you will have a test covering this chapter tomorrow. Rather than go to the movie and face the prospect of a failing grade, studying the text has acquired reinforcing value. Establishing operations resemble events often labeled as drives or motivational variables.

Establishing Stimulus

An establishing stimulus is a stimulus that is paired with an establishing operation. The response or stimulus change it evokes becomes a conditioned stimulus for that operation. In essence, an establishing stimulus cues or prompts the occurrence of an establishing operation. Establishing stimuli familiar to you are your textbooks. You cannot study if they are misplaced or unavailable. In these situations, you may find yourself seeking the books in order to study. Looking for the textbooks becomes an establishing operation.

COMPONENTS OF SELF-MANAGEMENT

Goal Selection

The initial step in changing behavior—goal selection—is one of the most important. It can be one of the more difficult steps in that we are not always certain of what we want to change. We may feel that we want to do something, such as improve our grades, but we do not know whether achieving this goal requires better time management, improved study habits, a change in majors, or a combination of actions. Or we may lack the skills required to change our problem. We may, for example, lack the skills required to perform well on either essay or multiple-choice examinations. Goal selection becomes difficult when we have to cooperate with someone to set goals jointly. If your doctor advises you to lose weight or to take medications to control hypertension, you have to arrive at a goal that both of you agree you should pursue. In these cases, goal setting may involve considerable give-and-take on the part of both you and your doctor.

Selecting a goal entails that you think about behavior change, analyze contingencies of behavior, and attend to specific aspects of behavior.

THINK BEHAVIOR CHANGE   In their book, Kanfer and Schefft (1988) offered six think rules that can help you select an appropriate goal:

1. Think behavior. This rule suggests that you consider both potential problems and how, through your actions, they can be resolved. Since you may spend considerable time and effort in altering a behavior or set of behaviors, you should give careful consideration to this facet of self-management.

2. Think solution. This think rule suggests that you consider a number of potential solutions to your problem before selecting the approach that seems most appropriate for you. More on the processes involved in selecting a solution for a problem will be presented in Chapter 4.

3. Think positive. This rule serves not only to remind you of your goals, but to develop positive ways of thinking in order to achieve the aims and goals you have established.

4. Think small steps. Breaking a problem down into components permits you to consider steps required to alter the problem. This process will help you resolve a problem by achieving a series of small steps rather than one large step that may not be attained.

5. Think flexible. With any change plan, it pays to be flexible. The plan you initially develop may not change the behavior problem to the extent you wish. When this occurs, you must alter the plan in order to attain your goal.

6. Think future. You do not want to develop and implement a change program if you do not believe it will be successful. Nevertheless, in changing any behavior, you should not become discouraged at what you perceive as a lack of progress. For this reason, focus on the future and the goals you have set for yourself.

ANALYZE CONTINGENCIES OF BEHAVIOR   Sulzer-Azaroff and Mayer (1991) describe what is referred to as a four-way contingency. This concerns the interaction between antecedents, behaviors, consequences, and contexts. When establishing goals, it is worthwhile to analyze your behavior in terms of a four-way contingency. By doing so, you can conduct a more refined analysis of what you believe to be a behavior problem; at the same time, you are likely to generate potentially better solutions for changing the behavior. Questions you may ask yourself about each of the four components include the following:

1. Antecedents. What are the antecedents to your behavior? Can you identify them? If identified, can they be changed or modified? Are new antecedents required in order for behavioral change to occur?

2. Behaviors. What actions are required for you to change a problem behavior? Do you know what skills are necessary for modifying the problem? Can you perform these skills?

3. Consequences. What consequences do you anticipate will occur because of your actions? Are these realistic outcomes for you to expect? Can you deal with any distress produced if you do not achieve your goals? Can you maintain behavioral change?

4. Contexts. Where do you want a behavior to occur? Do you want to perform skills in a particular context or in different contexts? How will context influence the performance of any necessary skills? Questions regarding antecedents, behaviors, consequences, and contexts are important to consider before selecting behavioral goals.

ATTEND TO SPECIFIC INFORMATION   Nothing is more complicated than the stream of behavior each of us performs. We are engaged in enacting some type of behavior from the moment we are born until the moment we die. Considering the constant stream of behavior that comprises each of our lives, it becomes important that we attend only to specific information. This becomes particularly relevant in establishing behavioral goals. Three suggestions for being competent in establishing goals include arriving at a precise definition of behavior, determining response competition, and calculating response effort.

1. Precisely define behavior. When selecting a behavioral goal, you need to be as precise as you can in defining exactly what it is that you want to change. If you say that you want to be more socially active, what does this mean? Does it mean that you want to increase the interactions you have with your roommates or to date more frequently? You need to be as specific as you can in defining the goal you want to pursue.

2. Response competition. When selecting a behavioral goal, it is important that you select a behavior that has little competition with other behaviors. It would be hard to study consistently, for example, if you study while at work or while in an environment where there are constant interruptions. Avoiding response competition can eliminate these potential problems.

3. Response effort. It is easier to perform responses if they require little effort on your part. If you decide to increase your exercise, it is helpful to do so by attempting to fit the activity within the time frame of your daily life. For example, you may wish to exercise in the morning before classes or in the afternoon after your last class. Whenever dramatic changes are required in your life-style, you are apt to be less successful in both initiating and maintaining a self-management program.

POSITIVE CONSEQUENCES OF GOAL SELECTION There are three positive consequences of goal selection (Ford, 1987; Karoly, 1993). First, goal selection permits you to establish preferences about what you think is a desirable outcome. In self-management, goal selection permits you to set the goals you want to pursue. Second, goal selection enhances your commitment to perform goal-relevant self-management skills. You will be more motivated to reach goals that you have set for yourself. Finally, goal selection establishes expectancies on your part that trigger and maintain your effort and performance. Ideally, success at selecting and pursuing the goals you set will enhance both your commitment and performance.

Information Collection

Self-management data is gathered via *self-monitoring*, which is the systematic observation and recording of behaviors that you target for change (Kanfer, 1972). There are two components of self-monitoring: self-observation and self-recording.

SELF-OBSERVATION This process involves your attending to specific aspects of your behavior. Self-observation can provide both the best and worst of information. If you carefully observe yourself, you are likely to discover that you engage in some behaviors more or less often than you thought. In these cases, the data you observe about yourself are accurate and useful to you. If you do not pay close attention to your behavior or you do so in a haphazard manner, any information you gather is not only inaccurate, but it may lead you to make erroneous conclusions about yourself.

SELF-RECORDING   This term refers to the act of recording observations about yourself. If you are going to record accurate information about yourself, you should record data shortly after it occurs. Recording information on a daily basis is useful for most behaviors; if you are observing behaviors that occur more frequently, you will need to record information several times throughout the day. Use of a diary and graph is recommended as a way to obtain accurate information on yourself.

The significance of self-monitoring in self-management cannot be overemphasized. It is necessary for self-management, although, in and of itself, it is insufficient for self-management to occur. No matter the model of self-management that is used, self-monitoring must be sustained to maintain effective self-management and to avoid self-regulatory failure (Kirschenbaum, 1987).

Information Processing and Evaluation

When you are involved in self-management, you are constantly gathering information about yourself. Much of the information may be private in that it is known only to you (e.g., negative thoughts); other information may be public in that it can be observed by others (e.g., smoking). Only you can monitor, process, and evaluate private information about yourself; with behaviors that are public, you may recruit someone to help you observe and record data on your behavior.

There are five distinct steps involved in information processing and evaluation (Creer and Holroyd, in press):

1. Detect changes. You must be able to detect any significant changes that occur in the information you observe, record, and process about yourself. This may not be difficult when you are using an objective measure, such as a scale to weigh yourself. The task becomes more difficult, however, when you are asked to monitor other aspects of your behavior, such as the number of negative thoughts you have. Vigilant self-monitoring is the only way you obtain the information required to detect changes that may occur in your behavior.

2. Establish standards. There are a number of commonly accepted public standards against which you can compare some behaviors. An example is the comparison you can make of your grade to the grades of other class members. With other behaviors, however, you need to develop a standard that is appropriate to you. If you are attempting to increase your exercise or to decrease the number of negative thoughts you have, you need to establish criteria against which you can compare your daily performance. This often occurs after you have monitored your behavior for a period and can use your recorded performance as a standard.

3. Evaluate and make judgments. Making judgments about your performance is not difficult when you have an objective criterion; it is easy to see if your weight has changed or your grades have improved. Matching your behavior to a standard is more difficult in the case of private events because you must acquire and refine your skills at matching your responses to what, at the outset of your performance, may be ambiguous and fuzzy standards.

4. Evaluate changes according to antecedents, behaviors, and consequences. In evaluating changes that may occur in your target behavior, you should consider the antecedent conditions that may have produced the change, the action you took to alter the change, if needed, and the consequences of your action. An analysis of change in terms of antecedents, action, and consequences will permit you to develop and refine decision-making skills.

5. Consider context. Because constant interaction occurs between contextual variables and behavior, you must consider how these factors could have generated a change in your responses. You may wish to consider the role of setting events, establishing stimuli, and establishing operations in altering your performance.

EXERCISE

This chapter introduced six components of self-management. In particular, three components—goal selection, information collection, and information processing—were discussed. In considering the behavior you select to change, consider the problem from the following perspectives:

What is the goal of my program?
What information do I wish to collect?
How will I process and evaluate this information?

REVIEW TERMS

Context
Discriminative stimuli
Establishing operations

Establishing stimuli
Self-monitoring
Setting events

QUESTIONS

Discuss the six components of self-management.
Discuss six think rules.
Discuss a four-way contingency.
Discuss five steps involved in information processing and evaluation.

Additional Components of Self-Management

CHAPTER 3

> "He had two lives; one obvious, which everyone could see and know, if they were sufficiently interested, a life full of conventional truth and conventional fraud, exactly like the lives of his friends and acquaintances; and another, which moved underground."
> —Anton Chekhov, *The Lady with the Toy Dog*

> "I don't do a bad job of setting personal goals and gathering data on myself. In fact, I think I'm pretty good. My problem is that I don't always make the best decision or do what's best according to what I know."
> —Jack

Chapter 2 introduced a self-management model consisting of six components. A description of three components—goal selection, information collection, and information processing and evaluation—served as the basis of discussion. If you select a goal, you must then learn to collect, process, and evaluate information relevant to your established aims. Depending upon your goal, the process may or may not be difficult. You set goals, and collect, process, and evaluate information on yourself each day. You had an aim in deciding which clothes you were going to wear today. The fact that you are reading these words suggests that you also have aims with respect to reading and processing information presented in the text.

The question to be answered in Chapter 3 is: How can I best use the information I have gathered, processed, and evaluated with respect to my goals? This requires your applying the remaining components of self-management—decision making, action, and self-reaction.

DECISION MAKING

Depending upon the information you process, you must make certain decisions. As will be described in Chapter 3, a number of variables are included in this process, including your knowledge, experience, and the context within which you make a decision. Decision making is a dynamic process where alternative solutions can be generated and tested. Different solutions may be required according to whether there are changes in the goal of a program, the settings where it is applied, or failure of the program to obtain its aims.

ACTION

Action entails the performance of self-management skills to change your behavior. There are a number of aspects of action: contingencies, antecedents, behavior, self-instruction, and consequences.

Contingencies

Contingencies are relations between responses and the events that precede or accompany them—their antecedents—and the events that follow them—their consequences. Contingencies can either occur naturally or as a result of self-management. If you consistently overeat and fail to exercise, you may gain weight. This would be a natural contingency. You may intentionally manage contingencies by presenting, withdrawing, or withholding stimuli to affect your behavior (Sulzer-Azaroff and Mayer, 1991). Using weight as an example, you may intentionally set about to reduce your weight by eating lesser amounts of foods that have fewer calories.

Antecedents

An antecedent is a stimulus that precedes or accompanies a given behavior. Antecedents set the stage for your behavior in that they convey to you the probability that a given behavior will lead to a particular consequence. Some antecedent stimuli, such as discriminative stimuli, are particularly significant because they control your responses. Stimulus control is the systematic influence of an antecedent stimulus or set of stimuli on the probability of the occurrence of a response. When stimulus control is complete, there is a high probability of behaviors occurring (or not occurring) in the presence of a particular antecedent stimulus or response, and a very low (or higher) probability of behaviors occurring in their absence (Sulzer-Azaroff and Mayer, 1991). We are all familiar with discriminative stimuli. The sound of an alarm clock and the sight of a red traffic light are discriminative stimuli. When the alarm sounds, there is a strong likelihood that you will arise and begin your day; at the sight of a red light, there is a strong likelihood that you will stop. You rely on other drivers stopping when their signal turns red and your signal turns green.

    Stimuli or responses can serve as discriminative stimuli in a number of different ways in that they may (a) *increase* a given behavior; (b) *teach* you new skills and knowledge; (c) *maintain* your behavior; (d) *generalize or extend* certain of your behaviors from one setting to another; (e) *restrict or narrow* the conditions which a particular behavior occurs; or (f) *reduce* a given behavior. In self-management, you can design a program to help produce any of these functions of discriminative stimuli. Antecedents that control your behavior can be established through a number of procedures, including (a) identifying stimuli or events that serve as antecedents; (b) modifying stimulus control; and (c) arranging new antecedents for behavioral control. Procedures suggested by Watson and Tharp (1993) are enumerated in Table 3–1.

IDENTIFY ANTECEDENTS   An initial step in behavioral change is to determine what stimuli or responses control your behavior. Three problems may occur if you lack this information (Watson and Tharp, 1993). First, you may not know the precise problem you should observe and record. Not only can this flaw result in your attempting to change the wrong behavior, but it can lead to your experiencing unwanted emotional reactions. Second, if you cannot identify the antecedents that control your behavior, it may prove difficult to determine how to change a problem behavior. You may alter the wrong stimuli. Third, if you cannot identify what antecedents control your behavior, you cannot use self-statements appropriately.

Discover self-statements. There are two types of self-statements: self-instruction and beliefs.

1. Self-instruction. Self-statements constantly guide and maintain our behavior. You are always talking yourself through the many events and interactions you experience each day. For this reason, you need to determine what self-statements serve as antecedent stimuli that control your behavior.

TABLE 3–1   Self-Management Skills (adapted from Watson and Tharp, 1993)

Identify Antecedents
    Discover self-statements
        Self-instruction
        Beliefs

Modify Antecedents
    Avoid antecedents
    Narrow antecedent control
    Reperceive antecedents
    Change chains
    Build in pauses
    Unlink behavioral chains

Arrange New Antecedents
    Initiate positive self-instruction
    Eliminate negative self-instruction
    Thought stopping
    Change the physical and social environment
    Stimulus generalization
    Precommitment and programming of the social environment

2. Beliefs. The role of beliefs as antecedent stimuli may be more difficult to discover. Inaccurate or false beliefs may control much of our behavior. For this reason, you should carefully and systematically analyze any of your belief systems that may serve as antecedent stimuli that influence your behavior.

Finally, a problem we face is that we often confuse stimuli that cause responses and those that are correlated with responses. If you are thirsty and drink a glass of water, it will likely quench your thirst. In this case, you would be correct in believing that drinking water caused a reduction of your thirst. If you experience stress, you may blame it on an impending test. You may be right in that thoughts of the test could cause stress. However, there could be other events, such as lacking money to pay your rent or a breakup with a boyfriend or girlfriend, that also generate stress. In this case, the upcoming test may not be the stimulus causing stress, but may be an event that is correlated with the increase in stress you experience. Correlation does not imply causation. The correlation of events and increase in stress may reflect any one of several cause-and-effect possibilities. In considering events, we often fail to recognize the difference between causation and correlation. This can lead to erroneous conclusions in analyzing antecedents to our behavior.

MODIFY ANTECEDENTS   A behavior can sometimes be altered through modification of the controlling antecedents. Table 3–1 lists a number of ways this aim can be achieved.

Avoid antecedents. Depending upon the behavior you select to change, you may wish to avoid antecedents to the behavior. If you decide to reduce the amount of alcohol you consume, you can avoid going with your friends to taverns or bars. Or, if you want to reduce your weight, it is useful to avoid purchasing snack foods to keep in your apartment. By avoiding the antecedents of behavior, you can often change your responses.

Narrow antecedent control. You may narrow the range of antecedents in order to alter a behavior. In losing weight, it is often suggested that you eat only when sitting down at the table. This helps you to avoid snacking. Or, if you suffer from insomnia, you might narrow the stimulus control of the bed to only sleeping and sex. Other activities, like watching TV, conversation, or worrying, should be done elsewhere. If you are still awake after ten minutes, you should leave the bed and return only when you believe you can fall asleep. This method of narrowing stimulus control appears to be one of the best self-management procedures for controlling insomnia (Bootzin, 1972).

Reperceive antecedents. By altering the way you think about an antecedent stimulus, you may change a behavior. Instead of thinking about the pleasurable aspects of eating an ice cream sundae, a person who wishes to lose weight can concentrate on the number of calories present in the sundae, the cost of the item, and the amount of exercise required to lose any weight gained through consuming the food.

Change chains. We sometimes find ourselves caught up in a chain of events that controls our behavior without realizing what is happening to us. You may have been decided yesterday that you were going to study. By the time you opened your book, however, it was late and you were tired. If you analyzed what occurred, you may have found that after a leisurely dinner, your friends gathered in your room to talk over the day's events. Naturally, you entered into the discussion. By the time they left, several hours had elapsed and you had not done what you set out to do: study. In such an instance, you may want to alter the behavioral chain in some manner. One way is to declare that you will visit only after you have completed studying. This approach will not only allow you to achieve the academic goals you have set for yourself, but to relax and more thoroughly enjoy the companionship of your friends.

Build in pauses. Watson and Tharp (1993) suggest several methods for building in pauses between events, particularly when you wish to alter behavioral excesses. To reduce smoking, the gradual increasing of pauses between the urge to smoke and actually smoking is effective in reducing the number of cigarettes smoked. To reduce the consumption of alcohol, taking a pause before ordering another drink is recommended. A pause of a couple of minutes in the middle of each meal may be an effective strategy in helping you eat less and, in turn, to lose weight. Finally, you may pause to make a record of your behavior. Remember that the earlier in the chain of events you make an interruption, the more effective pauses are as methods for changing behavior.

Unlink behavioral chains. When we are watching TV or reading, we often gravitate toward the refrigerator to find something to eat. In doing so, we may engage in poor nutritional practices or unnecessary weight gain. When this occurs, you may wish to interrupt the chain of behaviors. This unlinking of chains can occur early on by stopping and thinking of what you are about to do before you head for the refrigerator. A sign on the refrigerator door may serve as a reminder not to snack. We can also unlink this chain by not purchasing the snack items. Other methods for unlinking chains include the use of self-statements such as telling ourselves we are not hungry or that we will not eat anything until we read another thirty pages in our textbook. This method not only unlinks behavioral chains, but it helps us establish subgoals for positive behaviors.

ARRANGE NEW ANTECEDENTS   Arranging new antecedents can help us achieve our goal. There are several methods by which this can be accomplished.

Initiate positive self-instruction. Positive self-instruction can be powerful. Watson and Tharp (1993) asserted that designing a plan of self-instruction is simple: "The strategy is merely to substitute new instructions for the self-defeating ones you now use. Stop telling yourself, 'I can't do this!' Say, instead, 'I can (and tell yourself how)" (p. 146). Specific self-statements should be inserted into any program to help guide you to perform the chain of events that comprise the behavior you wish to perform, no matter how complex it may be.

Eliminate negative self-instruction. If you constantly tell yourself that you cannot perform a particular behavior, there is an increase in the likelihood that your negative self-statements will be self-fulfilling. Whenever you engage in negative self-instruction, you should replace these self-statements with incompatible statements, including thoughts that contain positive self-instruction.

Thought stopping. This procedure contains two elements: First, whenever an unwanted thought occurs, tell yourself, "Stop!" Say it sharply and, as suggest Watson and Tharp (1993), if you do not say it aloud, say it clearly to yourself. Second, immediately substitute another thought for the one you wish to halt. Think of something positive or pleasurable.

Change the physical and social environment. A way to change antecedents is to change your physical or social environment. If you want to improve your study skills, establish an environment where you can study. This setting should include good lighting and, for most people, little noise. Or you may wish to improve your social environment. Perhaps you choose to study with friends or roommates who are more academically oriented. Not only can they provide a good environment for your studying, but they can also provide support and reinforcement to you for your behavior.

Stimulus generalization. This is a process by which a behavior learned in the presence of an antecedent stimulus is performed in the presence of similar antecedent stimuli. If you study well in the library, you may wish to consider what stimuli help you engage in this behavior in this setting. You can establish similar stimuli to help you study in other environments. The result is stimulus generalization that is important not only with respect to establishing antecedent stimuli, but in helping you maintain self-management behaviors across settings.

Precommitment and programming of the social environment. Precommitment means that you arrange in advance for certain antecedent stimuli to occur (Watson & Tharp, 1993). It is common for many to decide who will be the designated driver before they go to a party where they are apt to drink alcoholic beverages. This entails the precommitment and programming of the social environment in order that specific antecedents occur (e.g., the selected driver eschews drinking and remains sober).

Behavior

Behavior is any directly measurable action that we perform. In considering behavior and self-management, we must consider the precise specification of the goals we wish to achieve, including (a) what behaviors are necessary; (b) the givens, situations, context, or conditions under which the behavior is to occur; and (c) what we will accept as a criterion level of performance (Creer, Kotses, and Wigal, 1992; Sulzer-Azaroff and Mayer, 1991). This process involves that we both acquire and perform the behav-

Self-Instruction

Skills involved in self-management have been described in this chapter. The method that guides you through the performance of these skills is self-instruction. Self-instruction refers to the statements we make to ourselves to learn, prompt, direct, increase, decrease, or maintain our performance. All of us use self-instructions, primarily in the form of self-statements, to direct our daily lives. Specific aspects of self-instruction include self-statements, self-generated stimulus change, and self-generated response change.

Self-statements. We use self-statements to guide all our conscious behavior throughout each day. You told yourself what you were going to do when you woke up this morning when you arose, took a shower, and had breakfast. Self-statements were then used to direct the many other actions you engaged in during the day. The effective use of self-statements is enumerated in Table 3–2. As many of these uses have already been described, they will only be reviewed in the current discussion. It should be emphasized that self-statements underlie the successful performance of all our behaviors, not merely those that you selected to change.

Analyze self-statements. We have described analyzing events in terms of a four-way contingency that includes antecedents, behaviors, consequences, and context. Such an analysis can provide invaluable cues as to why you act the way you do, as well as suggesting how you might change a particular behavior. Use self-statements to change and maintain behavior. Once you have analyzed your behaviors to determine what behavior you wish to change, you should constantly use self-statements to initiate and maintain your change plan. They are particularly impor-

---

TABLE 3–2   Effective Use of Self-Statements

Analyze self-statements

Use self-statements to change and maintain behavior

Use self-statements efficiently

Link self-statements to performance
  1. Self-generated stimulus change
  2. Self-generated response change
  3. Self-generated self-management

Review self-statements
  1. Link self-statements to rehearsal
  2. Avoid automatic and/or negative self-statements

tant at the outset when there may be no other reinforcement for your change except the statements you make to yourself.

Use self-statements efficiently. You already rely on self-statements to direct your behavior. You can often use self-statements more efficiently if you are systematic in their use to guide and direct the behaviors you wish to perform. To do so requires that you first conduct a careful analysis of exactly how you use these private events in your daily life.

Link self-statements to performance. There are three ways by which you can link self-statements to performance:

1. Self-generated stimulus change. This term refers to altering aspects of your environment in order to promote behavior change. As described, you may wish to change the setting to improve your studying or to avoid snacking.

2. Self-generated response change. This term refers to altering aspects of your performance. For the person who wants to increase exercising, it would involve engaging in various physical activities for longer periods of time or adding different types of exercise to his or her daily life.

3. Self-generated self-management. This term refers to the self-management skills you acquire and perform as a result of your own initiative. Many of us decide that we wish to lose weight or quit smoking. We design and implement a program of our own choosing to achieve this aim. Self-generated self-management programs are often effective in changing such behaviors as smoking and obesity (Schachter, 1982).

Review self-statements. It is important that you occasionally review the statements you are making to yourself. Are they positive? Are they maintaining the self-management program you have developed and introduced? If they are not, you may wish to consider the type of self-statements you need to make to yourself to direct your performance. Reviewing self-statements may also help you in two other ways: improving behavioral rehearsal and avoiding automatic or negative self-statements.

1. Link self-statements to rehearsal. There are times when you might imagine yourself performing in a certain manner, such as refusing an alcoholic beverage or having sex. Rehearsing what you will do, coupled with a review of the statements you are going to make to yourself to direct your behavior, is likely to increase the likelihood that you will actually behave as you wish.

2. Avoid automatic and/or negative self-statements. We often find that we begin thinking in an automatic way about a situation. In addition, the automatic thoughts are often negative, such as, "I'll never be able to pass this class!" For you and your self-management program to work, you must counter these statements with positive self-instruction. A periodic analysis of your thoughts will often reveal that you have been sabotaging your own progress by thinking automatic thoughts that suggest you will fail.

Consequences

Consequences are the relations between behavior and the events that follow them. Sulzer-Azaroff and Mayer (1991) point out that consequences depend upon behaviors in a probabilistic if–then relationship. If you exercise, you are apt to feel more energy, an example of a natural contingency. Specific consequences must be arranged so as to be appropriate to each of us and our circumstances. This is required because each of us is unique and our situations may change from moment to moment.

Certain behaviors may have stimulus changes as consequences; these are referred to as a reinforcer or a reinforcing event. The operation of the consequence occurring is referred to as reinforcement; the stimulus is called a reinforcer. A behavior may have four types of consequences (Creer and Christian, 1976):

1. Produce positive reinforcers. This occurs when certain stimulus events occur that result in an increase in your behavior. An example may be a grade of an A in a class. The grade will likely increase the amount of time you study for that class. This behavior, in turn, can result in generalization in that you begin to study more for your other courses.

2. Remove or avoid negative reinforcers. This occurs when you escape from or avoid certain stimulus events from happening by increasing your behavior. If you receive a low grade in a class, you may remove the grade or avoid receiving another low grade by increasing the amount of time you study for that course. There is also the prospect of generalization occurring in that you may study more for other courses in order to escape from or to avoid low grades.

3. Producing aversive stimuli. This occurs when you receive an aversive stimulus as a consequence of your behavior. Failing a course would be an aversive consequence. Under these circumstances, you might decide to study more to avoid receiving another failing mark, or you might decide that you are not meant for academia at the present time. Thus, an aversive consequence can either strengthen or weaken the effort you make in school.

4. Remove or avoid positive reinforcers. If you constantly talk in class, your instructor may ask you to leave. If this consequence occurs, you no longer have access to the materials covered in class that are essential to your passing the course. The result will be that you will likely show better classroom decorum in the future so as to pass the course.

SELF-REACTION

Self-reaction refers to the attention we direct toward reviewing and evaluating our performance in a given situation. This process permits us to set realistic standards and expectations, as well as to judge how our behavior compares to these standards or expectations. Positive self-reaction to our performance can assist us in self-management by allowing us to master whatever skills are necessary to perform in a given situation. Negative self-reaction to our performance, however, may influence not only whether we master self-management skills, but whether we will persist in performing these skills or competencies. Self-reaction to our performance is potentially a major factor in determining whether we acquire and later execute self-management behaviors.

A variable that can influence self-reaction is *self-efficacy*. Self-efficacy is the belief that we can perform adequately in a given situation. In the words of Albert Bandura (1977), "Given appropriate skills and adequate incentives . . . efficacy expectations are a major determinant of peoples' choices of activities, how much effort they will expend, and how long they will sustain effort in dealing with stressful situations" (p. 194). Considering the role of self-efficacy in influencing our behavior, the concept will be explored in more detail in a later chapter.

EXERCISE

Chapter 3 introduced the three remaining components of self-management: decision-making, action, and self-reaction. Consider these components in completing your selection of a behavior you want to change.

How will I make decisions concerning information I've collected on myself?

What actions can I take to change and manage my behavior?

What self-reaction procedures will I use to evaluate my performance?

REVIEW TERMS

Antecedents
Consequence
Contingencies
Self-efficacy

Self-generated response change
Self-generated stimulus change
Self-instruction
Stimulus generalization

QUESTIONS

List seven ways for modifying behavior by changing antecedents.

Discuss six ways for arranging new antecedents.

Discuss four types of consequences that may occur following a behavior.

Selecting a Problem: Decision Making and Problem Solving

CHAPTER 4

"Human life occurs only once, and the reason we cannot determine which of our decisions are good and which bad is that in a given situation, we can make only one decision."
—Milan Kundera, *The Unbearable Lightness of Being*

"I'm not cut out to make decisions, you know? My first husband, Floyd, was an S.O.B. He beat the hell out of me. After a couple of years, I left him. Then, I took up with George. He didn't beat me 'cause he was always drunk. I finally had enough and cleared out. Anyway, I met Al. He looked like some kind of a movie star. We had to have a romantic wedding that I ended up paying for. Sometimes Al was okay, sometimes he wasn't. We always owed money. Finally, he took the money I got when I was a waitress and disappeared. What a bastard! I can't pick men, you know?"
—Betty Lou, a waitress

The first step you must make in self-management is to determine your target behavior. In other words, you must decide which behavior or behaviors you want to change. Chapter 1 listed possible behavioral excesses or deficits students have elected to change. Table 4–1 is a checklist of behaviors; many of these behaviors may be relevant to you. If you have not decided what type of behavior you wish to alter, you may review this checklist. It may prompt you to select your personal target behavior. The behaviors listed have been classified into two categories according to whether they are considered behavioral excesses or deficits.

MODELS OF DECISION MAKING AND PROBLEM SOLVING

A number of different schemas have been proposed for learning to make decisions. Two models are presented in Tables 4–2 and 4–3. You will note that there is some commonality among the strategies suggested. The first model was proposed by Michael Mahoney (1979), an innovator in self-management; it is presented in Table 4–2. As noted, Mahoney developed a personal problem-solving strategy that is summarized by the acronym SCIENCE. The approach may seem simple, but it contains the basic elements of decision making and problem solving. In addition, you may re-

TABLE 4–1 Checklist of Behavioral Excesses or Deficits

Behavioral excesses I would like to change:

___	1. Drinking too much	___	13. Swearing
___	2. Smoking too much	___	14. Daydreaming too much
___	3. Eating too much	___	15. Procrastinating
___	4. Feelings of anxiety	___	16. Negative thoughts
___	5. Worrying too much	___	17. Overspending my budget
___	6. Feeling anxious around people	___	18. Getting upset
___	7. Worrying about my looks	___	19. Worrying about decisions
___	8. Biting my fingernails	___	20. Consuming too much caffeine
___	9. Twisting my hair	___	21. Test anxiety
___	10. Jealousy	___	22. Running up telephone bill
___	11. Using drugs	___	23. Anger
___	12. Lying	___	24. Fear of speaking

Any other behavioral excess you want to change _____

Behavioral deficits I would like to change:

___	1. Lack of assertiveness	___	10. Poor memory
___	2. Poor time management	___	11. Lack of social skills
___	3. Lack of exercise	___	12. Careless about personal appearance
___	4. Few dates	___	13. Poor study habits
___	5. Lack of interaction with others	___	14. Poor grades
___	6. Lack of sleep	___	15. Setting and achieving goals
___	7. Lack of positive thoughts	___	16. Plan realistically for my future
___	8. Being depressed	___	17. Acquire and maintain a job
___	9. Poor self image		

Any other behavioral deficit you want to change _____

member the method by its acronym. Thus, the model could become useful to you in the future.

A second and more complex model of problem solving was suggested by Bransford and Stein (1984). This is depicted in Table 4–3. The components of the model also form an acronym (IDEAL). This may help you remember the model in future attempts to solve problems.

The model suggested for use with the text is presented in Table 4–4. This model represents a synthesis of suggestions by D'Zurilla and Goldfried (1971), Mahoney (1979), Wheeler and Janis (1980), Watson and

TABLE 4–2 Seven Stages That Make Up the Basic Strategy of Scientific Inquiry (adapted from Mahoney, 1979)

Specify the general problem.
Collect information about the problem.
Identify possible causes of the problem.
Examine possible antecedents and how they might be changed.
Narrow potential solutions and experiment.
Compare your progress against baseline of where you started.
Extend, revise, or replace your solution as necessary.

> **TABLE 4–3 A Model for Problem Solving (adapted from Bransford and Stein, 1984)**
>
> **I**dentify the problem.
>   Before solving a problem, you must identify it.
>
> **D**efine the problem.
>   Define and describe the problem as carefully as possible.
>
> **E**xplore alternative solutions.
>   The importance of systematic analysis is relevant here.
>   Use general strategies such as:
>   1. Break a complex problem down into components. You can sometimes solve a complex or abstract problem by focusing on simpler and more specific solutions.
>   2. Work backward from the solution.
>   3. Avoid such blocks to creative problem solving as (a) tunnel vision, (b) emotional reactions, and (c) ignorance.
>
> **A**ct on your plan.
>
> **L**ook at the effects of your solution.
>   1. Evaluate the plan you implemented.
>   2. Be creative. Don't hesitate to explore other potential solutions in order to solve your problem.

Tharp (1989), Bransford and Stein (1984), Nezu and Nezu (1989), and Creer, Kotses, and Reynolds (1991). Each of the categories will be described.

Problem Definition

The first step in solving a problem is to identify and define it. This requires that you gather all possible information about the problem. Why is the behavior or situation a problem? You may wish to consider how serious the problem is to you, how frequently it occurs, and the likelihood that it can be changed. Differentiate between facts and assumptions regarding the problem. In all instances, you should describe the problem in a clear and unambiguous manner. Describing the problem in your own words and writing can assist you in this regard. Be honest and thorough

> **TABLE 4–4 A Model for Decision Making and Problem Solving**
>
> Problem definition
> Generation of solutions
> Decision making
> Application of selected solution
> Verification of success or failure of a solution
> Exploration of additional solutions

in listing details of the problem. Don't dwell too much on any negative feelings you may have; this may cause you to focus more on the consequences of the problem rather than the problem itself. Finally, consider what would be realistic goals for solving the problem. Do you have the necessary skills and resources to resolve the difficulty? Can the application of self-management techniques be of use to you? If you believe you lack the resources and competencies to manage a problem, seek the assistance of others.

Generation of Solutions

Experts in decision making and problem solving suggest that you generate as many potential solutions for resolving a problem as possible. Many propose that you brainstorm and produce a quantity of potential solutions. Brainstorming means that you generate ideas as you can without evaluation or criticism. The quality of a solution, they continue, can be considered later. Another suggestion is that you defer making critical judgment about a potential decision until later in the process of generating potential alternatives. This will allow you to avoid the possibility of tunnel vision noted by Bransford and Stein (1984).

Two other proposals are often proposed by experts in decision making and problem solving. First, you may wish to consider combining potential solutions. This approach, however, should be regarded as a viable option only after you have generated a number of potential and practical solutions. Second, once you have generated a number of alternatives, think of potential strategies for each solution. If two solutions are possible for working out a problem but one is easier or more likely to succeed, consider this factor in making your decision.

Wheeler and Janis (1980) summarized seven rules that can assist you in generating alternative solutions to problems:

1. *Do not evaluate at the beginning of the process of generating alternative solutions.* You may hit upon the most appropriate solution at the beginning of the process of deciding how best to solve a problem; in this case, you are fortunate. However, you are just as likely to consider a flawed solution as most appropriate. For this reason, it is best to consider all possible solutions and not contemplate what is wrong with any of them. You will make this judgment later in the decision-making process.

2. *Generate as many alternatives as possible.* Wheeler and Janis (1980) point out that the more alternatives you generate when brainstorming, the less apt you are to miss the best ones. You can reduce the number of choices later in the process. Wheeler and Janis (1980) warn, however, that there is a danger in emphasizing quantity because you may consider too many potential options. For this reason, it is important that you consider only those that are practical and potentially useful to you.

3. *Try to be original.* Almost all experts in decision making suggest that you add a few wild and far-fetched choices to your list of potential solutions. Daydreaming about solutions is often a waste of time. On the other hand, excursions into fantasy may result in a possible solution that you might not have otherwise considered. For this reason, you should always use your imagination in decision making and problem solving.

4. *Modify flawed alternatives.* Wheeler and Janis (1980) indicate that you use the alternatives you generate as springboards for new ideas. In doing so, you may break ideas apart, shift them around, or combine them to form a new idea. In keeping with the thought of being original, you do not have to connect new and old ideas directly. You may, in fact, only see the connection between potential solutions after you have solved your problem.

5. *Ask other people.* You may wish to ask other people for advice. Other people can offer helpful advice; many have already solved the problem that is a source of difficulty to you. In these cases, the advice of these individuals can be invaluable. By the same token, you can often learn how to solve problems by observing how others solve problems similar to those that you experience. If you have decided that you want to improve your social skills as your target behavior, you may find that observing others will provide a model for you to imitate in your own life. Your approach would not be unlike that taken by Meryl Streep or Robert DeNiro in preparing to play the characters they act on the stage and in the movies.

6. *Use contemplation as a source of ideas.* If you set aside time to engage in free-floating contemplation of a problem, almost any thought or external stimulus may serve as a source of a potential solution. By relaxing and thinking of how you can resolve a personal difficulty, you can generate ways to change your behavior and alter the difficulty.

7. *Avoid dichotomies.* Many of the decisions we make seem to have only two alternatives: either we do or do not perform a certain action. Dichotomies often form a type of tunnel vision in that we fail to consider other potential solutions to how we could solve a problem. When possible, we should attempt to avoid dichotomies in making decisions. As Wheeler and Janis (1980) suggest, "Whenever you are faced with an either/or choice, you should try to take a broader view of the situation and consider alternative ways of solving the main problem confronting you. This could change the yes/no choice into a problem for which there may be other acceptable solutions" (p. 48).

Decision Making

In most cases, we evaluate alternative solutions according to some predetermined scheme, such as the likelihood that the selected solution will solve our problem. This is a useful and practical approach to solving the daily problems we face. Nezu and Nezu (1989) suggest you evaluate each alternative solution according to three criteria. First, rate the likelihood that the selected solution, if implemented, will achieve your goals. What is the probability that your solution will work? This strategy is familiar to you; it is the tactic you take in solving most problems you face. Second, consider the selected solution in terms of the personal, social, and both the long-term and short-term consequences it has for you. What risks and benefits are associated with your proposed solution? Be certain you do not exaggerate either the risks or benefits of any given solution. Generally, risks we can control are more acceptable to us than those we believe are beyond our control. Finally, you should select the choice with both the greatest likelihood of success and the minimal expenditure of time and effort on your part.

Wheeler and Janis (1980) offered a four-pronged balance sheet to use in making decisions. First, they suggest that you consider the tangible gains and losses that a solution has for yourself. If you decide to quit smoking, for example, the gain would be overall health for yourself; a potential loss, however, might be a short-term weight gain. Second, there may be tangible gains and losses for others as a consequence of your action. If you decide to study more, for example, the result should be improved grades for you; this would be a personal gain. However, the time you require to study may mean that you have to quit a part-time job; this consequence, in turn, might be a loss to your parents if they are supporting you. Third, an expected consequence could be self-approval or self-disapproval. If you lose weight as a consequence of your action, the personal gain would result in self-approval. However, as most people on diets tend to experience plateaus in their weight loss, you may become overly harsh on yourself when a diet does not produce the results you expect. This reaction would be an example of self-disapproval. Finally, you may consider both social approval or disapproval. If you attempt to balance your budget by taking a part-time job, you will no doubt receive approval from your parents for your initiative and responsibility. Your girlfriend or boyfriend, on the other hand, may display disapproval because you no longer have the time to spend with her or him at other activities.

Application of Selected Solution

A number of approaches have been offered for solving problems. You will want to review these tactics and decide which is the most appropriate for changing the target behavior you have selected. In doing so, you will want to consider factors that have been discussed, such as the likelihood that the behavior can be optimally altered with the technique, and the time and effort you have to devote to bring about behavior change. You can then implement the chosen plan.

Verification of Success or Failure of a Solution

When you begin some form of self-management, you then begin to monitor the effects of your intervention strategy. The best way to determine if your solution works is to review the progress you have made in changing a target behavior. You may want to compare or match your progress against either a predicted or an actual standard that you have set for success. This assessment can be achieved through self-monitoring. As noted earlier, self-monitoring includes two components: self-observation and self-recording. By accurately observing and recording aspects of your behavior, you can reliably determine if you have successfully changed a behavior. You can decide whether the strategy you have taken was successful or whether you need to adopt a different tactic for behavior change. A more detailed discussion of self-monitoring is found in Chapter 5. If you have been successful, then you will want to reinforce yourself in some manner; if not, then you may wish to either consider other options or to recycle through the decision-making process that has been presented. It is imperative that you remain flexible. Careful monitoring of results will indicate whether you need to change your plans. Being flexible permits you to continue to improve and refine your ideas.

Exploration of Additional Solutions

In the past, about 15 percent of the students have found that their change program did not alter the target behavior that they selected. There is nothing wrong with this outcome; we all fail at tasks every day. What is required is that you explore other potential solutions for your problem. This can be achieved by reviewing potential strategies as presented later in the book. At the same time, you may have learned more about the nature of the problem than you knew when you started out.

There is a caveat that accompanies any discussion of decision making and problem solving: performing these tasks is particularly difficult for most people because they wrongly believe that all of their decisions should be correct and that they can solve any problem they face. This is never the case; no one is correct all the time and no one solves all the problems he or she faces. Townsend (1984) said he had been a success in business because one-third of his decisions were correct and he was wrong two-thirds of the time. He may have been modest in his claim of a .333 batting average, but not too much. We all make incorrect decisions, sometimes every day. They are a natural part of living. The best we can do is to follow the guidelines presented in the chapter in an attempt to make correct decisions and to solve problems. Failure is never a reason to abandon a systematic approach to decision making and problem solving. Rather, failure presents an opportunity for you to develop more refined and accurate methods of decision making and problem solving that can be useful to you in the future.

EXERCISE

In the space below, you may wish to jot down some ideas with respect to a potential target behavior that you decide to change. In doing so, follow the step-wise decision-making process outlined in the book.

Problem definition: What is the problem that you want to change? Describe and define it as precisely as you can.

Generation of solutions: What are the potential alternative solutions you could take to resolving the problem? Brainstorm and consider as many solutions as you can; later, you can refine your selection.

Decision making: What appears to be the best solution for resolving the problem you have selected to change? How likely is this solution to achieve the goals you have set for behavior change?

Application of selected solution: How are you going to apply the solution you have selected?

Verification of success or failure of a solution: How are you going to determine if your selection actually worked? What criteria are you going to use against which to match your success?

Exploration of additional solutions: If your original solution does not work, what are other possibilities that you may wish to consider?

REVIEW TERMS

IDEAL
Failure as opportunity

Problem definition
SCIENCE

QUESTIONS

Describe seven rules useful in generating alternative solutions to problems.
Discuss three criteria that can be used in evaluating alternative solutions.

Assessment and Behavior Change

CHAPTER 5

"The union of the mathematician with the poet, ferver with measure, passion with correctness, this surely is the ideal."
—William James, *Collected Essays and Reviews*

"The doc told me I could control my blood pressure by watching my weight. I try to. Around the holidays, I always gain four or five pounds. I get on the scales each morning and write down my weight on the calender. After the holidays, I cut down on what I eat and write down my weight. I return to my normal weight pretty quick. It's a lot easier to lose a few pounds than wait until I weigh too much and really have to diet."
—Fred, a sixty-five-year-old retiree

We are constantly measuring or assessing something in our life. Whether we are counting how many minutes we have left in a class or how much money we have in our purse or wallet, we determine the value, significance, or extent of whatever we are measuring. We do the same thing in assessing our behavior. You may do anything from dividing your homework up according to your study time or counting the number of cups of coffee you drink. You have no idea of whether there is any change unless you measure or assess some aspect of your behavior.

MEASUREMENT

There are four basic types of measures that you might consider to assess your target behavior. All have been used to assess self-management:

1. *Permanent Product Recording.* This means that you record the enduring outcome of a behavior. This might include the number of pounds you weigh, cigarettes you smoke, or class assignments you complete. The advantage of this method is that it is used by all of us in measuring changes that are relevant to us in our daily lives.

2. *Event Recording.* This involves assessing and recording the number of times a specific event occurs over a specific interval. You might count the number of calories you consume, the sit-ups you complete, or the miles you run each day. The method is appropriate for behaviors that have clearly definable beginnings and endings (Sulzer-Azaroff and Mayer, 1991).

3. *Duration Recording.* This is defined as the length or duration of time a behavior lasts. It is the appropriate measure to use if you assess daily increases in the amount of time you study or decreases in the amount of time you waste. It is easy to use because it can be precisely measured with a clock or watch.

4. *Interval Time-Sampling Recording.* This measure can be used if you wish to observe and record the presence or absence of a given response within a given interval of time. It would be a useful measure if you wanted to record whether you studied on certain days or went to bed within a given period of time each evening.

OBSERVING AND RECORDING BEHAVIOR

The specific measure you use will be a function of the behavior you decide to change. After you have selected the behavior and measure you will use, the next step is to gather baseline data. A *baseline* represents a period of time before you begin your program when you systematically observe and record information about your target behavior. A baseline will provide you with information regarding the occurrence or duration of the behavior. It may be that you discover that the behavior does not occur with the frequency or at the duration you initially thought; in this case, you might want to consider selecting another target behavior. Baseline data also determine the level of your behavior before you introduce a change procedure. You can then compare any changes that occur when you try and change the behavior against the baseline. Besides knowledge about the initial level of your target behavior, a baseline should also provide you with information regarding common antecedents and consequences of the behavior you have chosen to change. There are no basic guidelines for how long you should gather baseline data. Generally, you need to collect baseline data until you are able to identify the pattern of your responses.

EXPERIMENTAL DESIGNS

An experimental design permits you to determine if your program worked. When you carry out a self-management project, you need to use a design that will permit you to determine whether your program was a success or a failure. If you want experimental rigor, you will employ a design that gives you greater confidence that your program produced whatever change you recorded. This could require that you abandon your self-management program and permit your behavior to return to baseline, or that you use a sophisticated multiple baseline design. In most instances, however, you do not need such a degree of experimental rigor; you basically want to see if what you did produced any change. Three approaches will permit you to assess behavioral change.

A-B Quasi-Experimental Design

With this design, you collect baseline data before introducing your intervention procedure. The baseline comprises the A part of the design; self-management is represented by the B component. Data is plotted as a function of some unit of measure. In other words, rate, duration, or some other measure is plotted along the y axis; time, units, or some other measure is plotted along the x axis. This is shown, for a behavioral deficit, in Figure 5–1. As is noted, the rate, duration, or other aspect of a behavior is plotted from a low to a high point on the y (vertical) axis; time, units, or other measure is plotted on the x (horizontal) axis. It is further illustrated by a record presented by a student who increased the amount of hours he studied each day. As depicted in Figure 5–2, the student plotted the number of hours studied (duration) over a number of days.

An example of the use of an A-B quasi-experimental design for behavioral excesses is depicted in Figure 5–3. In this case, rate, duration, or

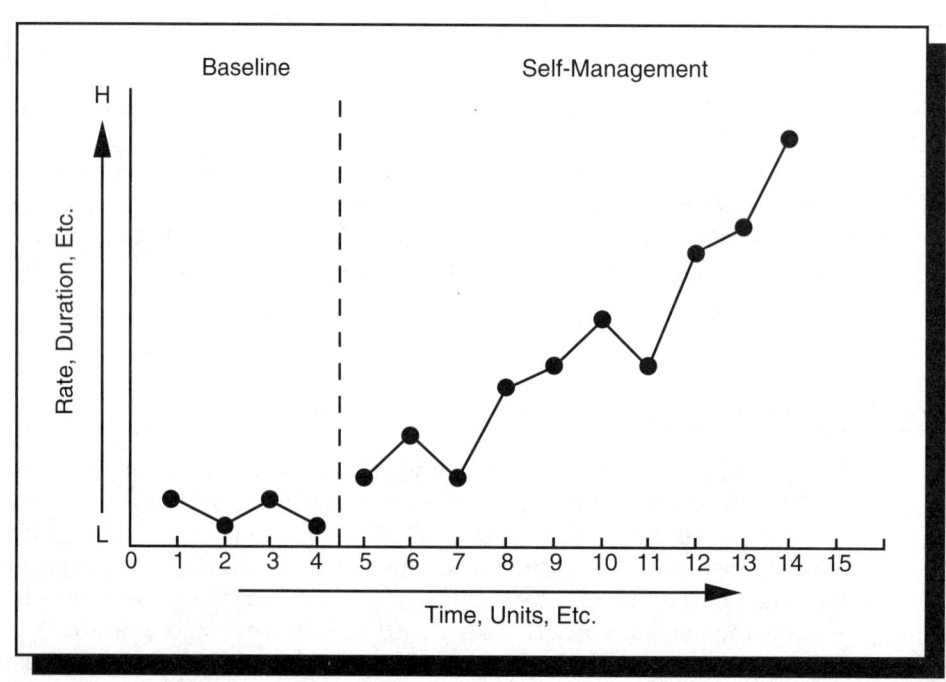

FIGURE 5–1
An A-B quasi-experimental design as applied to a behavioral deficit.

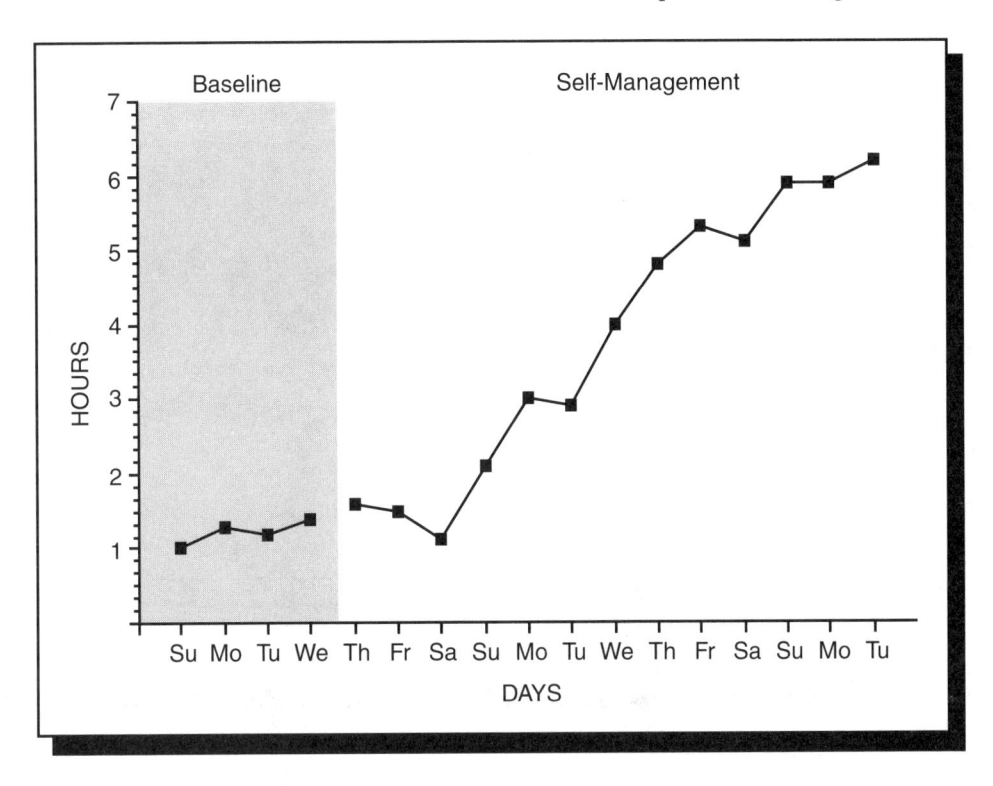

FIGURE 5–2
Increase in number of hours spent studying over time.

some other aspect of behavior is plotted, from low to high, along the y axis; time, units, or some other type of measure is plotted on the x axis. This is further illustrated by Figure 5–4, which shows the success a student had in reducing the number of times she swore over a number of days.

The A-B quasi-experimental design has been used by a majority of students conducting self-management programs. The problem with the design is that it is quasi-experimental, in other words, it really does not permit anyone to say with confidence that the program developed and implemented by an individual caused the change.

Multiple Baseline Design

With this design, baselines of several behaviors are obtained. The self-management procedure is then applied to one behavior while baseline measures continue with the remaining behaviors. The change procedure is then applied to a second behavior, and so on. Multiple baselines are relevant across behaviors, setting, or individuals.

A form of a multiple baseline design has been used by students, particularly when attempting to decrease negative thoughts and in-

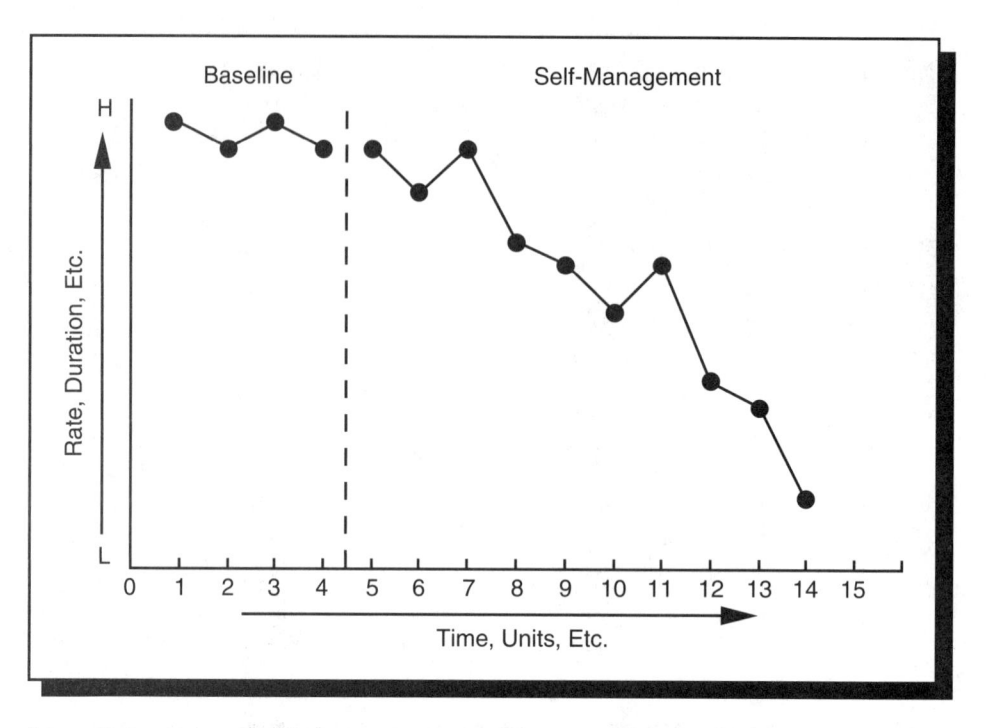

FIGURE 5–3
An A-B quasi-experimental design as applied to a behavioral excess.

FIGURE 5–4
Decrease in swearing over time.

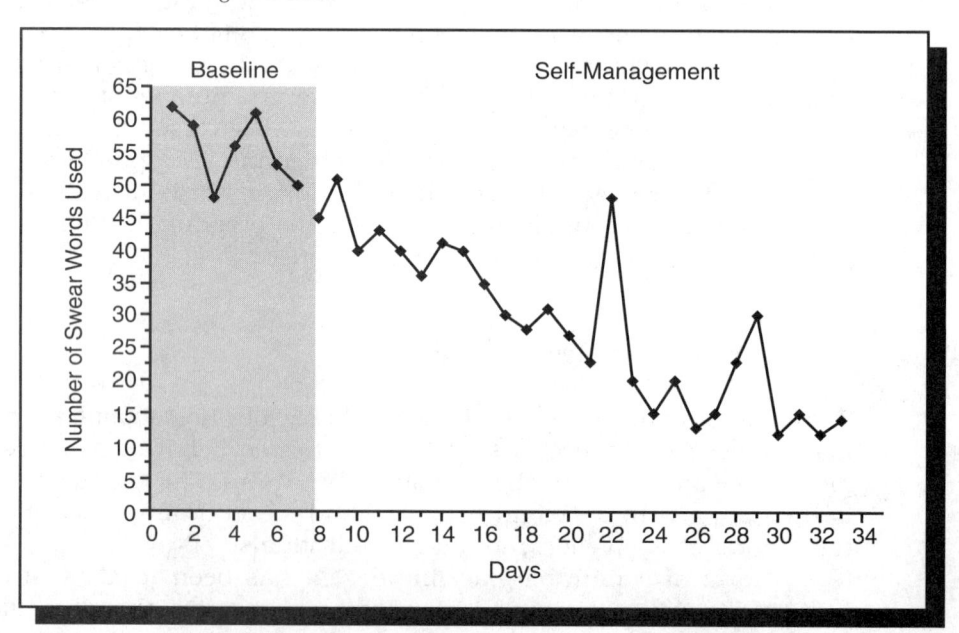

crease positive thoughts. An example of such a design is shown in Figure 5–5. In this instance, the number of negative and positive thoughts that occurred were recorded over time. As noted, the student decreased negative thoughts while she increased positive thoughts. A similar result is shown in Figure 5–6, with a student who reduced negative thoughts while increasing controlled and self-evoked positive thoughts. This type of design is not a true multiple baseline design. However, it is an appropriate design for use in recording the reduction of negative thoughts and the increase of positive thoughts through self-management.

Changing Criterion Design

In the form of this design, criterion levels are set beforehand. The individual can then determine whether or not he or she met a level, designated as a subgoal, in a particular period of time. An example of a changing criterion design for a behavioral deficit is depicted in Figures 5–7 and 5–8. In Figure 5–7, the subgoals and goals of a project have

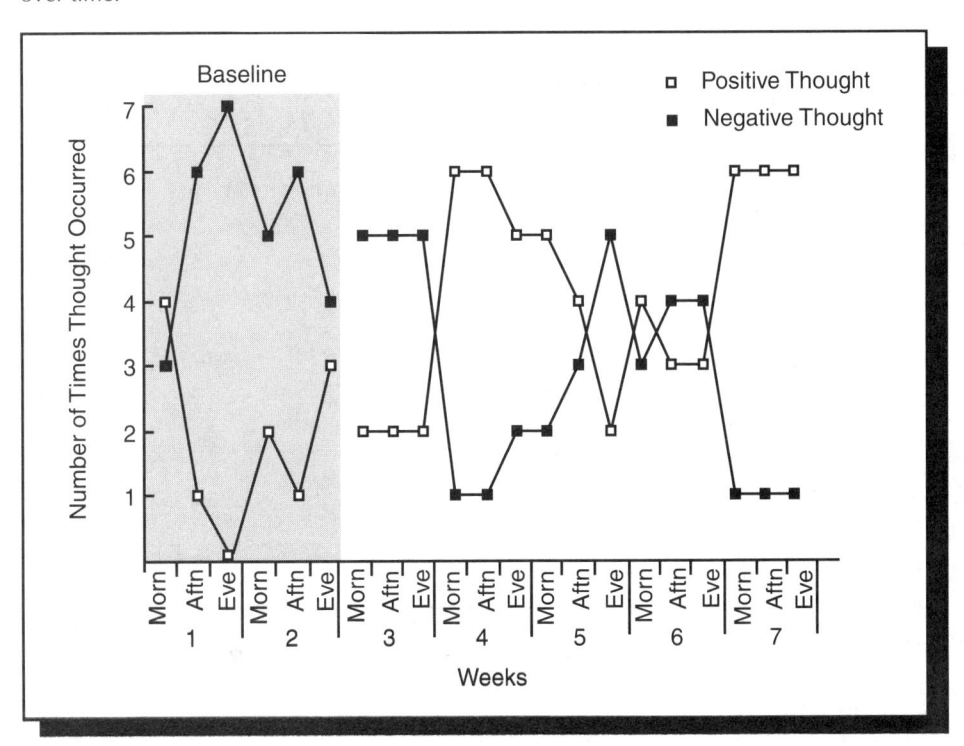

FIGURE 5–5
Example of a type of multiple baseline design in recording negative and positive thoughts over time.

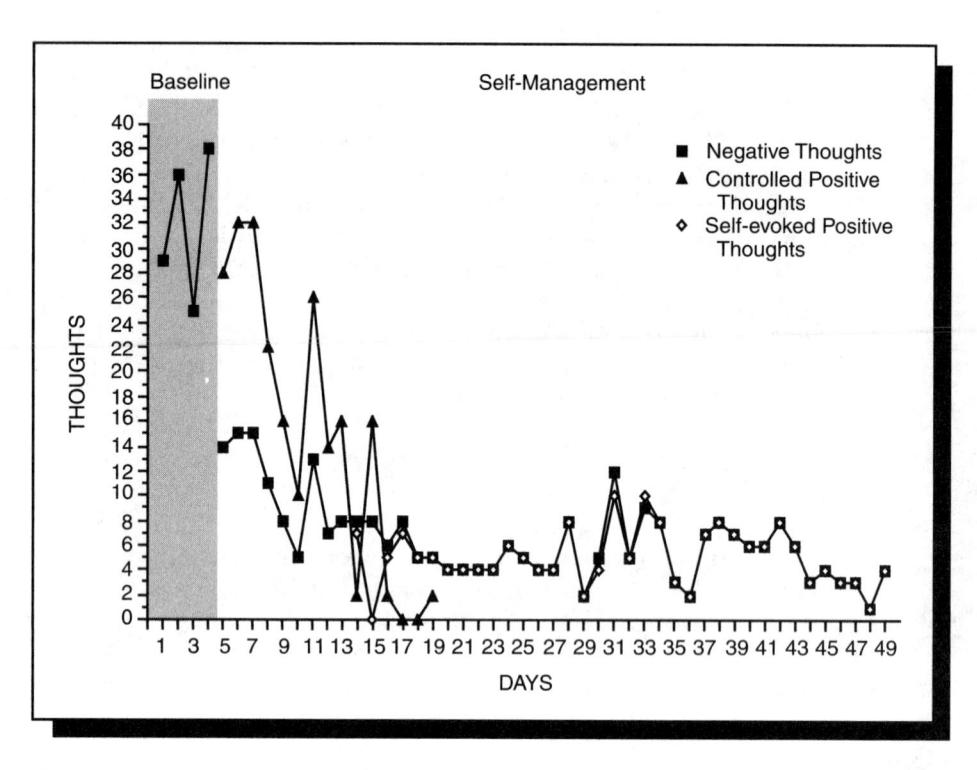

FIGURE 5-6
Example of use of a type of multiple baseline design in assessing positive and negative thinking.

FIGURE 5-7
Example of predetermination of goal and subgoals for program designed to change behavioral deficits.

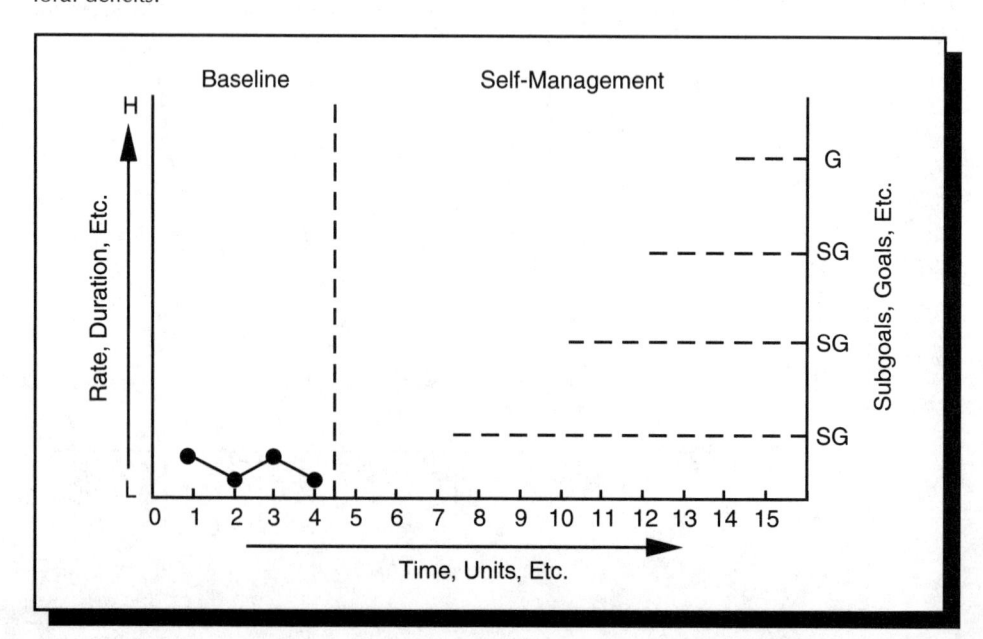

Experimental Designs **43**

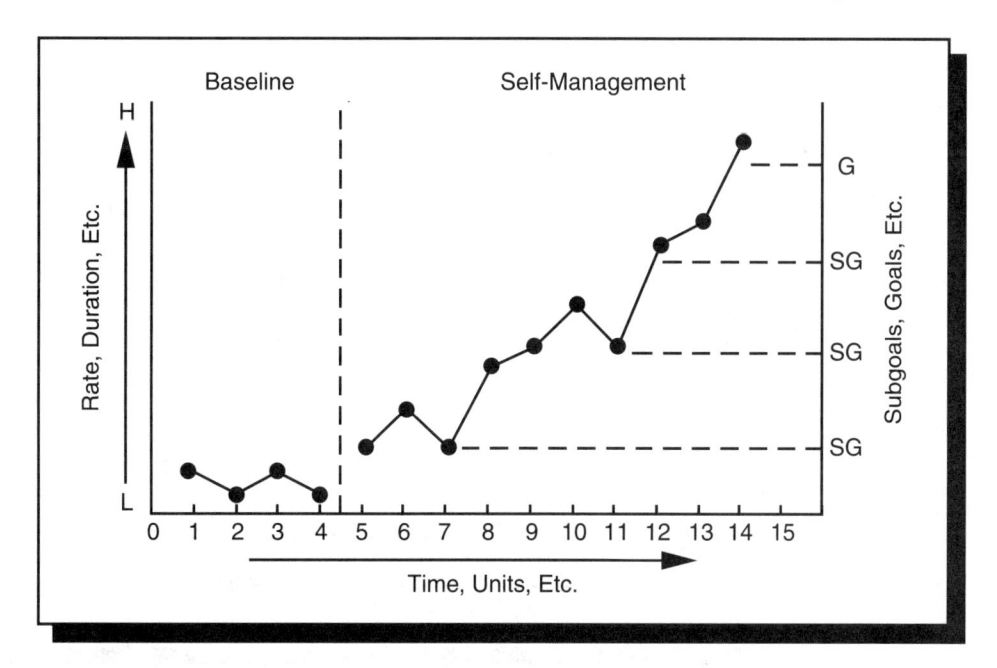

FIGURE 5–8
Success attained in changing behavioral deficit.

FIGURE 5–9
Example of predetermination of goal and subgoals for program designed to change behavioral excesses.

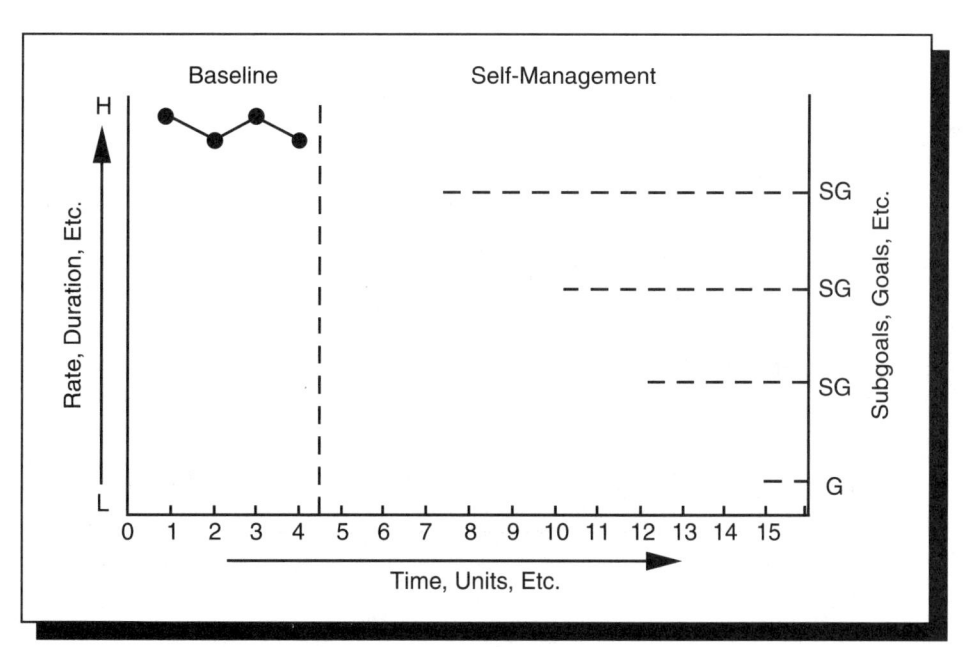

44 Chap. 5 Assessment and Behavior Change

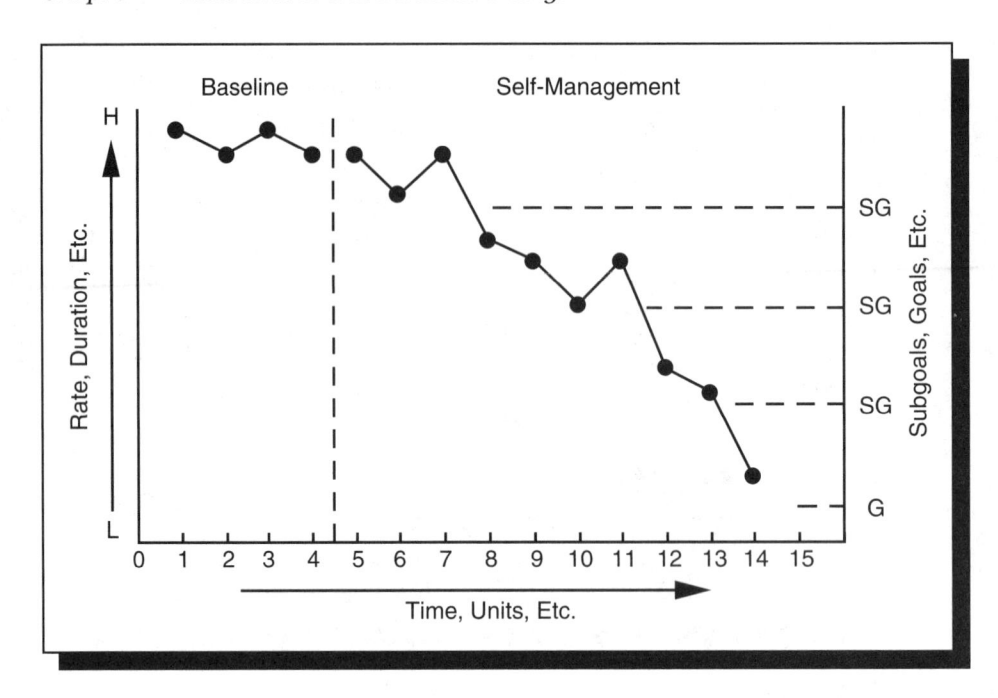

FIGURE 5–10
Success attained in changing behavioral excess.

FIGURE 5–11
Use of a changing criterion design in reducing complaining behavior.

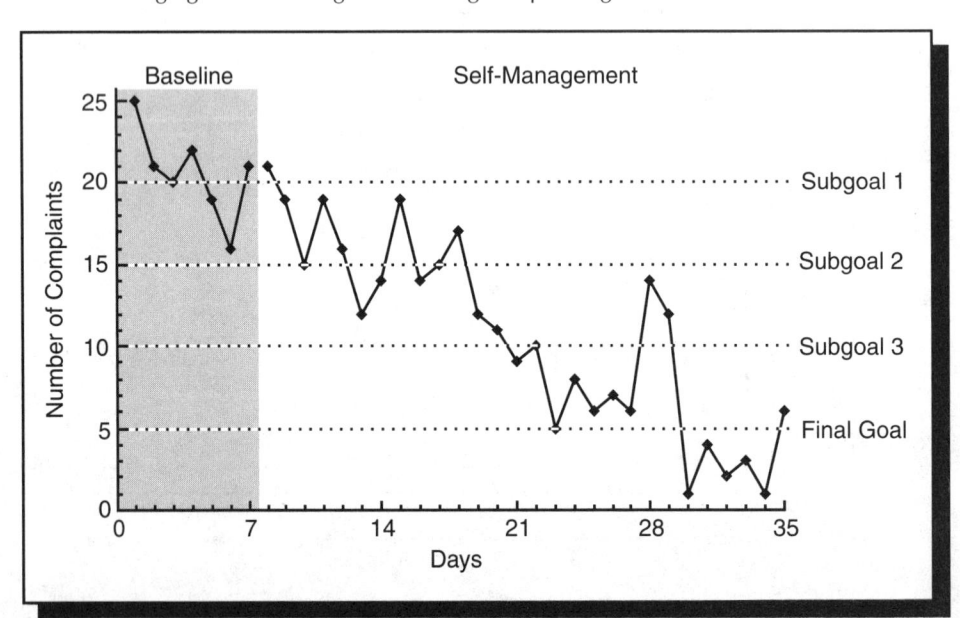

been preset as illustrated; Figure 5–8 illustrates the success attained with the change program. The changing criterion design, as applied to a behavioral excess, is shown in Figures 5–9 and 5–10. Figure 5–9 shows the goal and subgoals that were preset; Figure 5–10 shows the success attained with the change program. Figure 5–11 shows the use of a changing criterion design by a student who wanted to reduce the number of complaints she made. As noted, the student's program reduced her complaining over time. In addition, she met or exceeded most of the subgoals she set for herself (although, as can be expected, there were minor setbacks).

All of the projects presented in the remainder of the book use variations of one of the three designs presented here. The reader should be cautioned that these designs are modified from traditional single-subject designs. Anyone wishing to learn more about these designs should consult the excellent presentation in Sulzer-Azaroff and Mayer (1991).

PROBLEMS IN ASSESSMENT

There are a number of problems that often occur in assessing self-management, as enumerated in Table 5–1. They include the following:

Not observing and recording specific behaviors. It is impossible to attend to all of our behaviors; we would be overwhelmed if we tried to do so. For this reason, it should again be emphasized that you decide beforehand the specific behaviors you wish to attend to in a self-management program. By doing so, you should be able to observe and record any changes in these behaviors. Carry around a card in your pocket and jot down the frequency or duration of your target behavior when it occurs. Changing a given behavior is just one of the many behaviors you need to engage in during the day. If you become preoccupied with observing and recording changes as they occur in your target behavior, you may wish to reconsider target behaviors.

TABLE 5–1   Potential Problems That Can Arise in the Assessment of Self-Management

Not observing and recording specific behaviors
Too many target behaviors
Collecting inaccurate information
Recording information in automatic way
Waiting too long to record observations
Discouragement
Reactivity

Too many target behaviors. When they set out to change their behavior, many students decide that they want to change several responses at once. They may decide that in addition to studying more to improve their grades, they want to reduce their weight, exercise more, and be active socially. All too often, they fail; they simply are trying to do too much at once. The consequence of an individual's failure is often discouragement and feelings of failure. Rather than becoming overly ambitious in self-management, you should select one behavior, change it, and then select a second behavior to alter. If you break down all you want to change into specific behaviors, you are more likely to achieve success one behavior at a time. Success at changing one behavior also serves both to refine self-management skills and enhance your self-efficacy regarding your ability to alter your behavior.

Collecting inaccurate information. We are as capable of misleading ourselves as we are of misleading others. For this reason, it is imperative that you gather reliable and valid data concerning your target behavior. Be honest with yourself. If you need to redefine your target behavior, do so; if a program fails, note that it failed. It is not how successful you are at changing behavior that is important. What is important is that you learn how to observe and record aspects regarding your behavior. Successful behavior change, which generally occurs, is a bonus. If it does not occur, you will still have learned much about yourself and the behavior you should select to change.

Recording information in an automatic way. Sometimes, we enter information onto a graph or diary without considering our observations or recordings. This can produce inaccurate information. Take time to think through the observations you have collected and how they will be recorded. Data recorded in an automatic manner may be more misleading than helpful.

Waiting too long to record observations. Sometimes, we may forget to record the necessary information about ourselves and our program. It is usually no problem if you only forget a day. However, if you fail to observe and record information over several days, you often end up trying to reconstruct your behavior. The collection of remembered data becomes a hit-or-miss situation characterized more by guesswork than accurate observation and recording of data. For this reason, you should try to record your observations on a daily basis, and don't rely on memory.

Discouragement. In any behavioral change program, there is apt to be discouragement. You may not change your behavior as rapidly as you wish, or you may think that change should occur when it does not. The important point here is to anticipate that there will be failures in almost any program. When these failures occur, you then should be able to control them. There are more failures in our lives than successes. Most failure we deal with by trying harder, changing our environment, or modifying our behavior. A self-management program is no different from these daily setbacks in our lives.

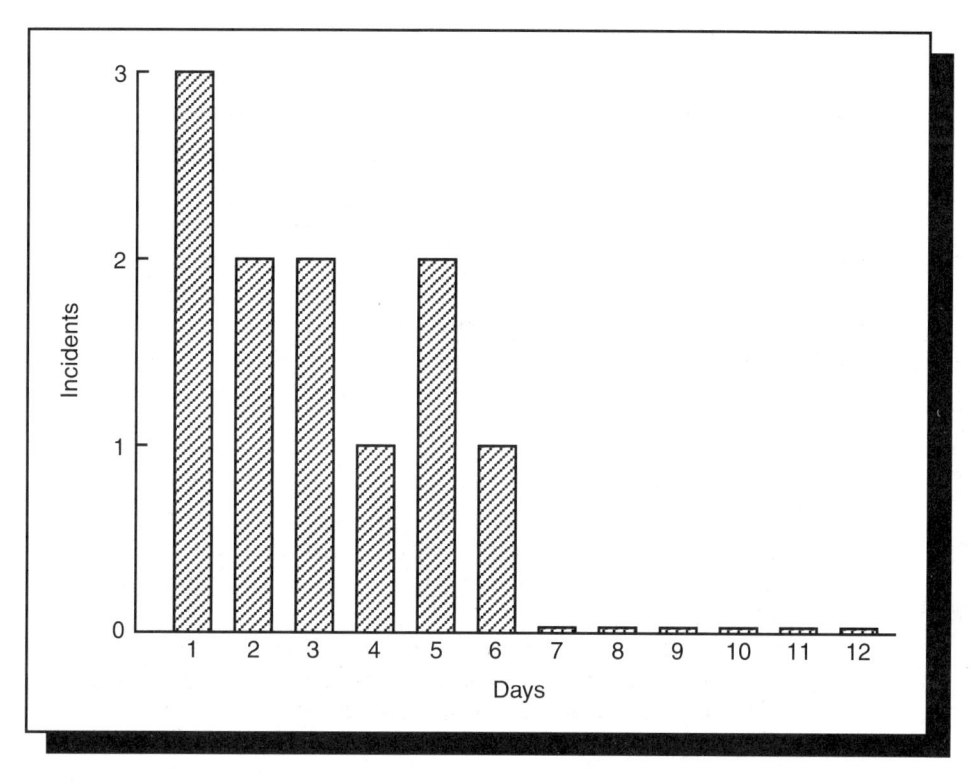

FIGURE 5–12
A case of reactivity changing an inappropriate behavior.

Reactivity. Reactivity is an effect produced by the assessment of a behavior, not by the introduction of a change program. Sometimes, our behavior can change through observation alone. This is not particularly bad; we welcome alteration of an appropriate behavior no matter what strategy evoked the change. An example of reactivity is depicted in Figure 5–12. The target behavior the student selected was lying; his goal was to reduce the behavior. When he started recording aspects of the behavior, however, he began to realize the troubles he created for himself because he was often untruthful. He discovered the act of recording these incidents was a type of intervention procedure. As a result, he halted his past behavior of lying to others. The truthfulness he developed continued to be maintained long after the course ended.

CHARACTERISTICS OF SUCCESSFUL PLANS

Before embarking upon your change program, you might want to review suggestions offered for a good plan. These suggestions were gleaned from a number of experts in self-management. Three models are offered.

Model 1

A successful plan might include the following features:

Written outline of change plan. This would include specific descriptions of the behaviors you want to change, as well as the techniques you plan on using to modify the behavior. The situations or contexts where the behaviors should occur should be clearly stated.

Subgoals and goals. Here, you would include the specific goals you wish to attain, as well as the subgoals that should be fulfilled along the way in order to reach your goal. These may be specified in writing and, as suggested, plotted along your graph. Both subgoals and goals can serve to prompt and motivate you to attain the aims you have for performing self-management.

Feedback on behavior. The best way to obtain feedback is to plot your progress daily. You can then review where you are with respect to achieving your goals and subgoals. At the same time, you can determine if you need to make changes in either your performance or, if necessary, your basic program.

Judge progress. Earlier, it was noted that information processing and evaluation were integral to self-management. To attain your goal, you repeatedly need to assess where you are with respect to your subgoals and goal.

Adjust program. In evaluating your progress, you may decide that some changes are required in order for you to achieve your goal. When this is the case, you should adjust the program to meet changing demands or conditions.

Model 2

This model is adapted from one proposed by Williams and Long (1991). There are five steps involved in their program:

1. *Select goal.* This entails that you select a goal for your program. A behavioral goal should be important, measurable, and positive.

2. *Assess progress.* Collect baseline data before you implement your change program. This may involve counting a behavior, but you may also use a diary, clock, or watch depending upon whether you use frequency or duration as a measure of your behavior. You should regularly plot your progress on a graph.

3. *Develop supportive environment.* You may need to alter an environment before beginning a program. This will include providing stimuli that support your program. Williams and Long (1991) suggest that you make arrangements so that requirements for reinforcement can be easily met and appropriate behavior immediately reinforced.

4. *Use self-statements.* The key role played by self-statements was emphasized in an earlier chapter. Self-statements not only permit you to determine cause-effect relationships, but to immediately reinforce yourself for appropriate actions.

5. *Maintain progress.* As noted, you can expect some failures in any self-management program. You might overcome these occasional setbacks by emphasizing the temporary nature of such failures, as well as enlisting the assistance of supportive individuals in your environment (Williams and Long, 1991).

Model 3

This represents an amalgamation of suggestions offered by others, including comments by students who have taken the course in the past. These suggestions, listed in Table 5–2, are as follows:

Establish target behavior. It has been reiterated throughout this book that you should precisely define the target behavior(s) you wish to change. In doing so, you should consider the four-part contingency of antecedents, behaviors, consequences, and contexts of the behavior. Consider conditions that either facilitate or compete with the target behavior. These may require change before you initiate your program. In selecting a target behavior, you may wish to perform a task analysis by breaking a behavior into different components and deciding what skills are required to achieve the desired behavior. This may require shaping, or the development of new behaviors by the successive reinforcement of closer approximations toward the behavioral objective. Decide what criteria will be used in order for you to demonstrate mastery of the skills involved in performing the target behavior(s).

Select goals and subgoals. Once you have selected your target behavior, establish realistic goals and subgoals that must be attained in order to bring about behavior change. The written descriptions of your target behavior, goals, and subgoals should be as clear as possible.

TABLE 5–2 Criteria for a Good Change Plan
Establish target behavior.
Select goals and subgoals.
Develop commitment.
Select reinforcers.
Collect data.
Develop change plan.
Adjust plans.
Develop future support.

Develop commitment. A commitment is the actual desire you have to change a given behavior. If you have a strong commitment, you will be highly motivated to change; if you do not, you are less likely to succeed. Ways of increasing your commitment are to make public statements about your desire to change, arrange your environment to assist you in reaching your goals, invest considerable time and effort into your project, and plan ahead for potential roadblocks that might hamper your progress.

Select reinforcer. In addition to commitment, some people like to add a reinforcer to their self-management program. Some reinforcers are *natural reinforcers* in that if you study harder, you obtain better grades. Others may be *extrinsic reinforcers* in that they are something tangible you give yourself contingent upon your performing a specified behavior. For example, you might save money to purchase a gift for yourself when you attain a specified goal. Other stimuli serve as *intrinsic reinforcers* in that they reinforce your behavior when you complete an activity such as homework. Other events are referred to as *activity reinforcers* in that you might do something you enjoy, such as playing basketball, contingent upon your achieving a given task. Punishment through application of time-out or response cost, two procedures to be discussed in a later chapter, has occasionally been used by students to reduce a target behavior. These methods are usually used in conjunction with a positive reinforcer.

Collect data. Once you have chosen your target behavior or behaviors, you should begin gathering data with respect to the behavior. Start by gathering baseline data; this will yield relevant information about how often a behavior occurs or the duration of its occurrence. Keep good records throughout your project.

Develop change plan. Decide what would be the most appropriate technique(s) to use in changing your target behavior. You will likely consider a variety of techniques before deciding what would be the most appropriate method for you. In this period, you may use trial-and-error in order to select the most appropriate technique. Be creative. Your basic aim is to arrive at a strategy that will permit you to replace an undesirable behavior with a more desirable behavior.

Adjust plans. You may need to adjust your plans as you learn more about yourself and your target behavior. As you become proficient at analyzing your behavior, you may detect competing consequences that need to be controlled. You will also determine what responses are most apt to reinforce your behavior. As you become more sophisticated at self-management, you will be better able to develop refined plans for effective change.

Develop future support. After you change a behavior, you want to be certain it is maintained. Who wants to lose weight, quit smoking, or acquire better study habits and have their progress disappear at the end of the formal program? Develop contingencies to maintain your progress. Be persistent in developing whatever personal and environmental support you need to maintain behavioral change. Life is the constant learning of new behaviors, as well as determining how they are changed by different factors. The self-management project you conduct in this class is but one of many you will develop and execute throughout your life.

EXERCISE

By now, you should be quite knowledgeable about developing a self-management program to change behavior. To assist you in planning the program you want to implement for this course, it is suggested that you review the following questions:

What target behavior(s) have you selected?

What are your goals and subgoals?

Have you the necessary commitment to carry out your program?

What kind of data should you collect and how will it be gathered?

What type of change plan have you developed?

How can you adjust your plans if needed?

What types of future support can be generated to maintain the success of your program?

REVIEW TERMS

Duration recording
Event recording
Interval time-sampling recording

Permanent product recording
Reactivity
Shaping

QUESTIONS

Describe three approaches to assessing behavioral change.

List eight criteria for a good change plan.

Describe four types of reinforcers.

CHAPTER 6

Behavioral Change Procedures

"I am the person I'm most concerned with controlling."
—B. F. Skinner, *Will Success Spoil B. F. Skinner?*

"I've never been able to take things one at a time, you know? I've always thought I needed deep psychotherapy, like, the kind that prove all my problems are related to my mother. She was the one who messed up, not me. Isn't this the way it's supposed to be? All the therapists and counselors I've seen tell me to change one of my problems at a time, but I don't believe them. I'll find somebody who will show that all my screwups are due to my mother, not to me."
—Bert, a twenty-five-year-old high school drop-out.

A number of procedures can be used to modify behavior; many are applied in what is referred to as behavior modification. Ten characteristics of behavior modification are listed in Table 6–1. These characteristics are empirical in that they are based upon systematic observations, not reasoning, speculation, or beliefs. They rest upon experimental psychology whereby a behavioral technique, an independent variable, was manipulated to alter a specific behavior, a dependent variable. The techniques have value both in self-management and in changing the behavior of others. Thus, while you might apply them to change your target behavior, you could use the same methods to alter behaviors or behavioral patterns in others, particularly your children. With these procedures, the discriminative stimuli that control behaviors are generally environmental. This means they are public events that can be observed by those other than yourself.

BEHAVIORAL TECHNIQUES

Behavioral procedures used in self-management are enumerated in Table 6–2. They have been categorized according to whether they are operant or classical conditioning techniques.

TABLE 6–1 Characteristics of Behavior Modification

Way to change behavior problem is to alter behavior
Concerned with the application of learning principles to manage behavior
Emphasis on precise definition of target behavior
Emphasis upon behaviors that can be observed and assessed
Change procedures often include the rearrangement of environment and activities
Change rationale and methods can be described precisely
Based upon empirical research
Techniques involve both operant and classical learning
Emphasizes demonstration of change
Wide applicability across problems

Operant Conditioning Techniques

Operant conditioning is a type of learning where behavior is controlled by its consequences. Behaviors affected by their consequences are called operants because they operate on the environment to produce consequences; operants are, in turn, modified by these consequences (Skinner, 1953). Most of the time we do something, our actions have consequences. These consequences determine whether specific actions are more or less likely to be repeated in the future. Several principles of operant conditioning were described in Chapters 2 and 3. They are repeated here both as a review and as an explanation of operant conditioning.

TABLE 6–2 Behavioral Techniques

Operant Conditioning Techniques
  Positive reinforcement
    Extinction
    Shaping
    Stimulus control
    Chaining
    Premack principle
    Conditioned reinforcers
    Generalized reinforcers
  Negative Reinforcment
    Avoidance learning
    Escape learning
  Punishment
    Time-out
    Response cost
  Generalization

Classical Conditioning Techniques
  Systematic desensitization
  Systematic self-desensitization

POSITIVE REINFORCEMENT   Positive reinforcement may be defined as the strengthening or maintenance of a behavior as a function of the contingent occurrence of a stimulus following the response or behavior. The stimulus that increases or maintains the behavior because of its presence is a positive reinforcer. If you received a star from your elementary school teacher when you did well in spelling, you probably made an effort to obtain a star the next time you had a spelling test. Later, praise for a good answer in a college course may have increased the number of times you responded to your instructor's questions. Positive reinforcers, whether they are the salary we receive for working or the high grades we obtain in a class, strengthen and maintain our responses and behavior. Whereas specific reinforcers may change as we go through various stages in our lives, the process of positive reinforcement controls much of our day-to-day behavior. This basic principle of positive reinforcement provides the foundation for many other techniques. Positive reinforcement can be significant to the success of a self-management program provided the following steps are taken.

First, you must select what behavior it is that you want to reinforce; in this case, we have referred to the behavior as the target behavior.

Second, you need to select a reinforcer that is positive to you. Reinforcers are unique to each of us according to our past history; a stimulus or response that reinforces a roommate may have no effect on you. You alone must decide what stimulus or response to use as a positive reinforcer.

Third, you must provide reinforcement to yourself contingent upon the occurrence of the target behavior. This process, in turn, will strengthen and maintain your performance.

Finally, at the beginning of self-management, it is imperative that you reinforce yourself immediately after the occurrence of a behavior (a positive self-statement can bridge the gap between the behavior and a tangible stimulus if you have selected this as a positive reinforcer). After the behavior is well established, you can gradually reduce the reinforcer so that you reinforce yourself after either a period of time (an interval schedule of reinforcement) or a number of responses (a ratio schedule). Use of these schedules, presented on fixed/variable time or fixed/variable ratio schedules, results in a stronger behavior that is more resistant to extinction.

Several processes influenced by positive reinforcement may be useful in designing a self-management program:

Extinction. Extinction is the decrease in behavior that occurs with the withdrawal or discontinuation of positive reinforcement. You can reduce and extinguish a response by removing the stimulus that reinforces your behavior. If you find you waste time in the library because you gravitate toward reading newspapers, you can halt the behavior and extinguish this method of wasting study time. In using extinction as a change procedure it is important that you have a specific behavior you wish to extinguish, select what plan you will use to extinguish the behavior, and execute the plan. *Spontaneous recovery*—the spontaneous performance of a behavior without it being reinforced—sometimes occurs. Don't be discouraged with spontaneous recovery as, with time and performance, the behavior undergoing extinction should again decrease.

Shaping. Shaping is a procedure whereby new behaviors are acquired by systematically reinforcing successive approximations toward a behavioral goal. We constantly use shaping in acquiring and refining new behaviors, whether they are in learning to interact with others or to acquire effective ways of expressing our ideas on paper. The use of shaping entails that you select the behavioral goal you wish to attain, decide upon an appropriate reinforcer to use in approximating this terminal behavior, and implement the change plan you have developed. In shaping, the reinforcer should immediately follow the desired behavior. This permits rewarding consequences to be associated with the behavior you wish to reinforce.

Stimulus control. Stimulus control is the influence that a stimulus or set of stimuli has on the probability that a behavior will occur. Stimuli that control our behavior are referred to as discriminative stimuli. We discussed stimulus control and the role of discriminative stimuli earlier. If you want to establish discriminative control, you must choose what stimulus or stimuli you will use to prompt your behavior, select an appropriate reinforcer, and develop discrimination so that the stimulus produces a specific type of response. As Sulzer-Azaroff and Mayer (1991) assert, "Stimuli are said to be discriminative when, after they have been present reliably when a response has been reinforced, their presence or absence systematically alters the probability of the rate of response. Discriminative stimuli influence given subsequent behavior" (p. 588).

Chaining. Chaining is a procedure whereby responses are reinforced sequentially to form more complex behaviors. When the step-by-step linkage of responses is complete, the chain appears as a single cohesive behavior. Chaining is a method by which we acquire many of the complex behaviors we perform on a regular basis. Riding a bicycle or driving an automobile are examples. If you use chaining in self-management, you should perform necessary components on a step-by-step basis with reinforcement occurring after each step. Eventually, you should perform what emerges as a single cohesive behavior.

Premack Principle. The Premack Principle states that for any pair of behaviors, the more probable one will reinforce the less probable one. This principle, proposed by David Premack (1959), has been used by many students to strengthen and maintain self-management performance. Think of all the possibilities in your life: you might make going out with your friends contingent upon your studying, or you might consider watching TV contingent upon some other behavior change such as exercising or losing weight. There are any number of ways that Premack's

Principle can be used; many of you, in fact, are already using the principle to regulate your performance. You postpone doing something you would like to do, such as go out with your friends, until you have completed studying. To use the technique effectively, you must determine which of your responses have low and high rates of occurrence. You can then make the future performance of the high-rate behavior contingent upon your performing the low-rate behavior.

Conditioned reinforcers. A stimulus that initially has no reinforcing value may acquire such properties if it occurs simultaneously with an unconditioned or strongly conditioned reinforcer. For example, grades for your school work performance were initially nonreinforcing to you. However, through pairings with praise from teachers and parents, they become conditioned reinforcers.

Generalized reinforcers. These are conditioned reinforcers that are effective for a broad array of behaviors as a result of pairing stimuli with a number of established reinforcers. Money is the best example of a generalized reinforcer in that it has been paired with and can be exchanged for a variety of reinforcers (Sulzer-Azaroff and Mayer, 1991).

NEGATIVE REINFORCEMENT Many confuse negative reinforcement with punishment; they are different processes. Negative reinforcement is a consequence that strengthens or maintains a behavior by being subtracted or removed from the environment. The occurrence of a negative reinforcer can be prevented either by avoiding or escaping from it. Negative reinforcement strengthens and maintains much of our behavior, whether we study to avoid failure in a class or abruptly leave to escape from an unpleasant confrontation with another person.

There are two types of negative reinforcement: avoidance and escape learning. *Avoidance learning* refers to the performance of behaviors that remove the possibility of an unpleasant consequence. Avoiding the consequences provides a strengthening or maintenance of the behaviors. It is doubtful that there is any driver who does not slow down at the sight of a police officer writing a traffic ticket for a motorist. The response of slowing down removes or reduces the probability that we will meet a similar fate. *Escape learning* refers to our performance of behaviors that terminate an unpleasant consequence. Escaping from the consequences provides a strengthening or maintenance of the behaviors. There are positive and negative aspects to both avoidance and escape conditioning. Avoiding a situation that could be dangerous to you, such as using an illicit drug, is positive. You may be so shy, however, that you actively avoid interactions with others; in this instance, avoidance behavior has a negative consequence. Escape conditioning has a positive consequence if you break up a relationship with a person who is abusive to you. It has a negative consequence if you attempt to escape from the situation by abusing alcohol or other addictive substances.

Negative reinforcement dictates much of our performance; the operation has implications for any behavioral change effort. If obese, you attempt to escape from or avoid health problems by exercising and reducing your weight. You attempt to avoid failure in school by studying for your classes. Considering the powerful effect exerted by avoidance and escape procedures, they are useful techniques to consider in developing and implementing a self-management program.

PUNISHMENT   Punishment is a procedure where an aversive stimulus (or punisher) is presented immediately after the occurrence of a behavior. The result is a reduction in strength of the behavior. Staddon (1995) recently pointed out the value of punishment in some situations. It is useful to parents who wish to keep children from touching a hot surface or from racing into the road. Staddon concluded that the scientific evidence is neutral in deciding between reinforcement and punishment. Each has its advantages and disadvantages. Punishment is better at suppressing behavior; positive reinforcement is better at generating behavior. Punishment tends to produce more persistent behavior than positive reinforcement; positive reinforcement is often better in the aqcquisition of behavior. Two forms of punishment—time-out and response cost—can be included in a self-management program.

Time-out. Timeout is a procedure whereby access to varied sources of reinforcement is removed or reduced for a given period of time contingent upon a specified behavior. Almost all of you are familiar with time-out; it was probably the technique used by many of your parents as a means of discipline. Students, too, have used time-out as a feature of their self-management program. The procedure can help reduce the frequency of specific target behaviors. If you decide to use time-out in a change program, including self-management, it is suggested that you follow the following steps: (a) take reinforcers away that support the behavior you want to change; (b) keep the duration of time-out relatively short (i.e., 5 to 10 minutes); (c) implement and maintain the time-out on a consistent basis; and (d) provide desirable alternative behaviors to yourself or others.

Response cost. Response cost is a procedure whereby a specified amount of available reinforcers are withdrawn contingent on the occurrence of a specified behavior. Some weight-reduction programs work according to response cost in that a person may initially pay a certain fee to the program. Portions of this fee may be either retained by the program or returned to the individual contingent upon their progress in losing weight. You may incorporate response cost into your self-management program. This could be achieved by giving your roommate a certain amount of money. He or she could then keep or return the money to you contingent upon attaining your preset goals.

GENERALIZATION   Generalization is programming environments so that a behavior that occurs in one setting will also occur in another setting. You may find it easy to study in the library. How can you create a similar environment in your room so as to study effectively? You may program the environment in your room by creating similar lighting, adding tables and chairs, and reducing noise levels. Use of similar study habits in both types of settings is an example of generalization.

Classical Conditioning Techniques

Classical or responding conditioning is the type of conditioning discovered by Ivan Pavlov (1927). Here, a neutral stimulus (a sound), followed closely in time by a stimulus (food) that elicited a reflexive response (salivation), comes to elicit a similar response (salivation). The stimulus of food is an unconditioned stimulus; the salivation to the food is an unconditioned response. By pairing the sound, which becomes a conditioned stimulus, with the sight of the food, a conditioned response, salivation, is created.

Classical conditioning is a procedure by which we acquire many emotional behaviors. Many emotional reactions are positive. Certain music or sights may lead us to recall pleasant times from our past. Some emotional reactions are unpleasant, however. A friend survived the Holocaust by hiding in a basement. From a window, he could see the Nazi soldiers marching and hear their band play military music. As might be expected, he still becomes anxious when listening to military music or to the sounds of soldiers marching.

As some emotions are maladaptive, there is need for procedures to change them. This aim can be reached through the application of counterconditioning procedures where a conditioned stimulus loses its ability to elicit a conditioned response by pairing the conditioned stimulus with a stimulus that elicits an incompatible response. It is difficult to remain anxious, for example, if one can relax in the face of what were formally anxiety-evoking stimuli. The most widely used procedure for counterconditioning is referred to as systematic desensitization.

Systematic desensitization. There are three components to the procedure (Wolpe, 1958). First, the individual constructs hierarchies of stimuli that may cause fear, anxiety, or some other maladaptive emotional response. Hierarchies are basically descriptions of stimulus events that have been broken down into specific items and rearranged into a hierarchy according to the intensity of the emotional reaction they arouse in the individual. Second, the individual learns a response that is incompatible with the emotional reaction he or she normally experiences when contemplating the items listed on the hierarchies. In most cases, the incompatible behavior is relaxation. Learning to relax is systematically taught to the individual; the goal of relaxation is achieved when the individual can detect which muscles are relaxed or tense and relax all muscles according to self-cue. Finally, there is a juxtaposition of the initial two steps in that the individual relaxes while imagining items presented on the hierarchy. By staying relaxed with the presentation of the items, the person becomes desensitized to stimuli that, in the past, elicited an emotional reaction. This is strictly a trial-and-error procedure, and it may take the individual some time to work through the hierarchy. The use of imagination to desensitize oneself is sometimes referred to as in vitro desensitization. Eventually, the individual might like to test his or her newly developed skills in the real world, a procedure called in vivo desensitization. As systematic desensitization is useful in changing any emotional reaction, it will be discussed again in later chapters.

Systematic self-desensitization. This is basically the same procedure as systematic desensitization, except that the patient goes through the various stages without the assistance of a therapist (Martin and Osborne, 1989). The basic change is that you jot down the hierarchies of stimuli on 3 x 5 cards that you carry around and use whenever you want to practice self-desensitization. The procedure has been useful to a number of students in reducing emotional reactions to a broad array of stimuli.

EXERCISE

In reviewing the various behavioral change techniques available, consider how any may be of use to you in your self-management program.

Technique:
Potential uses:
Describe how you could use it:

REVIEW TERMS

Avoidance learning
Chaining
Extinction
Positive reinforcer

Premack Principle
Spontaneous recovery
Stimulus control
Time-out

QUESTIONS

List ten characteristics of behavior modification.
Describe classical conditioning.
Describe systematic desensitization.

CHAPTER 7

Social Learning and Cognitive Procedures

"Our deeds determine us, as much as we determine our deeds."
—George Eliot, *Adam Bede*

"People who always talk but never do anything slay me. I know these guys who meet at this cafe almost every morning for breakfast and talk about what they are going to do when they grow up. They've been doing it ever since high school. What's funny is that they now are all in their fifties! You've got to think and plan what you're going to do, but that's not the main point. You got to act on your plans."
—Phil, an electrical engineer

Social learning theory is linked to the research and writings of Julian Rotter, Walter Mischel, and, in particular, Albert Bandura. The social context within which our behavior is acquired and maintained is central to their writings. Social learning theory emphasizes the role of learning, social factors, and cognitive processes on how we evaluate, process, interpret, and apply information to ourselves and others. Like behavior learning theory discussed in Chapter 6, social learning theory proclaims that the ways we think, act, and feel are the result of our learning history. Therefore, reinforcement and punishment are important as determinants of our behavior. Unlike behavioral learning theory, however, social learning theory emphasizes that our behavior is not only influenced by consequences of our behavior, but by our expectations of success and failure.

Three types of beliefs are central to learning theory: locus of control, self-efficacy, and delay of gratification.

Locus of control. Rotter (1966) indicated that locus of control refers to our beliefs regarding how much control we have over given situations and reinforcement. Our beliefs that we have some control over given situations and rewards form an internal locus of control. If you believe you can obtain better grades by studying more, your behavior exemplifies an internal locus of control. External locus of control occurs when you believe that you don't have any control over given situations and reinforcement. Some students believe it is impossible for them to do well in mathematics or statistics classes no matter how hard they try. They view fate as dictating the consequences of their performance.

Self-efficacy. As noted in Chapter 2, self-efficacy refers to our beliefs that we can perform adequately in a given situation (Bandura, 1977). The degree of self-efficacy you have regarding your performance also influences your feelings of locus of control. Self-efficacy is discussed repeatedly throughout the text, particularly in Chapter 32.

Delay of gratification. The concept of delay of gratification is that you voluntarily postpone an immediate reward in order to complete a task that promises a future reinforcement. Mischel (1993) pointed out the importance of delay of gratification this way: Consider, for example, the self-imposed referrals of pleasure required to achieve occupational objectives such as careers in medicine or science. The route to such a goal involves a continuous series of delays of gratification, as seen in the progression from one grade to the next, and from one barrier to another in the long course from occupational choice to occupational success (p. 453).

Empirical evidence for the importance of delay of gratification was provided by Mischel and his colleagues. Mischel, Shoda, and Peake (1988) found children who showed a high ability to choose delayed gratification at ages four and five years old were more successful and better-adjusted adolescents ten years later. A later investigation found the children best able to delay gratification at four years had higher SAT scores when they applied to college (Shoda, Mischel, and Peake, 1990).

SOCIAL-COGNITIVE THEORY

In his more recent writings, Bandura (1986) used the term *social-cognitive theory* to emphasize the role of cognitive influences and behavior. He suggests that change is influenced by four distinctive cognitive processes: language ability, observational learning, purposeful behavior, and self-analysis.

Language ability. Our ability to use words permits us to collect, process, and evaluate information. We can then take action based upon our interpretation of the information.

Observational learning. Observational or vicarious learning is a form of learning that we develop through watching others. It does not require that we perform any behavior or receive reinforcement. For observational learning to be effective, Bandura (1986) indicated we must perform four steps: (a) pay attention to what the model does or says; (b) use memory to encode what we see so we can later retrieve and use the information; (c) be able to perform the motor control required to guide our actions and imitate the behavior of the model; and (d) be motivated to imitate the model's behavior.

Purposeful behavior. This term refers to our ability to plan, anticipate events, and set goals. These abilities give our behavior a purpose and the motivation to act on our expectations.

TABLE 7–1 Characteristics of Social Learning Theory

Emphasizes operant and classical conditioning
Emphasizes observational or vicarious learning whereby we learn a behavior from observing others
Emphasizes cognitive processes, including locus of control, self-efficacy, and delay of gratification
Emphasizes social contexts in which behavior is acquired and performed
Emphasizes self-management
Emphasizes assessment and laboratory research

Self-analysis. Self-analysis is our ability to monitor our behavior and thoughts in order to achieve our goals. This term includes processes involved in self-management.

A number of social learning or cognitive procedures can be used to change behavior. Characteristics of social learning theory are noted in Table 7–1. In some instances, these factors are identical to those of behavior modification (Chapter 6); the reliance on operant and classical conditioning principles is a common characteristic. In addition, however, social learning emphasizes modeling in the acquisition of behavior, cognitive processes, social contexts in which behavior occurs, and self-control. With the exception of operant and classical conditioning, the experimental foundation of social learning and cognitive processes is not yet as solid as it is for behavior modification. There are a number of reasons for this, but a major difference is that social learning principles are still evolving both theoretically and experimentally. Therefore, much of the empirical basis for social learning theory must still be established. Cognitive processes are also not public, as are observable behaviors. Because they are private events, they are less open to experimental scrutiny by others. This characteristic has resulted in some ambiguity in interpreting data gathered in social learning and cognitive-behavioral research; this result has not negated the importance of these findings, however, as cognitive-oriented approaches mirror more closely what occurs in reality. As much of our behavior is controlled by private thoughts and self-generated actions, the degree to which these acts are open to public scrutiny remains a function of the behaviors we exhibit.

SOCIAL LEARNING TECHNIQUES

Social learning procedures used in self-management are listed in Table 7–2. In many instances, some might be more aptly classified as cognitive-behavioral approaches. However, for the purposes of this discussion, they are classified as social learning methods.

TABLE 7–2 Assorted Social Learning or Cognitive-Behavior Techniques

Self-Monitoring
   Self-statements
   Self-statements plus distraction
   Reperception of situation
   Thought stopping
   Thought substitution

Relaxation

Meditation

Imagery

Rehearsal
   Imagined rehearsal
   Imagined rehearsal plus relaxation
   Imagined rehearsal plus self-statements
   Fantasy

Modeling
   Imagined modeling

Stress Inoculation

Self-Statements and Incompatible Behavior

Self-Monitoring

Self-monitoring, consisting of self-observation and recording, is the single most effective ingredient of self-management. This finding consistently emerges in clinical studies involving self-management. Self-monitoring, in fact, can often change behavior without the addition of any other change procedure. This point cannot be overemphasized: regardless of the target behavior you select, the foundation for the change program will be self-monitoring. In addition to the behaviors involved in self-monitoring, there are three other characteristics of self-monitoring that deserve mention: self-statements, self-statements plus distraction, and self-reinforcement.

SELF-STATEMENTS Self-statements were discussed in an earlier chapter. To reiterate, the effective use of self-statements in self-management requires that you analyze and identify antecedents to the stimuli that control your behavior. The role of self-talk in influencing these stimuli should be identified and, if necessary, changed in order to induce behavior change. Two types of self-statements are prominent: Positive self-statements indicate you are thinking about positive aspects of the situation you face. You reassure yourself of your ability to handle the situation, and concentrate on recalling how you managed similar situations in the past. You should reinforce yourself for any success you experience. Finally, an evaluation of your experience can provide insight as to how you can use positive self-statements to better manage similar situations in the future. In using positive self-statements, it is important that they be used frequently; this establishes self-talk as a viable change procedure. Linking your performance to positive self-statements enhances and strengthens self-talk as a method both for modifying your behavior and maintaining behavioral change.

Negative self-statements indicate you think distressing thoughts about the current situation you face and how it can be resolved. You may grow agitated and not think productively about solving the problem you face. Under these conditions, negative self-statements may result in self-defeating behaviors. Because internally generated self-statements can be more effective in controlling behavior than externally imposed directions, the necessity to distinguish positive from negative self-statements is a major consideration in self-management.

SELF-STATEMENTS PLUS DISTRACTION   Self-statements may be combined with distraction to produce behavior change. Three types of distraction have been identified: external, internal, and fantasy. *External distraction* means that you attempt to divert your attention away from a situation by focusing on the immediate environment. If you experience pain, you might alleviate the distress you feel through use of this tactic. *Internal distraction* indicates that you attempt to divert attention away from a situation by focusing on some part of your body or physical sensation. If you are around friends who smoke when you are attempting to abandon the habit, you can concentrate on the healing that is occurring in your lungs or the fact that you cough less in the morning. Finally, *imagery* can be used as a distraction. This indicates you are thinking of some pleasant activity or event in order to divert your attention away from a given situation. If you are attempting to lose weight and are surrounded by tempting deserts, you might fantasize how much better others will think you will look when you can wear smaller clothes. Positive self-statements are at the core of these methods of distraction.

REPERCEPTION OF SITUATION   It was noted earlier that you may want to reperceive a given situation in order to change it. Reperception permits you to reinterpret your thoughts and, ultimately, alter your behavior. You might find that you come to enjoy performing a behavior, such as writing a paper or giving a talk, that you formerly avoided because you perceived it as distressing. A number of behaviors you currently enjoy performing fall into this category; where you once thought they would be unpleasant, you later came to enjoy engaging in the behaviors.

THOUGHT STOPPING   This procedure, described in Chapter 2, involves saying to yourself, "Stop!" whenever an unwanted thought occurs. After halting the thought, immediately substitute a pleasant or attractive thought for the one you wish to extinguish.

THOUGHT SUBSTITUTION   Whenever a negative thought intrudes, you may also use thought substitution. This may be a pleasant thought or, as often used in cognitive therapy, a thought that directly counteracts the unpleasant or irrational thought. If you constantly tell yourself that you are going to fail an examination, your ruminations may prove self-fulfilling. If, however, you counter a negative thought about examination failure with a thought such as, "I will pass this examination. I always have in the past," or "I will pass the exam along with most of the students in the course," you are using thought substitution. Consistently substituting positive thoughts serves to reduce the influence of any negative ruminations you have about a particular situation.

Relaxation

Relaxation is a major coping strategy used in self-management. In fact, many refer to relaxation as the aspirin of psychology: it can be used as a coping tactic in innumerable situations. If you relax when in the presence of stimuli that normally produce anxiety or panic, such as the classroom, blue books, and other students that surround you when you take a test, you should perform better. Being relaxed permits you to alleviate anxiety and concentrate on completing the test. A number of relaxation procedures can be used. All procedures have a similar basis: you learn to interpret bodily sensations and detect whether you are tense or relaxed. If you are relaxed, you can use relaxation exercises to maintain the state; if you are tense, you can apply relaxation exercises to achieve a relaxed state. An exercise often used to teach relaxation skills is given in Table 7–3. The exercise is based upon the ground-breaking research conducted by Jacobson (1938). In studies with asthma, relaxation instructions have either been recorded on audiotape and given to patients, or patients have been asked to record their own tape. They are asked to listen to and practice the relaxation exercises daily. Later, they can perform the exercises less often, without the tape, whenever they want to relax. You or a friend should tape the instructions described in Table 7–3. Listen to and practice the relaxation exercises daily, or until you can relax whenever you wish without the aid of the tape. You will notice that the approach teaches you to relax muscle groups one group at a time. As with most activities, the more you practice relaxation exercises, the greater will be your skill. You will not only be more capable of discriminating which of your muscles are tense or relaxed, but you will be able to relax on self-cue. Thus, relaxation can become invaluable to you if you set aside some time each day to practice and refine your ability to relax as directed by self-instruction.

Meditation

Meditation can achieve the same effects as relaxation in that it produces increased physical relaxation and a renewed sense of vigor. However, meditation differs from relaxation (Rudestam, 1980), in that instead of focusing on the body and concentrating on the release of physical tension, meditation emphasizes detachment both from physical states and from

TABLE 7–3   Deep Muscle Relaxation Exercises (adapted from Creer, Kotses, and Reynolds, 1991)

Make yourself as comfortable as possible. Close your eyes and relax. Take a deep breath and let it out slowly, feeling yourself release tension as you let out your breath. Just let yourself relax as much as possible, breathing in and out in a comfortable, relaxed way. Before you begin the tensing and releasing exercise, remember to pay attention to the muscles and to the way you feel when you tense them, and the way they feel when you relax them.

Let's begin. With both of your hands, make a tight fist and squeeze hard. Keep squeezing and hold it tightly. Feel the tension in your hands and lower arms. Focus on the tension (10 seconds). Okay, now relax. Let go all at once. Let the tension flow out the tips of your fingers. Notice the difference in the way your hands and lower arms feel. You may feel warmth spreading through your hands and arms. Feel how good it is to have your hands so relaxed. Focus on these feelings of relaxation (30 seconds).

Now tense your upper arm muscles. Push your elbows down to tense these muscles. Push them now and hold it. Hold that tension. Feel the tension throughout your upper arms (10 seconds). Now relax your arms completely. Feel the relaxation spreading throughout your upper arms and shoulders. Focus on the nice, warm feeling. Notice the difference between the feelings of tension and relaxation (30 seconds).

We will move the muscles around your face and neck. While tensing and relaxing these muscles, let your arm and hand muscles stay relaxed. Lift your eyebrows as high as possible and keep them there. Feel the tension around your eyes and forehead. Maybe it feels like a tight band. Focus on that tension (10 seconds). Now, let it go. Relax and feel your scalp smoothing out as you release tension. Focus on the calm feelings while relaxed and comfortable. You may feel a warm tingling after doing this exercise. Just relax and enjoy this feeling of relaxation (30 seconds).

Move down your face to your nose and cheeks. Squint through your eyes and wrinkle your nose at the same time. Do this now and hold it tightly. Feel the tension around your nose (10 seconds). Relax these muscles all at once. Feel the tension flow out of your face, across your cheeks, and away. A warm wave of relaxation flows over your face. Enjoy the feeling (30 seconds).

Now move to your lower face and jaw. To tense this area, bite down, holding your teeth together and pulling the corners of your mouth back. Feel the tightness in your jaw and cheeks. Hold that tension (10 seconds). Now relax. Let go of the tightness all at once. Your jaw will hang loose and relaxed. Your mouth may open slightly. Focus on the warm feelings of relaxation in your face. Stay with that feeling (30 seconds).

Next move to the neck muscles. Pull your head toward your chest. Feel the tension in the front and back of your neck. Focus on the straining muscles. Hold it (10 seconds). Now let it all go. Let your head ease back naturally, without tension. Let your neck muscles loosen and relax. Focus on the feelings of relaxation in your neck. Let the warm waves of relaxation sweep through your body (30 seconds).

Next move to the muscles of your chest and shoulders. Pull your shoulder blades together. Think of making them touch. Pull them tightly together. Hold the tension and feel it. Focus on that tension (10 seconds). Now let it all go. Let your shoulders slump down. Allow your shoulders and chest to relax completely. Focus on the warm feelings of relaxation as they flow into your shoulders and chest (30 seconds).

Next work on your stomach muscles. Suck your stomach muscles in as if someone is about to hit you hard in the stomach and take your breath away. Hold it. Focus on the knotted muscles in your stomach (10 seconds). Now relax. Let your stomach become loose. Try to release a little more tension each time you breathe out. Feel your stomach relax. Enjoy the warm feelings of the muscles as they loosen up, smooth out, and relax more and more (30 seconds). You are now feeling deeply relaxed from the waist up.

Let's move to the muscles around your buttocks and hips. Squeeze your buttocks together hard and hold it. Study the tension (10 seconds). Now relax. Let these muscles loosen as warmth and heaviness flow into this area. Focus on these feelings. You are now feeling more and more relaxed (30 seconds).

Now tense the muscles in your thighs by pinching your legs together. Feel how tight and hard these muscles become. Study the tension (10 seconds). And relax. Let all the tension flow from your thighs. Feel these muscles smooth out as warm waves of relaxation come over you. Focus on the warmth and the heaviness (30 seconds).

> **TABLE 7–3 Continued**
>
> Now tense your calf muscles. Bend your toes back and stretch your legs out in front of you. Bring your toes back as if you're trying to touch them to your kneecaps. Hold that tension (10 seconds). And now relax. Rest your legs. Feel their heaviness. Focus on these warm feelings of relaxation. Comfortable, calm, and relaxed. Enjoy these feelings (30 seconds).
>
> Last, tense the muscles in your feet. Point your toes straight ahead and hold that tension. Study the tightness (10 seconds). And let it all go. Feel your feet grow warmer as the relaxation spreads over them. Enjoy that feeling. Just relax (30 seconds).
>
> In your mind, review the muscle groups we have covered. If you feel any tension in any muscles, let that tension go. Focus on having feelings of relaxation, warmth, and heaviness flow into areas of tension. If you still have a lot of tension, tense and relax the muscles that remain tight.
>
> It is time to end the relaxation session. Do this slowly. Keep your eyes closed. Slowly count to four. As you do so, you will become more alert and aware of the room around you. You will still feel relaxed, however. One, softly move your hands and arms around to wake them up. Feel the fabric beneath them. Two, gently move your feet and legs around, feel the floor (chair or bed) beneath them. Three, slowly move your head and neck. Allow the sounds of the room to come back to you. Four, open your eyes and sit up slowly. Allow yourself to adjust to the lights in the room. Notice that even as you become alert, the feelings of relaxation are still with you. Move around, stretch, and stand up.

feelings and thoughts. The benefits of meditation, continued Rudestam, also appear more cumulative than immediate. Many people skilled at meditation claim that it produces a sense of relaxation and well-being that is deeper than that produced by relaxation. Those who take the time to perform meditation daily believe it plays a central role in their adjusting to and overcoming the daily hassles of life.

Rudestam pointed out that there are certain general principles that underlie meditation techniques. First, meditation involves a shift of attention away from ongoing concerns toward the exercise you are attempting to perform. In meditation, you attempt to attend exclusively to a meditation object, which may be a visual stimulus, your breathing, or a mantra. A mantra is a melodic word or phrase that may be the name of a deity or a meaningless word or phase. Perhaps the best known mantra is *Om,* often chanted aloud by groups of people; the words *Hare Krishna* are also a familiar mantra. Rudestam suggested there is similarity between meditation with a mantra and a Christian prayer.

There are many different forms of meditation. You may select a sound of your own in performing the following exercise adapted from Rudestam:

Assume a comfortable position. Concentrate continuously on your sound, repeating it to yourself slowly and rhythmically, over and over again. If your concentration weakens or wanders, as often occurs, return to the mantra or sound you selected; repeat it over and over again. The most important aspect of meditation is that you do not work at concentrating on your mantra or sound; instead, you should adopt a passive attitude and allow thoughts to move in and out of your consciousness. Let whatever happens to you happen. If memories, preoccupations, or mental images appear, observe them with detachment before they slide from your consciousness; return to repeating your mantra to yourself. At first, the mantra or sound may mean something to you. After a while, you stop thinking of meaning and focus on the sound. Eventually, any meaning disappears completely. The sound you make becomes totally compelling and achieves a life of its own.

Whether you meditate, pray, or use relaxation, the result should be the same: you determine if you are tense or relaxed and relax according to your own self-cue.

Imagery

Imagery may be used as part of a behavioral procedure, such as systematic desensitization, or on its own as a way to change behavior. There are several steps to using imagery effectively.

First, find a place away from distracting stimuli where you can relax. To many of you, this will be your own room. Rather than use your bed, it might be useful to find a comfortable chair in which to relax and practice visual imagery.

Second, become relaxed according to the relaxation instructions presented in Table 7–3. In order to use imagery effectively, you need to be relaxed.

Third, you may include soothing music if you think that it will help you both relax and visualize scenes better. Many students believe that music not only helps them attain these states, but that the stimulus filters out noises and other stimuli that could serve as a distraction.

Fourth, decide what type of imagery you want to perform. There are three types: (a) receptive imagery consists of relaxing, creating an ambiguous scene, asking a question, and waiting for a response to the question; (b) programmed imagery consists of generating an image complete with everything that might be present in the visualized scene or ambience; and (c) guided visualization consists of imagining your scene in detail. Programmed and guided imagery are the types of visualization to practice in order to perform systematic desensitization. Imagery is a significant component of self-management, particularly when using systematic desensitization or systematic self-desensitization. You must know not only how to relax on self-cue, but how to summon up in your imagination the stimuli you want to decondition.

Rehearsal

Watson and Tharp (1989) point out that simply rehearsing a behavior over and over in situations where you want it to occur is a way of master-

ing that behavior. The techniques described in this chapter can improve your ability to rehearse a behavior, although they are no substitute for your actual performance. You eventually must rehearse and perform a behavior in the real world if it is to be mastered. Several types of rehearsal are described in this section: imagined rehearsal, imagined rehearsal plus relaxation, imagined rehearsal plus self-statements, and the use of fantasy.

IMAGINED REHEARSAL   Imagined or covert rehearsal entails rehearsing behavior in your imagination. There is evidence that this approach can be effective, particularly in improving motor skills such as those involved in athletic performance. While they caution that actual performance is more effective than imagined performance, Watson and Tharp suggest that imagined rehearsal can be used to provide preliminary behavioral rehearsal, to allow extra rehearsal, and to permit rehearsal that emphasizes particular features of a behavior or situation.

There are certain steps to using rehearsal effectively, as enumerated in Table 7–4. If you are going to use these steps, it is suggested that you view yourself from the inside, eyes open or closed. This permits you both to feel your way through an activity and to see what you would if you were watching someone else perform the activity. The method can help you determine your actual reactions in a situation. Besides using imagined rehearsal before performing a task, it is also useful to imagine and rehearse a behavior *after* you have been successful. This reinforces your performance, thus making it more likely that you will be successful at performing the actual behavior in the future.

IMAGINED REHEARSAL PLUS RELAXATION   Watson and Tharp equate this procedure with systematic self-desensitization. It can be invaluable in helping you overcome past fears and failures. If you are going to use imagined rehearsal plus self-statements, it is suggested that you use it often, tie mental imagery closely to relaxation, and not overload yourself with too many verbal suggestions at a time. Emphasize that you will be successful

TABLE 7–4   Steps Involved in Using Imagined Rehearsal Effectively

1. Rehearse coping skills that you use in real life.
2. Actively imagine the situation as clearly as possible.
3. Imagine the situation and your behavior in complete, minute detail.
4. Rehearse your performance in the actual setting, if possible.
5. Practice any rehearsed activity in its entirety.
6. Imagined rehearsal should be successful.
7. At least one mental practice should precede actual physical performance.
8. Rehearsal should proceed at same speed at which behavior unfolds in real life.
9. In rehearsal, concentrate on imagining feel of situation.

in performing the actual behavior. If you use negative self-statements or imagine failure, the procedure is apt to be self-defeating.

IMAGINED REHEARSAL PLUS SELF-STATEMENTS   If you are successful at imagining an event or behavior, you can guide your performance in rehearsal through self-instruction. Following the suggestions offered in Table 7–4 can help lead you through all the steps you need to perform, as well as help you correct errors or mistakes. Rehearsal plus self-statements can help you correct potential problems before your actual performance, as long as you are not too hard on yourself. At the same time, self-statements can assist you in rehearsing behaviors that will help you achieve the goals you set for yourself. All rehearsal, in the long run, should be oriented toward attainment of your goals.

FANTASY   Fantasy can help you elicit materials that might otherwise be ignored. As Rudestam (1980) notes, "Fantasy begins where awareness leaves off. With awareness you stay in the present and attend to ongoing experiences; with fantasy you imagine and intuit, remember and plan" (p. 56). Rudestam suggests that the most important role of fantasy is that by allowing your fantasy to enhance a theme, you might contact feelings or memories that you would otherwise avoid. Fantasy has another role in that it might permit you to arrive at a goal that you would not otherwise have considered. The instructions provided for using imagery effectively should be employed to assist you in using fantasy effectively.

Modeling

We learn many behaviors—both desirable and undesirable—from observing others. There are few of us who have not acquired some behaviors from observing our parents. In self-management, the focus should be on the acquisition of desirable behaviors. Learning through observation follows the same principles as direct learning (Watson and Tharp, 1989). The consequences that occur to a model following a behavior will determine whether or not we imitate that behavior. If models receive positive reinforcement, we are apt to imitate their responses; if models are punished, however, we are less apt to model the behaviors. We learn what behaviors to imitate according to the cues and signals we observe from models. Modeling can be a useful component in a self-management program provided we find an appropriate model who exhibits behavior that we would like to perform in order to achieve a goal.

IMAGINED MODELING   With imagined modeling, you imagine someone, other than yourself, performing a behavior, being reinforced for it, and so on (Watson and Tharp, 1989). If you use imagined modeling, follow the steps outlined in Table 7–5. Some of these steps were suggested by Kazdin (1984); they have a proven utility in using imagined modeling to help you change a target behavior.

TABLE 7-5 Steps in Using Imagined Modeling

1. Break down problem behavior into series of discrete steps.
2. Imagine and write out your desired behavior.
3. Imagine the context in which the problem behavior occurs.
4. Imagine a model similar to you in sex and age.
5. Imagine the model began with a difficulty similar to yours, but that he or she mastered the ability to cope with the problem.
6. Imagine the person you model initially had difficulty with the problem, but gradually overcame and mastered it.
7. Imagine your model being reinforced for successful coping, particularly by reaching your desired goal.
8. Imagine your model using self-instruction. Think of coping statements that you might make to yourself in order to cope and master a situation.
9. Imagine different models in each situation, rather than one person only.
10. Perform in real life the desired behavior you have acquired through modeling.

Stress Inoculation

Sometimes we can avoid problems by successfully preparing for them. A strategy for coping with potential problems is stress inoculation (Meichenbaum, 1985). There are six basic steps to the procedure.

First, you construct mental pictures around some situation that you view as threatening. We will use giving a talk in public as an example because this is a leading fear for many of us.

Second, imagine yourself having a difficult time in giving the talk. Perhaps you begin to shake or your voice quivers. Let yourself feel the anxiety, embarrassment, and physiological responses you might experience under these circumstances. Your face blushes and you feel increasingly frightened.

Third—the key step in stress inoculation—think through exactly what you might do if the worst possible thing happened in a situation, in this case giving a speech. Let yourself go here, even if the effects arouse anxiety for you. Think of how you falter, stammer, and eventually go completely blank when speaking. You finally stumble back to your seat.

Fourth, develop a coping strategy to deal with the situation. Almost any of the procedures we have discussed in this chapter, as well as systematic self-desensitization described in Chapter 6, might be used as a coping strategy.

Fifth, work through the situation with your selected strategy so that you believe you could cope with the situation.

Finally, cope with the situation in real life. Remember that the more you rehearse and practice your coping strategy, the more successful you are likely to be in real life. Stress inoculation is an excellent procedure to

Self-Statements and Incompatible Behavior

This type of procedure could also have been described in Chapter 6, since it is similar to systematic desensitization. It is discussed in this chapter because of the effect of self-statements in cluing an individual to perform an incompatible behavior in a context where he or she formerly performed another behavior. Figure 7–1 illustrates this concept; in this case the subject is how a student reduced cigarette consumption by eating sunflower seeds. As noted, he was smoking over half a pack a week at the beginning of his program. Thereafter, when he was prompted to smoke either by self-generated or environmentally generated cues, he began eating sunflower seeds. He not only reduced the number of cigarettes he smoked, but he eventually reduced to zero the sunflower seeds he consumed. He therefore demonstrated that he was able to change both the target behavior he selected (cigarette smoking) and the incompatible behavior he selected (eating sunflower seeds) to modify cigarette smoking.

Two other approaches to combining self-statements with incompatible behaviors are illustrated in Figures 7–2 and 7–3. Figure 7–2 illustrates

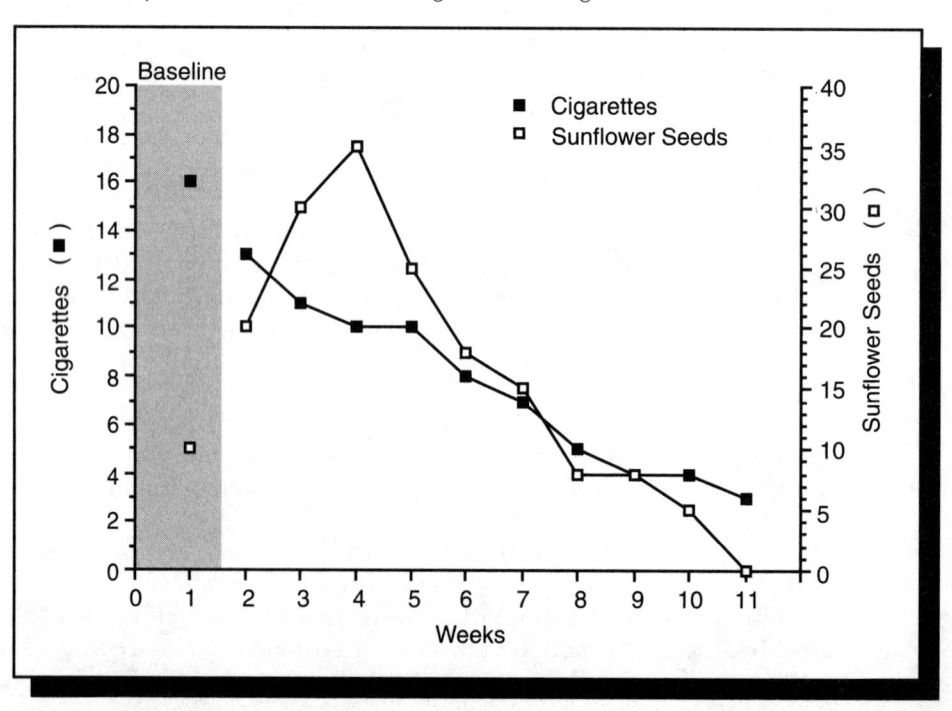

FIGURE 7–1
Use of incompatible behavior to reduce cigarette smoking.

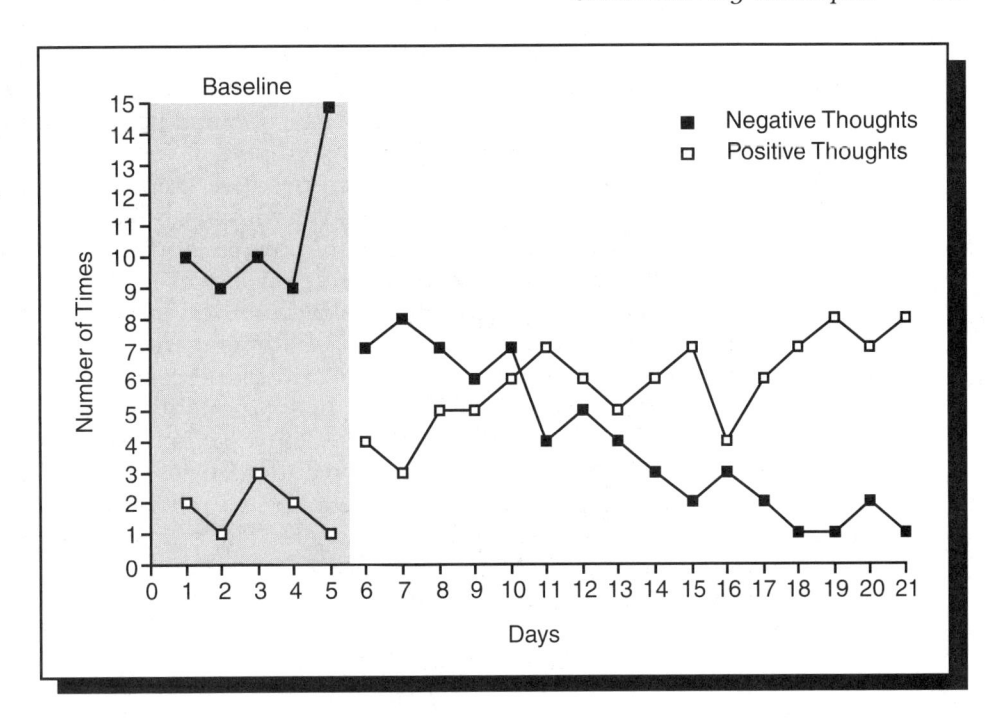

Social Learning Techniques   **73**

FIGURE 7–2
Decreasing negative thoughts and increasing positive thoughts of self.

FIGURE 7–3
Decreasing negative thoughts and increasing positive thoughts of self.

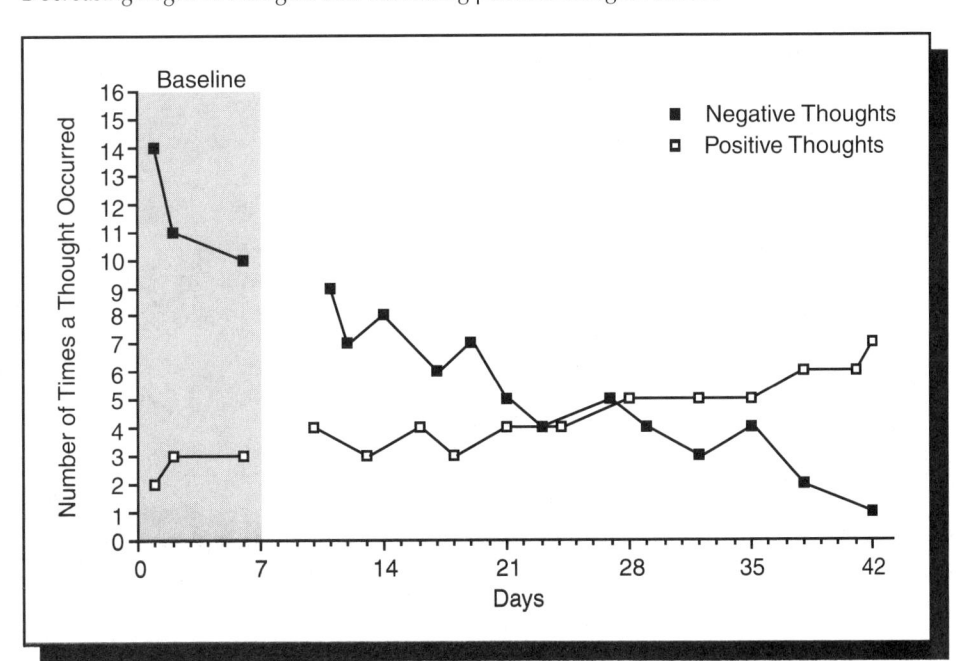

results of a program developed by a student who combined self-monitoring, self-statements, and thought stopping. As depicted by her baseline data, she had far more negative thoughts than she had positive thoughts. Her intervention consisted of saying "Stop!" to herself each time she had a negative thought. She then replaced each negative thought with a positive thought. Figure 7–2 shows that the student made solid progress. As she noted, "My program made me feel more positive and confident about myself and my appearance. This was reflected in my attitude in general." Figure 7–3 illustrates the progress made by another student who combined self-monitoring, thought stopping, self-statements, and environmental stimuli to reduce negative thinking and to increase the number of positive thoughts she experienced. She used thought stopping to decrease negative thoughts; she then made positive self-statements to herself. In addition, the student posted motivational messages around her room (e.g., "Happiness is a decision we make") to remind herself to replace negative thinking with positive thoughts. The student was pleased with her findings but thought they were just a beginning, commenting, "I believe this self-management program needs more time."

EXERCISE

In reviewing the different social learning and cognitive/behavioral techniques presented in this chapter, consider how any may be of use to you in your self-management program.

Technique:
Potential uses:
Describe how you could use a given technique:

REVIEW TERMS

Covert rehearsal	Internal distraction
Delay of gratification	Locus of control
Imagined modeling	Programmed imagery
Imagined rehearsal plus self-statements	Receptive imagery

QUESTIONS

Discuss six characteristics of social learning theory.
Discuss six steps involved in stress inoculation.
Discuss four processes involved in social-cognitive theory.

CHAPTER 8

Maladaptive and Dysfunctional Thoughts

"There is no trap so deadly as the trap you set for yourself."
—Raymond Chandler, *The Long Goodbye*

"I hate it to happen. Sometimes I wake up in the middle of the night and start thinking of things at work. It may be something large like a project we have to get out by a certain date or it may be something small like something said at work that day. Anyway, I start thinking and things just spiral. Before long, I'm worrying about whether I can do the job or if they'll fire me. It's like the thoughts have a life of their own. They just take over. When it happens, I'll lay awake for hours trying to shut them off and go back to sleep. I just can't turn the thoughts off."

—Fred, a forty-five-year-old manager

We all experience dysfunctional thoughts from time to time. We may find we are obsessed with certain ideas; no matter how hard we try, they never seem to go away. Or we may find that we constantly worry about an upcoming test. We repeatedly tell ourselves that we will do poorly, although we have studied and prepared ourselves for the examination. What appear as automatic thoughts about how poorly we will do if asked to present a talk in a class or a meeting are apt to consume much of our waking time.

Dysfunctional thinking is the result of learning inappropriate thought patterns, primarily through classical conditioning. We pair thoughts of giving the talk with a past experience where we were anxious; after a few pairings of the two types of processes, the idea of giving the talk becomes a conditioned stimulus that induces negative thinking. Other stimuli may become conditioned stimuli in arousing negative thinking through pairing of the previously neutral stimulus with either our anxiety or our thoughts of giving the talk. Much like ripples on the surface of a pond, an ever-expanding group of stimuli become antecedents to our behavior. These form the learning history that comes to dictate much of our future performance. Before reviewing ways for changing negative thinking, this chapter will describe characteristics of dysfunctional and maladaptive thinking.

CHARACTERISTICS OF MALADAPTIVE THINKING

A number of writers have described different characteristics of dysfunctional thinking. Table 8–1 indicates characteristics of automatic thoughts as suggested by McKay, Davis, and Fanning (1981), and Ellis, Sichel, Yeager, DiMattia, and DiGiuseppe (1989). As you read the list, you will likely agree that many of these characteristics of automatic thinking apply to the negative thoughts you experience. Other characteristics of dysfunctional thinking include faulty reasoning and illogical ideas.

Faulty Reasoning

A characteristic of maladaptive thinking is that it is based on faulty reasoning. Several experts have described, often with different terminology, features of faulty reasoning. Suggestions by Rudestam (1980) and McKay and colleagues (1981) exemplify these characteristics.

1. *Magnification.* This involves magnifying negative details while filtering out positive aspects of a situation. The result is that an event becomes far more stressful than warranted.

2. *Polarized thinking.* This is either/or type of thinking where things are either black or white, good or bad. There is no middle ground or shades of gray when we think in extremes. We overlook positive aspects of our behavior; since we are not perfect, we consider ourselves a failure.

3. *Overgeneralization.* This is the tendency to make broad conclusions based on little data. If something bad happens to us once, we tend to expect it will reoccur again and again.

4. *Mind reading.* You may believe that you know what other people are thinking or feeling toward you without their saying anything. This re-

TABLE 8–1 Characteristics of Automatic Thoughts (adapted from McKay, Davis, and Fanning, 1981)

1. They are specific and discrete messages.
2. They appear in shorthand form.
3. No matter how irrational they are, we almost always believe them.
4. They are spontaneous.
5. They are often couched in terms of should, ought, or must.
6. They tend to magnify and awfulize.
7. They are idiosyncratic.
8. They are hard to turn off.
9. They are learned.

action is often based upon a single response that you have misinterpreted.

5. *Catastrophizing.* This involves our making a catastrophe out of an event. We come to expect disaster, and begin to think in "what ifs": "What if I fail this test?" "What if I begin to stammer during this talk?"

6. *Personalization.* This is related to mind reading in that you believe everything a person does is somehow related to your behavior. You may begin to compare yourself to others in terms of who is smarter, better looking, and so on.

7. *Control fallacies.* If you think you have little control over an event, you see yourself as totally helpless. Your future is at the whim of someone or something else. If you believe you have some control over an event, you somehow feel you are responsible for the unhappiness experienced by others. If they experience failure, it is your fault.

8. *Fallacy of fairness.* In this case, you are resentful because you are certain you know what is fair even though others disagree with you. You may hold on to the idea that life is fair, although there is no evidence that this is the case.

9. *Blaming.* You hold others responsible for whatever problems you experience. It is currently popular to blame our parents for any problem we encounter, although there is usually no empirical evidence to support this premise.

10. *Shoulds.* We have rules about how we think others and ourselves should act. When others do not behave the way we think they should, we may become angry; when we do not act the way we think we should, we feel guilt or shame.

11. *Emotional reasoning.* Here you let your emotions dictate your should beliefs. If you feel dumb, you must be dumb. The fact that emotions do not obey the laws of reason is never considered in making your decision.

12. *Fallacy of change.* This suggests you can change people if you try hard enough to do so. If you do change them, it will increase your happiness.

13. *Global labeling.* In this situation, you generalize one or two qualities into a global judgment. If you perform poorly at one or two tasks, you think you must be stupid and incapable of performing any task well.

14. *Being right.* This point implies that you must continually be on trial to prove your behaviors and opinions are correct. Being wrong is unthinkable; you would go to any length to demonstrate that you are right.

15. *Heaven's reward fallacy.* You expect all your actions to pay off, as if someone is keeping score. You feel bitter when what you perceive as your just reward does not occur. At the same time, you may feel angry when someone receives what you perceive as a reward they do not deserve.

You may recognize that you regularly employ one or more of these methods of reasoning. As they can cause you concern and distress, you might elect to modify them in some manner.

Illogical Ideas

Long before social learning and cognitive-behavioral approaches became popular, Albert Ellis advocated that we induce and maintain much of the discomfort we feel because of the illogical ideas we acquire and maintain. He listed the following illogical ideas as especially common and destructive (Ellis, 1973). Check how many of these illogical thoughts and ideas apply to you.

1. It is a necessity for all of us to be loved or approved by every significant person in our lives.
2. We should be thoroughly competent, adequate, and achieve in all possible respects to consider ourselves worthwhile.
3. Certain people are wicked, bad, or villainous, and they should be severely blamed and punished for their evil.
4. It is awful and catastrophic when things are not the way we would like them to be.
5. Our unhappiness is externally caused, and people have little or no ability to control their terrors and disturbances.
6. It is easier to avoid than to face life's difficulties and responsibilities.
7. Our past history is an all-important determinant of our present behavior and, because something once strong affected our life, it will continue to do so.

If you were honest with yourself, you probably found that you cling to at least two or more of these common illogical ideas. They sneak into our thoughts and produce doubt, fear, and unhappiness. Consider only the first thought, "It is necessary to be loved or approved by every significant person in our lives." How many of us have felt sad, frustrated, or angry because we thought we did not achieve what others, such as our parents, believed we should achieve? Think of the anguish you have experienced because of your own self-generated thoughts. You may have spent a sleepless night having a conversation with yourself to try and explain why you were less than perfect. Consider how you attempted to change your behavior because of your irrational thoughts. You may have made some dramatic behavioral changes that were induced by your own unimportant and irrelevant ideas. Changing the illogical thoughts and ideas described by Ellis (1973) is a lifetime pursuit. Methods for modifying such ideas, including techniques offered by Ellis, include the following suggestions.

CHANGING MALADAPTIVE THINKING

Maladaptive thinking can have three consequences: (a) it can shape our thoughts and the actions we take; (b) it can determine how we perceive and interpret events; and (c) it can lead to a variety of behavioral problems.

A smorgasbord of techniques is available to help you alter maladaptive thought patterns, as listed in Table 8–2. Many social learning and cognitive-behavioral techniques were described in Chapter 7: imagery, meditation, modeling, rehearsal, relaxation, self-monitoring, self-statements, and stress inoculation. Other techniques that might be considered include: (a) altering the environment to change the stimuli that may be controlling maladaptive thought patterns; (b) self-reinforcement, where you reinforce yourself for appropriate behaviors; (c) practicing alternative responses, such as relaxation or differential reinforcement of other responses; and (d) practicing problem-solving skills. Five problem-solving skills that may be useful include: (1) alternative solution thinking, where you generate different problem-solving options; (2) means-end thinking, where you think of what you have to do to solve a problem; (3) consequential thinking, where you realistically identify what may occur as a consequence of your action; (4) causal thinking, where you attempt to determine how events may be related to one another; and (5) sensitivity to interpersonal problem thinking, where you perceive a problem that exists and identify the interpersonal aspects of any confrontation that may emerge in solving the problem. It should be emphasized that these techniques, particularly self-monitoring, are useful components of any package designed to change inappropriate and dysfunctional thought patterns and should be considered in any self-management program designed to change these behaviors.

TABLE 8–2 Techniques That Can Be Used to Change Maladaptive Thought Patterns

Cognitive restructuring
Imagery
Meditation
Modeling
Rational-emotive restructuring
Rehearsal
Relaxation
Self-monitoring
Self-statements and incompatible behavior
Stress inoculation
Thought control
Thought stopping

The remainder of the discussion will focus on four methods for modifying thought patterns: thought stopping, thought control, cognitive restructuring, and rational-emotive restructuring.

Thought Stopping

As noted earlier, Wolpe (1958) suggests we use a method called thought stopping to halt intrusive thoughts or ideas. This technique entails five steps:

1. Think about the problem thought (or feeling, if it is triggered by the thought).
2. When you have a clear image of the problem, yell "Stop!" to yourself. Since this may not always be possible to do overtly, you can do it covertly to yourself.
3. Eventually fade out use of the word *stop* when you find you no longer ruminate about the problem thought.
4. Substitute a positive thought in place of the unwanted thought.
5. When you have extinguished the unwanted behavior, reinforce yourself for your achievement.

Students have successfully employed thought stopping to reduce negative thoughts, as shown in Figure 8–1. This illustrates the progress of a student who combined thought stopping with positive thoughts to decrease jealous ideation or thoughts. A second student combined thought stopping with punishment (e.g., continued negative thoughts cost her use of her pillow), a response-cost procedure. Her progress is shown in Figure 8–2. This imaginative procedure resulted in a sharp decrease in negative thoughts. Thought stopping, either alone or in combination with another procedure, thus has demonstrated value in modifying maladaptive thoughts or thought patterns.

Thought Control

There are two aspects of thought control: reducing negative thoughts and increasing positive thoughts. Suinn (1986) suggests that we deal with negative thoughts by taking the following steps:

1. Use them in a positive way. Instead of letting them feed on themselves, determine if negative thoughts can be used to solve a problem. Do not avoid the thought, but use self-monitoring to analyze dysfunctional thoughts and develop plans for corrective action.
2. Control negative thoughts. You may achieve this goal by: (a) examining the thoughts to determine if they can be used in a positive way to suggest a solution; (b) analyzing the source of negative thoughts

Changing Maladaptive Thinking 81

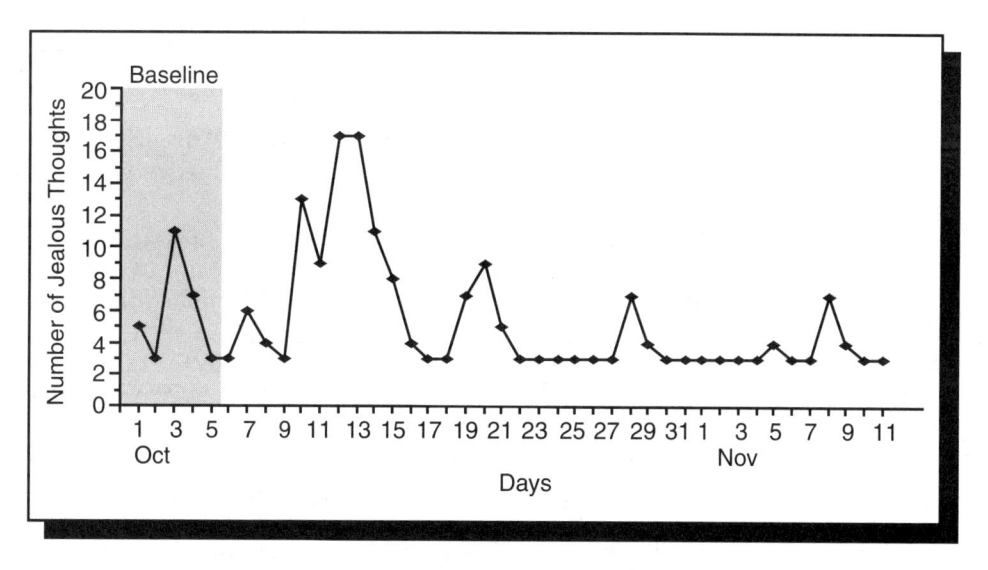

FIGURE 8–1
Use of thought stopping and positive thoughts to reduce jealous ideation.

FIGURE 8–2
Use of a combination of thought stopping and response cost to reduce negative thoughts.

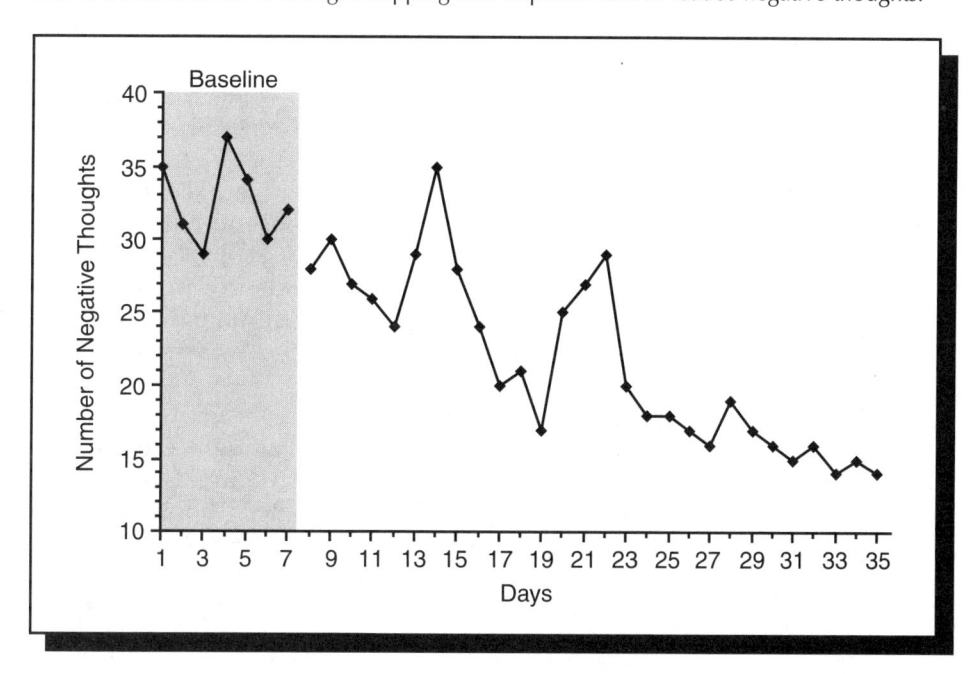

through self-monitoring, and taking action to remove their origin; and (c) making a realistic evaluation of whether or not you have a problem.
3. Replace negative thoughts with plans for the future. Set goals. Think of how you can use negative experiences to improve your future behavior.
4. Realistically consider what others think. As noted earlier, we are often too hard on ourselves because of our perceptions regarding what others may or may not think of us. Suinn (1986) noted that we forget others are likely to share the same doubts with us.
5. Review your strengths and how they can be used. Suinn (1986) suggested that recalling your strengths can be a positive way of controlling thoughts through distraction.
6. Substitute a neutral thought for the bothersome thought. The use of imagery can also be of value in this situation.
7. Contain negative thoughts that are unresponsive to other solutions. Suinn suggests two methods for achieving this aim. First, you can utilize thought stopping. Second, you can just let thoughts roam in and out of your consciousness. Eventually, you will become satiated with the ideas.

Suinn suggests that you can teach yourself positive thoughts in the following manner:

1. Value yourself as a person. If you do this, you should generate more positive thoughts about yourself.
2. Know where you are before you make a move. Before taking action, think of what you are going to do. You may want to use imagery and rehearsal to strengthen your plan.
3. Review your progress. You should look at where you are with respect to where you started. Keep looking at the total picture, and avoid feeling down about temporary setbacks. Identify your current strengths and constantly review them. As you recall your past successes, you can build upon these behaviors to enhance the positive statements you make to yourself.
4. Know what you want and what your goals are in social situations. The importance of goal setting has been emphasized, particularly in Chapter 4. It is important in developing positive thoughts.

The progress of a student in decreasing negative thoughts is depicted in Figure 8–3. Initially, he used only thought stopping in an attempt to control these thoughts. As noted on Days 9 through 13, this procedure proved ineffective. He then combined thought stopping with positive statements to himself. Except for one bad day (Day 32), he reduced the number of negative thoughts he had. The strategies outlined by Suinn are useful both in reducing negative thoughts and in building positive thoughts.

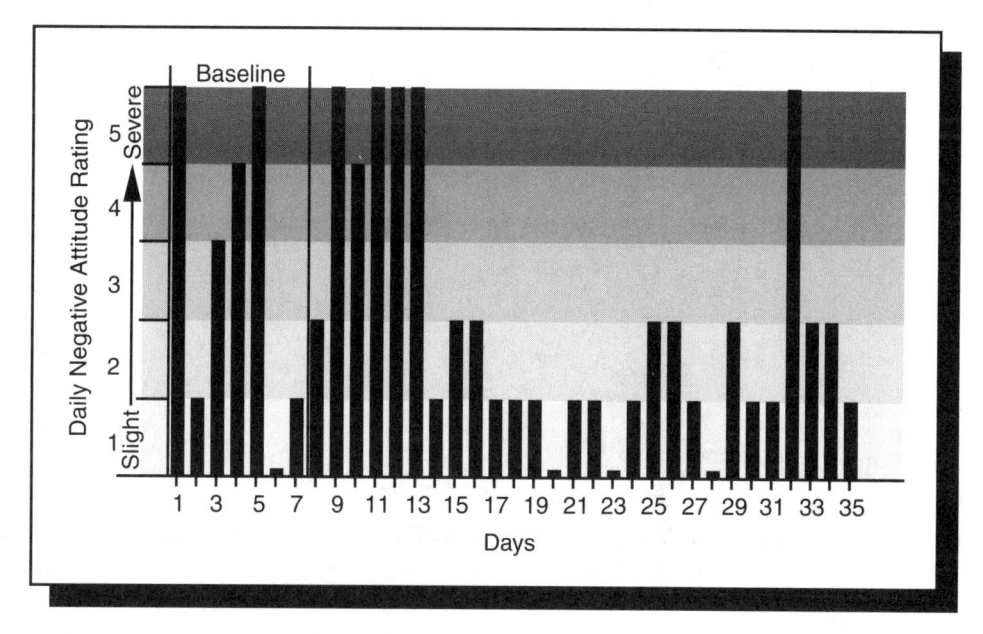

FIGURE 8–3
Using a combination of thought stopping and positive thoughts to change negative ideation.

Cognitive Restructuring

Beck, Rush, Shaw, and Emery (1979) proposed a method for restructuring dysfunctional cognitive behaviors. Aspects of the approach are applicable to self-management. To change maladaptive or dysfunctional thinking, Beck and colleagues suggest that we:

1. Clearly recognize and identify our negative, automatic thoughts.
2. Recognize the association between these negative thoughts, the emotions they generate, and their actions.
3. Self-monitor the occurrence of these thoughts in the same manner as we would any other behavior.
4. Test the thoughts and the inappropriate assumptions that distort our thoughts against reality by examining the evidence for and against them.
5. Change dysfunctional thinking by substituting more realistic thoughts.
6. Reinforce ourself for more appropriate thinking. This procedure is an empirical method that can be used in any self-management program we might design to modify maladaptive thinking.

Cognitive restructuring was employed by a student whose data is shown in Figure 8–4. The student attempted to reduce the number of

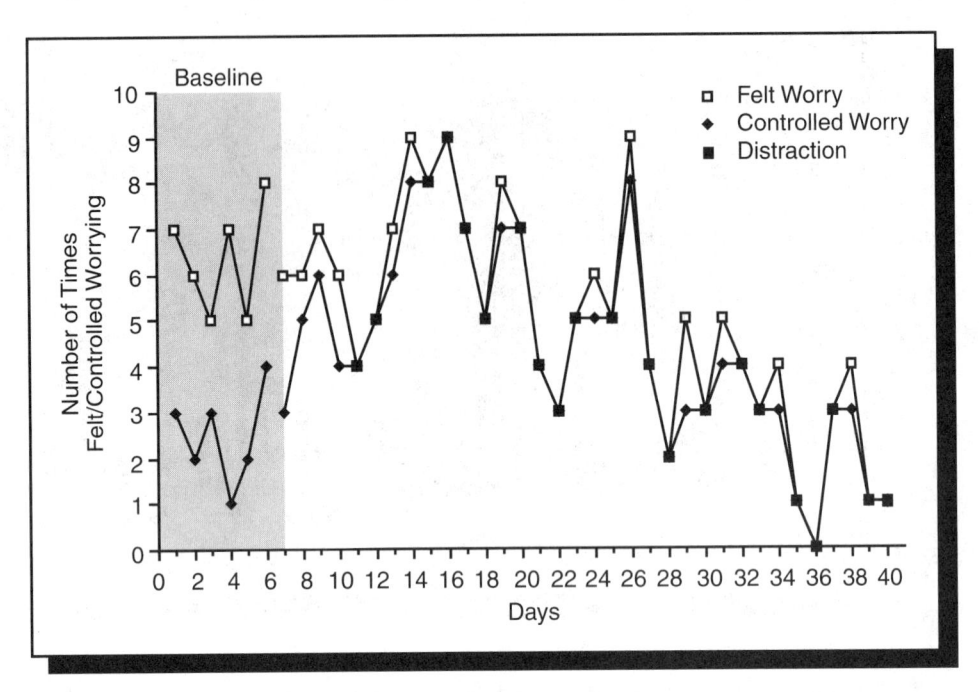

FIGURE 8-4
Decrease in the number of times the student spent worrying.

times she worried each day. Whenever a worrying thought occurred, she asked herself a series of what she referred to as reality-check questions. Answering these questions usually controlled the worrying thoughts. When the procedure did not, the student employed distraction. The combination of asking herself reality-check questions and distraction permitted the student to control the worry she experienced.

Rational-Emotive Restructuring

This approach by Ellis (1973) is also a form of cognitive therapy. Ellis believes that how we think dictates how we feel. Rational-emotive therapy focuses on our altering patterns of dysfunctional thinking to reduce maladaptive emotions and behavior. Ellis proposes an ABC sequence to describe his ideas:

A is the Activating event that produces the stress. It may be an action that occurs in your life, such as a failing grade, or just the thought that you may fail.

B is the Belief system, which represents the belief you have about the event, and your appraisal of the stress that occurs. As Ellis noted in his list of illogical ideas, we often tend to view minor events as disasters.

C is the Consequence of our negative thinking. When our appraisals of stressful events are negative, emotional distress is often a consequence.

To change a dysfunctional thought or thought pattern, Ellis suggests that you perform the following steps:

1. Review each idea to see how it influences you. You might consider the illogical ideas, discussed earlier, to evaluate any thought that disturbs you.
2. Monitor yourself carefully. It is important that you observe and record any self-defeating thought, particularly because of the automatic characteristics of such acts.
3. Identify stressful events and identify any negative thoughts associated with them. Through this procedure, you can determine whether any type of conditioning has occurred between your feelings and thoughts.
4. Try to counteract irrational and negative thoughts with positive and realistic statements. The discussion of controlling negative by positive thoughts, prominent in Suinn's proposal (1986), is relevant here.

It should be emphasized that a reduction in negative thinking is not causally linked to an increase in positive thinking. Those who have substituted positive thoughts for negative thoughts have deliberately sought to do so. In other words, when a negative thought was controlled, they at-

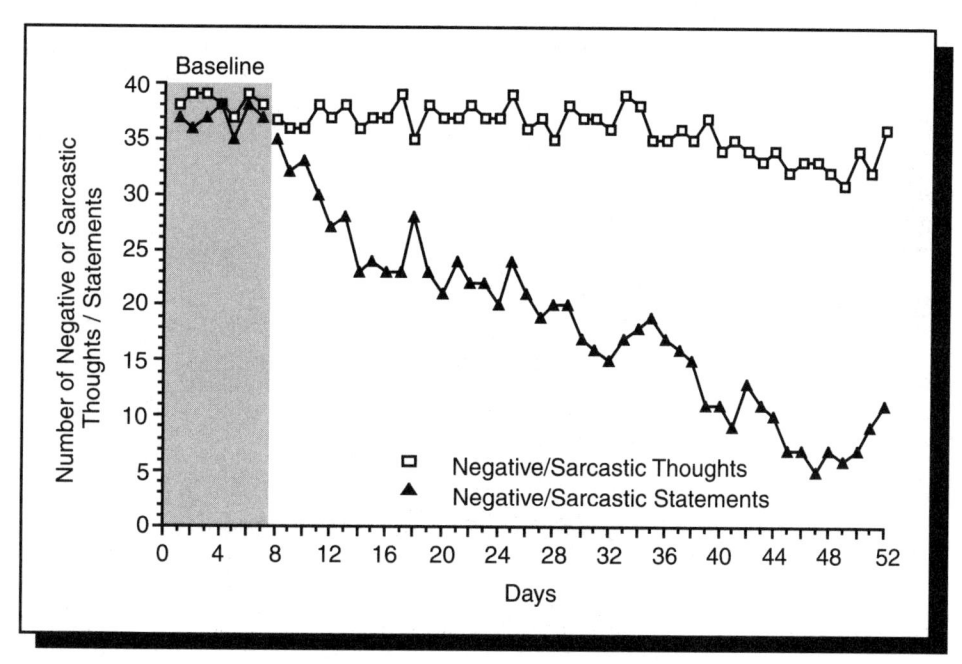

FIGURE 8–5
Attempt to reduce negative or sarcastic thoughts and statements.

tempted to substitute a positive thought in its place. As shown, the students were generally successful in achieving this goal. There is also no causality between negative thoughts and the public expression of such thoughts. This is graphically shown in Figure 8–5. The student was concerned about both the negative thoughts she experienced and the negative or sarcastic statements she made to others. She used a combination of self-monitoring, thought stopping, peer support, and negative reinforcement in an attempt to reduce both negative thinking and negative or sarcastic statements. At the completion of the program, the student said she did not achieve her goal of becoming more positive. However, the figure shows, while not reducing the number of negative thoughts she experienced, the program did result in a reduction in the number of negative or sarcastic statements she made. In this case, the lack of change in private events was not correlated with the change in public statements the student made.

EXERCISE

After reading ways of modifying problem thought patterns, consider the following:

What type of problem thoughts do I experience?
How might they be changed?
What would be the best strategy for me to use?

REVIEW TERMS

Fallacy of change
Fallacy of fairness
Heaven's reward fallacy
Means-end thinking

Negative thoughts
Rational-emotive therapy
Thought control
Thought stopping

QUESTIONS

Describe seven types of illogical ideas.
Discuss the six steps involved in cognitive restructuring.
Describe the ABC sequence proposed by Ellis.

CHAPTER 9

Emotional Reactions

"Seeing's believing, but feeling's the truth."
—Thomas Fuller, *Gnomologia*

"I'm very emotional. I cry through movies or even when watching soaps. I can't watch the news before going to bed because it scares me too much. I sometimes skip going to class because I'm afraid the teacher will ask me a question. What do you think I can do?"
—Jenny, a college sophomore

Emotions are one of the oldest topics of interest to humans. Part of the reason for the interest in emotions is that they are a fundamental part of being human. Furthermore, of all species, humans are the most emotional. In spite of their importance, emotions are difficult to define and measure and can be classified in many ways. Emotion, notes Millenson (1967), has "been a wastebasket category of behavior and the various phenomena discarded there have shown a strong resistance to systematic integration" (p. 433).

Despite past difficulties in defining, measuring, and classifying emotions, Kleinginna and Kleinginna (1981) define emotion as a complex pattern of physical and mental changes that include feelings, physiological reaction and arousal, cognitive processes, and behavioral reactions that occur in reaction to a situation that a person perceives as significant.

FEELINGS

Emotional reactions are similar in human cultures throughout the world. A reason for such similarity is that emotions are necessary for our survival both as a species and as individuals.

As infants, we cried when we needed the attention of our parents. This was a way we had of sending social signals to others. When in a situation where we experience fear, we may escape from the setting. The emotion of fear motivates us to take action. Feeling happy is a state all of us seek. We might engage in social interactions with others to seek happiness. Emotions add spice to our lives. We say we are happy or excited about events as we experience them. We take pride in our accomplishments or feel relieved and satisfied when we have successfully reached a goal.

At the same time, emotional reactions can cause us considerable distress. We may feel angry over someone cutting in front of us at a checkout line, or anxiety over an upcoming test. We feel sorrow over a loss. Martin and Osborne (1989) suggest that the feelings of emotion may be interpreted within an operant framework. To these authors, we experience pleasant or unpleasant emotions according to the contingencies of our behavior. In this scheme: (a) happiness is a pleasurable emotion caused by presentation of rewards; (b) anger is an unpleasant emotion induced by withdrawing or withholding rewards; (c) anxiety is an unpleasant emotion caused by the presentation of an aversive stimulus; (d) guilt is an unpleasant emotion based on a combination of anxiety and happiness; (e) pride is a pleasant emotion induced by a combination of happiness and anger; and (f) sorrow is an unpleasant emotion based on a combination of anger, anxiety, relief, and happiness.

We experience emotional reactions because of past experiences. If thoughts are paired with reinforcement, we acquire positive thoughts and expectations. If, however, thoughts are paired with aversive stimuli, we acquire negative thoughts and expectations. The learning process by which we acquire negative or positive thoughts and expectations is twofold. First, we learn many responses because of an association between an aversive or positive event and a thought; through such associations, often based on classical conditioning, we acquire thoughts that represent events in the real world to us. Second, once acquired, positive or negative thoughts may be maintained by either the occasional pairing of positive or negative stimuli with our thoughts (classical conditioning), or by the contingencies that occur as a consequence of our behavior (operant conditioning). As we look at emotional reactions, we are not always certain how we acquired or continue to experience specific emotional responses to different stimuli. In many instances, our current actions become more ambiguous because a combination of classical and operant conditioning helped create and maintain our emotional responses. Fortunately, we are not usually concerned over how we acquired or why we continue to experience negative and unpleasant reactions; what is significant is that, through self-management techniques, we might modify such reactions. Following a description of physiological and theoretical models of emotion, methods by which emotional reactions can be altered will be presented.

PHYSIOLOGICAL BASIS OF EMOTIONS

Internal or external stimuli from the brain activate or inhibit emotional reactions. The reactions begin with the arousal of the brain by the reticular activating system. The system serves as a general and nonspecific alarm system for the central nervous system (CNS) and the peripheral nervous system (PNS). The central nervous system consists of the brain and spinal cord; it is a highly organized system of nerve tissue that integrates and regulates body functions. The peripheral nervous system includes nerve pathways that spread out from the CNS throughout all the body, including our sense organs, muscles and glands. The PNS provides pathways for incoming sensory information about the environment and for outgoing commands that control bodily functions.

There are two components to the peripheral nervous system: the somatic and the autonomic nervous systems. The somatic nervous system is the part of the nervous system that controls movements of the skeletal muscles; it maintains body posture and permits the body to move as a whole. The autonomic nervous system is the part of the central and peripheral nervous systems that control internal activities such as heart beat, respiration, digestion, and glandular activity. These activities usually occur involuntarily without any conscious action on our part.

The autonomic nervous system prepares the body for emotional actions through the action of its two divisions: the parasympathetic and the sympathetic nervous systems. The parasympathetic division chiefly contains fibers that cause their targets to burn less energy; this function allows relaxation. The sympathetic division chiefly contains fibers that activate their targets to use energy; this function prepares our body for action. Strong emotions, such as anger or fear, activate the sympathetic nervous system. The system directs the release of two hormones, epinephrine and norepinephrine, from the adrenal glands. The release of these hormones leads internal organs to release blood sugar, raise blood pressure, and increase salivation and sweating. After the crisis is over, the parasympathetic nervous system restores calm by inhibiting the release of the activating hormones. Table 9–1 depicts the functions of both the sympathetic and parasympathetic nervous systems, including the

TABLE 9–1 Functions of the Parasympathetic Divisions of the Autonomic Nervous System

Parasympathetic	Sympathetic
Constricts pupils	Dilates pupils
Inhibits tear glands	Stimulates tear glands
Increases salivation	Inhibits salivation, increases sweating
Slows heart	Accelerates heart
Constricts bronchi	Dilates bronchi
Increases digestive functions of stomach and pancreas	Decreases digestive functions of stomach and pancreas
Increases digestive functions of intestine	Decreases digestive function of intestine
Controls bladder contractions	Inhibits bladder contractions

ability of both divisions to balance one another. The balance between the two divisions is significant to our emotional functioning.

The integration of both the neural and hormonal aspects of emotional arousal is controlled by the hypothalamus and the limbic systems. There are centers in the old portion of the brain that control emotions and patterns of attack, defense, and flight. Research suggests that part of the limbic system, the amygdala, acts both as a gateway for emotions and as a filter by interpreting information received from the senses.

THEORIES OF EMOTIONS

As noted earlier, emotions have always been a difficult subject matter for psychologists. This is not only because they are complex, but because we each have different histories with respect to our emotional reactions. Nevertheless, there are three well-known theories of emotions: the James-Lange Theory, the Cannon-Bard Theory, and the Schachter-Singer Theory. These are illustrated in Figure 9–1.

James-Lange Theory

This theory states that a stimulus or stimuli causes both arousal and an accompanying physiological change. The change is interpreted by the brain and reported as a specific emotion. The theory posits a unique pat-

FIGURE 9–1
Theories of emotion

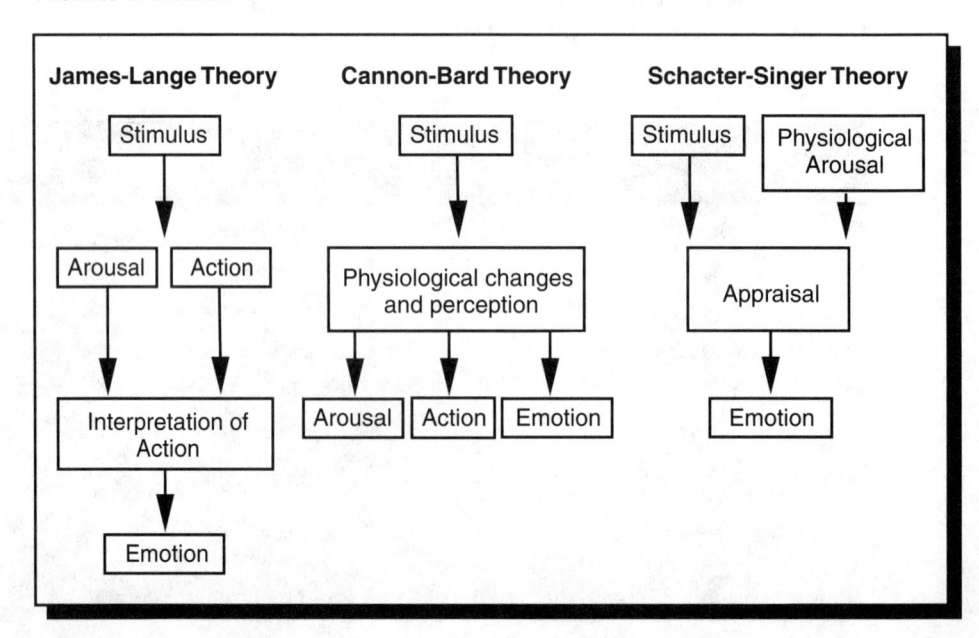

tern of physiological responses for each different emotional state; we, in turn, label these idiosyncratic patterns as they are experienced. For example, anger-evoking stimuli could lead to a distinct physiological state, anger, and a highly pleasant stimuli could lead to another distinct physiological state, happiness.

Cannon-Bard Theory

This theory states that a stimulus or stimuli causes both physiological changes and the perception of emotion. The events occur closely in time, but are independent of one another. The thalamus is thought to coordinate emotional reactions. Following the emotion-inducing stimulus, the thalamus simultaneously sends messages to another part of the brain where the emotion is experienced and to the body where physiological reactions take place. For example, an anger-evoking stimulus could send messages that simultaneously result in both physiological changes and the perception of anger, and a highly pleasant stimulus could send messages that simultaneously result in both physiological changes and the perception of happiness.

Schachter-Singer Theory

This cognitive theory of emotions states that an event causes both arousal and indistinguishable physiological changes. We appraise the arousal and search the environment for clues as to what stimuli produced the state. Physiological arousal depends upon our perception of the situation; physiological arousal will also determine the intensity but not the type of emotion we experience. For example, an anger-evoking stimulus will result in both cognitive appraisal of the situation and physiological arousal. The result may be anger, the intensity of which is determined by the extent of physiological arousal. A highly pleasant stimulus will also result in both cognitive appraisal of the situation and physiological arousal. The result may be happiness, the intensity of which is determined by the extent of physiological arousal.

From time to time, each of these theories of emotion has had proponents in psychology. At the moment, cognitive theory is the predominant theory of emotion within the field. It has implications for self-management in that it suggests that altering the perception of events that produce emotional reactions may change our behavior.

FOUR-STAGE THEORY

A particularly influential cognitive theory of emotions is that proposed by Lazarus (1991). Figure 9–2 depicts an outline of what is a four-stage, cognitive-motivational-relational model of emotion. According to the

92 Chap. 9 *Emotional Reactions*

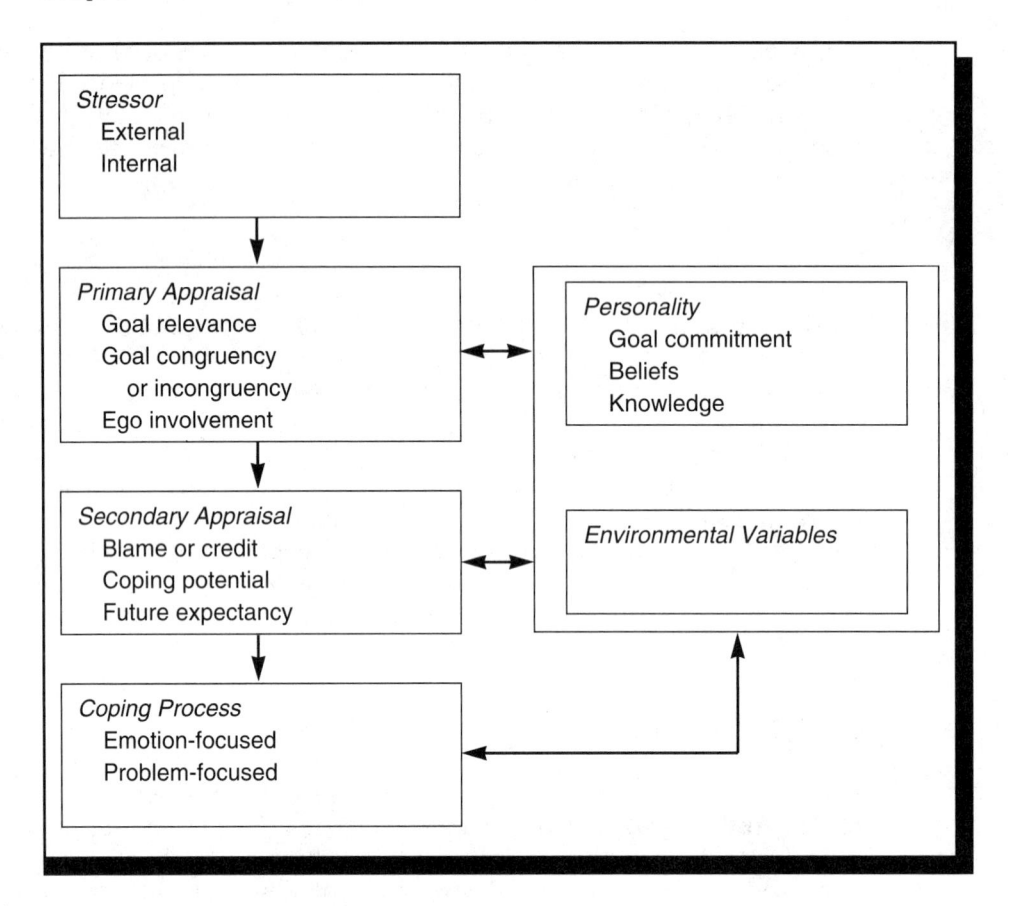

FIGURE 9–2
Four-stage model of emotion (adapted from Lazarus, 1991).

model, we appraise a situation in four stages to determine if we will react to it in an emotional manner.

Stage One: The occurrence of a stressor. This is the occurrence of an internal or external stimulus or event. An internal stressor may be how you react when someone tells you something that could be distressing; an external stressor may be a threatening gesture toward you by another person.

Stage Two: Primary appraisal. The term refers to our subjective evaluation of a situation. We determine the potential consequences of what could happen to us. For example, will the person making the threatening gesture hit you? In this stage, we balance what could occur against our ability to manage the situation. Lazarus suggested that three factors influenced the way we appraise a situation: goal relevance, goal congruence, and type of personal involvement.

Goal relevance refers to the extent to which a stressor touches upon your personal goal. If there is no goal relevance, there cannot be an emotion; if there is goal relevance, some type of emotional will occur.

Goal congruency or incongruency refers to the extent to which a transaction is consistent or inconsistent with what you want. If the event facilitates your wishes, goal congruence occurs; the result will lead to positive emotions. If the event thwarts your wishes, goal incongruence occurs; the outcome should be negative emotions. The specific emotion you experience will depend to some extent upon secondary appraisal components.

Type of personal involvement refers to diverse aspects of personal identity or commitments. Aspects enumerated by Lazarus include self and social esteem, moral values, personal ideals, meanings and ideas, other persons and their well-being, and life goals.

Stage Three: Secondary appraisal. The term refers to our deciding what we will do to manage or cope with a situation. Three components of secondary appraisal are blame or credit, coping potential, and future expectancy.

Blame and credit, either internal or external, derive from knowing who is accountable or responsible for frustration. You experience or assign credit or blame according to this knowledge.

Coping potential refers to how you manage the demands of an encounter. Coping potential is not actual coping, but your evaluation of the prospects of your action changing an event or stimulus.

Future expectancy concerns your perception that things will change for better or for worse.

Stage Four: Coping process. Coping consists of cognitive and behavioral efforts to manage specific external or internal demands.

Emotion-focused or cognitive coping processes refer to the way in which we attend to or interpret a situation. We attempt to manage the emotional distress produced by a harm or threat appraisal. We may use some of the techniques described in earlier chapters by employing distraction, thought stopping, engaging in thinking positive thoughts, or escaping from a situation. Lazarus pointed out that emotion-focused or cognitive coping processes mainly involved the use of cognitive processes rather than direct action to change the person-environmental relationship.

Problem-focused coping processes involve changing the actual relationship. We seek information about what we can do, we change our behavior, or we take whatever action is required to solve our problem.

As shown in Figure 9–2, there is a reciprocal interaction between personality and environmental variables and the primary appraisal, secondary appraisal, and coping processes. The interaction can facilitate or hinder the overall manner in which you manage emotions.

CHANGING INAPPROPRIATE EMOTIONAL RESPONSES

Throughout the text, a number of methods have been presented for use in modifying what you may perceive as an inappropriate emotional reaction. These include the following:

Extinction. Extinction may occur with responses acquired through both classical and operant conditioning.

1. Extinction of classically conditioned responses. This occurs through the repeated presentation of the conditioned stimulus without further pairings with the unconditioned stimulus. Eventually, the conditioned stimulus loses its ability to elicit a response. This often occurs naturally as you go through life. You may have been frightened of the dark because of stories told to you by an older brother or sister. When that sibling is not around you for a while, these fears extinguish.

2. Extinction of operant responses. Withholding a reinforcer following a response that was previously reinforced will decrease the likelihood of that response. This may be the procedure you use in changing your behavior. If you are reinforced by your peers for blowing up when angry, removal of their reinforcement should reduce your outbursts.

Stimulus control. You might try one of two approaches to establishing control over the stimuli or events that serve to induce emotional reactions. One approach is to change the environment; the other approach is to introduce cognitive procedures. Either approach may permit you not only to increase positive emotional stimuli or events, but permit you to avoid or escape from stressors that induce negative emotions.

1. Environmental changes. If you discover that you are unable to study in a particular environment and this induces frustration, you might consider altering the environment either by studying in the library or by seeking other living arrangements.

2. Cognitive changes. A number of cognitive techniques, including thought stopping, self-desensitization, rational-emotive restructuring, modeling, stress inoculation, and thought control, might be introduced to alter thoughts or feelings that lead to unwanted emotional reactions. The success of these procedures depends, to a considerable extent, upon your commitment and the imaginative way you apply them.

Self-monitoring. If you are experiencing more emotional outbursts than usual, you can monitor your behavior more carefully. You may find that certain events, such as arguments with a roommate, are triggering frustration or anger. Combining self-monitoring with self-instruction, such as "I won't let that comment bother me," may further facilitate you reaching a goal.

Self-reinforcement. You can add extrinsic or intrinsic reinforcers to increase and maintain positive emotions. When you have handled comments that formerly aroused anger, reward yourself with a frozen yogurt cone or by telling yourself that you managed the situation well.

Alternative response training. Techniques such as distraction may assist you to change emotional responses. In addition, you can differentially reinforce other responses that are incompatible with a negative emotion. Instead of listening to the complaints or remarks of your roommate, unless they are constructive comments, you can distract yourself by concentrating on something else or, even better, teaching yourself to relax in the face of negative comments.

Problem-solving skills. Problem-solving skills, such as those outlined in Chapter 4, can be invaluable in helping you manage situations that precipitate negative emotions. If the problems with your roommate are consistent, go through one of the problem-solving exercises to determine the best way to resolve the difficulty.

Systematic desensitization. This is a preferred method for changing anxiety responses. A form of systematic desensitization, systematic self-desensitization, was used by a student whose performance is shown in Figure 9–3. Her target behavior was to learn to speak in public without fear or anxiety. She followed three steps:

1. Relaxation. The student learned to relax by listening to a tape containing the instructions presented in Chapter 7. With repeated practice, she learned not only to discriminate whether she was tense or relaxed, but to relax on self-cue.

2. Hierarchy construction. The student constructed hierarchies of items developed from descriptions of situations that caused her to experience speech anxiety. She did this by imagining how she normally reacted in such contexts and carefully recording her thoughts.

FIGURE 9–3
Use of systematic self-desensitization to increase public speaking.

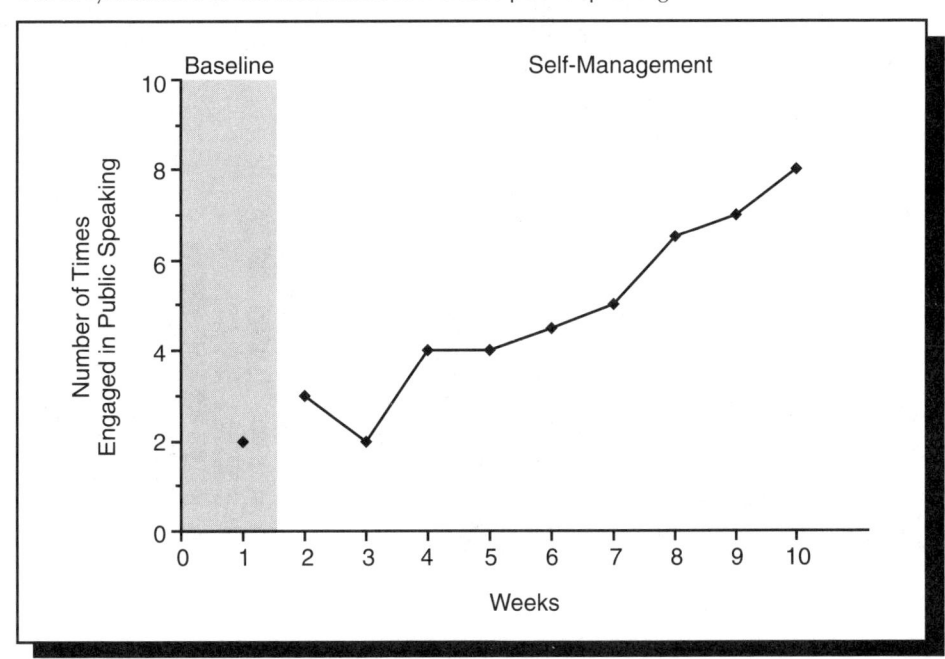

3. Desensitization. In the final stage, the student relaxed while imagining scenes she visualized from the hierarchies. She started with items causing the least amount of anxiety and gradually worked through the items that caused her the greatest amount of anxiety. As depicted in Figure 9–3, she desensitized herself to stimuli that, in the past, had generated anxiety. This was demonstrated by her increasing the number of times she was involved in public speaking. At the same time, she noted she developed greater self-confidence in her speaking abilities both in a public situation and when around her friends.

FIGURE 9–4
Use of a combination of procedures to increase social interactions.

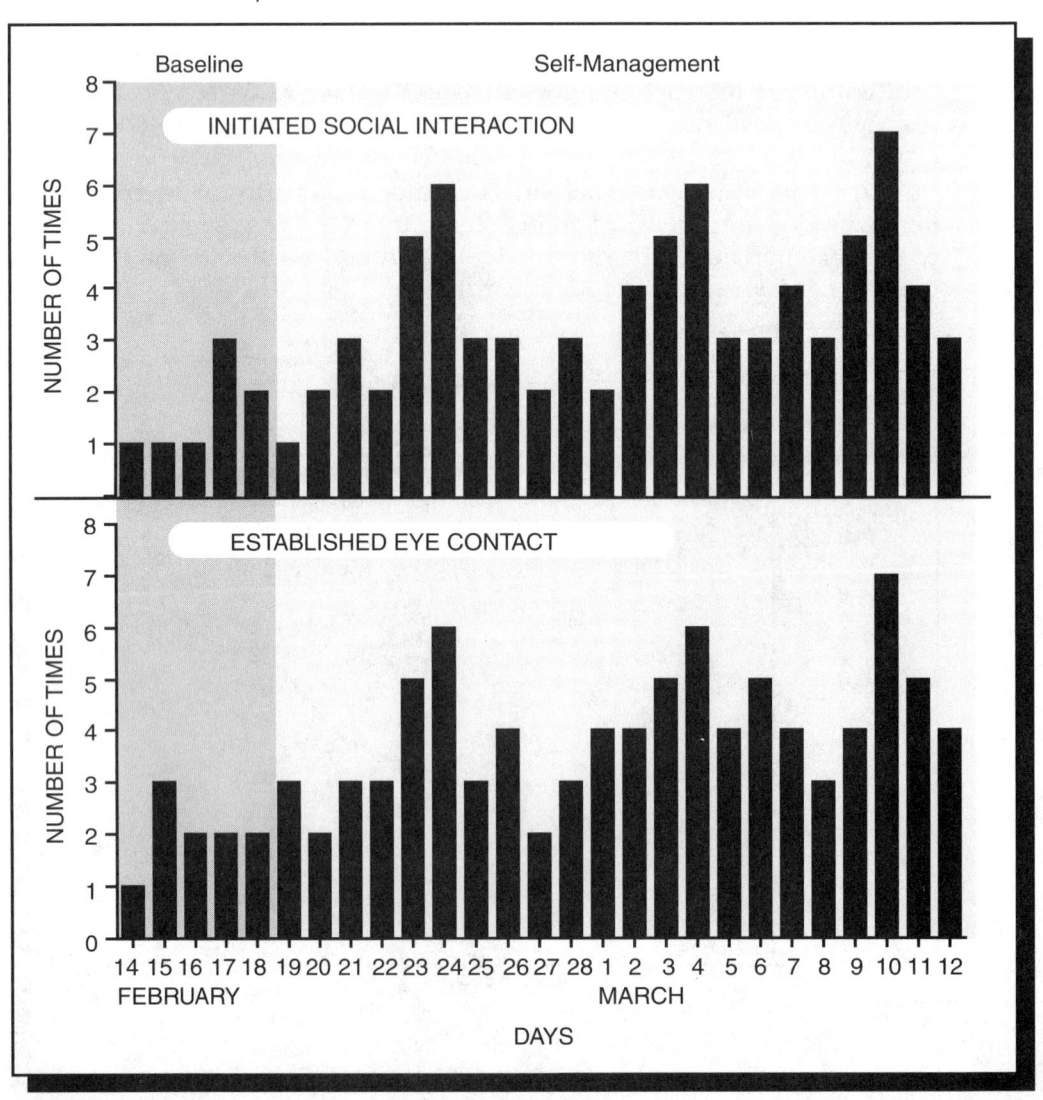

Combination of procedures. Most of the procedures described in Chapters 6 through 8 are applicable when changing emotional reactions. These might be used separately or in some sort of combination. Use of the procedures in combination is illustrated in Figure 9–4. In this case, the student was extremely shy and fearful of interacting with others. He developed a plan that involved the following strategies:

1. Relaxation. He learned deep muscle relaxation so that, in the presence of others, he could relax.
2. Imagery. He analyzed his behavior and imagined how he would like to behave. By doing so, he was able to select two target behaviors: initiating social interaction and establishing eye contact with others.
3. Rehearsal. The student established steps involved in successfully interacting with others. He jotted these down on paper. The student then rehearsed various strategies, using steps enumerated in Chapter 7, that he could use to reach his goal.

After performing the above steps, the student attempted to increase the number of times he initiated social interactions and established eye contact in the real world. As noted in Figure 9–4, he was successful. These skills, once acquired, proved useful to him in other contexts. The

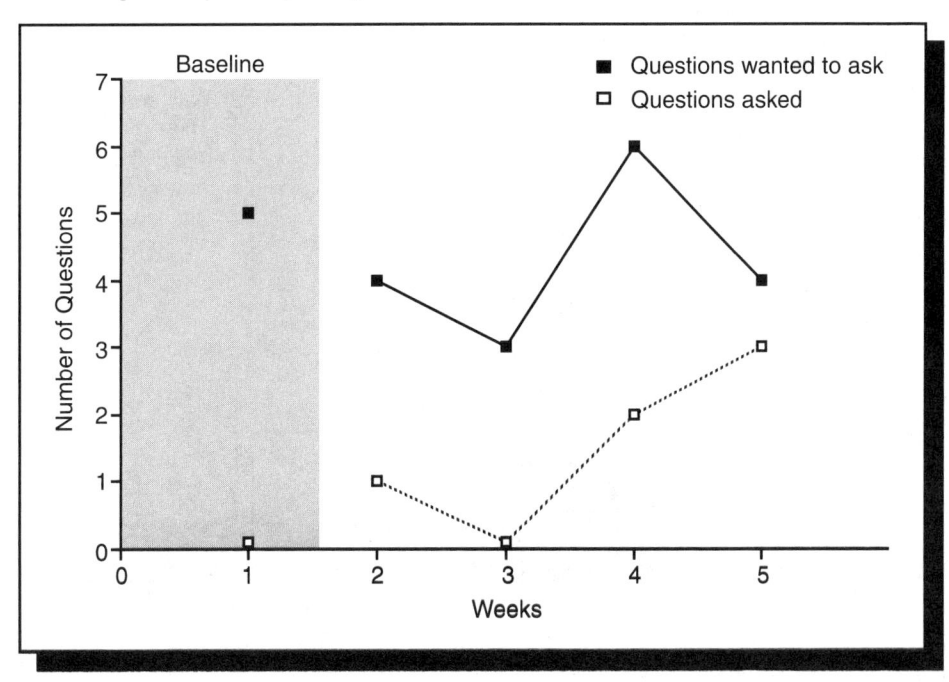

FIGURE 9–5
Decreasing fear of public speaking.

emotion of anxiety of fear that had been self-defeating was no longer a factor in his life.

SPECIFIC SELF-MANAGEMENT STRATEGIES

A number of students have sought to control emotional reactions through self-management. Figure 9–5 depicts a program where a student combined self-monitoring and in vivo desensitization to increase the number of questions he asked in class. He explained that he often wanted to ask questions but was fearful to do so. Use of desensitization proved useful to the student, although he felt his program only achieved minimal success because of the lack of opportunities to speak up in class. A number of students selected anger control as a problem. Figure 9–6 shows, after collection of baseline data, the percentage of times different strategies were effective in managing the anger experienced by a student. As noted, thinking before acting and not speaking were the most effective tactics. She made progress in performing strategies for anger management, but, considering the number of times she was angered, the student added that she had only made a start in controlling her anger. Figure 9–7 depicts progress made by another student who used a combination of self-monitoring and thought stopping to control her anger.

FIGURE 9–6
Determining most effective strategy for dealing with anger.

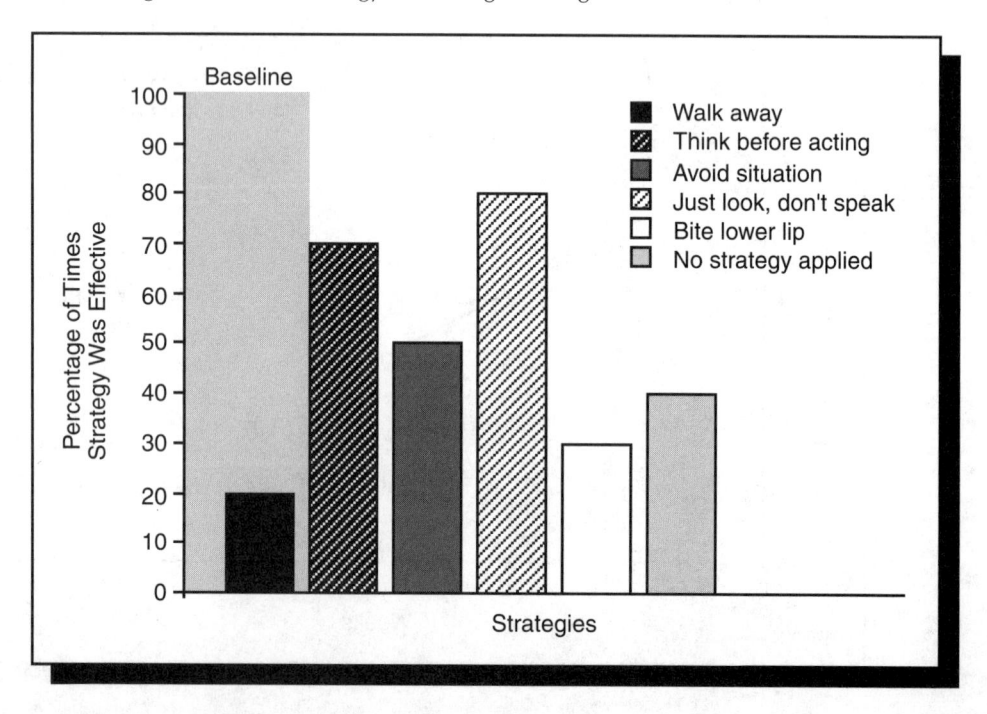

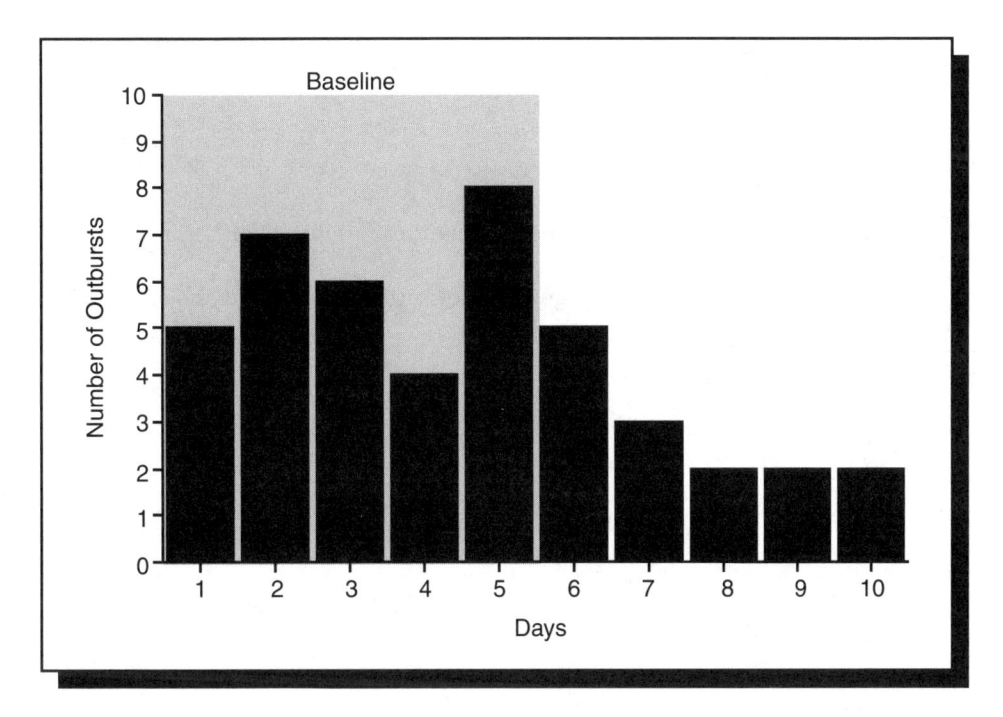

FIGURE 9–7
Controlling anger.

Sometimes it is difficult, if not impossible, to resolve an emotional problem by ourselves. When this occurs, don't hesitate to seek professional assistance. A skilled professional may provide you with more assistance in a shorter time than you can achieve through the development and implementation of self-management strategies.

EXERCISE

Think of an emotional reaction that you would like to change.
Describe the reaction as precisely as possible:
Describe how you might assess the emotion:
Think of ways that the emotion can be changed:
Think of the goal you want to achieve in changing the behavior:

REVIEW TERMS

Amygdala
Cannon-Bard Theory
Central nervous system

Extinction of operant responses
Goal relevance
James-Lange Theory

Limbic system
Peripheral nervous system

Schachter-Singer Theory

QUESTIONS

List eight functions of the parasympathetic division of the autonomic nervous system.

Discuss the four-stage, cognitive-motivational-relational model of emotion proposed by Lazarus (1991).

CHAPTER 10

Coping with Stress

"Take away your opinion, and then there is taken away the complaint, 'I have been harmed.' Take away the complaint, 'I have been harmed,' and the harm is taken away."
—Marcus Aurelius, *Meditations*

"I used to hate being under stress, but it really works to my advantage. I don't do very much in my classes unless I feel under some stress. I sometimes try to generate stress so that I'll get my work done. As long as I'm not under too much stress or get stressed out, stress serves to motivate me."
—Jack, a senior

Most of us only think about the negative aspects of stress. We focus on the stimuli referred to as stressors that produce the stress and the effect such stressors have on our health and well-being. We think about the physical and behavioral problems we may have when experiencing stress. These problems may include: (a) behaviors such as chewing our fingernails, insomnia, clenching our teeth, smoking too much, or alcohol abuse; (b) physical difficulties such as digestive disorders or tension headaches; and (c) emotional changes such as anxiety, depression, anger, or an overreaction to minor events.

Stress, however, can sometimes be good. It may prompt us to perform at a higher level than we would if we did not experience some stress. Stress results from our interaction with the environment. The amount of stress we experience is determined by our perception of whether the situation strains or overwhelms our ability to cope with the stress and endangers our well-being. You might experience some stress if you are playing in an intramural basketball game, but it is likely less severe than if you were suddenly thrust into playing in the Final Four NCAA basketball championship.

Considering the number and variety of stressors that impinge upon us each day, why do some enhance our performance and others lead to distress? An answer lies in a brief discussion of stress.

101

CONCEPTION OF STRESS

Hans Selye is regarded as the father of stress research. He described stress as the nonspecific response of the body to a demand, pleasant or unpleasant, made upon it. The adaptation we make to the stress depends upon the intensity of the demand. Selye (1976) suggested we react in three distinct stages to any stressor. He referred to the set of signs or symptoms as the General Adaptation Syndrome. The three stages to the syndrome—alarm, resistance, and exhaustion—are depicted in Figure 10–1.

Alarm

In the alarm stage, the body automatically activates physiological resources to defend itself against the perceived stressor. We may immediately feel these physical changes as our muscles tense up, our blood pressure increases, and both our heart rate and breathing accelerate. Our palms may begin to sweat, our mouth may seem dry, and we may feel a knot in our stomachs. We may begin to feel anxious and experience an increase in our level of alertness.

The alarm stage is characterized by an increase in adrenalin secreted from the adrenal glands. The increased adrenalin acts like a red alert to the body as it prepares for "fight or flight." At this point, stress may be helpful in that all our systems are ready for action to manage both the stress or the stressors producing the reaction.

FIGURE 10–1
Resistance.

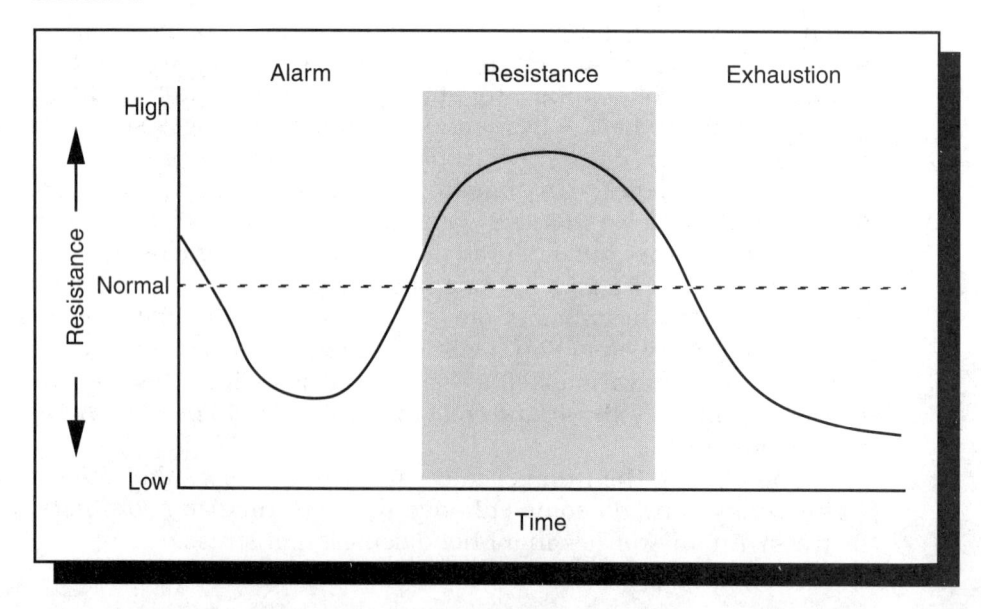

Resistance

As shown in Figure 10–1, in the second stage resistance is raised as the body reacts to protect itself and adjust to the stress. Body resources are mobilized to overcome the fight or flight response; internal systems attempt to return to normal, although to achieve this state requires that energy be diverted from other bodily functions. We attempt to increase and intensify our use of coping mechanisms; in addition, we often show a tendency to engage in defense-oriented behaviors.

Resistance is a form of adjustment in that it lasts until stress ceases. If the stressor remains over a period of time, then the third stage, exhaustion, can occur.

Exhaustion

If stress continues long enough, we cannot function normally and the symptoms of the alarm stage return. As our bodily defenses have been depleted, we are particularly vulnerable to even a small amount of stress. If the stress cannot be halted or reversed, sickness, tissue damage, or, in small animals, death may occur. Psychologically, you may experience an exaggeration of defense-oriented behaviors, a disorganization of thinking, and personality changes that may include depression. In his experiments, Selye (1976) showed that animals placed under continuous stress showed enlarged adrenal glands with loss of steroids, decreased levels of salt in the blood, and malfunction of the kidneys. As the animals died from exhaustion, it appeared as if they succumbed because of an excess of hormones produced by their bodies in an attempt to halt stress.

Considerable research is being conducted to determine how humans react to stress. A promising area of research is referrred to as psychoimmunology or psychoneuroimmunology. This is the field of study that investigates the relationships among the central nervous system, psychological factors, and the immunology system. The interaction among these three systems appears to strengthen or suppress the immune system (Ader, Felton, and Cohen, 1991). This interaction, in turn, could explain why some of us are more apt than others to experience colds or other infections during periods of stress (e.g., Kiecolt-Glaser et al., 1993).

GENERAL STRATEGIES FOR COPING WITH STRESS

There are a number of tactics that we can use to cope with stress; these are depicted in Table 10–1. While it is likely that you already employ some of these methods, all deserve brief discussion.

TABLE 10–1 Methods of Coping with Stress

Acknowledge that you will experience stress; it is unavoidable.

Appraise the situation.

Consider possible coping strategies.
1. Do not take on more than you can handle.
2. Deal with stressful events at once.
3. Be flexible.
4. Realize that you do not always have to be right or perfect.
5. Be assertive.
6. Learn to say no.
7. Consider locus of control regarding events.
8. Avoid making too many life changes at once.
9. Anticipate and prepare for stressful events.
10. Express your feelings.

Develop ways of managing time and resources.
1. Set realistic goals and priorities.
2. Organize time in accordance with priorities.
3. Break complex events down into components.
4. Attack one thing at a time.
5. Be realistic.
6. Schedule time for relaxation and leisure.
7. If overwhelmed, eliminate some events.
8. Protect yourself against boredom.

Care for personal health.
1. Get enough rest.
2. Eat properly.
3. Exercise.
4. Avoid substance abuse.
5. Avoid poor behavioral habits.

Develop friendships.

Help others.

Accept yourself.

Acknowledge that You Will Experience Stress

All of us experience stress; it is an unavoidable part of life. Rather than let it cause you mental and physiological pain, you should accept the inescapable nature of stress and prepare to cope with it. Use stress in a positive manner when you can. Theoretically, everyone can learn strategies for managing stress. How successful you are in this quest will determine, to a large degree, how much effort you expend in acquiring and performing stress-management skills.

Appraise the Situation

How you appraise a situation will determine the amount and type of stress you experience. Four factors that influence our appraisal of a situation are our familiarity with the situation, the controllability of events, the predictability of a situation, and the imminence of a potential threat.

1. Familiarity. How familiar are you with stressful demands? The less familiar you are with a situation, such as interviewing for a job, the more likely you are to experience stress. Improving job-seeking skills, on the other hand, permits you to become familiar with the challenge of a job interview. Familiarity increases your confidence and makes interviewing for a job less stressful.

2. Controllability. How much control do you perceive you have over a situation? The concept of locus of control, or how we perceive events, was discussed in an earlier chapter. As you recall, internal locus of control is the perception that positive or negative events are under your control (Rotter, 1966). In these cases, you see yourself as playing a major role in determining how these events will unfold. An example of internal locus of control is if you believe you will do better on tests if you study. External locus of control is the perception that positive or negative events are not under your control. In these cases, you see yourself as having little effect over an event. An example of external locus of control is that we are all going to experience colds sometime or another despite our best efforts to avoid such infections.

Locus of control is a major psychological construct. How much effort you expend toward achieving a goal will be a function of whether or not you see the event as a consequence of your behavior. If you believe it is a consequence, you are likely to expend more effort. Another facet of locus control is that, as we grow older, we begin to realize that many events shift from being under our control toward being under the control of other factors. An example is the aging process itself; despite millions of dollars spent on cosmetics and other products, we all eventually age no matter how much we try to delay or reverse the process. It is the wise person who is constantly aware of events he or she cannot control. It is the wiser person who not only knows what events he or she can control, but who can maximize control over events that can be controlled while minimizing the effects, wherever possible, of events perceived as having an external locus of control.

3. Predictability. How predictable is an event? If you accept a temporary job, you expect to be eventually terminated. If you accept a position that you think will last you for your entire career, you do not anticipate termination of your job. When the latter occurs, it is unexpected; the unpredictability of the event, in turn, is likely to create stress. Potential stressors have less of an effect when you anticipate that a stressor may occur somewhere in the future and prepare to deal with it when it occurs.

4. Imminence. How imminent is a potential stressor? If you have a test scheduled for next week, you probably are not experiencing much stress at the moment. If, however, the test is to be given later today or tomorrow and you have not prepared for it, you may see the examination as a powerful stressor.

Consider Possible Coping Strategies

The better you are in controlling stress, the happier you are. If you know beforehand what events generate stress, you can anticipate and prepare to handle them. For this reason, making a list of potentially stressful events can be of assistance. In addition, you can take the following steps:

   1. Do not take on more than you can handle. There is only so much time in the day for you to perform daily tasks. Only you know how you will spend each day; thus, only you can decide whether you should take on any task that may require more time and effort than you can realistically spare.
   2. Deal with stressful events at once. If there is an event that you know is stressful, it is better to deal with it as quickly as you can. If you procrastinate, this response is only going to intensify the stress. It is better to deal with the event and move on to something more pleasant.
   3. Be flexible. There is always something unexpected that disrupts the best of plans. If you are flexible, you can manage these unanticipated situations. This presupposes that you always allow yourself time to be flexible. Starting now on a paper that is due the end of the quarter permits you flexibility.
   4. Realize that you do not always have to be right or perfect. Earlier, we discussed some of the factors Albert Ellis pointed out that create misery. You may want to reread those; in the meantime, you should always be cognizant that you cannot be right or perfect at everything you do. Centering your life on being correct or perfect only causes you more stress than would otherwise be induced by life's daily events.
   5. Be assertive. You alone can determine if you are assertive enough in dealing with others. In a later chapter, we will discuss ways that you might enhance your ability to be assertive in your life.
   6. Learn to say no. Sometimes it seems as if everyone wants a different part of your life. As it is apt to be impossible to do everything others ask, you must learn to say no if you do not have time. This is not always an easy task, but the costs of not saying no will be borne by you.
   7. Avoid making too many life changes at once. We are sometimes forced to make major changes in our life, such as accepting a job in another part of the country. The new job may not only create stress, but the move itself may be stressful. If we could take only one step at a time, the process should be less stressful to us.
   8. Anticipate and prepare for stressful events. We all know that events, such as an upcoming talk, are going to generate stress. If we can anticipate and prepare for them, they are likely to prove less stressful to us.

9. Express your feelings. There are times when you may feel angry with a roommate over something. Rather than stew about the situation, it is better to express your true feelings. At other times, you may feel like crying. There is nothing wrong with crying. Either behavior—expressing your anger or having a good cry—can reduce your level of stress.

Develop Ways of Managing Time and Resources

Most of these strategies will be discussed further in the discussion on time management (Chapter 11). However, the tactics are of value in coping with stress.

1. Set realistic goals and priorities. As you only have twenty-four hours in each day, you need to set goals and prioritize them. This will allow you to make optimal use of your time and resources.

2. Organize time in accordance with priorities. By setting and following priorities, you can focus on those activities that require your immediate attention; this practice, in turn, should reduce stress.

3. Break complex events down into components. If you have a complex ask, such as writing a long paper, you can reduce stress by breaking the task down into separate parts and completing them one at a time. This might entail reviewing the literature this week, outlining the paper next week, and so on. The process reduces stress engendered by attempting to complete a complex project all at once, usually within a short period of time.

4. Attack one thing at a time. It is impossible to do everything you have to do at once. For this reason, you should perform only one task at a time. By doing this, you can carry out a series of assignments within a set period.

5. Be realistic. Some activities you are asked to complete may be beyond your abilities; when this occurs, discuss the matter with others. Or, you may not have time to complete everything you want to do; again, be realistic in allocating how much time it will take you to perform an activity.

6. Schedule time for relaxation and leisure. Regardless of how busy you are, you should take time to relax. This may entail nothing more than taking time off to watch your favorite TV program. Another activity that we all should engage in is quiet time. It is important that you take time off and do something by yourself even if it is nothing more than basking in the sun for a few minutes.

7. If overwhelmed, eliminate some events. If you find you are unsuccessful at juggling school, work, and a personal life, you may want to list everything you need to do and see if there are some events that can be eliminated or delayed. This will permit you to experience less stress.

8. Protect yourself against boredom. When bored, we waste time. Try to set goals that will be satisfying to you and work toward them.

Care for Personal Health

The strategies to be described are common sense to most of you. They are useful not only in permitting you to live more satisfying lives, but in reducing stress.

1. Get enough rest. A number of students have taken as a project the self-management of the amount of sleep and rest they obtain each day. As the amount of rest we each need varies from person to person, this is a prime topic for self-control. You alone know how much sleep you need; if your roommates require less, this does not mean that you should adjust your life to meet their needs. Rather, adjust your schedule to meet your requirements.

2. Eat properly. We know that good nutrition is a necessity. However, the type of foods you eat becomes even more critical when you are under stress. Some foods may lead to stomach pain or distress. As this is idiosyncratic to each person, good nutrition rests on self-management.

3. Exercise. Exercise is important not only in keeping us physically capable of fulfilling daily demands of living, but in helping us control stress. Working out daily is a proven way for managing stress.

4. Avoid substance abuse. No matter how much stress you experience, it is unwise to attempt to control it through substance abuse. Not only might you become more reliant upon such substances, but they generally do not control stress in any meaningful way.

5. Avoid poor behavioral habits. Some individuals chew their nails or twist their hair when they are under stress. Neither behavior reduces stress; rather, both habits have a tendency to increase the stress you experience.

Develop Friendships

Making friends with others is an excellent method for reducing stress. Not only can you share your concerns with friends, but they may offer you suggestions for reducing the stress you experience. If both of you experience stress, you can work on a strategy that will allow you to resolve the problems that generate these feelings.

Help Others

Attempting to help others can also help you reduce the types and amount of stress you experience. You may find that you not only feel satisfaction in helping others, but that the stress you experience may be alleviated through your efforts.

Accept Yourself

You all have something to offer both to someone else and to yourself. As Hafen and colleagues (1988) note, "You are a human being, and you have talents and abilities that are unique to you. Concentrate on your good points, and make friends with yourself" (p. 58). As you do so, you are apt to discover that you develop more positive attitudes toward yourself and begin concentrating about more positive aspects of your life. As the late song writer Johnny Mercer declared, "You have to accentuate the positive and eliminate the negative." His words are as true today as when he wrote them almost fifty years ago.

SPECIFIC STRATEGIES FOR COPING WITH STRESS

Methods for coping with stress were described earlier. Those that seem especially useful are self-monitoring, all forms of relaxation, time management, imagery, rehearsal, stress inoculation, systematic desensitization, and exercise. Methods described in Chapter 9, including establishing stimulus control, self-reinforcement, performing alternative responses, and problem-solving, may also be used to help control stress. Use of some of these methods to reduce various facets of stress are noted in the following four figures.

Figure 10–2 depicts the results obtained when a student carefully observed and recorded aspects of his nailbiting. As noted, careful monitoring reduced the frequency of nailbiting engaged in by the student. Figure 10–3

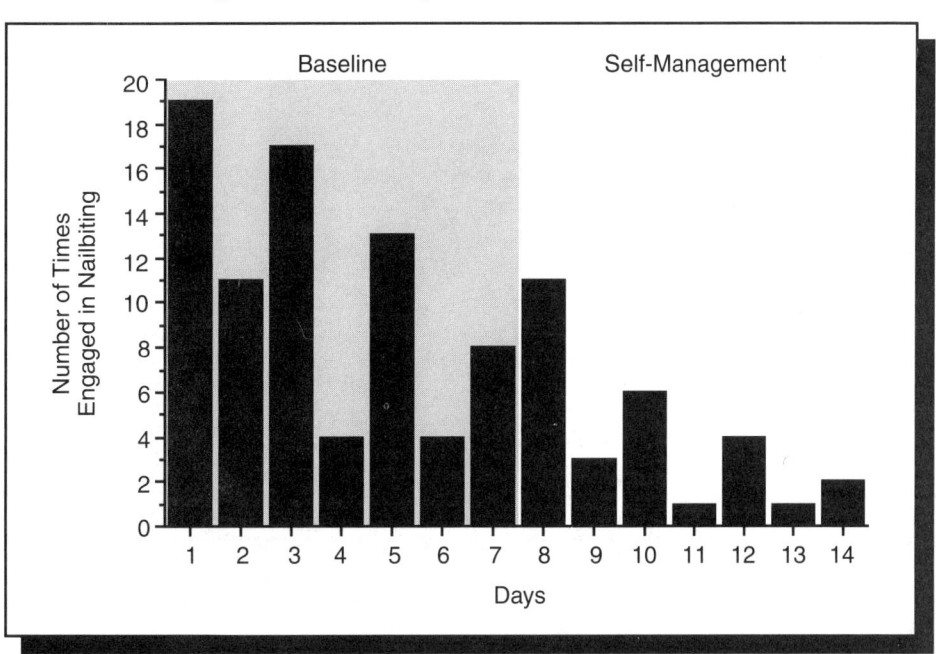

FIGURE 10–2
Use of self-monitoring to reduce nailbiting.

110 Chap. 10 Coping with Stress

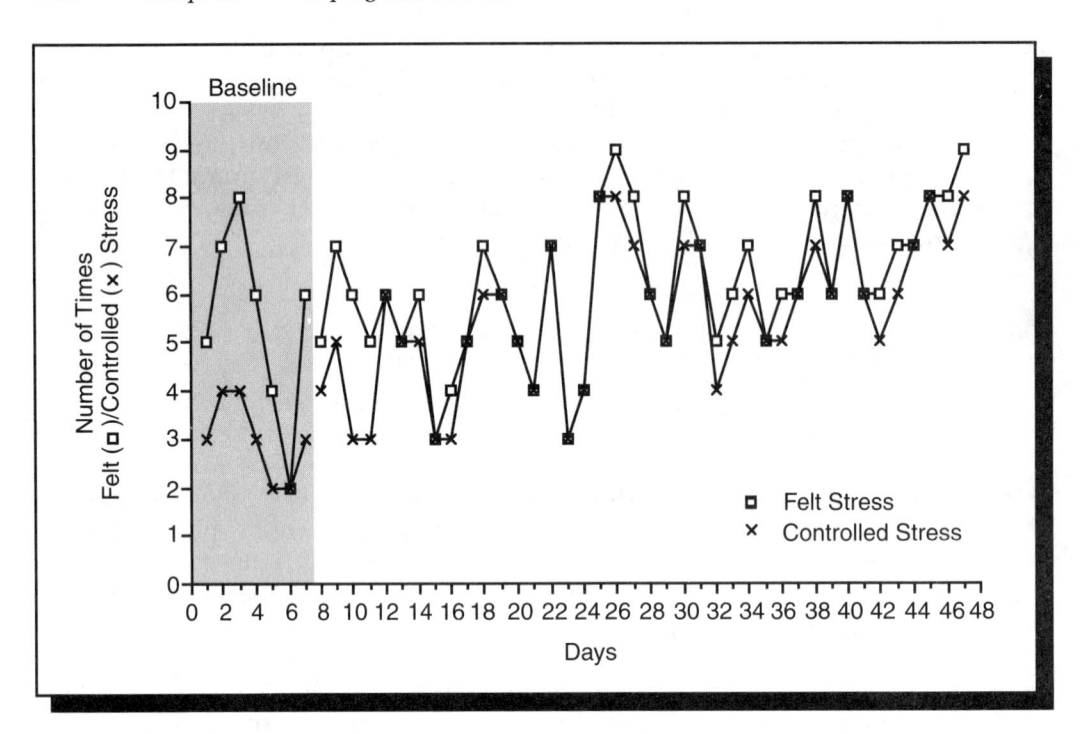

FIGURE 10–3
Use of self-monitoring and relaxation to control stress.

FIGURE 10–4
Use of running to decrease blood pressure.

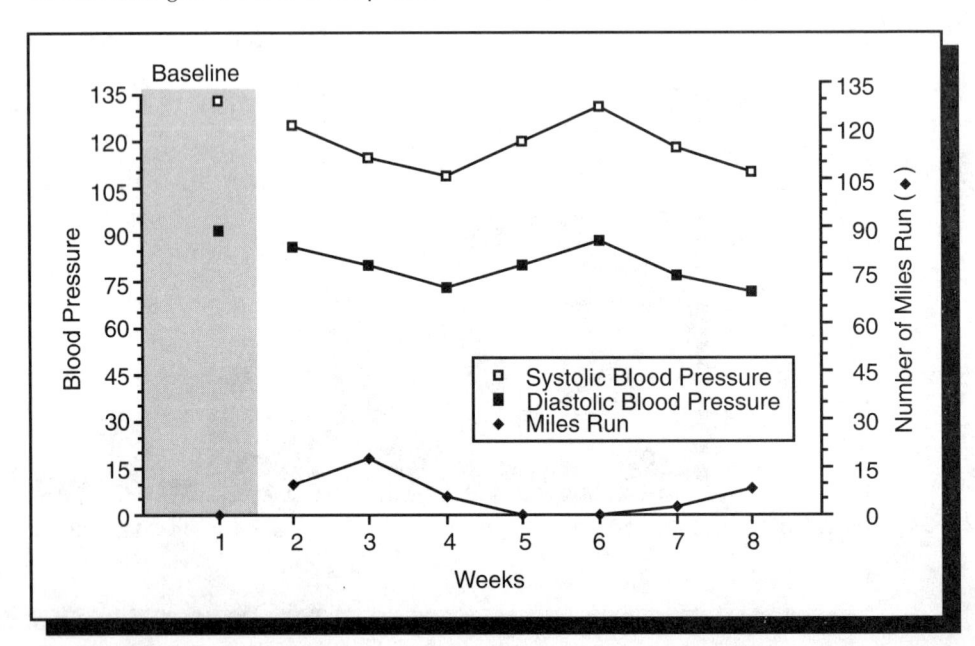

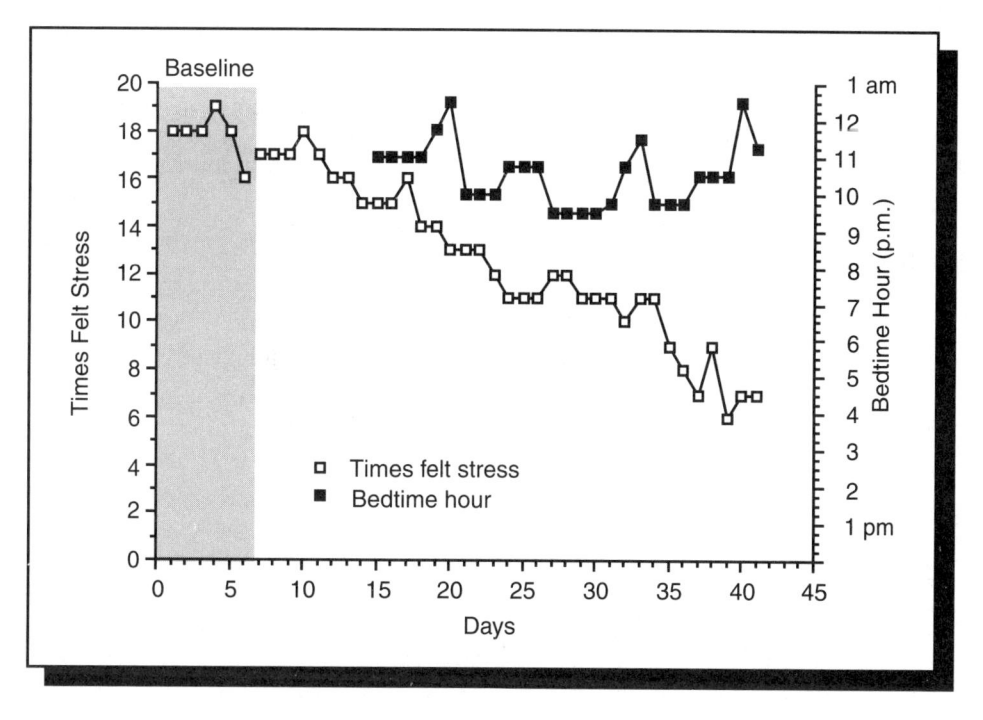

FIGURE 10–5
Use of a number of procedures in combination to control stress.

shows how another student established control over the stress he experienced. In this case, he found that by carefully observing his behavior and relaxing when he experienced stress, he could control the behavior.

Figure 10–4 depicts what occurred when a student attempted to control his blood pressure by increasing the number of miles he ran each week. As noted, a reduction in both his systolic and diastolic blood pressure occurred when he ran faithfully; his blood pressure increased, however, when he did not run on a regular basis. Finally, Figure 10–5 illustrates what occurred when a student used a combination procedure involving exercise, relaxation, listening to music, and thinking positive thoughts to reduce stress. As noted, this strategy, when applied before bedtime, reduced the student's level of stress.

EXERCISE

Think of most stressful situation you currently face.
Consider methods you might use to control stress.
Attempt to control stress with the method you select.
Determine if your strategy was effective in reducing stress.

REVIEW TERMS

Alarm
External locus of control
Hans Selye
Internal locus of control
Perception of stress
Psychoimmunology

QUESTIONS

Discuss the stages of the General Adaptation Syndrome.
List eight coping strategies that you might use to manage stress.

CHAPTER 11

Time Management

"Those who make the worst use of their time most complain of its shortness."

—La Bruyere, *Les Caracteres*

"Each term, I think I'll do things differently. I don't. I mess around for the first few weeks every term. Then midterms hit. I'm never prepared. I have to work day and night to get ready for them. So far, I've managed to barely pass. Do you think I learn from this? I don't. I continue to screw around and all of a sudden finals are here. I don't know how many all-nighters I have put in trying to study or to finish a paper, you know? I just don't have the knack of using my time right."

—Jeff, a fifth-year junior

You may notice that some people seem to be able to do everything they want during the day while others, perhaps yourself, struggle to accomplish some of their daily tasks. You may think some people are lucky or that they just seem to know how to get things done. The problem becomes even more acute when you recognize that there are only twenty-four hours in each day. You are apt to hold any number of misconceptions about why others achieve their goals and you do not. Many of your ideas may reflect what Martin and Osborne (1989) refer to as misconceptions about time management. They describe four:

1. Managing time is a matter of reducing time spent in various activities. Martin and Osborne point out that this is a misconception because it fails to recognize the distinction between high-priority and low-priority activities. To manage time, you must learn to decrease time spent on low-priority activities and increase time spent on high-priority activities.

2. People who concentrate on working efficiently are more effective performers. This misconception, note Martin and Osborne, fails to consider the difference between efficiency and effectiveness. Efficiency refers to the amount of time and cost required to do something; effectiveness refers to achieving high-priority goals and objectives. Ineffective people can spend their time on low-priority goals and objectives, but effective performers concentrate on high-priority activities with the greatest poten-

tial payoffs. Efficiency thus entails doing the job right, whereas effectiveness entails doing the right job.

3. The busiest people get the best results. This is a misconception, caution Martin and Osborne, because there is again a failure to consider high-priority versus low-priority activities. Those who are effective at managing time are able to prioritize their activities. Prioritization involves the identification of the goals and activities with the highest potential payoffs. Almost all effective and efficient time managers use prioritization.

4. Most people can resolve their time problems by working harder. Martin and Osborne warn that this is not necessarily so. Good time managers work smarter, not harder. They always consider what they are doing rather than what they might be doing. In doing so, they may continually ask themselves, "How could I best use my time right now?"

Considering these misconceptions, how can you best manage your limited time and resources? The following are strategies offered by experts in time management.

TIPS FOR EFFECTIVE TIME MANAGEMENT

There is considerable agreement among experts on how to manage time. The following suggestions may be of value to you.

Evaluate current skills. The way to evaluate your current time management skills is to self-monitor your behavior for a week or so. In particular, look at whether you plan out events and assess results. See if you perform activities that waste your time. As Martin and Osborne explain, determine whether you: (a) overschedule your time so that you have so many tasks, they are all impossible to perform; (b) fail to delegate activities that might be better fulfilled by someone else; (c) lack assertiveness and fail to say no when asked to perform a task; (d) waste time such as by watching too much television or hanging out too long at a restaurant; or (e) practice excessive briefcasing by carrying considerable work home, but not performing any of the tasks.

Set priorities. Do you occasionally list all of the tasks you should complete and prioritize them in some order? You should. By doing so, you can determine which goals have the greatest potential payoff for you at any given moment. This will permit you to determine which short-term tasks require immediate attention and which are longer-term goals.

Set deadlines. All of you are familiar with deadlines. Almost every course you take has deadlines for tests, papers, talks, and so on. In time management, you should examine what work assignments you must fulfill and establish deadlines. This not only permits you flexibility, but it allows you to control your own time and resources. As was emphasized in the last chapter, by setting your own deadlines you experience less stress and the problems it can produce.

Plan your schedule. Along with prioritizing tasks, planning your schedule is a major component of time management. Planning entails that you think ahead of the goals you wish to set, as well as estimating the time required to achieve each goal. You must be realistic in planning a schedule. Do not overschedule yourself or underestimate how much time a given task will take. A variation of Murphy's Law is that everything takes longer to accomplish than you anticipate. There is considerable truth to this so-called law. On the other hand, Parkinson's Law states that achieving a task will consume all the time you allow for reaching this goal, no matter how insignificant the task may be. If you allow yourself more time than required for performing a task, you will find that you fill the time by dallying and generally waste time. Both laws illustrate the importance of planning in time management.

Use a planning calendar. A planning calendar allows you to plan ahead for days, weeks, months, or even years. You can think of what you need to do each week and break up these tasks into separate parts so that one or more of the parts are performed each day. This practice also lets you consider what experts refer to as your peak or alert time when you seem to be able to study or work better. Preserve this time for those activities that require the greatest amount of concentration on your part. You are not only better able to take responsibility for your own performance, but you are usually more efficient and effective.

One caveat should be noted regarding planning calendars. Some people become so obsessed with planning and writing down future events that they complete few of the tasks they plan. If you find that using a planning calendar becomes a preoccupation, you may want to jot down one or two tasks and go about performing them.

Martin and Osborne offer additional tips for effective time management. Many of these suggestions were described earlier, but they bear repeating. The tips include:

1. Work at only one thing at a time. In the last chapter, it was pointed out that you experience less stress if you concentrate on performing only one task at a time. You will also find that you will be more successful if you adopt this practice.

2. Break up large tasks into parts. This approach was discussed in Chapter 9. Martin and Osborne advocate use of the "pineapple" method. This involves breaking a large task down into smaller parts, each of which can be completed in the time you have available.

3. Protect alert time. Be highly protective of the time of day when you are most alert and capable of working at your highest level.

4. Reserve a given place exclusively for work. This topic will be described more thoroughly in Chapter 12. It involves establishing an area exclusively for such activities as studying, sleeping, and so on. By doing this, you can more effectively create stimuli that prompt you to accomplish whatever goal you want to attain. In the present context, this means work.

5. Deal with low-priority items in groups. When a number of low-priority items accumulate, take time off and accomplish them all at once. You might be able to do your laundry while you write letters to your friends or family. This would be an example of successfully accomplishing a couple of what may be low-priority activities. (Unless, of course, you have run out of clean clothes or have to write your parents for needed money!)

6. Give up waiting time. If you have to wait to see someone, always take along your books or something else that you can do while waiting. This will not only make the time go faster, but it will permit you to achieve a higher-priority goal.

7. Reward good time management behavior. As is the case following the attainment of any goal, reward yourself for your behavior. If you turn a required paper in before a deadline, you may want to take off the evening and do something you enjoy, such as going out to eat or to a movie.

Other Ways to Save Time

A major force in the field of time management is Alan Lakein, who burst upon the scene in 1973 with an influential book entitled *How to Get Control of Your Time and Your Life*. His book offered a number of ways that he used to save time. You may or may not agree with some of his suggestions, a partial listing of which is enumerated in Table 11–1. However, the list does include ways of managing time that may be relevant to each of us.

A Final Comment about Time Management

A final statement should be made about time management: life is too complex without planning what we are going to do with each moment of every day. Many people become obsessed with managing their time; they feel naked without their omnipresent day planner. Life is just too short for such obsessions. Use whatever time you have available to complete projects in the most effective way you can. Time management can be helpful in helping you achieve these goals. However, there are moments when you want to do nothing more than take time to relax and listen to music or just think about your life. These moments are as significant to your overall happiness as managing time effectively. Those who balance what they have to do against what they want to do are the ones who achieve the good life.

TABLE 11-1 A Partial List of Ways to Save Time as Offered by Lakein (1973)

1. Get satisfaction out of every minute.
2. Enjoy whatever you are doing.
3. Be a perennial optimist.
4. Build on successes.
5. Don't feel guilty over past failures or what you don't do.
6. Remind yourself that there is always time for important things.
7. Find a new technique each day that will help you gain time.
8. Get up at 5:00 A.M. (and go to bed early).
9. Eat a light lunch so as not to be sleepy in the afternoon.
10. Don't read newspapers or magazines.
11. Skim books to search for ideas.
12. Don't own a TV set.
13. Walk to work or school.
14. Eliminate useless habits.
15. Use waiting time usefully.
16. Keep watch 3 minutes fast.
17. Carry blank cards around, jot down notes and ideas.
18. Review lifetime goals daily.
19. Use signs to remind you of goals.
20. Plan each day and set daily priorities.
21. Be flexible.
22. Reward yourself when you have achieved goals.
23. Do first things first.
24. Work smarter rather than harder.
25. Stick to priorities.
26. If you procrastinate, ask yourself why. Take head on the tasks you tend to avoid.
27. Start with most profitable parts of large tasks; you may not have to do more.
28. Cut off nonproductive tasks as quickly as possible.
29. Focus on high-priority items.
30. Learn to concentrate for longer stretches of time.
31. Concentrate on one thing at a time.
32. Focus on items that have long-term benefits.
33. Push and be persistent when you sense you have a winner.
34. Go down "to do" list without skipping over difficult items.
35. Think on paper.
36. Work creatively in morning; use afternoons for other tasks.
37. Set deadlines for yourself and others.
38. Listen actively in all discussions.
39. Don't waste others' time.
40. Delegate as much as possible.
41. Generate as little paperwork as possible; throw everything away that you can.
42. Handle each piece of paper only once.
43. Keep your desk cleared for action.
44. Have a place for everything.
45. Save all trivia for one session.
46. Put aside time for yourself.
47. Try not to think of work on weekends.
48. Recognize that you do not have locus of control over all activities.
49. Look for action steps to take to further your goals.
50. Continually ask yourself, "What is the best use of my time right now?"

SELF-MANAGEMENT AND TIME MANAGEMENT

Time management is a solid topic to take for a self-management project. Accordingly, there are always students who select this topic. Most achieve some success, although the strategies taken often vary from student to student. Figure 11-1 indicates an approach taken by one student. Each night, she set four goals for herself that were to be fulfilled the next day. In the morning, she reviewed and altered any goals that did not seem important. The student then set about achieving her goals; she monitored her progress and recorded her success each evening. As noted in Figure 11-1, she accomplished her goals most of the days she conducted her project. Toward the end of the month's program, she stated that she had difficulty in setting four goals a day: she had caught up with her assign-

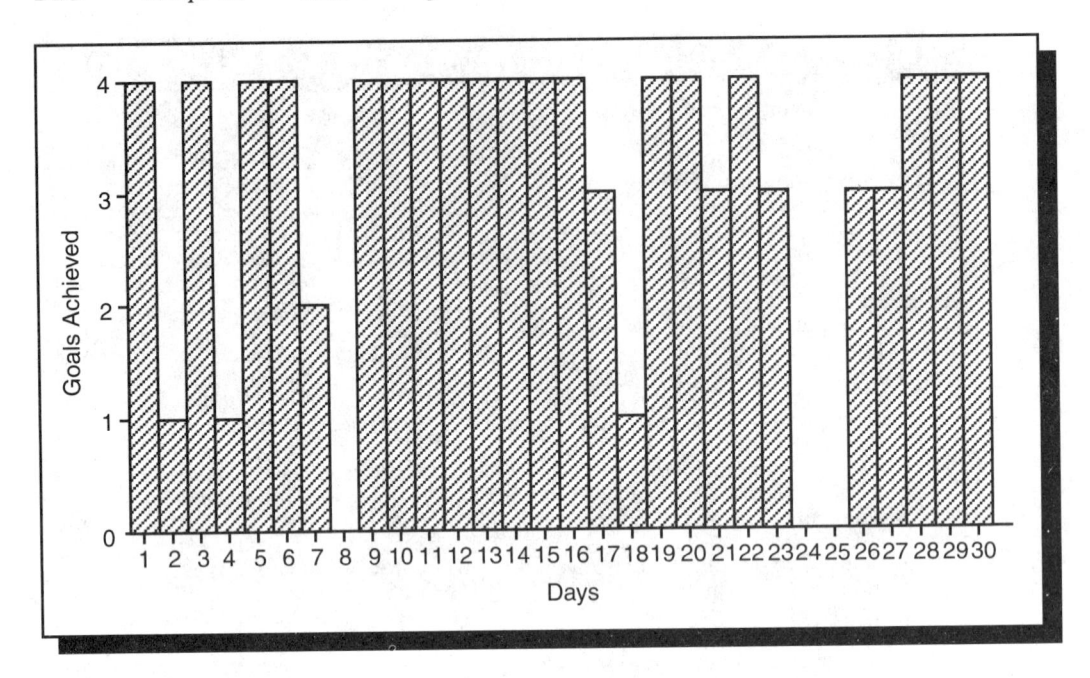

FIGURE 11–1
Use of goal setting and self-monitoring to reduce procrastination.

ments and other work earlier in the month. Thus, there were days when she set fewer than four goals for herself. In addition, she was able to take off a weekend (days 24 and 25) because she had performed all the goals she had to achieve for the quarter. Another student took a similar approach in that she set goals for herself each morning, monitored her progress during the day, and recorded her success in the evening. Her data are shown in Figure 11–2. As depicted, the percentage of tasks she completed ranged from 30 percent to 100 percent with introduction of her program. She achieved 100 percent of her goals on twenty-one of the forty-six days she conducted her program.

The student whose data are shown in Figure 11–3 found that he tended to procrastinate; consequently, he did not perform all his assignments and other work. He adopted a tactic that included self-monitoring, thought stopping, and self-reinforcement to reduce procrastination. As depicted, this approach was immediately successful in the first week (Week 2) he introduced the method. However, in Week 3, he found that he again tended to procrastinate. To control the behavior, he added a date book with a listing of the goals he had to achieve that day to the other procedures he was using. He checked off each goal as it was performed. As shown, this approach, combining several methods, resulted in a significant reduction in the number of times he procrastinated each day. The student whose findings are shown in Figure 11–4 wrote down the goals she set for herself in the morning. She then checked off each

Self-Management and Time Management **119**

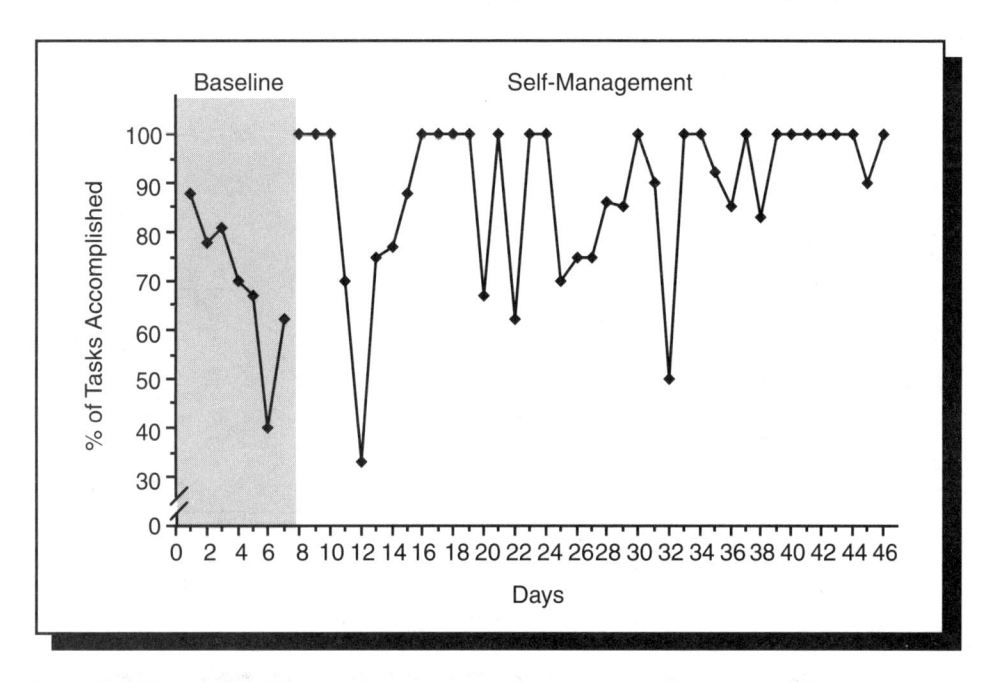

FIGURE 11–2
Use of goal setting and self-monitoring to improve time management.

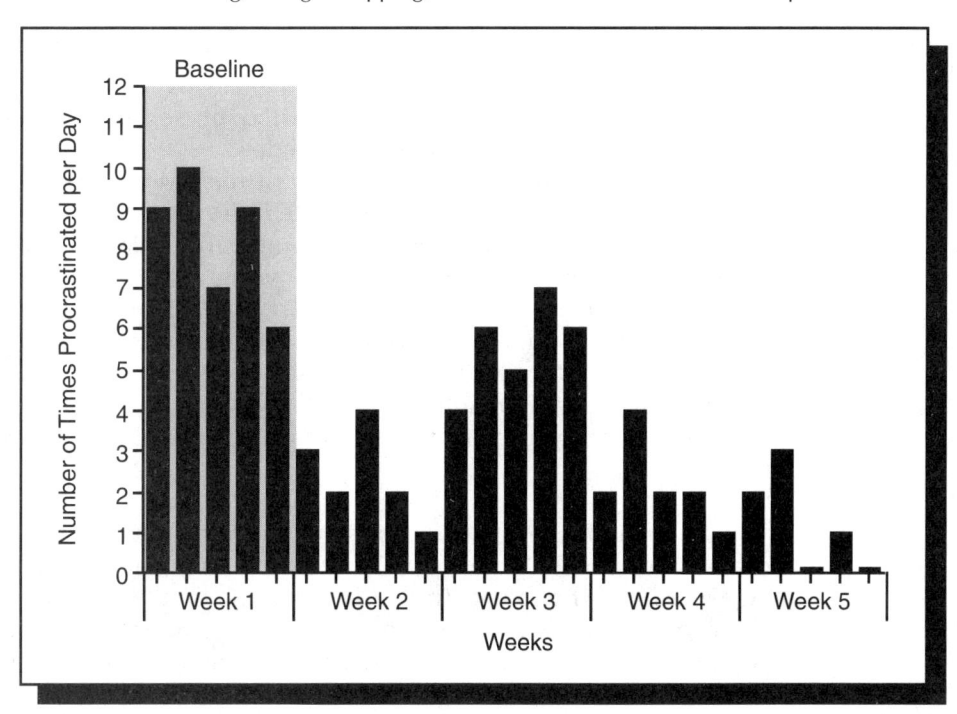

FIGURE 11–3
Use of self-monitoring, thought stopping, and self-reinforcement to decrease procrastination.

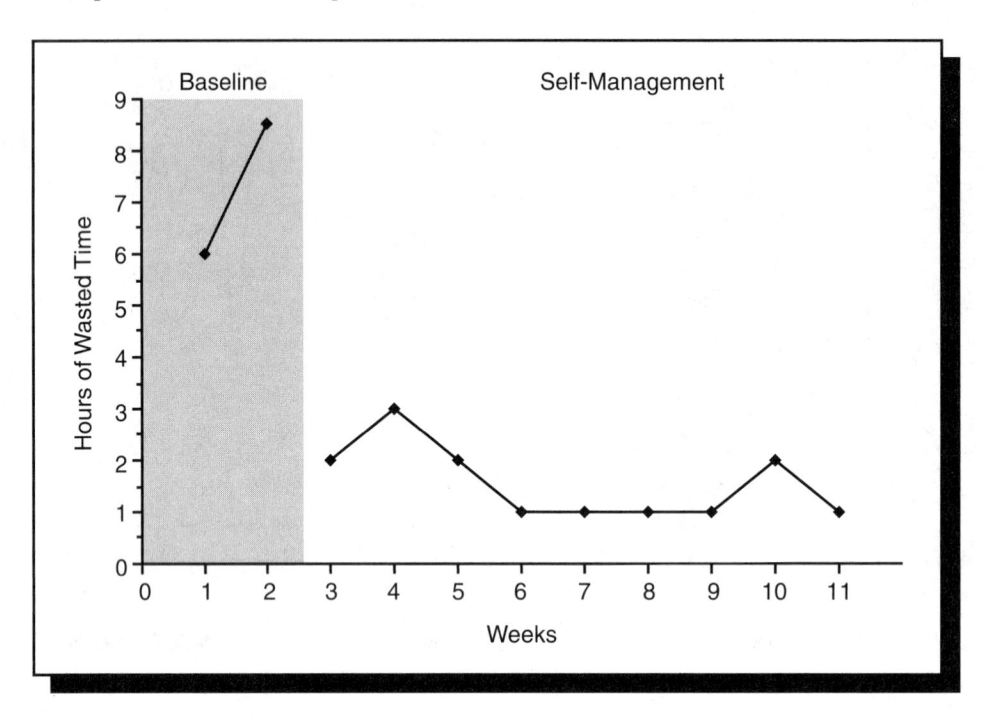

FIGURE 11-4
Use of self-monitoring to decrease wasted time.

goal as it was attained. Through this method of self-monitoring, she greatly reduced the amount of time she wasted.

Figure 11-5 shows the approach a student took in an attempt to improve his grades. On school days, he plotted the number of hours he spent each day in going to class, walking to and from classes, studying, eating, and in personal time. He felt that, overall, there was some improvement in his grades. However, he found, as noted in the figure, that he still did not use his time appropriately, particularly on weekends. His conclusion was that he would need to improve his time management if he were to be truly successful in school.

Almost any successful venture involves time management. As Kaye (1992) notes:

> It helps you "chunk out" the day, so that your activities reflect the plan you set for yourself. Without time management, you may experience the frustrating sense that "your life is running you." With careful time management, however, you can balance many areas in your life without undue stress. You can reward yourself at the end of the day for work well done (p. 86).

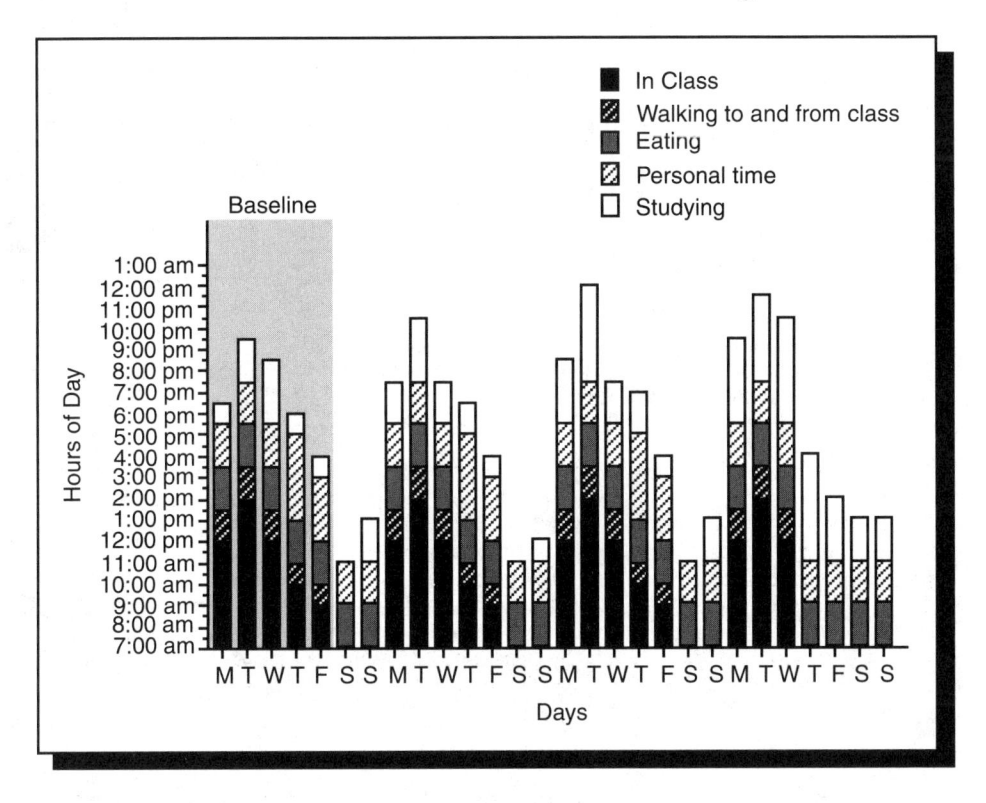

FIGURE 11–5
Use of self-monitoring to increase study time.

EXERCISE

What goals would you like to achieve each day?
What would be a proven strategy for achieving your set goals?
How are you going to implement and record any behavioral change?
What criteria will you set to determine if your goals have been achieved?

REVIEW TERMS

Effectiveness
Efficiency
Alan Lakein

Parkinson's Law
Peak or alert time
Pineapple method

QUESTIONS

Describe four misconceptions about time management.
Describe five components to effective time management.
List the eight tips for effective time management offered by Martin and Osborne.

CHAPTER 12

Effective Studying

"What one knows is, in youth, of little moment; they know enough who know how to learn."

—Henry Adams, *The Education of Henry Adams*

"I never had to study much before I came to college. Things came easy for me and I always managed to slip by. My first term was a mess. I never had received a C before. I got four that term. My parents were really pissed. They said that if I didn't shape up, they wouldn't pay my tuition. I was ticked too. I sure as hell didn't want to work at the service station with my dad. I started learning how to study my second term. It took me a while to learn how to get my routine down, but I now have my grade point average above a 3 point."

—Matt, a sophomore

All students are concerned about effective studying. You would not be in college if you did not think about your study habits and how they might be improved. The approach taken by students in studying varies according to a number of variables, including natural abilities, time constraints, past experiences, and the context within which learning occurs. Because each of us is different, we vary from one another in the approach we take to learning academic materials. As we are all unique in our approach to studying, there is no one plan that is suitable for everyone. For this reason, a variety of approaches to studying will be presented.

CHARACTERISTICS OF SUCCESSFUL STUDENTS

Zimmerman (1986) points out fourteen characteristics of successful students. As these general characteristics are appropriate for all of us, they will merit discussion. They are:

1. Self-evaluation. You should continually review, analyze, and evaluate your behavior. You might ask yourself, "Am I doing as well as I can in this class? If not, what can I do to increase my success?"

2. Organization. You should carefully organize to study. In particular, you should employ time management skills, discussed in Chapter 11, to enhance your abilities and overall success.

3. Transformation of information. You should be able to transform the ideas you acquire in the classroom or textbooks into whatever conceptual framework is appropriate for the information. This is often easy with practical information, but more difficult when the material is abstract. Nevertheless, all information you learn should become an integral part of your knowledge base.

4. Setting subgoals. Besides setting long-term goals, you should establish subgoals that must be attained along the way to your goals. You will want to review constantly and, where necessary, change your goals to meet both your short-term and long-term needs.

5. Planning. As noted in the last chapter, you should plan out your life. This involves establishing schedules of when you attend class, study, and perform other duties and tasks.

6. Seeking information. If you are unclear about a topic, ask questions. In addition, you may want to seek out additional sources, such as materials in the library, to buttress your knowledge.

7. Keep records. Until studying becomes an integral part of your day, you will want to keep written records noting how much time you spend studying each day. This material will help you balance the time you spend in studying, working, or performing other activities.

8. Self-monitoring. Self-monitoring is a significant component in any studying you undertake.

9. Structuring the environment. Individual students require different environments within which to study. Some students like it quiet; others like listening to loud rock music when studying. You should decide the type of environment that is most conducive to successful studying.

10. Self-consequences. You should reinforce yourself for successful performance. It might sometimes be necessary to consider the consequences of your behavior if you do not study. To avoid or escape from these potentially aversive consequences, you may want to increase studying.

11. Rehearsal. Before taking a test or giving a talk, you should rehearse the behaviors you expect to perform. Arguments for rehearsal as a technique for behavior change have been presented; the same arguments hold true for improving study skills.

12. Memorization. Although many of you do not like to memorize material, overlearning is a key to the success of any good student. For this reason, memorization can be invaluable to successful academic performance.

13. Seeking assistance. Everyone in school needs help from time to time. Don't be too shy or proud to ask for assistance when required.

14. Reviewing notes and textbooks. It is useful to review notes and textbooks before class. This not only sets the stage for the next lecture, but it reinforces your memory of what you have learned.

DEVELOPING EFFECTIVE STUDY HABITS

Now that you have reviewed the qualities exhibited by good students, you may want to consider ways to develop effective study habits. The following suggestions are useful to all of us, although some of you may find certain skills are more relevant to you than to others. Nevertheless, the skills that will be discussed are important for you not only in learning in the classroom, but in acquiring other knowledge throughout your life. There is consensus among a number of educators about the importance of a common set of factors, including the following.

Setting

The first item to consider in studying is to establish the proper environment. Environmental characteristics that should be present include: (a) good indirect lighting; (b) a temperature that is neither too cold nor too hot; (c) a desk or table clear of everything but your study materials; (d) a quiet place or a place where there are no distracting sounds (you might use white noise if you find other noises are distracting); and (e) a minimal number of distracting sights. You prepare beforehand by having all the materials you will need for your studies (e.g., pencils, paper, books). As noted in an earlier chapter, it is helpful if you only study in whatever area you designate as your studying area. The stimuli in these environments can become discriminative stimuli for studying.

Schedule

Before making out a schedule for studying, you should determine exactly how much time is required for each class you take. Some classes require considerable work while others require less effort. In addition, some classes require intense study at certain periods, but less intense study at other times. As noted in the previous chapter, it would be helpful if you scheduled your studying when you are most alert. For many of you, this could mean the early morning hours; for others, it could mean late at night. It is further recommended that you study your tougher subjects during your peak or most alert periods; this should enhance your chances of success at learning the subjects. Write down your study schedule. A schedule will not only serve as a reminder to you, but increase your commitment to study your course materials. You should occasionally review your schedule to be certain it is compatible with course demands. Occasionally take breaks based on progress rather than the passage of time. Taking a break following a period where you make progress and feel alert will reinforce making progress and being alert. The result should be strengthening of your study habits. Finally, you should always reward yourself for studying.

Studying Effectively

In the past few chapters, suggestions have been offered for improving your study skills. All these strategies require activity on your part, including breaking large projects into smaller components; such tactics should be considered in deciding how you will study. In addition, a number of writers advocate the SQ3R method (Robinson, 1961), which is a system for study that is designed to promote effective learning. It involves five steps:

1. Survey. Before reading a chapter, skim over it to obtain an overview of the topics covered. You should review a chapter outline or summary if one is provided. Write down any questions that you want answered when you do study the chapter. These tactics also permit you to better organize the materials when you read the chapter.
2. Question. Once you have performed an overview of a chapter, proceed through it one segment at a time. Pay careful attention to the headings of sections to see if they generate more questions for you.
3. Read. This step involves actually reading the chapter. You may want to underline what you consider relevant material in the text. In addition, attempt to answer the questions that were generated in surveying and reviewing the material.
4. Recite. After you answer the questions you have raised, recite the answers to yourself in your own words. This permits you to transform what is written into your own terminology. Go through sections one at a time. It is suggested that you put the book down while you recite significant information; this enhances your memory of what you are learning.
5. Review. After you have completed the other four steps, review what you have read. Continue to recite to yourself what seemed to be the key points of the chapter. Establish the habit of reviewing because, no matter how much you learn, you constantly find that you must review what you have learned.

You need not adhere rigidly to the SQ3R method. However, as noted by Weitan, Lloyd, and Lashley (1991), the SQ3R method is effective because it permits you to break down a reading assignment into manageable segments. It also requires that you understand what you are reading before you move on.

Active Listening

There are a number of ways you can improve on how you take lecture notes. Weitan and colleagues provided the following suggestions:

1. Be an active listener. This not only involves listening to what the instructor says, but also looking for nonverbal signals. See if you can tie in material covered in lectures with topics discussed in your textbooks, or with the knowledge you have already acquired.

2. Prepare for lecture. In many instances, you can prepare, particularly for difficult subject matter, by reviewing your notes of past lectures and reading the textbook. This may help set the stage for the lecture.

3. Don't be a human tape recorder. If you are an active listener, you can translate what the lecturer is saying into your own thoughts. You may also develop a style of taking notes that relies on a form of personalized shorthand. Use an outline format with headings. This can help you in jotting down more information when it is required. Don't attempt to rewrite this material; the scribbled notes often contain stimuli that trigger memories to you when you review your notes.

Improving Memory

There are a number of proven methods you can use to improve your memory. These include:

1. Engage in adequate practice. Retention of material improves with increased rehearsal. While many of you dislike memorizing material, it pays to overlearn what you have been taught. Overlearning refers to the repeated rehearsal of material after you believe you have mastered it. It not only improves retention of what is being taught to you, but enhances incidental learning that may take place. Incidental learning features no intention to learn on your part. Learning is incidental when no instruction is given to learn the material on which you may be later tested. This type of learning plays a major role in our everyday life.

2. Use distributed practice. It pays to spread out your studying and not try to cram. Retention is improved with distributed practice and not the mass practice that occurs with cramming.

3. Minimize interference. You may forget information because of competition from other learned material. One way to manage interference is to direct your attention to a given subject just before a scheduled test. If you have used mass practice, this tactic also permits you a final review of what you have learned.

4. Organize information. Retention is usually greater when information is well organized. By outlining materials, you can organize it in a way that assists you in learning.

5. Use verbal mnemonics. A mnemonic is a device that enhances your memory. It may be a word or a nonsense sentence; other mnemonics include: a) acrostics or phrases where the first letter serves as a cue;

(b) an acronym or a word formed by the first letters of a series of words; (c) narrative methods where you create a story out of what you are learning, and (d) rhymes. Whatever approach you use, it should be useful to you.

6. Imagery. There are three types of imagery that might be used to help you learn: the link, loci, and peg methods.

The link method involves your forming a mental image of what you want to remember by linking items together. For example, you might visualize someone performing a series of behaviors you need to know for a psychology course. The image may not be rational; often, the more bizarre the image, the more likely you are to recall it.

The loci method involves your taking an imaginary walk along a path where you have associated images of material you want to remember with certain locations or items. You might use a familiar setting, such as your room, and associate particular items with the materials you are trying to remember.

The peg method involves your creating associations between number-word rhymes and items to be memorized. The rhymes can then serve as "pegs" on which to hang items to be memorized. The rhyme will probably be nonsensical to anyone but you; if it helps you memorize material better, that is all that matters.

In a self-management manual developed for children with asthma, Creer, Backial, Ullman, & Leung (1986) used rhymes to teach children steps to perform in the event of an asthma episode. One rhyme went, "Think, drink, be calm, tell Mom, maybe a med, maybe to bed" (p. 8–3). The rhyme included possible steps the children could take when they had an attack. They were taught to perform the steps according to the severity of their asthma. In the case of a severe exacerbation, for example, they would immediately tell their mother, take an inhaled dose of medication, calmly wait a period before taking a second inhalation, and so on. Children as young as five learned how to control their asthma through the use of rhymes and pegging their treatment to the steps outlined in the rhymes (Creer et al., 1988).

TEST TAKING

As most of you have learned by now, taking tests requires certain skills. General skills include:

1. Stay relaxed. If you can stay relaxed, your memory is improved. If you panic, you are apt to forget everything you studied.

2. Prepare beforehand for a test so as to avoid cramming. Mass practice can lead to a lack of retention; thus, you should engage in distributed practice whenever possible.

3. Within the time limits of the class, set your own pace. Even if your classmates finish tests fast, you may not be ready to wrap up your exam. Set your own pace; if you require the entire testing period, take it.

4. Answer those questions first where you know the proper response. Don't ponder over questions where you are uncertain about the answer, but go on to those questions that you can answer. You can come back later and answer the questions that require more thought and consideration.

5. Adopt proper level of sophistication. Don't read things into questions, particularly those that may seem simple to you.

6. Unless forbidden, don't hesitate to ask an instructor to clarify a question that you are uncertain about. Let's face it: all test items are not necessarily clear to everyone, particularly students.

7. Review the test. Allow yourself a few minutes to look over and review your test. This may permit you not only to correct any mistakes you may have made, but to be certain that your answers are readable.

Multiple-Choice Exams

Weitan and colleagues (1991) offered several tips for taking multiple-choice exams. These may or may not be useful to you.

1. Anticipate the answer. You may want to consider the potential answer to a question before reading the possible options.

2. Read all options. Even if you are certain the first item is the correct answer, read all options before checking what you think is the most appropriate answer.

3. Eliminate highly implausible options. You can learn to do this quickly. Once the skill is mastered, you can concentrate on selecting the most appropriate choice from the remaining options.

4. Look for cues to one answer from other questions. Sometimes, there is a cue to a later answer provided in an earlier question. Be alert for such signals.

5. "All of the above." These can be tricky answers. Weitan and colleagues provide the following advice: "On items that have 'all of the above' as an option, if you know that just two of the options are correct, you should choose 'all of the above.' If you are confident that any one of the options is incorrect, you should eliminate both the incorrect option and 'all of the above,' and choose from the remaining options" (p. 26).

6. Detail of options. Options that are more detailed tend to be correct.

7. Broad generalizations in options. Options that create broad, sweeping generalizations tend to be incorrect. In contrast, options that create carefully qualified statements tend to be correct.

Identification and Essay Exams

Suggestions for these exams include:

1. Memorize key points and key terms. This practice is useful not only in identification exams, but in writing concise essay answers.

2. Rephrase material. Once you have learned a term or another topic about a subject area, rephrase the material in your own words. This is useful not only in learning the subject matter, but in helping you later write an essay answer.

3. Write answers you know first. When writing identification answers, jot down the ones you are certain of first. You can later go back and contemplate the questions that require more attention.

4. Outline. It is an excellent idea to outline an essay answer before you begin to write. This is especially helpful if you use one of the mnemonic devices, particularly acronyms, described earlier.

5. Rewrite. Allow yourself time to rewrite an essay answer. This permits you not only to determine if you have correctly answered the question, but to be certain that the answer you have written reads well.

STRATEGIES FOR STUDYING

Improving study skills is always a popular topic for students. Most use self-monitoring to achieve their goal. This technique was used by the student whose progress is noted in Figure 12–1. She felt that she did very well in the latter stages of the program, but rued the fact that she started so poorly. She noted that she paid because of her lack of studying in weeks 1 through 3. Figure 12–2 depicts the progress in studying made by another student who used self-monitoring. She reported that she not only increased her study time, but that her grades improved. The student wrote that her interest in the subject matter increased dramatically as she studied more.

Figure 12–3 depicts the increase in study time reported by a student who used both self-monitoring and time management. He stated that by using distributed practice, he not only eliminated "all nighters" before exam time, but he learned more than he had in the past. The student whose results are shown in Figure 12–4 set goals and attempted to reach them through self-monitoring. He not only achieved his subgoals, but he attained the overall goal he set for himself.

Figure 12–5 depicts the strides made by a student who used a combination of procedures to increase his study time. He changed environments by going to the library to study, he studied during his peak peri-

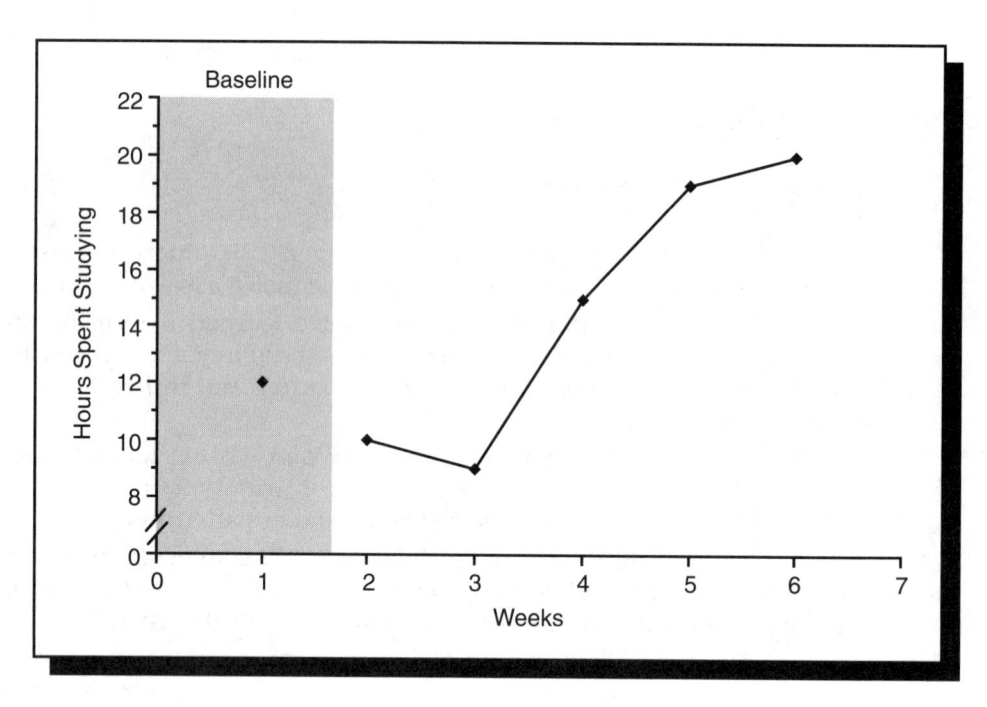

FIGURE 12–1
Use of self-monitoring to increase study time.

FIGURE 12–2
Use of self-monitoring to increase study time.

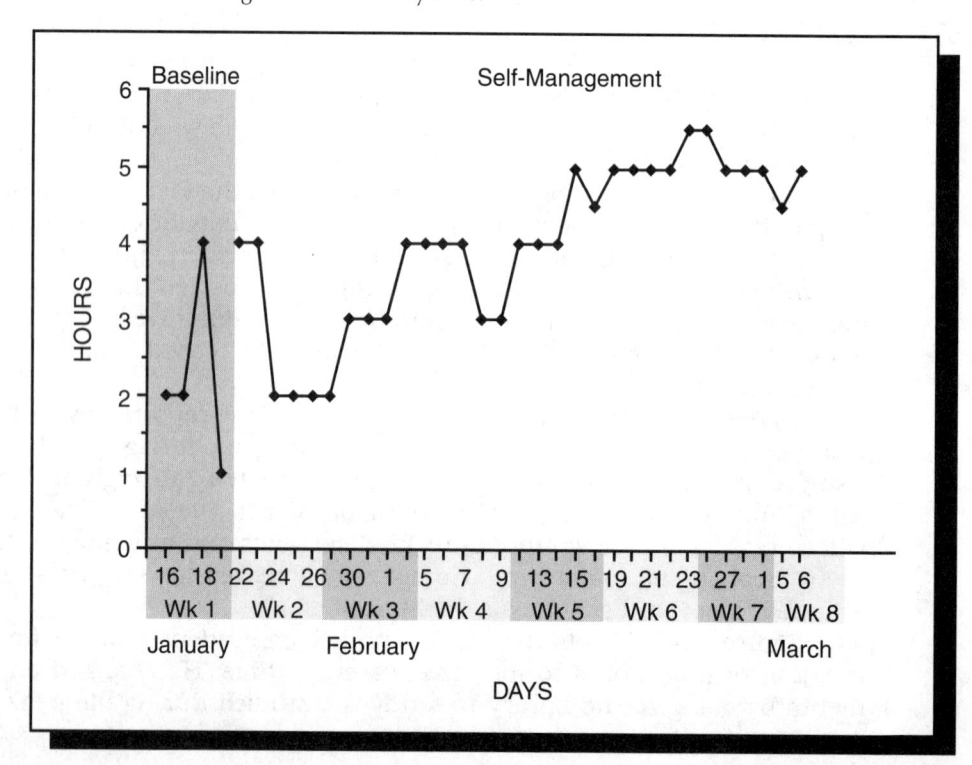

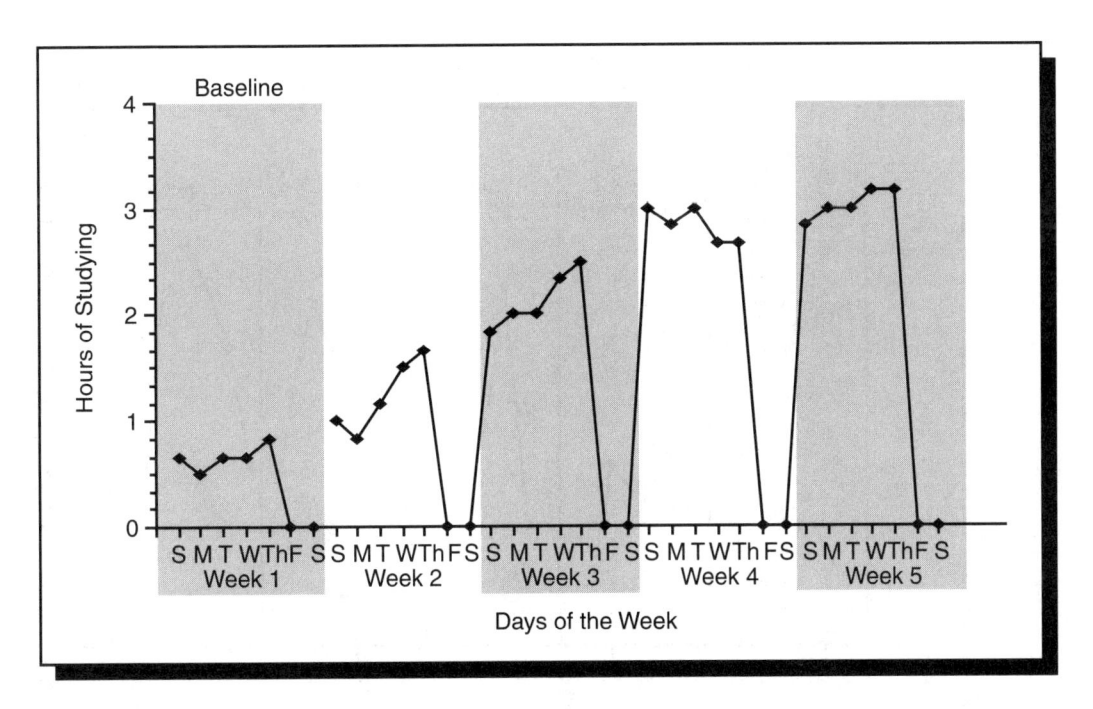

FIGURE 12–3
Use of self-monitoring and time management to increase study time.

FIGURE 12–4
Goal setting and self-monitoring to improve study habits.

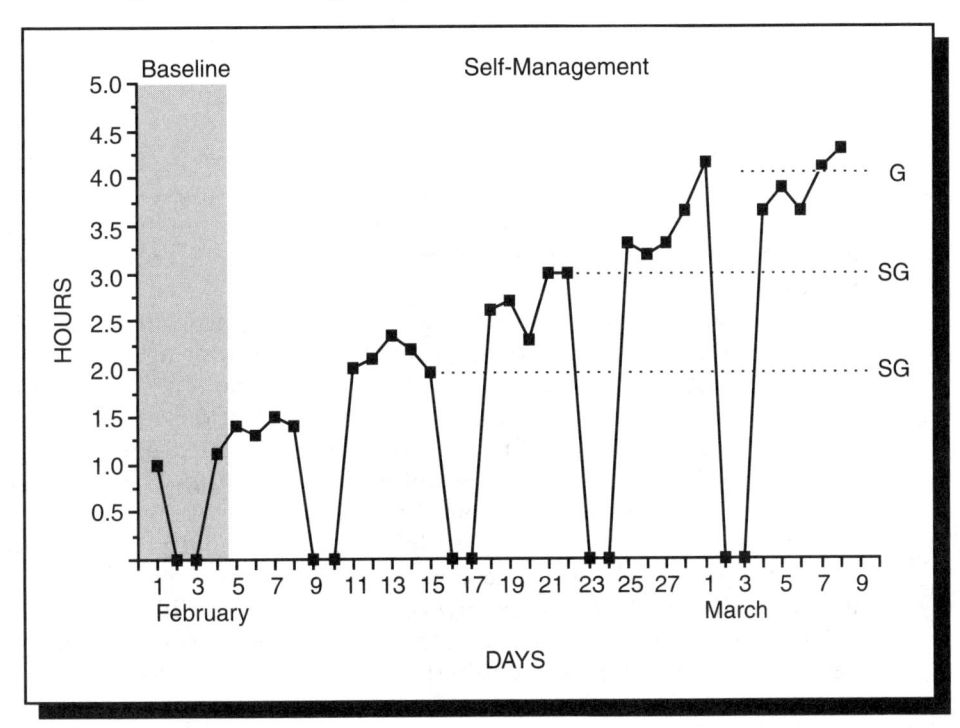

132   Chap. 12   *Effective Studying*

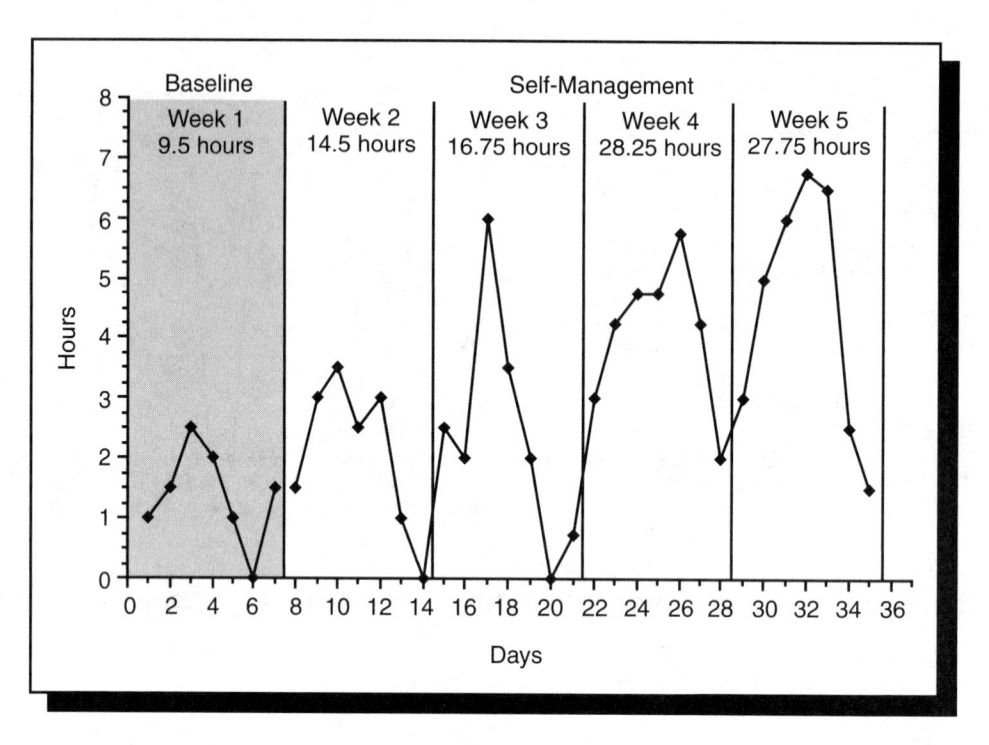

FIGURE 12–5
Use of a combination of environmental change, scheduling, distributed practice, and self-monitoring to increase study time.

ods, he used distributed practice to learn materials, and he carefully monitored his behavior. He concluded that he became not only more efficient at studying as a result of his project, but that there had been a marked improvement in his memorization and retention of acquired knowledge.

Finally, the project depicted in Figure 12–6 involved a student using time management, distributed practice, self-monitoring, and systematic self-desensitization to increase the amount of time she studied and, as a consequence, to improve her grades. After she self-desensitized herself to fears engendered by studying, she worked out a schedule that helped her plan her assignments according to her own schedule. The clever strategy she took resulted in the progress she reported.

Most students who take studying as a personal project do improve their study skills. Those who do not improve, however, inevitably learn why they do not study as effectively as they should. This analysis of their behavior later permits them to make adjustments in their lives so as to develop the competencies required for success in the classroom.

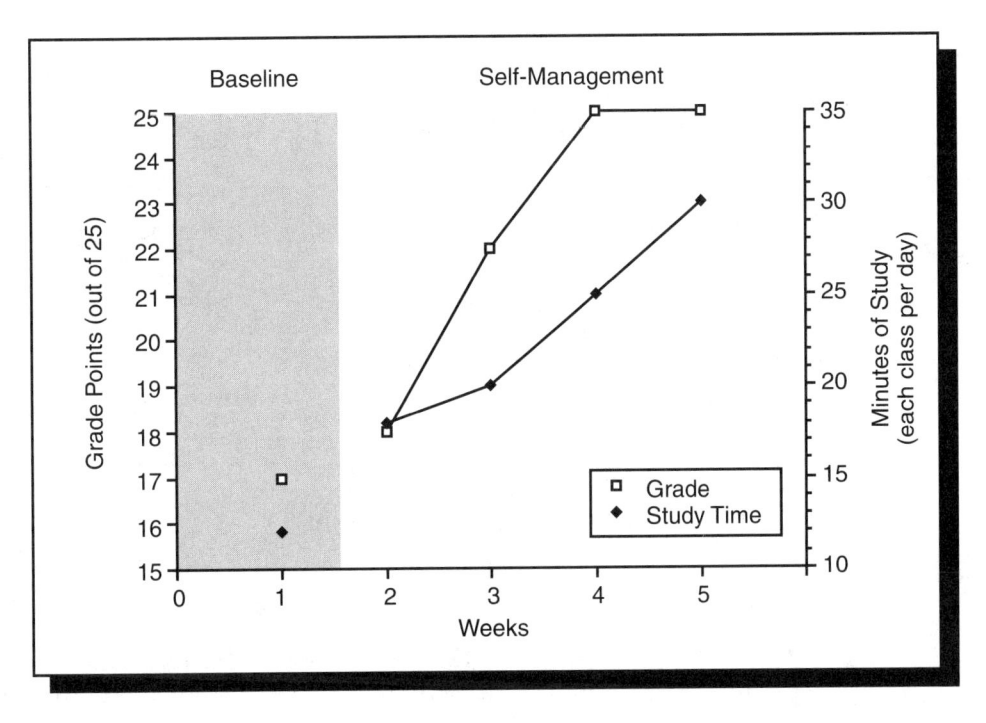

FIGURE 12–6
Use of systematic self-desensitization, time management, self-monitoring, and distributed practice to increase study time and, as a consequence, improve grades.

EXERCISE

Analyze your study skills. Are they in need of improvement?
What strategies can you take to improve your studying?
How are you going to assess your progress?
What criteria will you establish to determine if your program is a success?

REVIEW TERMS

Acronyms
Acrostics
Incidental learning

Link method
Loci method
Overlearning

QUESTIONS

List fourteen characteristics of successful students.
Discuss the SQ3R method of studying.
Discuss seven test-taking skills.

CHAPTER 13

Health and Wellness

"Life is not merely being alive, but being well."

—Martial, *Epigrams*

"I don't know why I have to be sick all the time. I know I'm overweight and never exercise, but it doesn't seem fair that I catch every cold that comes along. My roommates say I should get more sleep and eat better, but I think I just have bad luck."

—Gary, a college senior

Hafen, Thygerson, and Frandsen (1988) point out that most of us think of health as the absence of illness or some physical disorder. From this perspective, health would be easy to measure: we would use available medical techniques to measure whether a person is healthy. However, as Hafen and colleagues state, health is in reality difficult to define and almost impossible to measure. The World Health Organization, for example, defines health as a state of complete physical, mental, and social well-being, and not merely the absence of disease or infirmity. The word *well-being* introduces the concept of wellness. As Hafen and colleagues note, there is a difference between "health" and "wellness":

> Health is a state of being; either you are healthy or you are not. And when you are ill, you cannot at the same time be healthy. Wellness, on the other hand, is a process—a continuous moving toward a greater awareness of yourself and the way in which environmental, interpersonal relationships, nutrition, fitness, stress, and other factors influence you. . . . Illness and "health" are opposite states but you can be ill and still enjoy "wellness" if you have a purpose to life, a deep appreciation for living, and a sense of joy (p. 2).

In this discussion, wellness assumes a position more dominant than health. However, the degree of wellness we experience is still likely to be a function of our overall health. For this reason, our goal should be to improve our health and enhance our wellness. In order for us to achieve this goal, we need to review the characteristics experts have reported that describe both healthy and well people.

CHARACTERISTICS OF HEALTHY PEOPLE

Hafen and colleagues discuss a number of features that characterize the healthy individual. As we will note, there is overlap between these characteristics and those of people considered to be well. The difference between the two classes of individuals, when there are differences, would probably only be in the degree to which they display given characteristics or behaviors. Characteristics of healthy people include:

1. Freedom from aches and pains. Healthy people are generally free from the occasional sore muscle or headache. When they experience these problems, there is no dampening of their confidence or optimism with respect to their ability to care for their problem.

2. Remarkable resistance to disease. In addition to their perennial optimism, healthy individuals are more resistant to disease; they often do not experience the common infections, such as colds, that incapacitate their friends and relatives.

3. Intelligent about their health. People who are healthy not only know how to prevent many physical problems from occurring, but they are able to relieve many ailments once they occur. The emphasis of these people is on preventing illness, not in attempting to alleviate ongoing diseases or infections.

4. Exercise. Healthy people exercise on a regular basis. As a result, their reaction time is good, they are strong, and they exhibit high endurance.

5. Display active life-style. Individuals who are healthy love to be involved with life. They have considerable energy to do whatever task they undertake, whether it be studying for an exam or going on a brisk run.

6. Respect their bodies. Healthy people respect and enjoy their bodies. They make the most of their physical abilities, and take delight in themselves and their health.

7. Mentally strong. Healthy individuals are mentally alert. They are able to think clearly. In addition, they recognize the link between good health and their mental confidence and enthusiasm.

8. Creative. Healthy people are creative. They approach problems with different and unique perspectives; the approaches they take, in turn, often lead to a quick resolution of problems.

9. Curious. Healthy individuals are curious about both themselves and their world. They are always looking for new and challenging tasks to perform.

10. Stimulating and capable. Healthy people are alert and skilled. They relish the prospect of improving themselves or learning something new.

11. Have vision and promise. Healthy individuals are able to see opportunities and plan for them. Hafen and colleagues note that, more

than anything, they are open-minded and accepting of others. The self-confidence of healthy individuals guarantees that they can take their place in the world among others without sacrificing themselves or requiring others to be like them. Healthy people enjoy others and are not threatened by what other individuals might do or say.

12. Experience deep and abiding happiness. Healthy people have a deep happiness that is not ephemeral, but stems from a powerful inner contentment.

13. Accepting of themselves. Healthy individuals are accepting of themselves. They value themselves as people who have something to contribute and who are worthwhile.

14. Stable. Healthy people can look at success and failure and move in a predetermined course. They are goal-oriented, but, at the same time, firmly rooted in the present.

15. In touch with feelings. Healthy individuals are in touch with their feelings. Because they are self-confident, they do not worry about expressing their feelings or sharing them with others. They are not overly concerned about what others think of them.

Hafen and colleagues conclude their discussion of healthy people by noting:

> Healthy people have the unique ability to see beyond the isolated event—to, in a word, envision the whole picture. A healthy person sets realistic goals and sets about reaching them with hope, enthusiasm, and determination, but those goals are never the end result. Instead, they are part of the whole, cogs in the larger machine of life. Healthy people are always enthused about what lies ahead, not content with what has been accomplished in the past (pp. 10–11).

CHARACTERISTICS OF UNHEALTHY PEOPLE

Dr. Lester Breslow, a public health specialist, followed the lives of nearly 7,000 adults living in Alameda County, California, over the past three decades. His early research in 1965 indicated that the more poor health habits practiced by people, the greater the chances they had of dying within ten years. Recently, Breslow and Breslow (1993) reported that more people than originally thought are guilty of performing unhealthy health habits. These habits not only predict early death for many individuals, but chronic and costly disabilities for those who survive. Seven habits in particular were singled out by Breslow and Breslow (1993). Their study found that individuals who exhibited six or seven of these poor health practices in 1965 were twice as likely to be disabled ten or more years later than were their neighbors who displayed no more than two of the habits. The habits merit special discussion:

1. Excessive alcohol consumption. Alcohol abuse is discussed in Chapter 16. Recent data reported by McGinnis and Foege (1993) indicated that excessive alcohol consumption was responsible for approximately 100,000 deaths in the United States in 1990.

2. Smoking. Smoking is discussed in Chapter 16. Recent data compiled by McGinnis and Foege showed that tobacco consumption contributed to an estimated 400,000 deaths in the United States in 1990. This estimate is lower than that suggested by the Centers for Disease Control, which reported that 418,690 deaths were caused by tobacco in 1990, including approximately 30 percent of all cancer deaths and 21 percent of cardiovascular deaths. The dangers of smoking are magnified as the number of deaths from smoking increases each year because of the popularity of smoking from 1940 through 1960.

3. Excessive weight. Diet and weight control are described in Chapter 15. Deaths from obesity fall under the category of diet and activity patterns discussed by McGinnis and Foege. They estimated that this contributed to 300,000 deaths in the United States in 1990. Breslow and Breslow found that 66 percent of Americans were found to be overweight in 1991. This reflects an increase in comparable reports of 61 percent in 1991 and 58 percent in 1983.

4. Sleeping too little or too much. Breslow and Breslow found that 50 percent of the respondents in their study reported they obtained as much as seven to eight hours of sleep a night. This is down from 64 percent in 1983. It was suggested that sleeping too little or too much was not on par with smoking or overconsumption of alcohol as a health risk. Rather, Breslow and Breslow suggested these practices are likely to indicate that people had chaotic life styles and were unlikely to pay attention to their overall well-being.

5. Lack of exercise. Exercise is discussed in Chapter 14. The lack of adequate exercise and activity patterns, along with poor diet, were estimated to be linked to 300,000 deaths in the United States in 1990 (McGinnis and Foege, 1993). In the study by Breslow and Breslow, 33 percent of the respondents indicated they exercised vigorously three or more times a week. This was down from 37 percent who reported they actively exercised in 1991.

6. Eating between meals. Snacking is also not a health habit that is on par with smoking, alcohol consumption, or poor diet as predictors of poor health. However, Breslow and Breslow reported that such a practice was suggestive of a chaotic life-style.

7. Not eating breakfast. Like snacking, not eating breakfast is not a major health risk in and of itself. However, it does suggest a chaotic lifestyle, according to Breslow & Breslow. Along with the other information they reported, they concluded, "The data indicate that good personal health practices, which may be termed a modern hygiene, strongly favor both longer survival and curtailment of disability" (p. 94).

CHARACTERISTICS OF WELLNESS

As described, healthy people provide good models for all of us. Individuals who are considered as unusually well exhibit many of these characteristics, as will be noted. Well individuals are:

1. Committed to outside causes. People who are unusually well are committed to others. They have both the time and the energy to be involved in activities involving others. A similar characteristic was noted for healthy people.

2. Physically strong. Unusually well individuals are like healthy people in that they are in excellent physical condition. As a result, they can perform whatever activities they wish with great energy. As occurs with healthy people, those who are unusually well are seldom sick.

3. Caring and loving. People considered unusually well care about and love others. They are the type of individuals others lean on in crises. Again, this characteristic was noted for those considered as healthy.

4. In synthesis with spiritual. Individuals regarded as unusually well are in tune with the spiritual in that they have a clear sense of purpose and direction. As noted, this was also a quality reflected by healthy people.

5. Intellectually strong. Usually well people are intellectually strong. They are able to handle and process information quickly. They are also reported to be curious and to have a good sense of humor. These characteristics apply as well to healthy individuals.

6. Well organized. Unusually well individuals are organized. They are able to accomplish great quantities of work irrespective of time constraints. Although it was not described, a similar characteristic would likely apply to people regarded as healthy.

7. Live in present. Unusually well people live in and enjoy the present. They plan ahead, but are not always looking at the future. They also benefit from past experiences, but they are not rooted in the past. The same comments could be made about healthy individuals.

8. Comfortable with full range of human emotions. Unusually well individuals are able to experience the full range of emotional reactions in a positive manner. They optimistically bounce back from distressing events with vigor and enthusiasm. At the same time, they are willing to share both their own feelings with others as well as the emotional feelings of others. These attributes are also typical of healthy individuals.

9. Accepting of limitations, handicaps, and mistakes. Unusually well people are accepting of their own limitations and handicaps. They know the boundaries that frame their abilities. At the same time, they recognize that they make mistakes. Unlike others, they know that they often learn only through making mistakes. These remarks are similar to those described for healthy individuals.

10. Take charge of own life. Unusually well people are able to take charge of their lives. They know what events can be controlled by themselves and what events are under the control of external factors. These are the individuals most apt to optimize the control over events that they can control, while minimizing the impact of external factors. This characteristic, too, would apply to healthy people.

It is likely that both healthy and unusually well people exhibit what is referred to as hardiness. Hardiness is a personality syndrome comprised of three personality characteristics—control, commitment, and challenge—that are associated with resistance to the potentially harmful effects of stress (Kobasa, 1979). If you are challenged by a problem, are committed to solving it, and can control whatever is required to resolve the difficulty, you exhibit hardiness. While there is as yet little evidence to link hardiness to health, a number of investigators in health psychology consider the construct in their research.

IMPROVING HEALTH

The Department of Commerce estimated that health spending would rise $118 billion to $1.06 trillion, and would account for a record 15 percent of the total output of goods and services in the United States in 1994 (Pear, 1993). Reducing spending for health care is fast becoming a national goal. Self-management approaches can be used in two ways to improve your health. The first approach is to apply self-management techniques both to improve your health and to prevent illness. A blue-ribbon panel (Fries et al., 1993) recently suggested that health-care costs in the United States could be reduced by shrinking the need and demand for medical services. They emphasized that the application of self-management procedures was the key to the success of their proposal. As we all hold dual citizenship in the kingdoms of the well and the sick (Sontag, 1978), the second approach is that we learn to become good consumers of health-care services. Tables 13–1 and 13–2 suggest ways you might achieve this aim. Table 13–1 has a number of suggestions from Inlander and Weiner (1992) on how you might avoid or correct medical abuses. Table 13–2 offers ways to be certain that your medical bill is correct, and Table 13–3 suggests questions you should consider before enrolling in a health maintenance organization. As only you are apt to be aware of the potential of medical abuses, it is up to you to review these suggestions and apply them whenever you are involved with the medical system.

TABLE 13–1 The Self-Management of Medical Abuses (adapted from Inlander and Weiner, 1992)

1. When in doubt, obtain a second or even a third opinion.
2. Determine how often your physician and/or hospital has performed a particular procedure. The more often a practitioner or hospital performs a procedure, the more likely it is to be a success.
3. Determine if your physician has ever been disciplined or had his or her license suspended.
4. Determine if your physician is trained in the speciality in which he or she claims expertise. You can acquire this information by asking your physician or by checking registries in a university library.
5. Ask your physician or an attending technician the last time a piece of equipment was inspected or calibrated, if you have concerns.
6. Read and thoroughly know your health-insurance policy. If you are about to transfer jobs or health-insurance policies, look for clauses that indicate payment will not be made for preexisting conditions.
7. In picking a physician, look for expertise rather than bedside manners if a distinction is to be made. Pick a physician who is a strong diagnostician and who has a solid reputation in his or her area of expertise. Pick a physician who will answer all your questions or seek to answer them, no matter how many questions you may have.

TABLE 13–2 Self-Monitoring Your Hospital Bill (adapted from Inlander and Weiner, 1992)

More than 90 percent of all hospital bills have errors; 75 percent of these errors are in favor of the hospital. To avoid having to pay unnecessary hospital expenses, consider the following strategies

1. Check fees in advance by comparing quoted fees against hospital bill.
2. Don't pay your bill on the way out of the hospital as you may not be alert enough to analyze it.
3. Demand an itemized hospital bill. Make certain that you understand the bill.
4. Check to see if you were billed for:
   a. The correct kind of room and number of days
   b. The correct time spent in specialized units
   c. Only those X-rays and tests you received
   d. Only those medications, dressings, injections, and so on that you received in the quoted quantities
   e. Only bedpans, humidifiers, thermometers, personal items, and so on that you received or were allowed to take home
   f. Correct number of daily hospital visits by your physician
   g. Consultations with only those specialists you spoke to and
   h. Only labor rooms and nursery care used by you or your baby
5. If you don't understand something on your bill, ask your physician or a hospital administrator to audit that portion of the bill. Don't pay that portion of the bill until the situation is remedied.
6. If you suspect that there is a problem with a bill to be paid by your insurance, contact your insurance company.

TABLE 13–3 Selecting the Right Health Maintenance Organization (HMO) for You

1. What is the basic cost of the HMO to you?
2. Where are the locations of the nearest HMO service facilities with respect to where you live?
3. What is the policy of the HMO with respect to preexisting conditions, including pregnancy?
4. What percentage of a plan's network doctors are board certified and what percentage leave each year?
5. If the plan has a "quality report care," or has been audited by the National Committee of Quality Assurance or other organizations, can you inspect the report?
6. What's in the sample benefits contract?
7. How many complaints filed with the state insurance department against the plan have been upheld?
8. Must primary care physicians receive permission from the H.M.O. before making referrals to specialists? For women, does that rule include gynecologists?
9. How easy is it to file an appeal when medical treatment is denied?
10. What portion of the plan's premium dollars is spent on medical care?
11. What sort of financial incentives do doctors receive for holding down the cost of medical care?
12. What type of preventive care, like immunizations, does the plan offer?
13. What kind of pre-authorization is needed for hospitalization?
14. Is a prescription drug you regularly take on the plan's list of medications approved for payment?
15. What sorts of treatment does a plan not cover because it considers them "experimental"?
16. Is the plan stable enough that it is likely to pay claims quickly and keep doctors, as you, happy?

SELF-MANAGEMENT PROJECTS

Upcoming chapters will describe how you can improve your health by eating appropriately, maintaining proper weight, quitting smoking or chewing tobacco, avoiding alcohol abuse, and exercising on a regular basis. There have been students who have elected to work on specific health-related problems; these are illustrated.

Figure 13–1 depicts the change in playing with her hair that occurred in a self-management project. The student had the habit of twisting her hair in class; this behavior, in turn, damaged her hair. She attempted several strategies, such as asking her friends to tell her to stop when they observed her, but it was only when she began to closely monitor her behavior that she was able to reduce the habit. Whether she maintained her gains is uncertain: The sharp decrease in the behavior occurred on Day 5 when she had her hair cut. Thereafter, there was a trend for her to again play with her hair. Greater self-monitoring appeared as a likely solution for the problem.

Figures 13–2 and 13–3 indicate how students used self-management

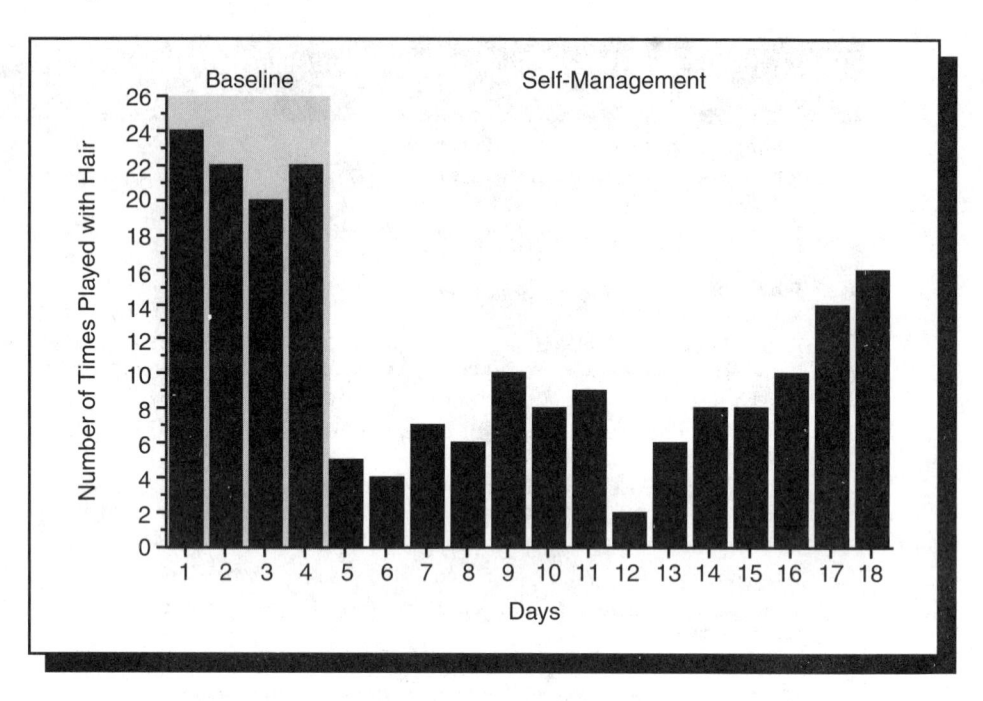

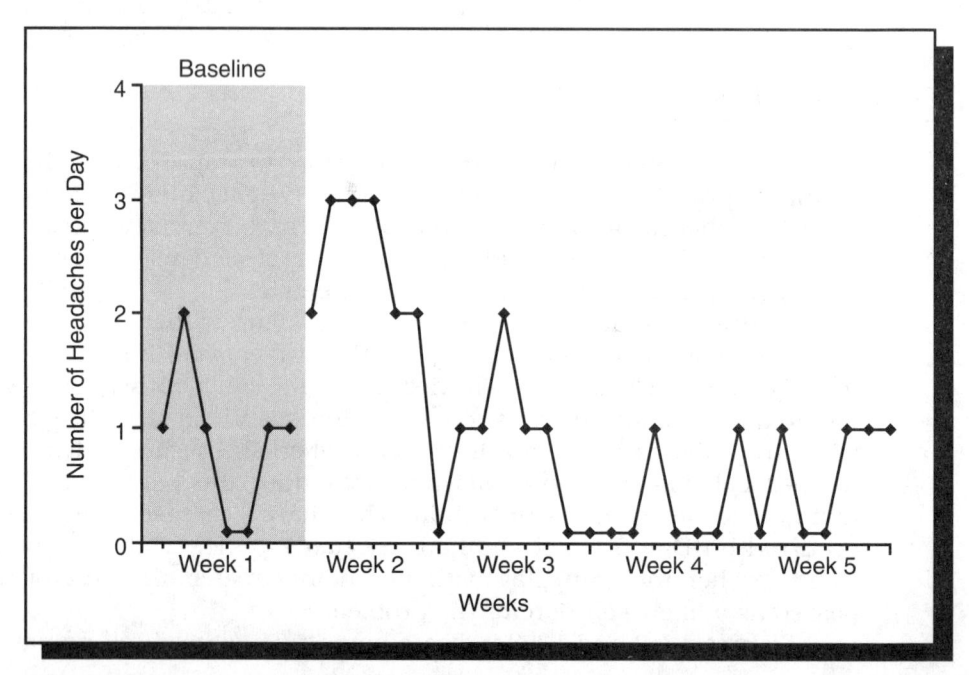

FIGURE 13–1
Use of self-monitoring to reduce hair twisting.

FIGURE 13–2
Use of self-monitoring, relaxation, coping self-statements, and a reduction in consumption of caffeinated soda to decrease headaches.

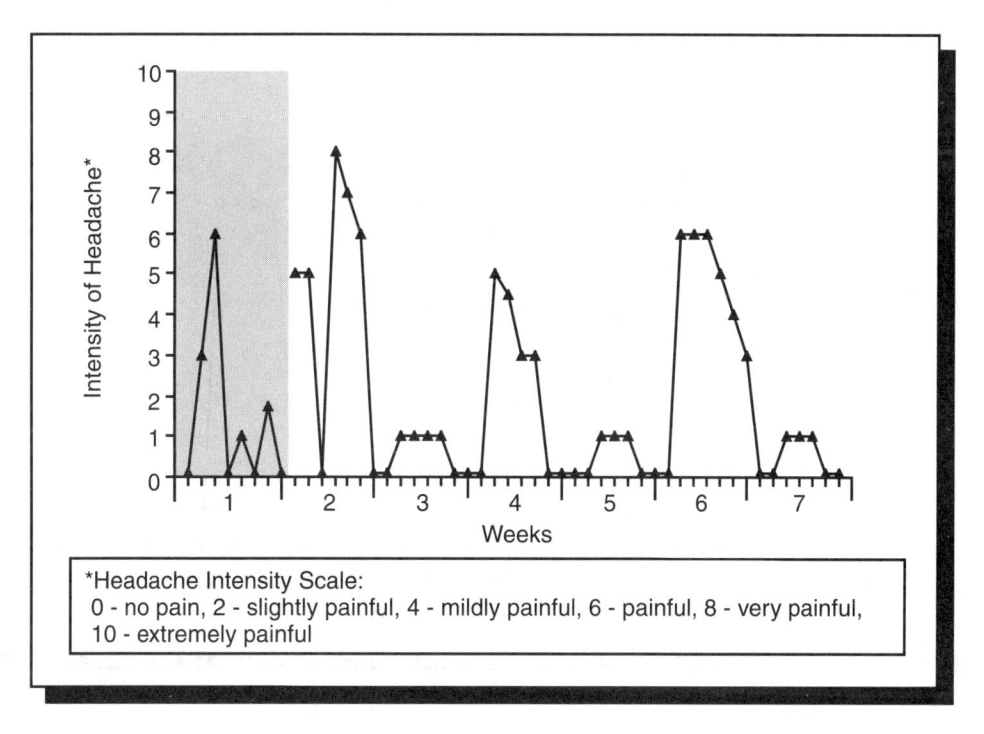

FIGURE 13–3
Use of self-monitoring to manage headaches.

to control the headaches they experienced. The data in Figure 13–2 were reported by a student who thought that anger, stress, and caffeinated soda contributed to her headaches. She developed a strategy that combined self-monitoring, relaxation, coping self-statements, and a reduction in the consumption of caffeinated beverages to decrease her headaches. The tactic worked. In Figure 13–3, the student attempted to monitor closely the headaches she experienced in an attempt to control them. She experienced some success, although she reported that the knowledge she acquired about her headaches through self-monitoring was the most useful aspect of her project. She added that she believed she could learn to control the headaches because she had more knowledge about when and why they occurred.

Figure 13–4 presents an interesting project. The student took a prescribed antibiotic to clear up a skin ailment. The problem was that she became psychologically addicted to the medication. The program she developed involved shaping her behavior by gradually reducing the number of pills she took each day. She went from taking four pills a day to taking none of the medication. Besides extinguishing her dependence upon the medication, the student reported that there was no difference in the appearance of her skin. As she exclaimed, "My self-management program has a very happy ending!"

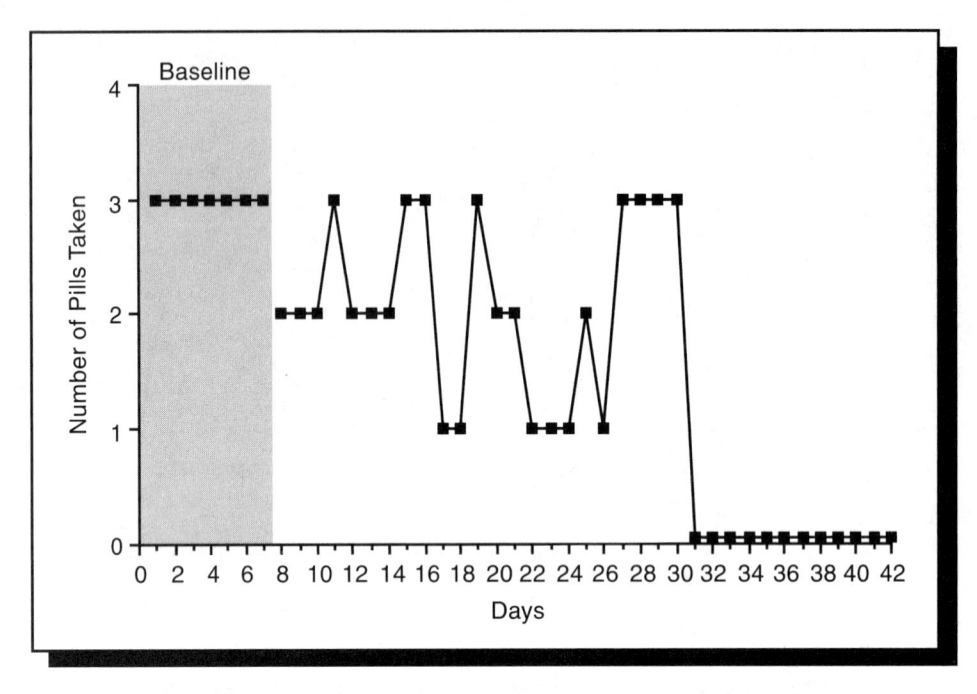

FIGURE 13-4
Application of a shaping procedure to reduce use of a skin medication.

EXERCISE

Is there any health-related problem you experience and would like to change?

What strategies can you take to self-manage the problem?

What plan will you use to achieve your desired goal?

What criteria will you use to determine if you have achieved your goal?

REVIEW TERMS

Hardiness
Health
Wellness

QUESTIONS

Describe seven habits that contribute to poor health.

Describe ten characteristics of wellness.

Describe seven ways for managing medical abuse.

CHAPTER 14

Exercise

"Those who think they have not time for bodily exercise will sooner or later have to find time for illness."

—Edward Stanley, Earl of Derby, *speech*

"I've been active all my life. When I worked, I walked a lot. On weekends, I spent time in the garden. I also got caught up in the jogging craze that hit the country when I became middle aged. I ran in a number of races and marathons. When I retired, I found that my knees hurt when I ran. I bought an exercise bike and use it half an hour at least three times a week. I feel like I'm in good condition for my age."

—Vern, a retired postal clerk

Along with weight reduction, more students elect to plan and execute self-management projects related to exercise than on any other topic. They make a good decision: establishing and adhering to an exercise regimen can provide benefits during the entire life of an individual. Most experts believe three benefits result from regular exercise: improved health, lower medical bills, and longer life spans. These topics will be discussed in detail.

HEALTH BENEFITS: IMPROVED HEALTH

Table 14-1 lists a number of health benefits attributed to exercise. In some cases, there is empirical evidence to support these claims; in other instances, the data consists of anecdotal reports. However, even the lack of firm evidence developed under laboratory conditions does not negate the latter reports. Exercise physiology is a growing topic for research; hence, many physical and psychological benefits attributed to exercise will likely be supported through scientific investigation (Dishman, 1985). In addition, a number of psychologists are devoting their attention to the area of exercise. The result is the burgeoning of what is referred to as sports psychology. It is a rare professional sports team that does not employ the services of a psychologist or psychiatrist to serve as a consultant to its players. A large number of sports psychologists are involved with athletes at the amateur level, particularly with the United States Olympic

> **TABLE 14–1 Reported Benefits of a Regular Exercise Program**
>
> **Physical Benefits**
> 1. More energy and less fatigue.
> 2. Fewer physical complaints.
> 3. More effective digestion and fewer constipation problems.
> 4. Stronger bones and minimization of risk of osteoporosis.
> 5. Easier pregnancy and childbirth.
> 6. More restful sleep.
> 7. Increased cardiovascular efficiency and possible protection against coronary heart disease.
> 8. Stronger muscle tone, improved posture, and a more flexible body.
> 9. Fewer aches and pains, including back pain.
> 10. Better weight control and body composition.
> 11. Possible lowering of blood pressure.
> 12. Possible postponement or prevention of adult-onset diabetes.
> 13. A more attractive, streamlined body.
>
> **Psychological Benefits**
> 1. More enjoyable and active leisure time.
> 2. Healthier, more alert appearance.
> 3. Greater mental efficiency, including improved concentration.
> 4. Improved ability to handle stress and crisis situations.
> 5. Possible psychological benefits, including a reduction of mild anxiety and depression.
> 6. Sense of well-being, with more vitality and zest for life.
> 7. An end in itself, including the sensuous pleasure of movement.

Team. The exact contribution of this area of psychology must still be demonstrated, despite a number of reports that suggest sports psychologists can make a contribution to the overall performance of some athletes.

The benefits of a regular exercise program are classified into two categories: physical and psychological.

Physical Benefits

A number of physical benefits of exercise have been reported. They include:

1. More energy and less fatigue. It is assumed, at least as well as it can be assessed, that regular exercise results in more energy and less fatigue. The reasons for this finding are difficult to pin down because those who exercise are also likely to practice other health-related behaviors, such as eating correctly and keeping their weight under control. They also tend not to smoke cigarettes.

2. Fewer physical complaints. There is some evidence to support this claim. However, the growth in the number of physicians who treat sports-related injuries suggests that there are athletes who go beyond their limits and overexercise.

3. More effective digestion. There have long been reports that regular exercise improves digestion. Why this occurs is unknown, although some experts claim that exercise enhances the metabolism of foods. In addition, there is evidence that constipation is reduced with exercise.

4. Stronger bones. Depending upon the type of exercise performed, there is apt to be a strengthening of a person's bones. Whether this result delays the risk of osteoporosis is still unclear. The role of widely advertised calcium supplements is still unknown with respect to altering the risk of osteoporosis.

5. Easier pregnancy and childbirth. There are reports that regular exercise during pregnancy results in fewer physical pregnancy-related complaints and easier childbirth.

6. More restful sleep. Those who exercise regularly report that they sleep better and suffer less insomnia than those who do not exercise or do so on an erratic basis.

7. Increased cardiovascular efficiency. The lack of exercise increases the risk of the cardiovascular disease 1.9-fold (Simon, 1994). Physical inactivity places more Americans at risk for cardiovascular disease than any other factor (Simon, 1994), and accounts for 205,000 deaths from cardiovascular disease annually. Regular exercise, on the other hand, has a number of beneficial effects on cardiovascular disease, including increased high-density lipoprotein levels, lower blood pressure, improved glucose tolerance and decreased insulin levels, enhanced fibrinolytic activity, decreased platelet adhesiveness, and improved myocardial efficiency (Simon, 1994). Consequently, physicians should recommend to their patients that they undertake regular exercise programs. Cardiovascular fitness means the heart can withstand progressively greater loads during exertion. Cardiovascular endurance is the maximum amount of work you can perform continuously with large muscle groups; it is a function of the ability of your body to use oxygen efficiently (Hafen, Thygerson, and Frandsen, 1988). Whether regular exercise protects against coronary heart disease is less clear. While it likely does so in the majority of individuals, this depends upon the given individual. All one has to do is recall some of the past gurus of exercise, including Jim Fixx, a noted authority on running who suffered a fatal heart attack while running.

8. Stronger muscle tone, improved posture, and a more flexible body. Depending upon the exercise program you establish and perform, there is evidence that you can improve your muscle tone. You should achieve both muscular strength and endurance. Three types of muscle exercise programs—isotonic, isokinetic, and isometric—can be engaged in by those interested in weight training. Lifting a barbell or dumbbell is re-

ferred to as an isotonic exercise; here your muscle shortens during contraction with varying tension while you lift a constant weight. Isokinetic muscle exercise, such as that performed with Nautilus equipment, is exercise where your muscle shortens during contraction to provide constant tension over the entire range of motion. Isometric muscle exercise involves constant resistance, with a fixed bar, that produces muscle contraction but does not involve movement of joints or extremities. The exercise regimen you select should also influence how flexible you are. Whether exercise results in improved posture is probably more anecdotal and less scientific than are other findings regarding exercise and muscles.

9. Fewer aches and pains, including back pain. There seems to be a reduction in aches and pains as a result of regular exercise. Whether there is an improvement in back pain would be dependent upon the type of exercise you select; without attention to selecting the type of exercise you engage in, there is the possibility that you could further aggravate existing back pain.

10. Better weight control and body composition. There is strong evidence that, in combination with the proper diet, regular exercise can assist you in attaining and maintaining weight control. This point is reflected in the number of student projects where eating prudently is combined with regular exercise to achieve a desired weight. There is also evidence that regular exercise enhances body composition, or the ratio of fat to lean muscle and bone.

11. Possible lowering of blood pressure. There is compelling evidence that regular exercise can lower blood pressure, particularly in those individuals whose blood pressure is at the borderline level for hypertension.

12. Possible postponement or prevention of adult-onset diabetes. It is a common practice for physicians to recommend exercise for patients who have what many refer to as a prediabetic condition. The usual recommendation is to combine exercise with weight control to reduce the threat of diabetes.

13. A more attractive, streamlined body. There seems little doubt that regular exercise and weight control produces a more attractive and streamlined body. The importance of having such an appearance is particularly important for adolescents and young adults.

Psychological Benefits

While there is an increasing trend for psychologists and exercise physiologists to collaborate on research regarding exercise, there is, as yet, little evidence to firmly support many reported psychological benefits of exercise. This does not mean that benefits do not occur; it merely means that the evidence of these benefits are based upon anecdotal reports and not scientific data. What is required is that valid and reliable instruments for measuring these benefits be developed and tested; as yet, this has not occurred to any great degree. Not withstanding the need for such assessment techniques, reported psychological benefits of exercise include:

1. More enjoyable and active leisure time. People who exercise on a regular basis believe that they more thoroughly enjoy their active leisure time.

2. Healthier, more alert appearance. People who exercise on a regular basis report that they look healthier and are more alert.

3. Greater mental efficiency, including improved concentration. There is some evidence suggesting that regular exercise enhances mental efficiency, including improving an individual's ability to concentrate. This finding has also been reported by a number of students who have chosen exercise as a self-management project.

4. Improved ability to handle stress and crisis situations. This finding is reported by people who exercise; however, there is little empirical evidence to buttress their claims.

5. Possible psychological benefits. There are reports that regular exercise reduces anxiety and depression. Although the evidence is meager, there are scientists who claim that physical activity may be as good as long-term psychotherapy or medications in relieving mild to moderate depression. These suggestions require more intensive scientific scrutiny, however.

6. Sense of well-being. People who exercise describe that they experience a sense of well-being when they exercise. While the question has not been investigated in studies, there is likely some truth in their reports.

7. An end in itself. People who exercise report that exercising is, by itself, a reward. There is no doubt that many people who exercise faithfully experience such a feeling. They may find exercising so satisfying that they center their lives around their daily workouts.

HEALTH BENEFITS: LOWER MEDICAL BILLS

During your lifetime, there has been a sharp escalation in health-care bills. This was reflected in a report from the Health Care Financing Administration in 1992. In 1980, the total bill for health care in the United States was $250.1 billion, representing 9.2 percent of our gross national product, and per capita health-care expenditures of $1,063 for every man, woman, and child in the United States. By 1990, the total bill for health care in the United States had soared to $666.2 billion, representing 12.2 percent of our gross national product, and per capita health care expenditures of $2,566 for every man, woman, and child in the country. By the year 2000, it is projected that the total bill for health care expenditures will be $1.6 trillion, representing 16.4 percent of our gross national product, and reflecting per capita expenditures of $5,712 for every man, woman, and child in the United States.

A number of proposals have been put forth for curbing health-care expenditures. More will be presented in the months and years to come. At the moment, however, the two methods with proven value are, first, that each of us makes a contribution to remaining healthy and well. We can do this by following the suggestions offered in Chapter 13. Second, as suggested by Fries and colleagues (1993), we should use self-management principles and techniques to make a difference in the total health-care bill of the United States. The self-management procedures you are learning to apply have been used with patients to help control health-care expenditures due to cardiovascular disease, headaches, asthma, high blood pressure, diabetes, hypertension, and gastrointestinal disorders (Holroyd and Creer, 1986). If each of us makes a contribution, we can, in conjunction with whatever plan is eventually adopted in the country, make a significant dent in health-care expenditures.

HEALTH BENEFITS: LONGER LIFE SPAN

You might think that if you exercise regularly, it would increase your life span. There is some evidence to support this view, but, until recently, it was weak. Recent studies, however, suggest that regular exercise does help to maintain muscle tissue. This, in turn, helps to prolong life. Recent evidence strongly supports this claim. A study by Manson and colleagues (1995), for example, examined the relationship between body weight and mortality among 115,195 U.S. women between the ages of thirty and fifty-five. It was found that among women with body-mass indexes of 32.0 or higher who had never smoked, the relative risk of death from cardiovascular disease was 4.1 and from cancer was 2.1, as compared with the risk among women with body-mass indexes below 19.0. Body weight and mortality from all causes were directly related among these women. Even a moderate gain of twenty-two pounds or more above a person's weight at age eighteen increases the person's risk of an earlier death. In an editorial accompanying the report by Manson and colleagues, Byers (1995) contended that one thing was clear from the hundreds of studies of weight control conducted in the past twenty years: "Without regular physical activity, weight control can usually not be achieved. Conversely, regular physical activity can improve longevity, even for those with body-mass indexes in the 'overweight' range" (p. 724).

TYPES OF EXERCISE

If you decide to exercise on a regular basis, it is important that you select an activity you enjoy. You might consider the strengths, as well as potential weaknesses, of each of the following types of exercise:

1. Aerobics. This is the most popular exercise performed by college women. It is an excellent exercise in that aerobics increase total blood volume and lung capacity. Aerobics also strengthen heart muscles; there is evidence that high-density lipoprotein (HDL) increases and the total cholesterol/HDL ratio decreases (Cooper, 1982). To be effective, aerobics should be performed for at least twenty minutes during three or four sessions per week. This will produce an elevated heart rate and produce sweating. Possible injuries due to aerobics include stress fractures, ankle sprains, and shin splints.

2. Jogging. This is a good exercise if you wish to improve your cardiovascular functions. It requires a proper outfit and surface. As with most exercises, it is recommended that you jog for at least twenty minutes three or four times a week. Possible injuries due to jogging include Achilles tendonitis, shin splints, muscle cramps, stress fractures, and knee injuries. Heat exhaustion can occur if you fail to take precautions in warm or hot weather. Exercise-induced respiratory problems, including wheezing or asthma, can occur when exercising in cold, dry weather. Contact your physician if this happens to you.

3. Swimming. Swimming is a solid selection for an exercise regimen provided you swim strenuously and do not just float around. It is recommended for pregnant women and for those who may suffer asthma or other respiratory disorders. Potential injuries from swimming include otitis externa (inflammation of the ear), muscle strains and tears, conjunctivitis (inflammation of the eye), and dental enamel erosion.

4. Cycling. This is also an excellent exercise if you want to increase your heart and lung capacity. As with other exercises, it should be performed on a regular basis. Potential injuries of cycling include abrasions, lacerations, fractured limbs, and head injuries. Proper equipment is recommended if you select this as an exercise.

5. Racquet sports. These are good exercises to select if performed on a regular basis. Racquet sports can improve heart and lung functions. Potential injuries of these activities include tennis elbow and damage to the eye, head, or leg.

6. Stair-climbing. This is an increasingly popular exercise. Stair-climbing ranks with jogging and cycling in developing thigh and leg strength, as well as in increasing heart and lung functions. Potential injuries include shin splints and muscle pain.

7. Golf. This provides mild exercise. The only way golf can benefit your heart and lungs is if the course is hilly and you carry your own clubs. Potential injuries include muscle strain or tears and elbow injuries. In most instances, however, these injuries are unlikely to occur.

8. Dancing. Dancing provides a great workout. In addition, you may find that it is more interesting to you than are other exercises. Outside of an occasional sprained ankle, injuries are rare. The potential problem with dancing is the lack of opportunities for participation on a regular basis.

9. Lifting weights. This is a good exercise if you want to concentrate on building muscle; it does little to enhance cardiovascular fitness. You should also be in good condition before you start weight lifting because potential injuries include muscle strains and tears.

10. Walking. Walking is increasingly becoming an exercise of choice to many individuals, particularly older people. Walking a mile has the same benefits as jogging a mile, but without the potential of injury. If you do nothing more with respect to exercise, be certain to walk as much and as often as you can.

In selecting an exercise for you, consider first the goal of your regimen. You may want to choose one of the above exercises according to whether your aim is to improve cardiovascular endurance, muscular endurance, muscular strength, flexibility, or body composition (Hafen, Thygerson, and Frandsen, 1988).

GENERAL PRINCIPLES OF EXERCISE

At one time, it was thought that you could make no gains without pain. This proved a fallacious statement; as noted, walking is a safe and useful exercise for everyone. Martin and Osborne (1989) and Hafen and colleagues suggested several general principles of exercise; most experts in the area of exercise share these views. The principles are depicted in Table 14–2.

Components of an Effective Exercise Program

A number of components have been suggested for an effective exercise program. Several of these components, particularly those on which there is consensual agreement among experts, include:

1. Assess your level of fitness. Before you select a particular exercise, you should consult with your physician or an exercise expert to de-

---

TABLE 14–2 Suggested Principles of Exercise

1. Do warm-up exercises for 7 to 12 minutes at beginning of each exercise session.
2. Gradually increase the level of exercising across sessions until desired level of fitness is attained.
3. Individualize your exercise in accordance with your pre-exercise fitness level.
4. Consider that specific training brings specific results.
5. Do not overexercise, particularly at beginning of program.
6. Develop maintenance program for long-term fitness goals.
7. Cool down for 5 to 10 minutes at end of session.

termine the shape you are in. Not only can this provide you with baseline information, but it can help you set the goals for your program. Use self-monitoring to insure that you achieve the goals you set for yourself.

2. Select an exercise program. Choose and develop an exercise program that will help you attain your goals, whether you want to control your weight, improve your cardiovascular function, or develop muscle strength. At the beginning, consider how the program can be performed on a regular basis without cutting into other responsibilities, such as your studies or work.

3. Make a commitment. At the beginning, you should make a commitment that you wish to become involved in an exercise program. Without such a commitment on your part, the probability is high that your program will fail.

4. Develop a supporting environment. You should find a place and time to perform whatever exercise you select. If you choose swimming, you should be certain you have access to a swimming pool at the time you want to swim. If you pick weight lifting, you should be certain that you have access to a weight room. In developing a supportive environment, you may want to choose a partner, usually a friend. Not only can a friend cue you to perform your exercise, but can also reinforce you for performing such behavior.

5. Reinforce participation. It may be a period before you see or feel any tangible results of exercising. During this period, it is imperative that you obtain reinforcement from someone, even if it is self-reinforcement. After a while, you may come to enjoy and look forward to the activity; at this time, you actually may miss exercising when unable to do so. You can always build in extrinsic reinforcement for exercising. Once you are in shape, you have more latitude in the foods you select to eat. Without eating to the point where you are again out of shape, you might reinforce your attaining of a goal by eating a yogurt sundae or similar nonfattening foods.

6. Use supportive self-statements. Everyone who exercises regularly uses self-statements to remind themselves of their goals. These self-statements usually come before or during the early stages of a regular exercise session. You must sometimes prod yourself into exercising and, once underway, keep going until you achieve your aims for the day. Self-statements automatically come with exercising on a regular basis; they become critical ingredients of any successful program.

7. Adjust for competing responsibilities or injuries. Sometimes, we are forced to halt exercising because of competing responsibilities or injuries. As will be noted, a number of students who have taken exercise as a project sharply curtail their exercise activity toward the end of a term. This is understandable since they often have to increase their studying. Competing responsibilities and, from time to time, illness or injuries may lead you to abandon your exercise regimen. When this occurs, take time off to do whatever you have to do; be certain, however, that as soon as the competing activity or health problem has been controlled, you bounce back and resume your exercising. Obtaining proper amounts of exercise is a lifetime pursuit. While you may change activities according to your age, never abandon regular exercise.

8. Prevent injuries. There are several methods by which you can prevent injuries. First, don't overdo it. Watch for warning signs that suggest a muscle pain, fatigue, localized throbbing, or a tingling sensation. As noted, the idea of "No gain without pain" is nonsensical: you do not need to experience pain to exercise and be fit. Second, wear appropriate equipment. If you jog or play tennis, wear proper-fitting shoes. They should fit snugly and have sufficient support. If you lift weights, wear the proper equipment around your stomach. Third, it is wise to cross-train by engaging in a number of activities that exercise all major muscle groups, and reduce the wear and tear on specific joints. This also reduces the possibility of muscle imbalance contributing to injury.

SELF-MANAGEMENT PROCEDURES TO ENHANCE EXERCISE

Almost any type of self-management procedure can be used to increase the quantity and quality of your exercise. These include:

1. Stimulus control. You can use both environmental and cognitive stimuli as ways to manage your exercise regimen.
   a. Environmental stimuli. You can attempt to establish stimulus control by exercising at the same time each day. The time on the clock, for example, can serve to cue in your activity. You may also exercise with friends. They provide both stimuli and reinforcement for exercising.
   b. Cognitive stimuli. You can remind yourself, though self-instruction and self-statements, of when it is time to exercise and what activity in which you are going to engage. Self-statements can assist you to complete your daily exercise regimen, and thought stopping can be used when you think of quitting before you have achieved your exercise goal on any given day.

2. Self-monitoring. Carefully observing and recording aspects of your behavior can enhance the quality and quantity of your exercise. Recording accurate information can serve as an environmental stimulus that helps you control the time and type of your exercise activity.

3. Self-reinforcement. You can use self-reinforcement, in the form of self-instruction and self-statements, both throughout and after exercising. Not only will it permit you to continue exercising, but it will reinforce you for successful performance.

4. Add alternative responses or behaviors. Many people may believe that an exercise such as jogging or riding a bicycle is boring. Use of a small radio or tape recorder with a headset may stimulate you to perform such activities and help keep the activity interesting to you.

5. Problem solving. You can use the technique of problem solving to increase your exercise performance. This can be utilized in several ways. First, identify the best time for you to exercise. Attempting to exercise at the same times each week permits you to establish a regular schedule. Second, think of what exercise you want to perform. Look at both the exercise that you enjoy the most and the exercise that offers you the best chance to reach whatever goals you have set for yourself. You may find that you like some activity that is totally different from that engaged in by your peers; what matters here is your interest in selecting the most appropriate exercise for you. Third, act on your plan. All the consideration and thought in the world will do nothing to improve your health unless you actually perform the exercise. Finally, carefully monitor and record your behaviors. These can serve both to prompt future behavior, and to act as a reinforcement. If your data shows that you are not exercising to the extent you desire, consider other options you might pursue using problem-solving skills.

EXERCISE REGIMENS

Because a large number of students take exercise as a project, the results from several will be presented. They are representative of approaches taken by all students. Figure 14–1 depicts the progress of a student who prepared for a cycling marathon. As noted, he used self-monitoring to in-

FIGURE 14–1
Use of self-monitoring to increase daily cycling.

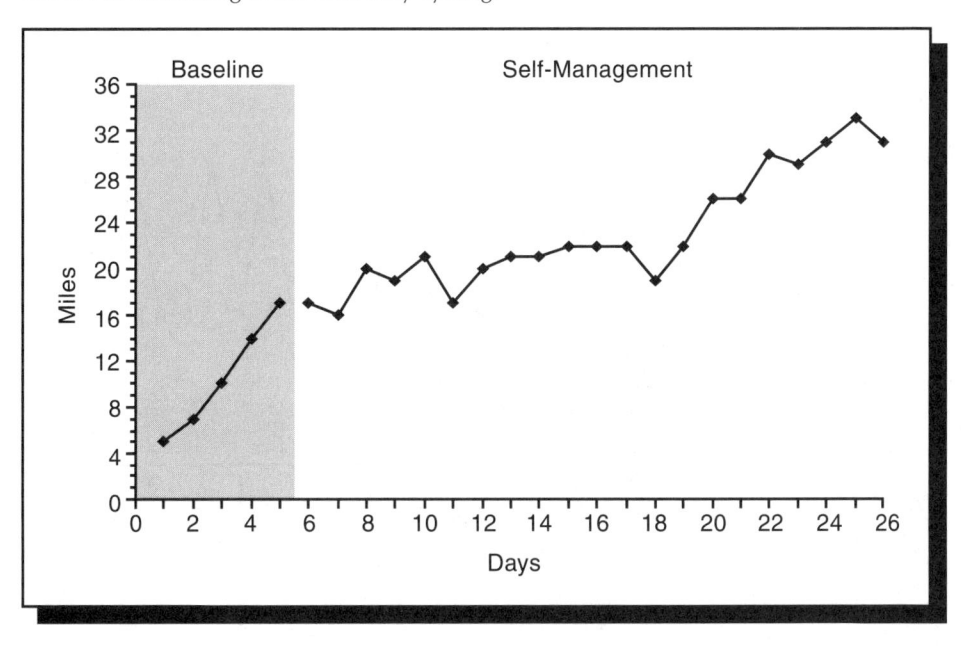

crease the distance he cycled each day. Figure 14–2 shows what occurred when a student combined self-monitoring with an extrinsic reward (e.g., a trip to the mall) when she achieved her goal. As noted, she became consistent at performing regular exercise, in this case aerobics. Figure 14–3 depicts the success a student attained when she used self-monitoring to improve her ability to shoot basketballs. As depicted, the number of shots she made increased over the course of her program.

The student whose data are shown in Figure 14–4 had undergone reconstructive surgery on his knee. In an attempt to strengthen his knee, he developed a program, based on self-monitoring, that increased his stretching, and use of a stationary bike and leg weights. As noted, he became very regular at performing his exercises; the overall result was a strengthening of his weakened knee. Figure 14–5 depicts progress made by a student in increasing his physical fitness and, as a result, his grades. Through self-monitoring, he increased the number of times he jogged each day; this behavior, in turn, enhanced his classroom grades.

Figure 14–6 shows what happened when a student attempted to increase his exercise and grades through self-monitoring. He admitted that increasing the times he exercised was a flop; this he blamed on

FIGURE 14–2
Use of self-monitoring and an extrinsic reward to attain consistent level of exercise.

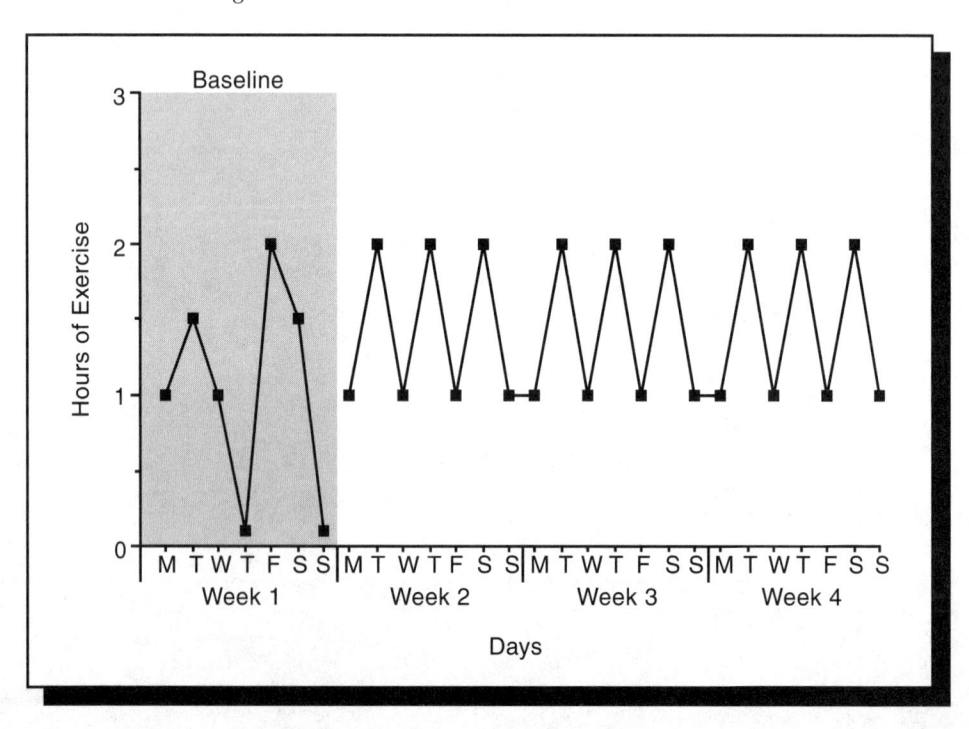

Exercise Regimens **157**

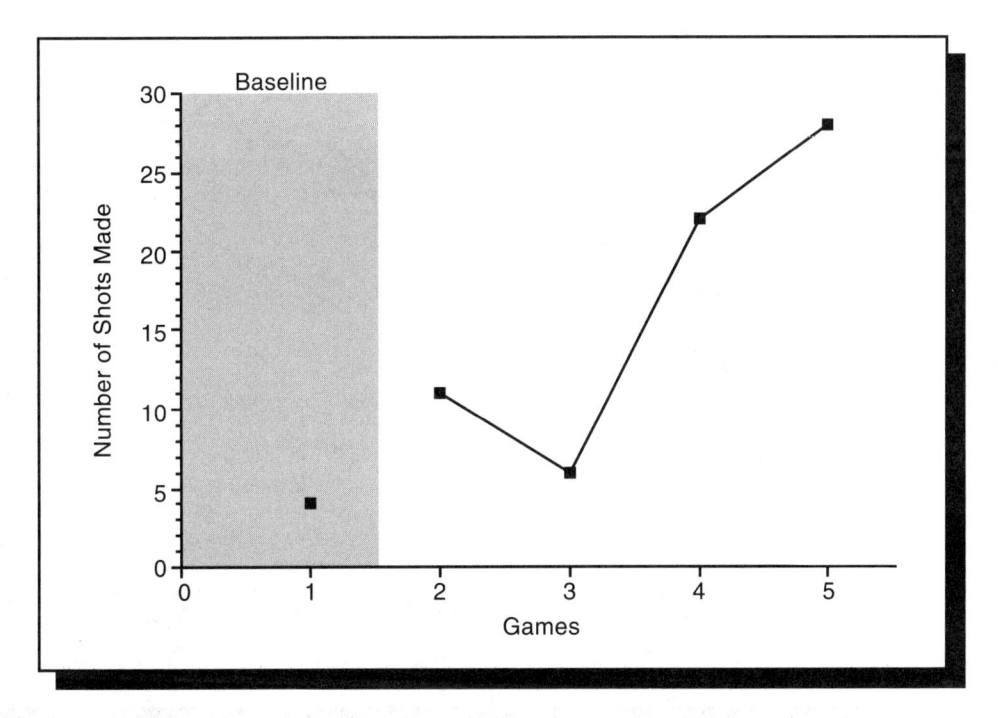

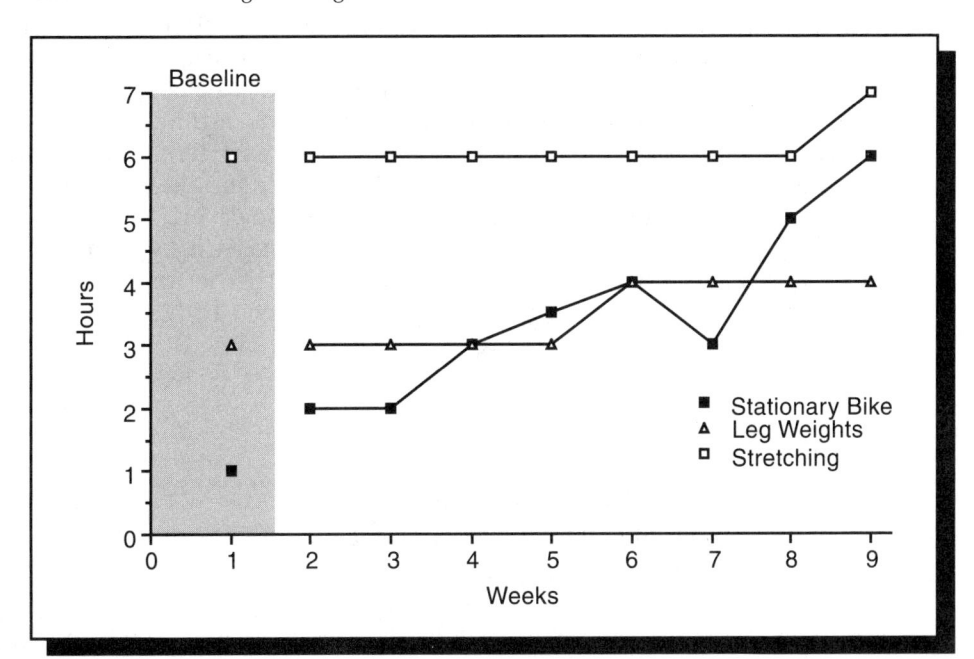

FIGURE 14–3
Use of self-monitoring to increase basketball shooting.

FIGURE 14–4
Use of self-monitoring to strengthen a weak knee.

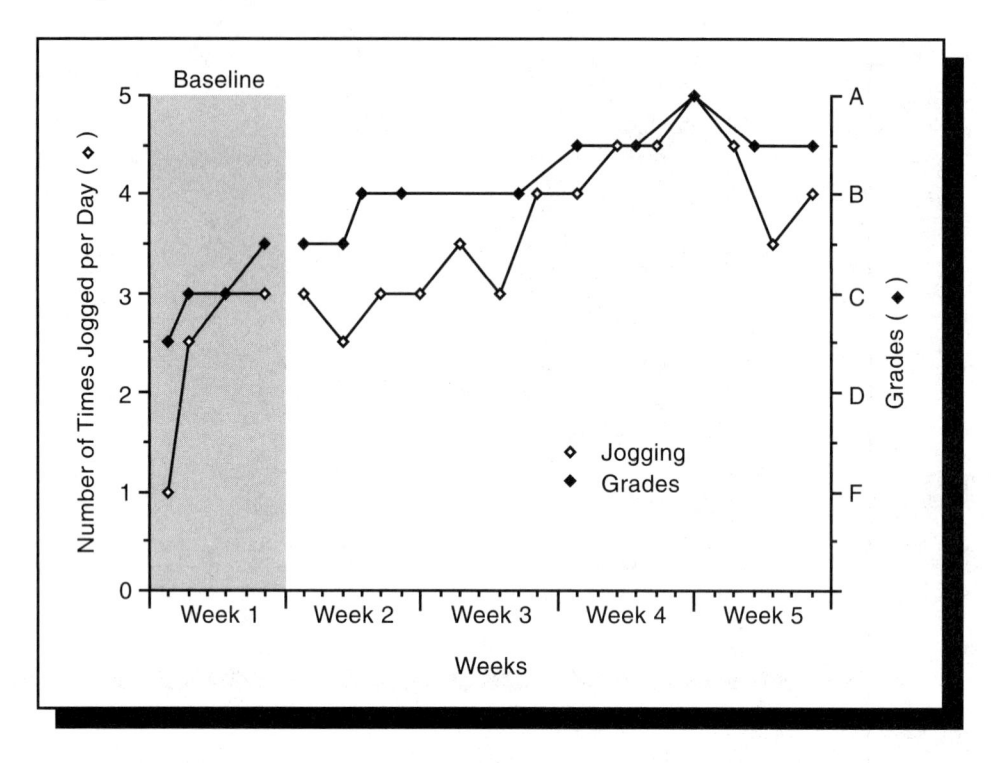

FIGURE 14–5
Use of self-monitoring to increase jogging and improve grades.

poor weather. However, he continued, the attention he paid to self-monitoring paid off handsomely with his improved grades. Thus, while he did not achieve the goals he set with respect to exercising on a regular basis, he improved his grades. The final illustration, Figure 14–7, reflects a common problem in exercise programs. Here, the student increased the number of times he exercised over his baseline. In fact, he managed to exercise four times in Week 5. However, this performance fell sharply toward the end of the term as competing activities, namely his increased studying, began to interfere with the amount of time he had available to exercise. Hopefully, he returned to his exercising once the term ended.

EXERCISE

What type of physical shape are you in?
What goals would you set for an exercise program?
How could you achieve these goals?
How would you monitor your progress?
What criteria would you select to indicate that you have attained the goals you set?

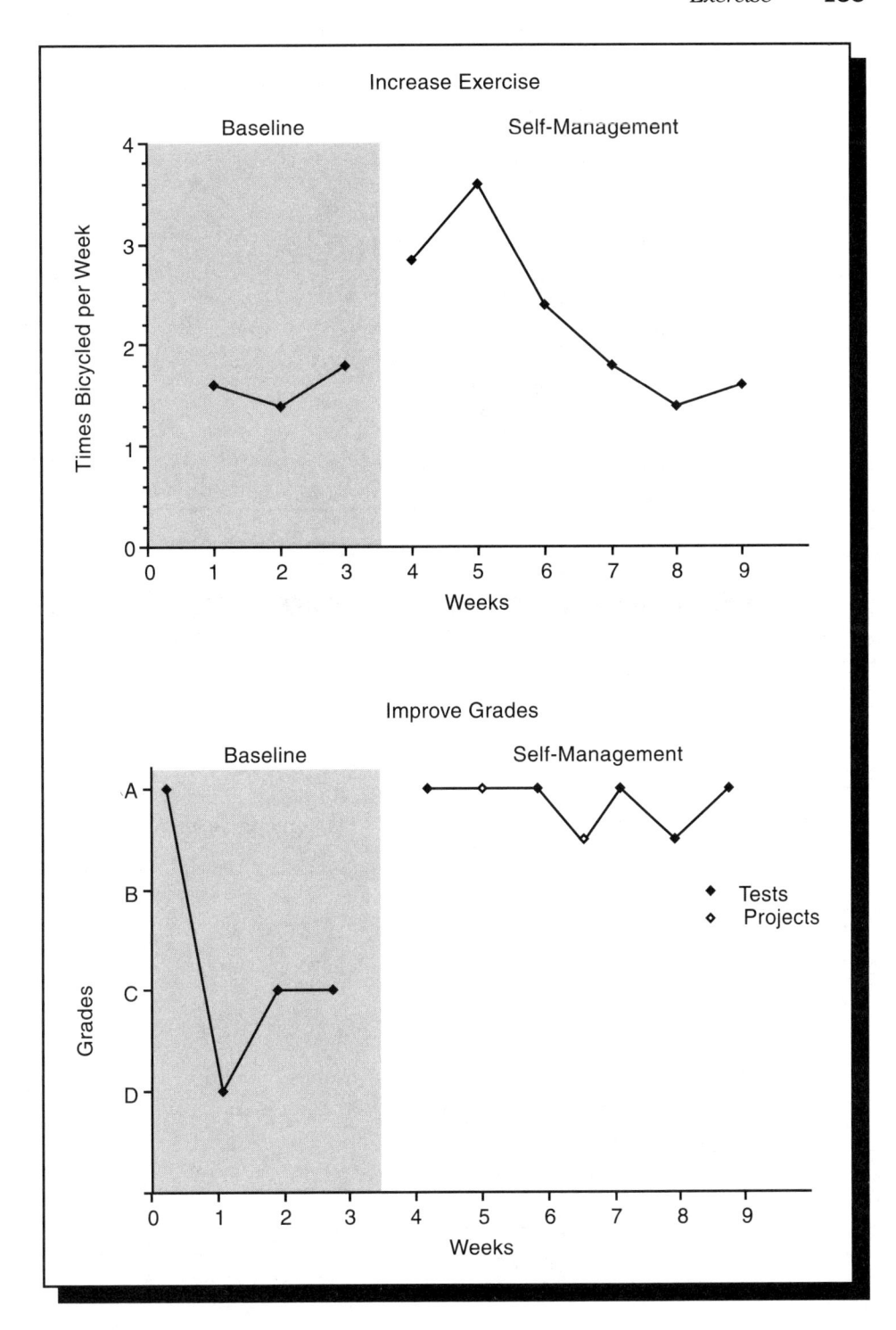

FIGURE 14–6
Use of self-monitoring to increase exercise and improve grades.

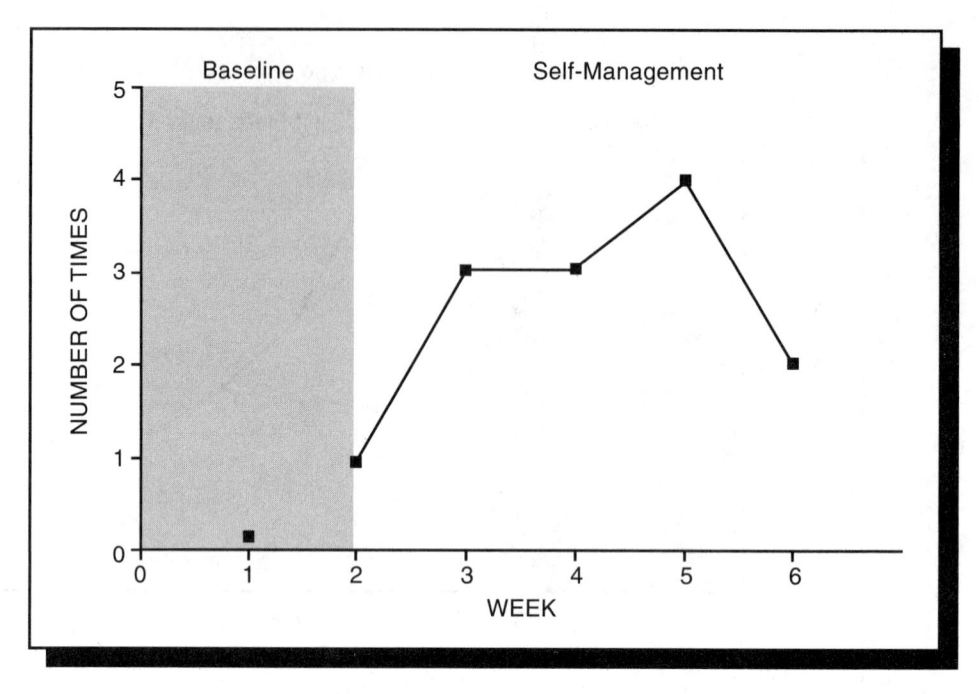

FIGURE 14–7
Use of self-monitoring in an exercise program.

REVIEW TERMS

Isometric muscle endurance   Isotonic muscle endurance

QUESTIONS

List advantages and disadvantages of the following exercises:

    Aerobics   Jogging
    Cycling   Swimming

List thirteen physical benefits of a regular exercise program.
List seven psychological benefits of a regular exercise program.
Describe seven principles of exercise.
Describe eight components of an effective exercise program.

CHAPTER 15

Diet and Weight Control

"According to the saying of an ancient philosopher, one should eat to live, and not live to eat."
—Moliére, *L'Avare*

"I just can't lose weight. I go on diet after diet, but they don't work. I lose weight for a while, but it all comes back. In fact, I get heavier each year. Is anyone able to lose weight and keep it off?"
—Jenny, a middle-aged homemaker

Despite all we read in newspapers, there is not a strong scientific basis for directing us about what we should and should not eat. Periodically, guidelines are issued by authorities as to ideal dietary requirements. Generally, the guidelines state nothing more than that we should eat a varied and balanced diet that provides the nutrients essential to good health, that we increase our consumption of starch and fiber, and that we decrease fat, sugar, sodium, and alcohol. The standards say nothing about what would be an appropriate diet for a given individual, in part because the nutritional needs of each of us will vary according to our sex, age, health, body size, and other factors. In addition, the guidelines are aimed at those in good health, not at anyone with diseases or other physical conditions that have an impact on nutrition (Hafen, Thygerson, and Frandsen, 1988). Such guidelines as those noted above, however, provide a way to outline what are considered as ingredients of an ideal diet.

NUTRITION BASICS

Eat a variety of foods. A way to insure variety and a well-balanced diet is to eat food from each of the selected major groups each day. These groups are fruits, vegetables, whole-grain products, milk and dairy products, meats, poultry, fish, eggs, dried beans and peas. You should adjust the number and size of your portions to reach and maintain your desired body weight.

Eat foods that provide proper nutrients. There are six types of nutrients: proteins, carbohydrates, fats, vitamins, minerals, and water. Generally, we supply our bodies with enough nutrients by eating foods from the major groups each day. The six groups of nutrients and their functions are:

1. Proteins. These are formed from chemical components called amino acids. They are the building blocks of the body essential for growth, maintenance, and replacement of body cells. They also form hormones and enzymes used to regulate body processes.

2. Carbohydrates. These are the starches, sugars, and dietary fiber. There are two types of carbohydrates, unrefined and refined. Unrefined carbohydrates are found in foods such as potatoes, whole-grain products, beans, rice, and corn; they are sources of fuel for the brain and muscle tissue. They produce glucose, a form of blood sugar that feeds the brain, and glycogen, a form of sugar in the muscles and liver that provides energy for the muscles. Refined carbohydrates include such foods as table sugar; while they alleviate hunger, they basically provide empty calories. Carbohydrates also provide the dietary fiber that promotes regular elimination of wastes from the body.

3. Fats. These are nutrients that provide energy, carry soluble vitamins throughout the body, form cell membranes and hormones, and transfer substances across cell membranes. While they are a source of fuel for low to moderately intense exercise, they can increase the risk of heart disease when consumed in the form of high cholesterol and high saturated fats.

4. Vitamins. These are food substances needed by the body for normal functioning. They do not supply energy, but they help release energy from carbohydrates, fats, and proteins. They also assist in other chemical reactions in the body. There are two general types of vitamins: water-soluble vitamins and fat-soluble vitamins. Water-soluble vitamins, including vitamins B and C, are dissolved by water in the body and washed away in urine. Fat-soluble vitamins, including vitamins A, D, E, and K, are dissolved only through interaction with fats. If they are not dissolved, they can become poisonous.

A list of vitamins is presented in Table 15–1. In most instances, you will receive most of the daily amount of vitamins you require if you eat a balanced diet. If you do not eat a balanced diet, you may need to take a vitamin supplement; you should consult with your physician or a nutritionist if you think you need vitamin supplements. For most people, vitamin supplements are not recommended, for three reasons: (a) vitamins may be unsafe, particularly if you take too much of a fat-soluble vitamin; (b) they are a waste of money if you eat a balanced diet each day; and (c) they can provide you with an excuse to eat an unbalanced diet.

5. Minerals. These food substances are essential for normal daily functioning. They help build strong bones and teeth, and keep hemoglo-

TABLE 15–1   Sources and Functions of Vitamins
(adapted in part from Hafen, Thygerson, and Frandsen, 1988)

Vitamin A	Found in liver, eggs, fortified milk, carrots, tomatoes, apricots, cantaloupe, and fish. Vitamin A promotes good vision, helps form and maintain healthy skin and mucous secretions, and may help prevent some types of cancer.
Vitamin C	Found in citrus food, strawberries, and tomatoes. Vitamin C promotes healthy gums, capillaries, and teeth; it aids in healing wounds and possibly assists in controlling common colds.
Vitamin D	Found in fortified milk and fish. Vitamin D promotes strong bones and teeth; it is necessary for the absorption of calcium.
Vitamin E	Found in nuts, vegetable oils, whole grains, olives, asparagus, and spinach. Vitamin E protects tissue against oxidation, is important in the formation of red blood cells, and helps the body use Vitamin K.
Vitamin K	About half our daily needs are produced by our bodies; the remainder is found in cauliflower, broccoli, cabbage, spinach, cereals, soybeans and beef liver. Vitamin K aids in the clotting of blood.
Vitamin B-1 (Thiamine)	Found in whole grains, dried beans, lean meat, and fish. Vitamin B-1 helps release energy from carbohydrates. This is necessary for healthy brain and nerve cells, as well as functioning of heart.
Vitamin B-2 (Riboflavin)	Found in nuts, dairy products, and liver. Vitamin B-1 aids in the release of energy from foods; it interacts with other B vitamins.
Vitamin B-3 (Niacin)	Found in nuts, dairy products, and liver. Vitamin B-3 aids in the release of energy from foods and is involved in synthesis of DNA; it maintains normal functioning of skin, nerves, and digestive system.
Vitamin B-5 (Pantothenic Acid)	Found in whole grains, dried beans, eggs, and nuts. Vitamin B-5 aids in the release of energy from foods; it is essential for the synthesis of numerous body materials.
Vitamin B-6 (Pyridoxine)	Found in whole grains, dried beans, eggs, and nuts. Vitamin B-6 is important in chemical reactions of proteins and amino acids. It is involved in normal function of the brain and the formation of red blood cells.
Vitamin B-12	Found in liver, beef, eggs, milk, and shellfish. Vitamin B-12 is necessary for the development of red blood cells; it also maintains normal functioning of the nervous system.

bin in red blood cells. They also help maintain blood fluids, as well as assist in other chemical reactions in the body.

A list of minerals is provided in Table 15–2. In most instances, you should obtain a recommended amount of each mineral daily by following a balanced diet. For this reason, the same warning that was made regarding vitamin supplements should be heeded here.

6. Water. Hafen and colleagues (1988) refer to water as the forgotten nutrient. It replaces body water lost through normal body functioning. Water also helps transport nutrients, regulate body temperature, and remove wastes.

Calories are not nutrients, but a measure of energy supplied by food when used by the body. We need such energy to perform work. Nutrients that provide calories are carbohydrates, fats, and protein.

TABLE 15–2 Sources and Functions of Minerals (adapted in part from Hafen, Thygerson, and Frandsen, 1988)

Calcium	Found in milk and milk products, sardines and salmon, dark green leafy vegetables, shellfish, and hard water. Calcium builds bones and teeth, maintains bone density and strength; it plays a role in regulating heart beat, blood clotting, muscle contractions, and nerve conductance.
Chloride	Found in table salt, fish, pickled and smoked foods. Chloride maintains normal fluid shifts, balances pH of the blood, and forms hydrocloric acid to assist digestion.
Magnesium	Found in wheat bran, whole grains, raw leafy green vegetables, nuts, soybeans, bananas, apricots, hard water, and spices. Magnesium aids in bone growth and functions of nerves and muscles, including regulation of normal heart rhythm.
Phosphorous	Found in meats, poultry, fish, cheese, eggs, dried peas and beans, milk products, soft drinks and nuts. Phosphorous aids in bone growth, strengthening of teeth, and in energy metabolism.
Potassium	Found in oranges, bananas, dried fruits, peanut butter, dried peas and beans, potatoes, coffee, tea, cocoa, yogurt, molasses, and meat. Potassium promotes regular heartbeat, is active in muscle contraction, regulates transfer of nutrients to cells, controls water balance in body tissues and cells; it contributes to regulation of blood pressure.
Sodium	From salt. Sodium helps regulate water balance in the body and plays a role in maintaining blood pressure.
Chromium	Found in meat, cheese, whole grains, dried peas and beans, peanuts, and brewer's yeast. Chromium is important to glucose metabolism and may be a cofactor for insulin.
Copper	Found in shellfish, nuts, beef and pork liver, cocoa powder, chocolate, kidneys, dried beans, raisins, and corn oil margarine. Copper is important in the formation of red blood cells and is a cofactor in absorbing iron into blood cells. It interacts with zinc and assists in the production of several enzymes involved in respiration.
Fluorine (Fluoride)	Found in fluoridated water, foods cooked in fluoridated water, fish, tea and gelatin. Fluorine contributes to bone and tooth formation.
Iodine	From iodized salt, seaweed, vegetables, and vegetable oil. Iodine is necessary for normal function of the thyroid gland and normal cell function. It also keeps skin, hair, and nails healthy; it prevents goiter.
Iron	Found in liver, kidneys, red meats, eggs, peas, beans, nuts, dried fruits, green leafy vegetables, grain products, and blackstrap molasses. Iron is essential to formation of hemoglobin, is the oxygen-carrying factor in the blood, and is part of several enzymes and proteins in the body.
Manganese	Found in nuts, whole grains, vegetables, fruits, instant coffee, tea, cocoa powder, beets, and eggs. Manganese is required for normal bone growth and development, normal reproduction, and cell function.
Molybdenium	Found in peas, beans, cereal grains, organ meats, and some dark green vegetables. Molybdenium is important for normal cell function.
Selenium	Found in fish, shellfish, red meat, eggs, chicken, garlic, tuna, and tomatoes. Selenium complements Vitamin E to fight cell damage by oxygen.
Zinc	Found in oysters, crabmeat, beef, liver, eggs, poultry, brewer's yeast, and whole wheat bread. Zinc maintains normal taste and smell acuity, growth, and sexual development. It is also important for fetal growth and wound healing.

SELF-MANAGEMENT OF NUTRITIONAL NEEDS

From your early days in school, good nutrition has been stressed in different classes. By the time you come to college, most of you are aware of what is a balanced diet, as well as whether you eat foods that comprise such a diet. Many students do not eat a balanced diet daily, however. Perhaps it is for this reason that a number of students have developed, as their project, programs designed to improve their diet. As will be noted in the five figures presented, they have attempted to change a variety of nutritional problems.

Figure 15–1 reflects a program developed by a student to eat more nutritionally. She devised a scoring system where, if she ate the required number of servings from each of the major food groups, she could earn 12 points a day. She then observed and recorded her diet each day. As noted, there was a trend toward her achieving her desired goal of earning 12 points a day, although she did not achieve this goal by the end of the recording period. Figure 15–2 shows a typical program developed by many students: attempting to cut back on the consumption of soft drinks, particularly beverages with caffeine, while drinking more milk and water. This student thought that she drank too much soda. This not only interfered with her diet, but created other health problems for her. She worked out a strategy whereby she not only monitored her behavior

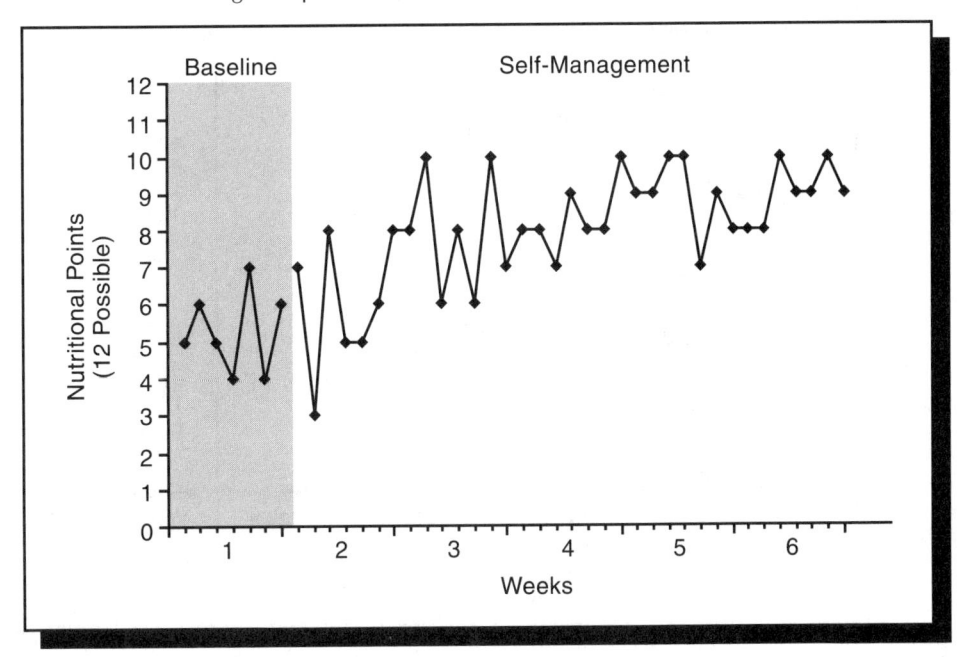

FIGURE 15–1
Use of self-monitoring to improve diet.

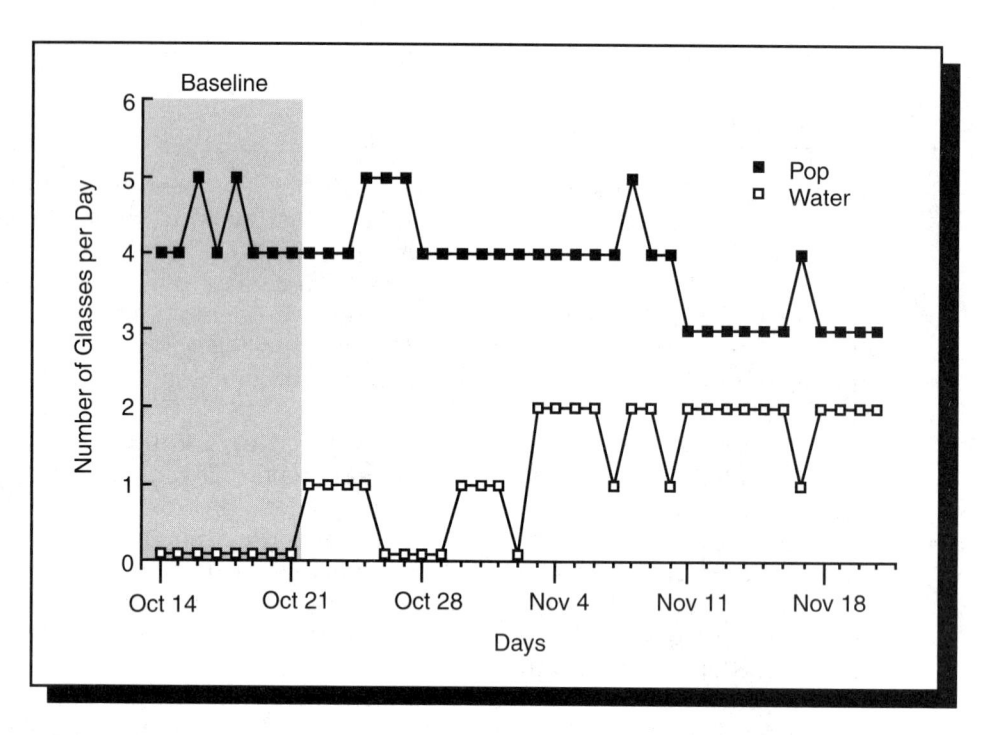

FIGURE 15–2
Use of self-monitoring to reduce consumption of soda pop and increase intake of water.

FIGURE 15–3
Use of self-monitoring to reduce consumption of red meat in diet.

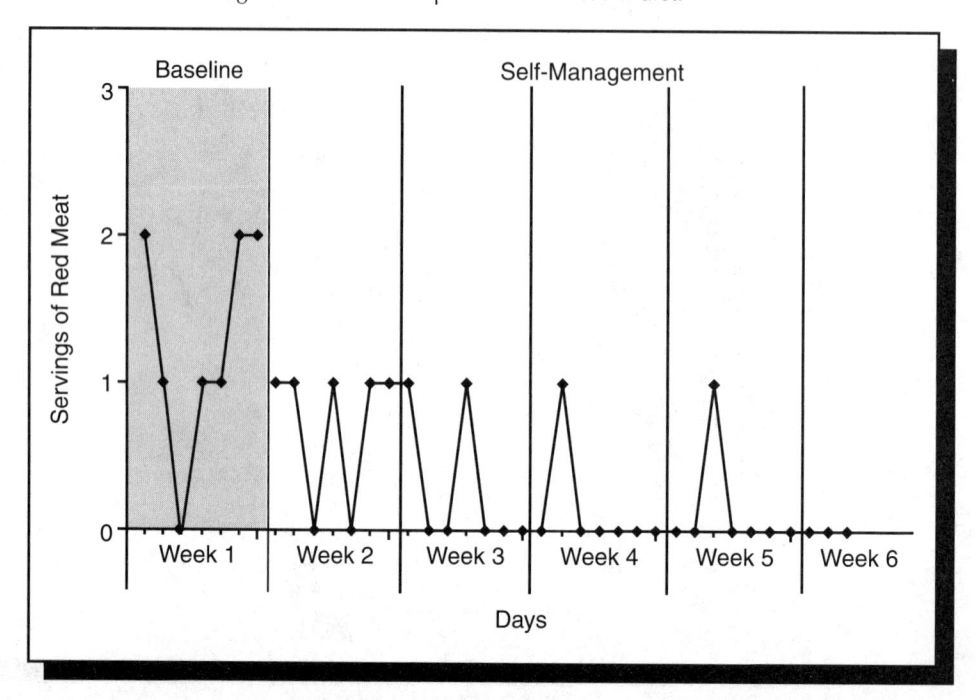

carefully, but she cut down on her purchases of soft drinks when she shopped. As noted, she did not entirely cut out her consumption of soda; on the other hand, she did increase her intake of water.

The student whose results are presented in Figure 15–3 wanted to cut down on the consumption of red meat because her family had a history of high blood cholesterol. She carefully monitored her behavior; at the same time, she substituted nonmeat products into her diet. As is shown, her program was successful. Figure 15–4 depicts a program where a student monitored the times she snacked, and drank caffeine products or alcohol. Through self-monitoring, she was able to reduce her consumption of these three products; in fact, her behavior was stable during the latter days of her project. Figure 15–5 illustrates the progress made by a student to decrease overall fat intake and intake of unrefined sugars, while, at the same time, increasing her consumption of fiber and complex carbohydrates, and her exercise. Through self-monitoring, the student felt that although there were times she fell short of her expectations, she achieved her goal for the program.

FIGURE 15–4
Use of self-monitoring to reduce times eating snacks, and consumption of caffeine and alcohol.

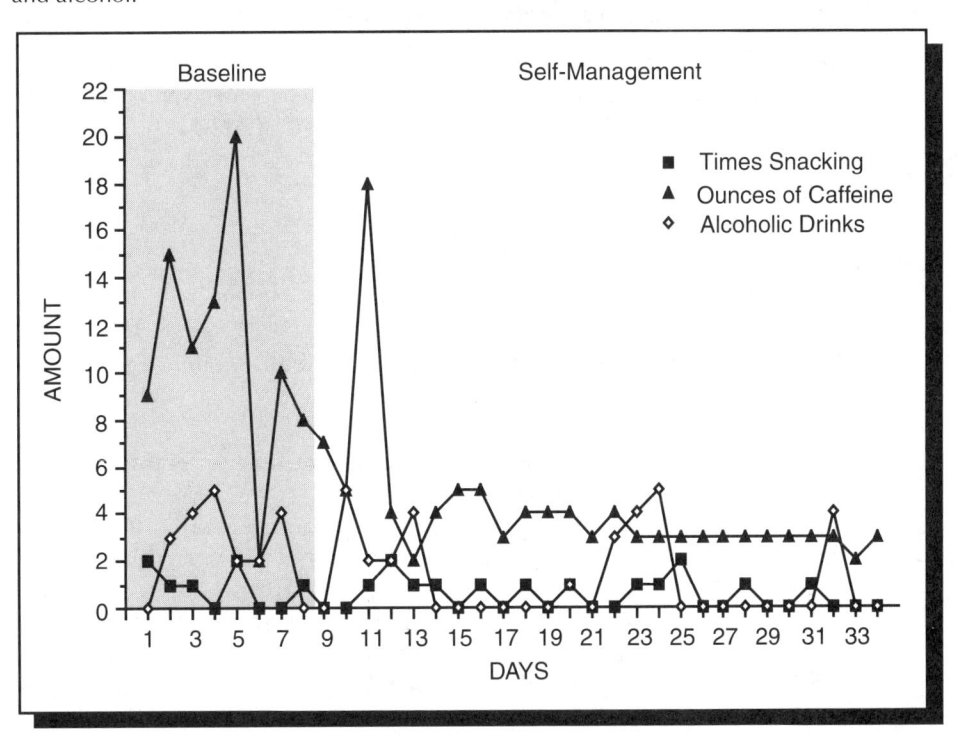

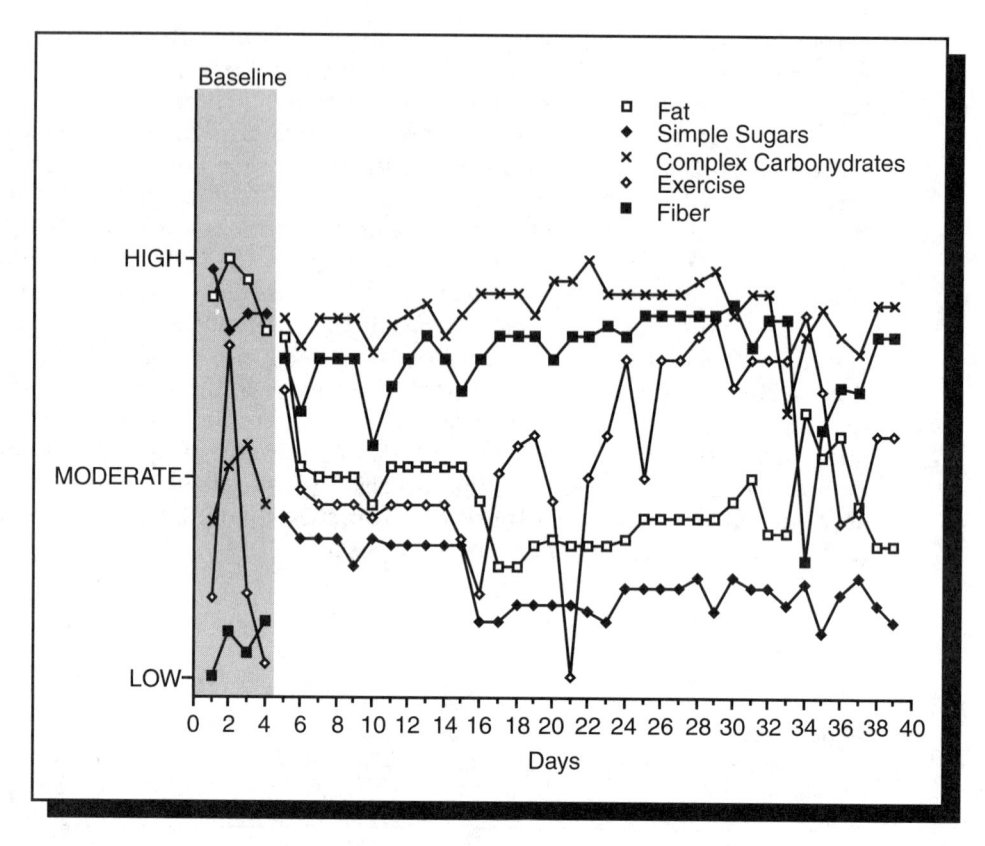

FIGURE 15–5
Use of self-monitoring to increase exercise and consumption of complex carbohydrates and fiber, and to decrease consumption of fat and unrefined sugar.

SELF-MANAGEMENT PROCEDURES FOR ESTABLISHING A PROPER DIET

We all need to establish and maintain a healthy diet. Techniques useful in helping you achieve this aim include:

1. Stimulus control. Both environmental and cognitive stimuli may be used to help establish stimulus control.

Environmental stimulus control. Environmental stimuli can be extremely influential with respect to your diet. If you think that you are snacking too much between meals, you can opt not to purchase those foods on which you snack. This removes discriminative stimuli for eating. Or, if this is an undesirable strategy, you can post signs on the refrigerator door to remind you not to snack. While you are in college, it is helpful if you can imitate those who seem to maintain a good diet. At the same time, you should avoid modeling those who tend to overeat or eat too much of certain foods. Not only is this not a good diet, but it is apt to promote unwanted weight gain.

Cognitive stimulus control. A number of tactics can be used. You will need to use self-instruction and self-statements to guide you through your daily diet. Adjusting these so they promote good eating habits may be all that is necessary to establish and maintain a healthy diet. Thought stopping is useful in helping you avoid situations that may cause unhealthy eating habits. Finally, you can use rehearsal to help you decide beforehand how you are going to behave in a situation where you believe you will not maintain a diet or imagery to consider ways you want to behave.

2. Self-monitoring. Self-observation and self-recording can serve as effective prompts for your diet. This data, when plotted, can be a discriminative stimulus to guide your behavior, as well as a source of reinforcement when used as a contingency.

3. Develop alternative methods. There are a number of techniques that can be employed to help you maintain a diet. There is a wide variety of tasty, low-calorie foods that offer alternatives to other foods you may be eating. If you decide not to go this route, you may wish to eat smaller portions of the foods you eat or to increase the time that expires between meals.

4. Problem-solving skills. These are particularly useful in helping you develop and maintain a diet specifically for you. First, explore the best possible foods you can select without sacrificing foods from various food groups. With the products available at today's grocers, you have a wide variety of options. Second, think ahead in planning meals and considering what foods you should purchase. If you plan beforehand, you can develop a list to guide your shopping (as well as to save money). Third, act on your plan. Not only will this involve obtaining the foods you need, but preparing them in a proper manner. Fourth, be prepared for setbacks or plateaus in your program. We all fail to follow our planned diets all the time (indeed, we have holidays, particularly Thanksgiving, when we are expected to deviate from our regular diet). Rather than let these setbacks serve as a source of discouragement, prepare and take advantage of them to refine your future diets. Finally, if your diet fails to meet your needs, whether it concerns obtaining the energy you need or maintaining the weight level you desire, consider your present diet and how it might be changed to attain your goals.

PRINCIPLES OF WEIGHT CONTROL

Weight control is of major interest to everyone, particularly young adults. If you decide you want to lose weight, you may wish to review the following steps.

Assess the Problem

There are a number of weight charts that suggest what your ideal weight should be for a particular height and body frame. You may want to compare your weight against such a chart. Many college students, particularly female students, believe their weight should be lower than that depicted on these charts. Consequently, they go on diets when they do not need to do so. Remember that you are not considered obese unless you weigh more than 20 percent above your ideal weight. For this reason, carefully consider whether you are indeed overweight and need to go on a diet. Thompson (1986), for example, found that 95 percent of women overestimated their body size to be a fourth larger than it was. Men also overestimated their body size, but to a lesser degree than did women. Cash, Winstead, and Janda (1986) found that 38 percent of women and 34 percent of men were dissatisfied with their bodies. Part of their reaction may be due to inaccurate perceptions of physical appearance. Martin and Osborne (1993) suggest that you elicit the opinions of people you trust when considering a diet. They are likely to make a more accurate judgment of whether you need to go on a diet than you are.

Analyze Current Diet

The second step is to analyze your diet to see if it is contributing to your weight problem. Hafen and colleagues point out that there are certain basics that apply to everyone, including:

1. To lose weight, you must use up more calories than you take in. In analyzing your diet, determine if you are eating more than you need to in relation to your activity level. This may lead you to adjust your diet, activity, or, as usually occurs, both diet and activity. Byers (1995) pointed out that calorie intake has been increasing in the past twenty years in the United States, in part because of the increased intake of foods low in fat. Cholesterol levels are, therefore, dropping. However, because levels of physical activity have changed little, Americans are getting fatter.

2. All calories count. Regardless of the food from which they come, calories count with respect to the total number you consume daily. However, some foods, such as fat and alcohol, have twice the number of calories as carbohydrates and protein.

3. Consider ingredients contained in a balanced diet. As noted in an earlier section, you should eat a balanced diet consisting of foods selected from the five food groups. If you are consuming too many empty calories, such as from sweets or alcoholic beverages, this diet will have to be altered for you to achieve your desired weight.

4. Avoid too much fat, sugar, and alcohol. While you can still eat these foods, they should be taken in moderation. Analyze expenditure of calories. In Chapter 14, it was noted that certain activities, such as golf or weight lifting, burn fewer calories than aerobics or jogging. You will want to determine what calories are expended in the activities in which you participate. If few calories are used, you may wish to become involved in activities that consume more calories.

Make a Commitment to Change

If you have a weight problem, you already know how difficult diets are to follow. Indeed, the literature suggests that long-term outcomes from dieting are bleak. In a study released by the National Institute of Health in April 1992, it was found that after five years: (a) 11.1 percent of those who had followed a diet of 800 calories a day maintained a weight loss of 22 pounds or more; (b) zero percent of those who had followed a behavioral therapy program of 1200 calories a day maintained a weight loss of 22 pounds or more; and (c) 9.1 percent of those who had followed a combination behavior therapy program and diet of 800 calories a day maintained a weight loss of 22 pounds or more. These results are not only disheartening, but are contributing to the emergence of a counterdiet movement in the United States. It is therefore imperative that you have a strong commitment to achieve and maintain whatever your desired weight may be.

Develop a Self-Management Program

A diet program should contain the following elements:

1. Set a realistic goal. You are not going to lose 20 pounds overnight. Nor, for that matter, do you want to lose the 20 pounds as rapidly as you can. You should attempt to lose one or two pounds a week. This is not only a realistic goal, but it is a healthy goal.

2. Chart your progress. Record the foods you eat, as well as your weight.

3. Emphasize consistent change, not occasional failures. Everyone who has undertaken a diet may succumb to comsuming foods they should not eat, or find that they occasionally reach plateaus in their diet. These barriers should be expected. If you find you gain weight during a day or week, double your efforts the next week to regain the level you were when you experienced your setback. This is much easier than abandoning your diet. If you do this, you will find that you quickly regain or surpass your weight level prior to the diet.

4. Change your environment. There are two ways you can alter your environment. First, you can eliminate snacks and other foods that contributed to your weight gain. If the foods are unavailable, you can't eat them. Second, you can place discriminative stimuli in conspicuous places, such as on the refrigerator door, to remind you of your diet. This may consist of the graph of your results or a sign that suggests you *stop* or *think* before opening a refrigerator or cupboard. It is useful if you only eat at one place, such as the kitchen table, rather than at other places in your environment.

   5.   Use self-statements. Not only can self-statements help you overcome periods when you begin to feel hungry and it is not time to eat, but they can help defeat automatic eating that occurs when you watch television or a movie. Self-statements should be integral to guiding you throughout any diet or weight loss program.

   6.   Involve others. Losing weight with a friend is a good strategy. Friends provide reminders and support for one another. In addition, you may want to negotiate a contract with a friend when you go on a diet. This may stipulate the consequences of what will occur if you go off your diet. For example, if you slip off the diet, you might do all the dishes for yourself and your roommates for a month. That should help you maintain your diet.

   7.   Maintain weight loss. Once you have lost the weight, you should make every effort to keep the pounds off. As noted earlier, long-term results are not encouraging; however, you cannot let these data influence your own behavior.

   8.   Genetic factors are involved in weight loss. Brownell and Rodin (1994) note that estimates of variance in body mass explained by genetics range from 25 percent to 70 percent. A recent study of Zhang and colleagues (1994), for example, described the isolation of an obese or ob gene in mice. It is thought that mutations of the ob gene could be responsible for disrupting the body's energy metabolism and appetite control center. The mutation, in turn, could be responsible for some types of obesity. You undoubtedly have heard of three biological or genetic factors that could influence weight: metabolic rate, fat cells, and set point theory.

   Metabolic rate. This refers to the rate at which your body converts food into tissue and energy. Some people are said to have high metabolic rates; consequently, they burn off what they eat and it does not convert to fat. Others may have slower metabolic rates; although they may consume no more than those with higher metabolic rates, much of what they eat is converted to fat. Why this should occur is as yet unknown, although it is speculated that metabolic rate may be a function of genetic factors.

   Fat cells. Fat cells are those cells within which our fat is stored. The number of fat cells you have is inherited. These cells may change in size (i.e., the amount of fat they contain), but never in number.

   Set point theory. This theory proposes that we all have an inherited homeostatic mechanism, located in the hypothalamus, that regulates food intake, metabolism, and fat reserves to keep us at some predetermined weight. The set point theory, according to some proponents, accounts for why some of us find it easy to lose weight and why others find it so difficult.

9. Dieting can be dangerous. In most cases, going on a diet is healthy, particularly if you are overweight. Obesity contributes to a number of health problems, including the onset of diabetes and cardiovascular diseases. Three types of problems can occur with diets, however, which may be harmful: yo-yo dieting, bulimia, and anorexia nervosa.

Yo-yo dieting. After losing weight by reducing the amount of food they eat, some people find that the pounds return with halting the diet. These individuals may then put themselves on another diet, lose weight, and find that they regain the weight when they stop dieting. A yo-yo effect is created by the constant losing and gaining or cycling of weight. This may be harmful to your health in that there are higher rates of cardiovascular disease and death among those with highly variable weight changes—either from losing or gaining weight—of 5 percent or more. The National Task Force on the Prevention and Treatment of Obesity (1994), however, concluded that the evidence on weight cycling is not sufficiently compelling to override the potential benefits of weight loss in significantly obese individuals. Wing, Jeffrey, and Hellerstedt (1995) declared, based on their investigation of overweight individuals, that there were no negative effects of weight cycling on cardiovascular risk factors. Rather, the findings confirmed previous research showing the positive effects of weight loss on risk factors.

Bulimia. Technically called bulimia nervosa, bulimia is characterized by at least two binge-eating episodes in a period of at least three months; fear of not being able to stop eating; regular self-induced vomiting; overuse of laxatives; rigorous dieting and fasting; and excessive concern about body shape and weight (American Psychiatric Association, 1994). Approximately 90 percent of those with bulimia are said to be young white females.

Anorexia nervosa. Anorexia nervosa is a serious eating disorder characterized by maintaining body weight 15 percent or more below normal, having an intense and irrational fear of gaining weight or becoming fat, starving oneself, and having a disturbed body image (American Psychiatric Association, 1994). Those with anorexia nervosa are almost exclusively white females between the ages of fifteen and twenty-four.

10. Losing weight is hard. Kirschenbaum (1994) notes that the weight-control industry emphasizes that you can lose weight easily and quickly. He points out that this is both a grave exaggeration and oversimplification of weight control. As he so cogently states, "Losing weight is a personal choice; losing weight is very difficult; if you decide to lose weight, you deserve admiration and support; if you decide not to persist, you deserve understanding acceptance" (p. 28). In the long run, you must decide what is your ideal weight. If, after careful consideration, you decide to diet, you need to develop and pursue your program. Remember that the only successful diet programs are those that include self-management.

SELF-MANAGEMENT WEIGHT LOSS PROGRAMS

A variety of approaches to weight loss are illustrated in this section. Figure 15-6 shows the progress made by a student who carefully reduced snacks, ate three meals at regular times each day, and exercised more. She stated that she wanted to continue with her program when the class ended. Figure 15-7 depicts the progress made by a student who monitored her weight over a period of two months. She relied upon reducing her food intake and increasing the amount of exercise she engaged in each day. Figure 15-8 shows what occurred when a student monitored her weight and exercised on a regular basis to reduce. The consistency of the student in exercising seems particularly important in helping the student reduce.

Figure 15-9 illustrates the results of a student who reduced her intake of calories and increased the amount of time she exercised to reduce her weight. Finally, Figure 15-10 shows what occurred when a student carefully monitored calorie intake and output. As noted, she lost 8 pounds through application of this procedure.

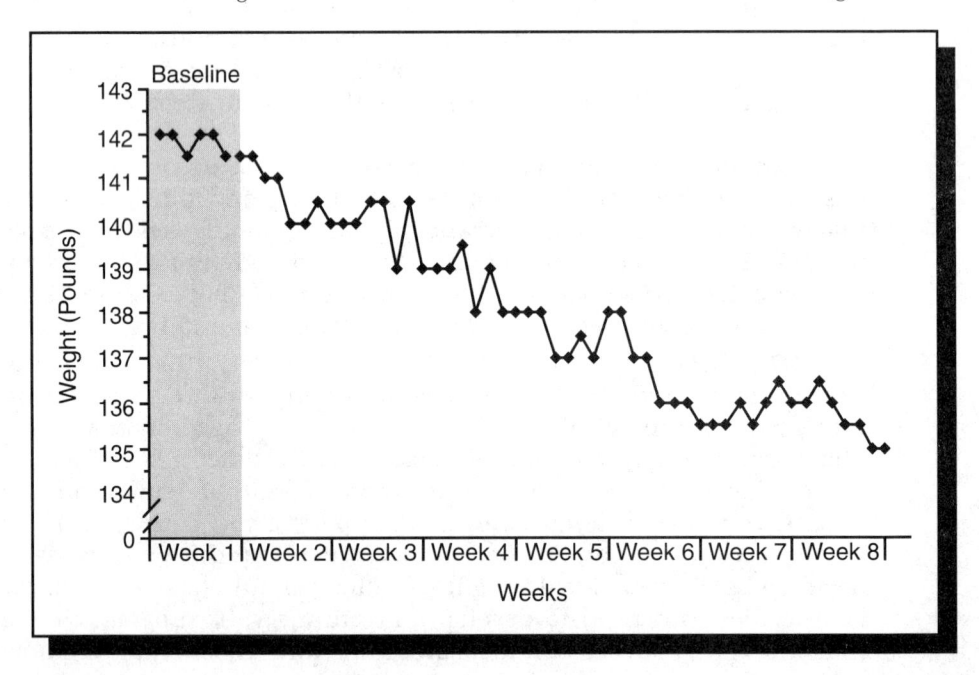

FIGURE 15-6
Use of self-monitoring to reduce food intake and increase exercise to reduce weight.

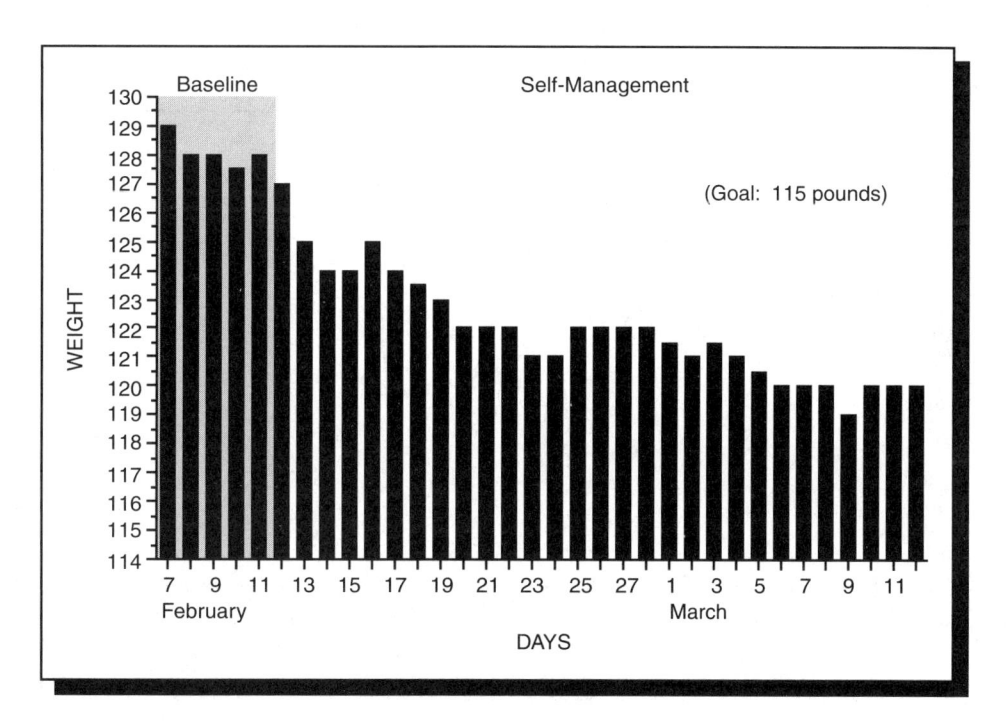

FIGURE 15–7
Use of self-monitoring to reduce weight.

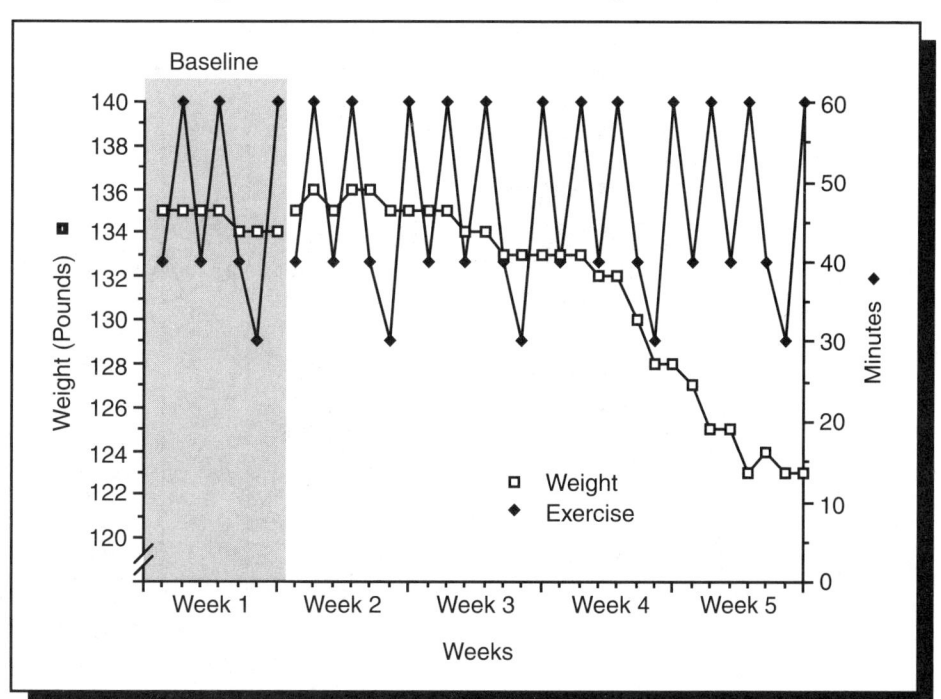

FIGURE 15–8
Use of self-monitoring and consistent exercise to reduce weight.

176 Chap. 15 Diet and Weight Control

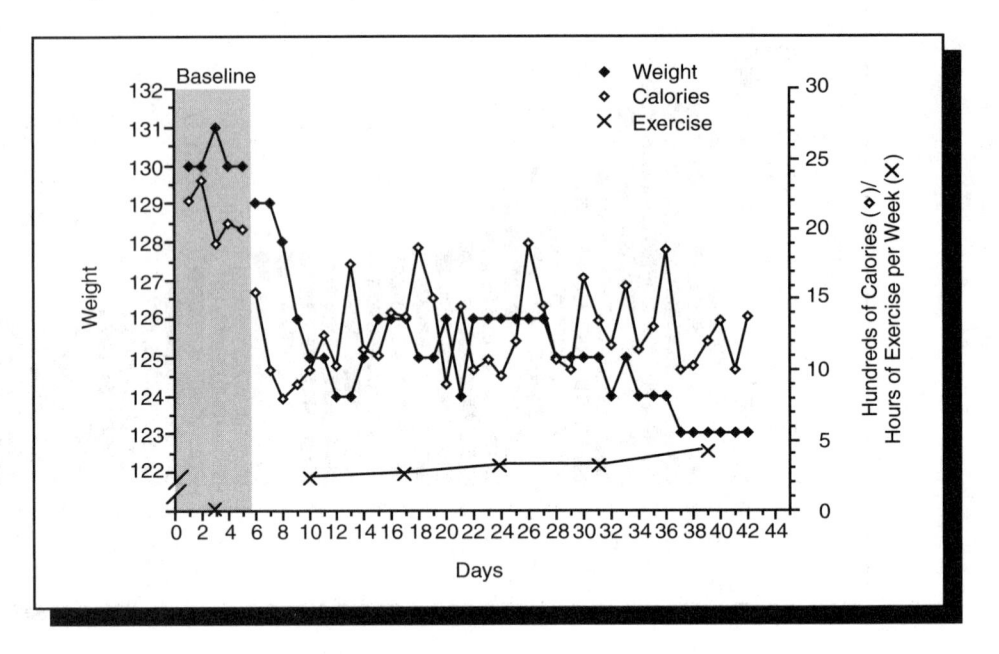

FIGURE 15–9
Use of calorie maintaining and increased exercise to reduce weight.

FIGURE 15–10
Self-monitoring of caloric input and output to reduce weight.

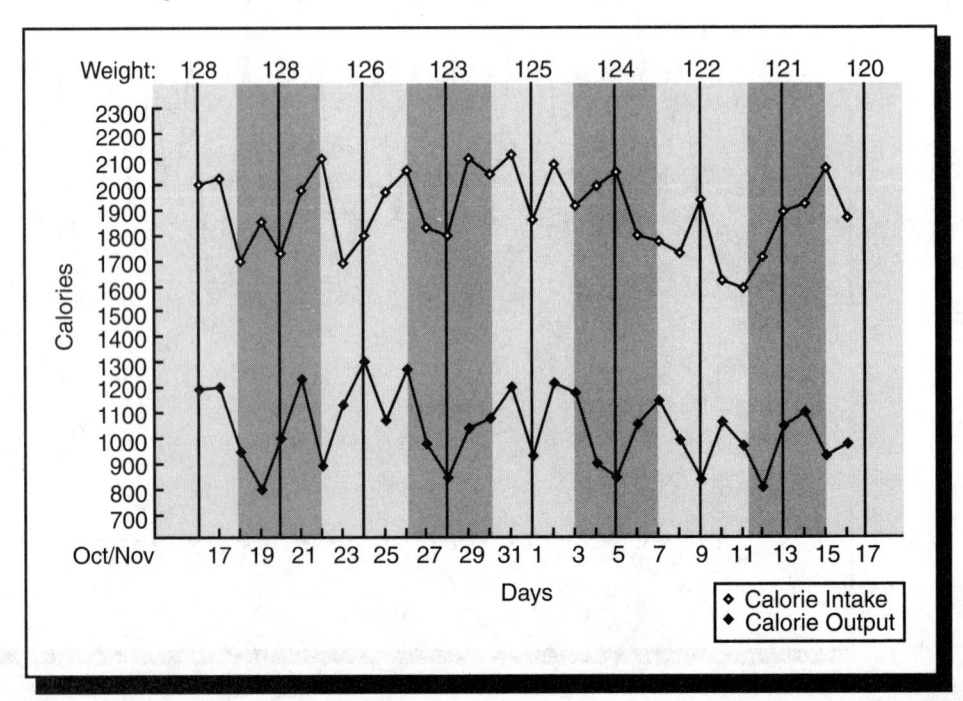

EXERCISE

Are you eating a balanced diet?
Do you need to make changes in your diet because it is unbalanced or because you are overweight?
What procedure should you follow if you decide to change your diet?
What criteria will you use to determine if you achieve your goal?
What steps will you take to maintain any progress you make?

REVIEW TERMS

Anorexia nervosa
Folacin
Glucose
Glycogen
Iodine

Molybdenium
Potassium
Vitamin B-5
Vitamin K
Yo-yo dieting

QUESTIONS

Describe six types of nutrients and their functions.
Discuss five weight-control steps.
Discuss three genetic factors thought to be involved in weight loss.

Tobacco Use

CHAPTER 16

"For thy sake, tobacco, I would do anything but die."
—Charles Lamb, *A Farewell to Tobacco*

"I've smoked cigarettes since junior high. For a while, I smoked a pack and a half a day. I thought it would be really hard to stop. It was for a couple of my buddies. However, when I saw an X ray with a spot on my lungs that could have been cancer, it scared the hell out of me. I threw away my cigarettes when I came out of the doc's office and haven't smoked since. That was five years ago."
— Gil, a construction worker

Tobacco use has a huge impact on our society. Currently, 46.3 million adults in the United States (25.7 percent of the population) smoke, including 24 million men (28.1 percent of the total) and 22 million women (23.5 percent of the total). Tobacco use is the leading preventable cause of disease, disability, and premature death in the United States. Meltzer (1994) asserted that tobacco costs our economy up to $85 billion annually because of the price of health care, property damage, increased accidents, insurance premiums, second-hand disease, and decreased earnings because of premature mortality, absenteeism, and poor productivity. Bartecchi, MacKenzie, and Schrier (1994) pointed out that a total of 414,960 deaths in the United States were attributed to smoking in 1990. Smoking-related illnesses accounted for nearly one in five deaths and more than one quarter of all deaths among those thirty-five to sixty-four years of age. A report, *Mortality from Smoking in Developed Countries, 1950–2000,* published by the Imperial Cancer Research Fund, the World Health Organization, and the American Cancer Society in 1994, noted that smoking kills more than all the other causes of death in Western countries put together. It is responsible for the deaths of 3 million people worldwide, or one person every ten seconds, each year. Around the year 2020, the report predicted that deaths would reach 10 million a year if current smoking trends continue. Projecting smoking data worldwide, the report concluded that about half a billion of the 5.5 billion people now alive will eventually be killed by tobacco.

There is increasing evidence that passive smoking, whereby you inhale the second-hand smoke of others, causes deleterious effects that are equal to one-third to one-half of those of direct smoking. Some 50 percent to 75 percent of the nonsmoking population is exposed to environmental cigarette smoke. As Sockrider and Coultas (1994) point out, sidestream smoke—that which enters the air through smoldering cigarettes—contains the same carcinogens as exhaled smoke, but may actually be more harmful because of greater concentrations of such substances as carbon monoxide and benzopyrene. Diseases that occur following regular exposure to environmental smoke, conclude Sockrider and Coultas, are similar to those observed in active smokers. Simon (1994) pointed out that passive smoking is ranked third among the preventable causes of death in the United States.

Smokeless tobacco also exacts a toll. The Center for Disease Control estimated that 5.3 million Americans used smokeless tobacco in 1991. Of these, 4.8 million were men; this represents 5.6 percent of all men in the United States. It was estimated that 533,000 women or less than 1 percent of all women in the United States used smokeless tobacco. The highest use was among men ages eighteen to twenty-four, although the total number of users has remained unchanged since 1987. Smokeless tobacco is often used because it delivers three times more nicotine than does cigarettes. It is increasingly associated with diseases of the mouth, including the teeth and gums, and is a leading contributor to mouth and throat cancer.

Fortunately, there is bright news with respect to tobacco use. The number of Americans who smoke cigarettes has dropped sharply in the past four decades. Smoking is lower in those in college or with college educations. In addition, survey after survey indicates that there are more former smokers than current smokers. Attempts by the tobacco industry to target potential groups for their products, primarily less-educated and minority populations, have met with strong opposition. The tide for tobacco use seems to be shifting; we can only hope it continues to go in the direction it is heading.

For those who continue to smoke, halting the habit may be difficult. Despite the introduction of such products as chewing gum that contains nicotine and patches that can be worn on the arm to dispense nicotine into the blood stream, many individuals still find it difficult to quit. Those who continue to smoke or chew tobacco cite a number of reasons for continuing their behavior:

Tobacco stimulates. Nicotine reaches the brain seven seconds after the inhalation of smoke from a cigarette. Those who smoke or chew tobacco report that nicotine provides them with a high. Nicotine is an addictive stimulant; it releases acetylcholine and betaendorphine. These transmitters may serve to calm anxiety and reduce sensitivity to pain. Nicotine reportedly improves attention, concentration, memory, and mental performance. It also stimulates the sympathetic nervous system, responsible for arousing the body, by increasing blood pressure, heart rate, and the secretion of stimulating hormones. While nicotine is the major additive ingredient in tobacco, there are over 4,000 other substances.

Over 40 of these chemicals are carcinogens; many others produce deleterious effects to the cardiovascular and pulmonary systems. Meltzer (1994) noted that the substances include tars, nitrosamines, polycyclic aromatic hydrocarbons, hydrogen cyanide, formaldehyde, and carbon monoxide.

Tobacco provides energy. Because it is a stimulant, it may provide a brief burst of energy. However, this energy is short-lived and overshadowed by the potential harm of tobacco.

Taste of tobacco. Those who smoke or chew tobacco-based products sometimes say they continue with their habit because of the taste. There is some truth to this claim, in part because tobacco companies have attempted to add substances to their product to enhance taste. Tobacco companies have also made cosmetic changes to lure people to smoke cigarettes. Filters were added to reduce hand stains and create a perception of safety; consequently, approximately 95 percent of consumers smoke filtered brands of cigarettes. Filters, plus the addition of reduced tars, creates a picture of a safer product; many smokers, however, compensate by increasing frequency and depth of puffing (Meltzer, 1994).

Tobacco provides a feeling of comfort. Many who smoke claim that they feel more comfortable, particularly in social situations, when they smoke. As the habit of smoking is often of long duration, there may be truth to their perception. For this reason, smokers may need to acquire other skills, such as relaxation on self-cue, before they quit smoking. They can then perform these skills, instead of smoking, in social situations.

Tobacco offers oral gratification. Those who smoke or chew tobacco often say that they receive oral gratification when they engage in such behaviors.

Fear of weight gain. A reason often cited for not quitting smoking or chewing tobacco is that the person fears he or she may gain weight. Many people who do quit using tobacco experience weight gain. However, weight gain is usually of a short duration. In addition, a person would have to gain 75 pounds to produce a risk comparable to that of using tobacco.

COMPONENTS OF TOBACCO CESSATION PROGRAM

There are a number of steps to halting the use of tobacco products. Many of these pertain to both cigarettes and smokeless tobacco. If you are attempting to abandon the use of tobacco, the following suggestions may be of value whether you want to halt smoking or to quit using smokeless tobacco.

Prepare to quit. Before quitting, you should reduce your overall level of stress. Procedures such as relaxation, meditation, systematic self-desensitization, imagery, or rehearsal can be used to achieve this aim.

Improving other health habits, such as obtaining more sleep and initiating an exercise regimen, are recommended.

Preparing to change is a major component of a self-management program advocated by Prochaska, Norcross, and DeClemente (1994). They have marshaled an impressive amount of data in support of this model of behavior change. For this reason, you may wish to consider the stages of the model in planning and conducting any behavioral change program. The model has six stages that constitute the spiral of change:

1. Precontemplation. In the initial stage, you become aware of the problem and what may be involved in changing your behavior.
2. Contemplation. In this stage, you want to change but must consider what behaviors you should alter and how you are going to produce change.
3. Preparation. In this stage, you develop an effective plan of action.
4. Action. In this stage, you learn the methods and obtain the support you need to be successful.
5. Maintenance. In this stage, you create a plan for controlling lapses and achieving long-term success.
6. Termination. In the final stage, you find that while you may not totally eliminate temptation, you still achieve lasting change.

Prochaska and colleagues (1994) provide many useful insights to changing your behavior, including ceasing to smoke.

Assess target behavior. If you want to quit using tobacco, you should gather baseline information as to the number of cigarettes you smoke or the amount of smokeless tobacco you use. You should identify the internal and external cues that trigger your behavior. For example, the use of tobacco is often under the control of external stimuli that prompt its use. You may light up a cigarette after a meal or when having a cup of coffee. These responses become discriminative stimuli for tobacco use. Your identification of these external stimuli, as well as such internal cues as anxiety or fear, will allow you to change them before ceasing the use of tobacco.

Change setting or discriminative stimuli. Suggestions for those who want to quit smoking or using smokeless tobacco include:

1. Set a target date for total cessation. If you attempt to halt the use of tobacco, allow yourself one month to prepare for a target date. This will allow you to develop alternative responses to employ when you quit using tobacco.
2. Develop nonsmoking alternatives. Strategies that can be used to replace tobacco use include the performance of such behaviors as chewing sugarless gum or eating low-calorie candies. You should have ample supplies of gum or candies on hand prior to abandoning tobacco use.
3. Reduce the range of stimuli associated with tobacco use. If you use tobacco, you can reduce the range of stimuli associated with the

stimulus by such strategies as decreasing the number of cups of coffee you drink—if you smoke cigarettes when drinking coffee—or occupying yourself by clearing the table if you formerly smoked following a meal. Switching to decaffeinated coffee is also recommended as a way to reduce tobacco use. You can also reduce the range of stimuli associated with tobacco use by avoiding areas where you formerly used the product or individuals with whom you smoked or used smokeless tobacco. Select some out-of-the-way place to smoke.

4. Rank situations in which tobacco is apt to be used. Once this task has been achieved, you can prepare to cope with the same situations without tobacco. Any of the self-management tactics described earlier, including relaxation, meditation, systematic self-desensitization, self-monitoring, imagery, or rehearsal, may be used to achieve this aim.

5. Once tobacco use has been reduced, you should control other stimuli. One effective method is to increase the duration between tobacco use through means of a timer. This method will allow you to shape your behavior by gradually lengthening the time between your use of tobacco. When the urge hits to smoke, wait five minutes. Gradually increase the amount of time before you smoke. Other strategies include not carrying around cigarettes or other tobacco products, or not having a lighter with you. Inhaling only half of each puff and smoking only half of each cigarette is also recommended.

6. Neutralize fascination of tobacco use. Martin and Osborne (1989) and Williams and Long (1991) suggest a commonly used strategy for decreasing the attractiveness of smoking: carry around a butt jar of your discarded cigarettes. The contents of the jar eventually look disgusting. Carrying around a jar of tobacco juice, for those who use smokeless tobacco, would be equally effective.

7. Mobilize social support. Let your target date be known to others, particularly those who can help you abandon tobacco. You might also identify those who do not use the products and begin spending more time with them.

8. Refocus your thinking. You should use self-statements throughout any self-management program designed for the cessation of tobacco. If you can, increase the positive thoughts you provide yourself; at the same time, avoid negative thinking, such as, "I don't think I can go through with this." More and more people quit using tobacco, so you stand an excellent chance of success.

9. Reinforce yourself. You should remember to use self-statements to maintain your avoidance of tobacco. Another excellent reinforcer is to put aside the money you normally spend for tobacco. After a period, this will allow you to have a nice spending spree at a local store or mall.

10. Prepare for withdrawal symptoms. Common symptoms of withdrawing from nicotine, particularly cigarettes, include an intense craving for tobacco, increased appetite, heightened irritability, poor sleep, and gastrointestinal disturbance. You should prepare for such potential problems. You might counter them by imagining how your lungs are beginning to rid themselves of the black tar and nicotine that coated them. With the removal of these substances, your lungs can begin to heal themselves. You should be prepared to engage in alternative activities, such as chewing gum or increasing your level of physical activity. Halting tobacco use increases your ability to participate in and enjoy many additional recreational activities.

    11. Maintain change. Several strategies should be considered to maintain your change. First, you want to maintain a supportive environment. Attempt to build your social life around not using tobacco; this can be of assistance. Keep whatever stress you experience under control with self-management strategies, and be prepared for social pressures for you to abandon your program. When failure occurs, start the tobacco cessation cycle over. Eventually, you can abandon tobacco. Another tactic may be that you consult with your physician. He or she may prescribe either nicotine gum or nicotine-laden patches. Either product may help you achieve your ultimate goal: quitting the use of tobacco forever.

SELF-MANAGEMENT OF TOBACCO USE

There are a number of self-management techniques that can be used to promote the cessation of tobacco products. These include:

    1. Stimulus control. You could change the stimuli that serve as discriminative stimuli for the use of tobacco products. As noted earlier, this could include altering environmental or cognitive stimuli or both.

Environmental stimuli. The use of tobacco by many people is under the control of environmental stimuli. You may smoke following meals or during breaks. The meals and break times serve as discriminative stimuli. Those who use tobacco products may do so when engaging in outdoor activities, such as playing sports or doing yard work. Changing these discriminative stimuli may modify your use of tobacco products. The person intent on not smoking may establish other stimuli as discriminative stimuli for not smoking. Carrying around gum to chew when tobacco products were formerly used would be an example of a discriminative stimulus for not smoking. Being careful to avoid modeling the tobacco use of friends or families could also alter environmental stimuli.

Cognitive stimuli. A number of cognitive stimuli may be changed, subtracted, or added to a situation to avoid the use of tobacco products. Those trying to halt smoking or use of smokeless tobacco might refocus their thinking. Instead of automatically reaching for a cigarette, grab a piece of sugarless candy. When coupled with self-instructions and self-statements, halting the use of tobacco may occur. The person who wants to quit using tobacco may also use imagery or rehearsal to change cognitive stimuli. Imagine the smoke and other chemicals that are polluting your body. Thinking of ways to handle situations where tobacco was formerly used and rehearsing these steps also suggests how cognitive stimuli may help you quit smoking.

2. Self-monitoring. Increasing or refining self-observation and self-recording may also enhance your ability to halt the use of tobacco. An accurate depiction of your progress can serve to reinforce your behavior.

3. Self-reinforcement. You may reinforce yourself when you have successfully avoided the use of tobacco in a context where it was formerly used. If tempted, use thought cessation; reinforce yourself when this proves useful in permitting you to avoid tobacco use. Self-reinforcement can also be combined with the use of alternative stimuli to strengthen tobacco cessation efforts.

4. Self-punishment. Carrying around a jar containing smoked cigarettes or tobacco juice would likely be disgusting to you (as well as others around you). This is the best example of the use of self-punishment when used in tobacco cessation programs.

5. Develop alternative ways of occupying yourself. Instead of smoking or using smokeless tobacco, you can carry around other stimuli, such as sunflower seeds, that can be used as a substitute for tobacco. Doing something to occupy your hands, such as playing with a paper clip or rubber band, also represents an alternative habit to smoking or using smokeless tobacco.

6. Problem-solving. Problem-solving strategies can again be used to consider how to quit using tobacco. This would involve: (a) thinking ahead of activities where you may be tempted to use tobacco, such as during breaks or after meals; (b) exploring alternative behaviors that can be used; (c) developing a plan to counter the use of tobacco; (d) acting on your plan; (e) evaluating the plan; (f) managing any setbacks that may occur; and (g) considering alternative strategies that might be tried.

SELF-MANAGEMENT SMOKING CESSATION PROJECTS

Students seem to be able to quit using tobacco far more successfully than was originally anticipated. Figure 16–1 depicts the record obtained from a student who used self-monitoring to reduce her smoking. Through self-monitoring and chewing gum, she was able to decrease the number of cigarettes she smoked to less than a half a pack a day. Figure 16–2 reflects the progress made by a student who used self-monitoring and positive thoughts to reduce her consumption of cigarettes. Whenever she wanted to smoke, she thought of how her lungs were beginning to heal; this approach proved successful. Figure 16–3 depicts an interesting approach taken by another student to halt cigarette smoking. She combined the support of her friends, use of a butt jar, gum chewing, and self-monitoring to decrease cigarette smoking. Unfortunately, as she noted, she was under stress during the latter part of her program and increased

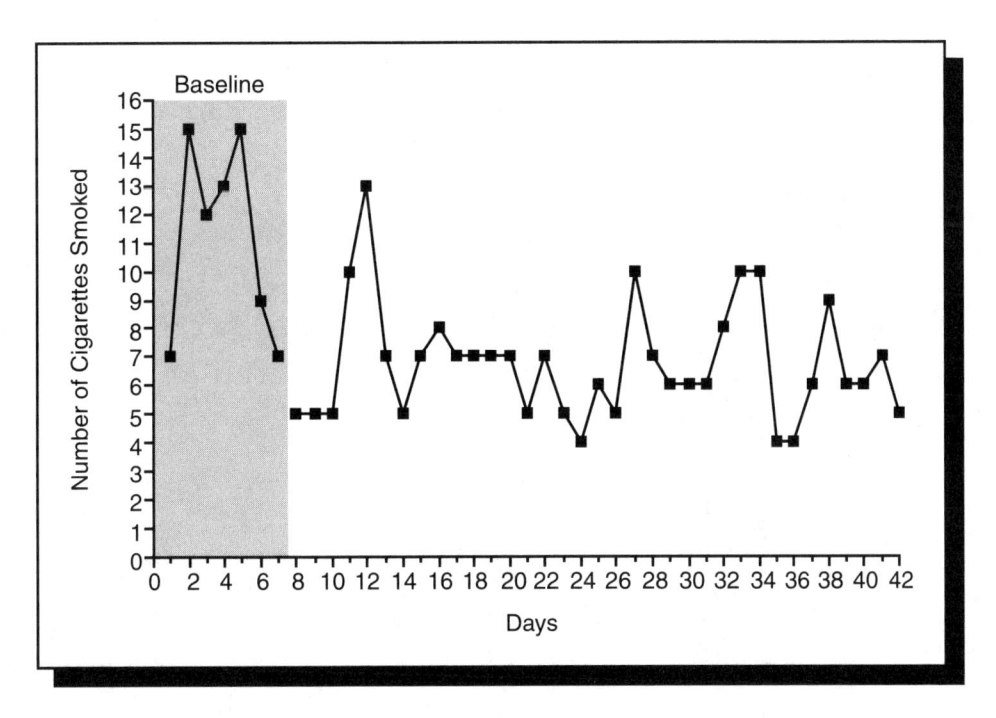

FIGURE 16–1
Use of self-monitoring and chewing gum to reduce cigarettes smoked.

FIGURE 16–2
Use of self-monitoring and positive thoughts to reduce cigarettes smoked.

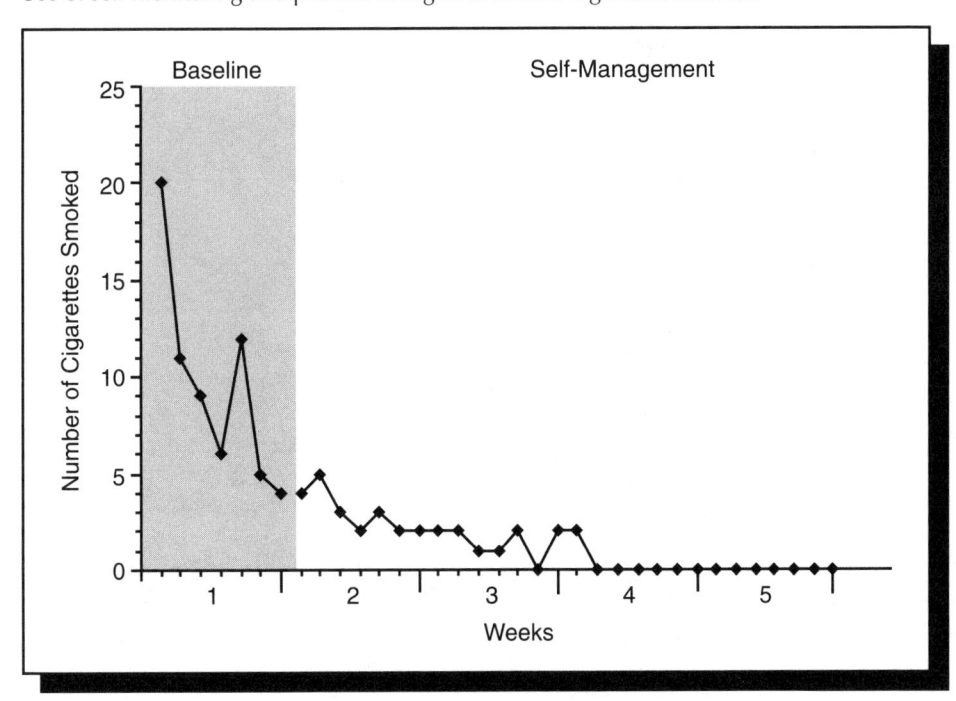

185

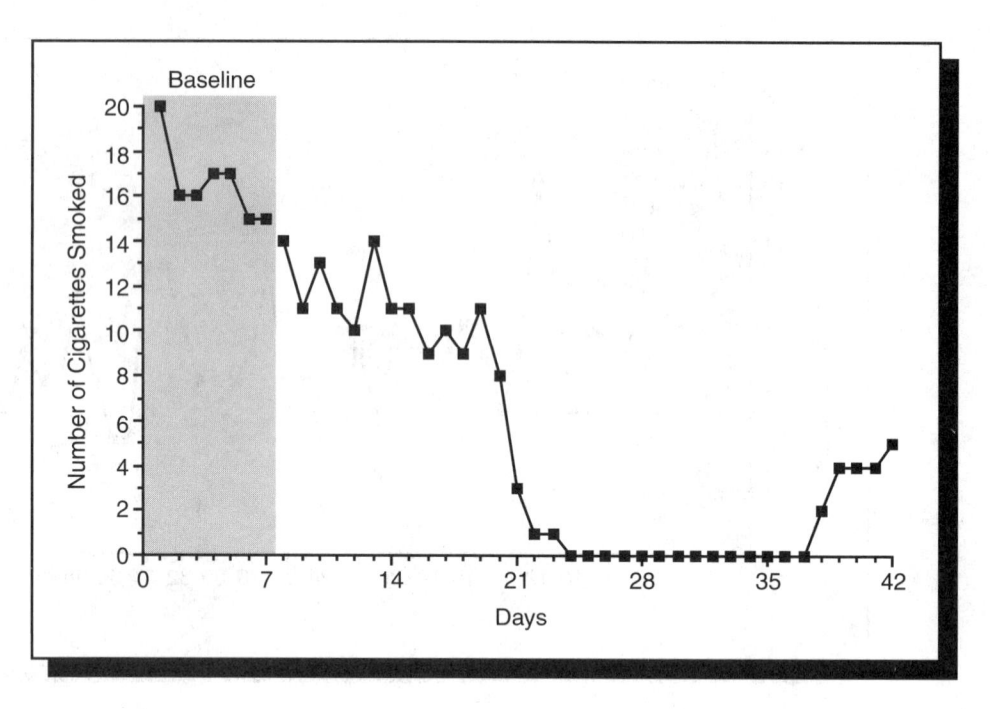

FIGURE 16–3
Use of peer support, gum chewing, a butt jar, and self-monitoring to quit smoking.

FIGURE 16–4
Use of self-monitoring to reduce cigarette consumption.

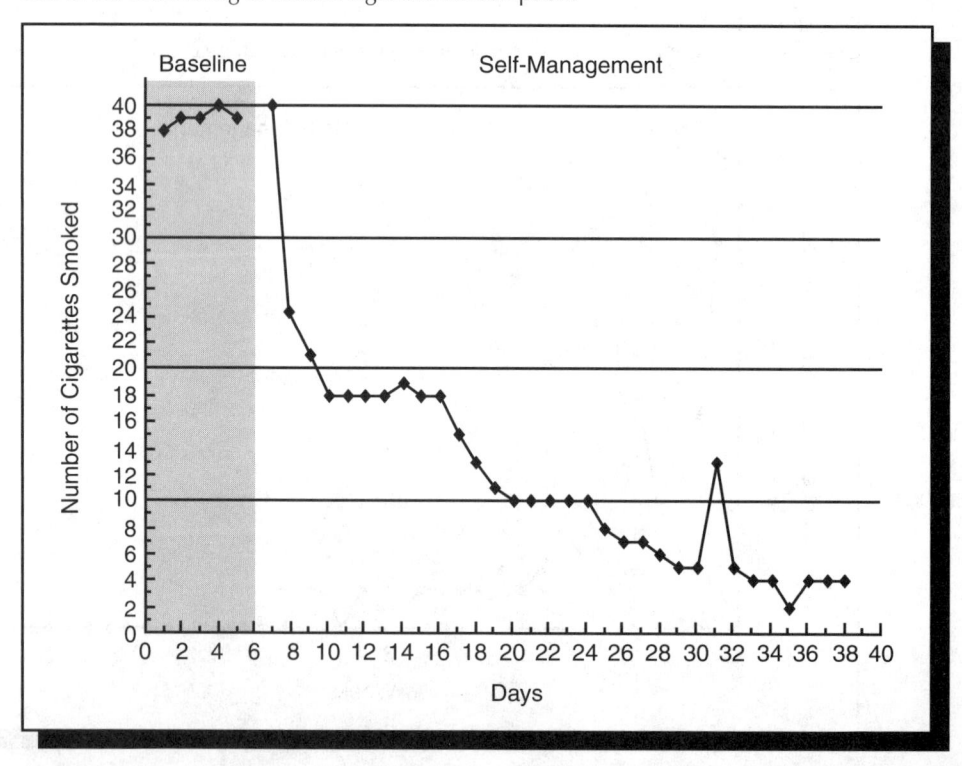

her use of cigarettes. However, she said she believed that her past success showed that, if she wished, she could quit again in the future. Whether she actually ever abandoned her use of cigarettes is unknown. Figure 16–4 depicts the progress made by a student in halting his use of cigarettes. Through self-monitoring, he was able to reduce the number of cigarettes he smoked from two packs a day down to four cigarettes. He eventually quit smoking altogether. The student remained a nonsmoker for two years. At that time, he again began smoking, but at a lesser amount than before. However, he anticipated that, based on his past experience, he could completely quit when the hectic quarter he was experiencing ended. Hopefully, he succeeded.

Figures 16–5 and 16–6 illustrate progress made by two students who wanted to abandon the use of smokeless tobacco. The student whose data are shown in Figure 16–5 experienced solid progress. However, as he noted, he believed he needed to improve his self-monitoring if he were to reach his goal of total abstinence. Figure 16–6 depicts progress made by a student who used self-monitoring, gum chewing, alternative activities, and a reduction in TV viewing to reduce his use of smokeless tobacco. He was highly successful. In addition, the student stopped by several months later to say that, with the exception of one episode that occurred when he was home with his friends, he had not returned to using smokeless tobacco. He was extremely proud of his accomplishment.

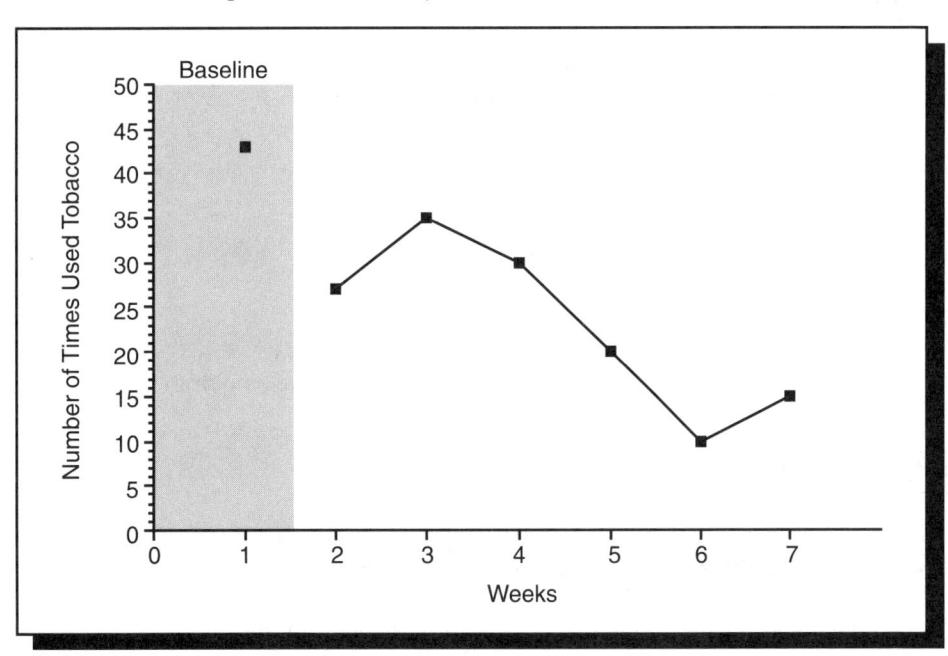

FIGURE 16–5
Use of self-monitoring to reduce consumption of smokeless tobacco.

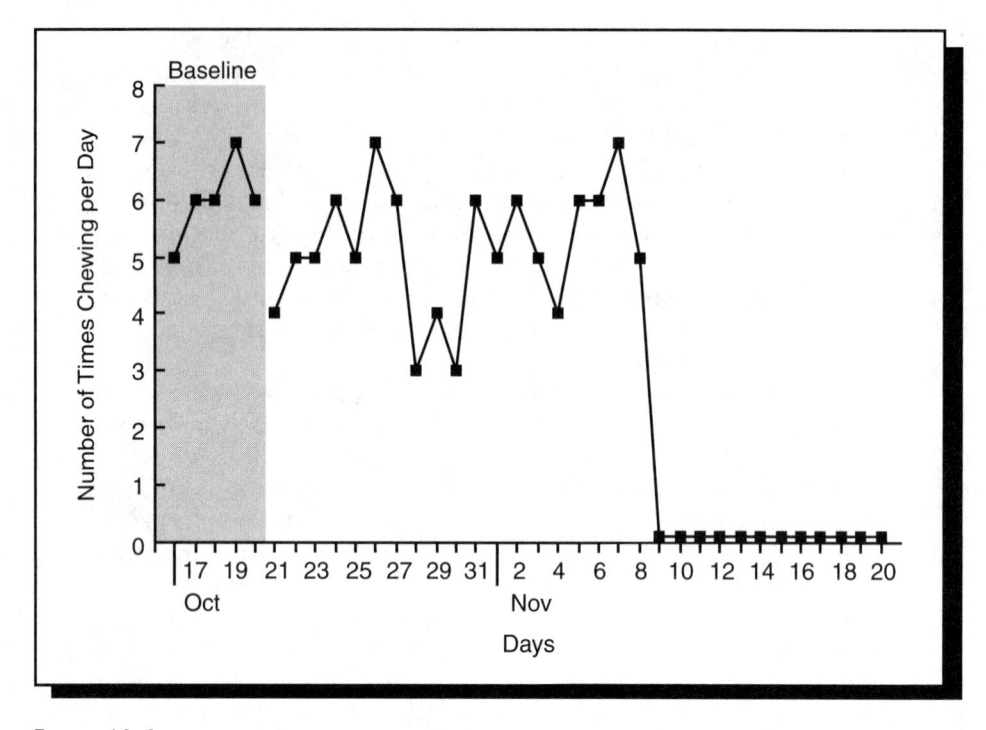

FIGURE 16–6
Use of a procedure combining self-monitoring, alternative procedures, gum chewing, and avoidance of TV to quit chewing tobacco.

EXERCISE

If you use tobacco, how often do you use it?
What are the compelling reasons for you to stop?
What strategies would you use to halt tobacco use?
What criteria would you establish to demonstrate the success of your program?
How would you maintain your success?

REVIEW TERMS

Betaendorphine
Butt jar
Nicotine
Passive smoking

QUESTIONS

Describe six reasons for using tobacco products.
Discuss the six-stage program for changing behavior developed by Prochaska, Norcross, and DiClemente (1994).
List eleven ways of changing discriminative stimuli for smoking.

CHAPTER 17

Alcohol Abuse

"Tis not the drinking that is to be blamed, but the excess."
—John Seldon, *Table Talk*

"I know I shouldn't drink, but I do. I wake up almost every morning with a hangover. I always swear that I won't have anything to drink that day. Come late afternoon or early evening, I need something. I figure one beer will do it. It doesn't take me long to go to a bar and have a beer. One brew leads to another and before long, I'm drunk. I've got to break the pattern somehow, you know?"
—Max, a sometime college student

It is estimated that one in ten Americans abuses alcohol. Almost a billion dollars is spent each year on treatment for the disorder; in addition, the cost to the U.S. economy because of alcohol abuse is approximately $50 billion each year. Alcohol abuse is second only to smoking among the preventable causes of death in the United States.

Reasons for the abuse of alcohol are many and varied. Some who abuse alcohol obtain positive reinforcement from drinking alcoholic beverages. It may make them feel euphoric and in control of their lives. Drinking can also become a conditioned reinforcer, particularly when a person drinks with peers or friends. The TV program "Cheers" illustrates the conditioned reinforcement that occurs when drinking with people you know in a setting you enjoy. Others drink because it removes them from what they perceive as aversive stimuli. These people may be involved in an unhappy relationship or may hate their job. Finally, individuals may become psychologically or physiologically addicted to alcohol to the point where they experience withdrawal symptoms, including physical discomfort and intense craving for a drink, when they don't drink alcohol. The reasons cited for abusing alcohol are as numerous as the number of individuals who are considered as borderline or full-blown alcoholics.

DEFINITIONS OF ALCOHOL ABUSE

Alcohol abuse is the use of alcoholic beverages to the point where it has a negative influence on your social, psychological, or physical well-being. Your life begins to revolve around that first drink in the morning; it may not end until you help close a bar late at night or fall into a drunken stupor. Some who abuse alcohol may believe their drinking cannot be controlled or stopped; other people may not perceive they have a drinking problem. Anyone who has lived with alcohol for a period knows the omnipotent impact that alcohol abuse can have not only on the chronic drinker, but on his or her family and others involved with the individual.

A recent study by Wechsler and colleagues (1994) examined the extent of binge drinking by 17,592 college students at 140 four-year colleges in the United States. The results indicated almost half (44 percent) of college students classified themselves as binge drinkers; almost one fifth (19 percent) of the respondents said they were frequent binge drinkers. There were other findings reported by Wechsler and colleagues concerning binge drinkers:

1. Almost half (47 percent) of the frequent binge drinkers experienced five or more different drinking problems, including hangovers, injuries, school absenteeism, and engaging in unplanned sex, since the beginning of the school year.
2. Binge drinkers created problems for classmates who were not binge drinkers, including arguments, physical attacks, damaged property, unwanted sexual advances, and disruption of sleep or studying.
3. Students who were not binge drinkers at schools with higher binge rates were more likely than students at schools with lower binge rates to experience problems created by binge drinking.
4. Most binge drinkers did not consider themselves to be problem drinkers, and had not sought treatment for an alcohol problem.

The results of this large, representative national study confirmed that binge drinking is widespread on college campuses.

Do you have problems with drinking and alcohol abuse? Martin and Osborne (1989) offer a dozen questions that you should ask yourself with respect to your use of alcohol, as listed in Table 17–1. If you answered yes to any of these questions, you may want to evaluate where you are with respect to the use of alcohol. Your evaluation will determine if you should develop a program to change your behavior or if you should seek assistance from others. There are two approaches you can take: protect yourself against alcohol abuse and develop a self-management program.

PROTECTION AGAINST ALCOHOL ABUSE

There are a number of strategies you can take to prevent abusing alcohol (Martin and Osborne, 1989). These tactics include:

1. Practice avoidance. You can avoid friends and places where you are apt to abuse alcohol. It is not necessary to go bar hopping at night, or even stroll along a street with many bars.

TABLE 17–1 Questions About Alcohol Use (suggested by Martin and Osborne, 1989)

1. Do you often drink more than you plan on a particular occasion?
2. Does anyone believe you are an alcoholic?
3. Do you require larger amounts of alcohol than you did in the past in order to feel the same effect?
4. Have you experienced memory blackouts while or after drinking?
5. Have you been treated for alcoholism or attended a meeting of Alcoholics Anonymous (AA)?
6. Do you regularly drink large quantities of alcohol, including beer?
7. Do you have persistent problems at home, school, or work that are related to drinking?
8. Do you take alcohol with you when traveling?
9. Do your friends drink heavily, sometimes passing out in your presence?
10. Have you ever tried to disguise or hide the amount that you drink?
11. Do you usually drink at home, often by yourself, rather than socially?
12. Does alcohol ever lead you to discard the belief system you have when you are sober?

2. Perform alternative behaviors. When you are around alcohol, such as at a cocktail party, you can ask for a nonalcoholic beverage. A number of possibilities are usually available, including seltzer water, soft drinks, coffee, and even nonalcoholic wines and beer. You will increasingly find that more and more people are joining you in abandoning the consumption of alcoholic beverages. There are just too many reasons to select options other than a drink containing alcohol.

3. Develop natural highs. Some experts claim you can develop natural highs from exercising; others, including those who exercise on a regular basis, are dubious about such comments. There are a number of recovered alcoholics, including writers and artists, who have described the sense of achievement they feel once they quit drinking (e.g., Hamill, 1994). They explain that they not only have more time to do activities they enjoy, but that the quantity and quality of their output sharply increases.

4. Develop alternative ways to handle behavior problems. If you drink to avoid or escape from problems at work, school, or home, or to overcome feelings of stress, frustration, or depression, you should develop other ways to cope with these feelings or situations. Exercise, plus any of the self-management procedures described in this book, represent a large pool of alternatives to drinking.

5. Be assertive. In the long run, it is up to you to decide whether you want to stop drinking. You can always say no when asked if you want to drink. You are the one who ultimately decides to drink; you will likely be the one who may suffer aversive consequences because of your behavior (although friends and family members also suffer consequences).

SELF-MANAGEMENT OF ALCOHOL USE

If you find that none of the methods for preventing alcohol abuse work, there is self-management. The format you may want to follow in developing a self-management program includes these components. Select a goal. You need to decide whether you wish to achieve a goal of total or partial abstinence. If your goal is the former, then you will want to think of not consuming any alcohol at all. This would be the appropriate goal if you find you are habitually drunk and/or perceive yourself as unable to stop drinking. In these situations, you not only want to include methods for prevention of alcohol abuse discussed above, but you may want to attend regular meetings of a chapter of Alcoholics Anonymous (AA). The overall impact of Alcoholics Anonymous on reducing alcohol consumption is debatable (e.g., Seligman, 1994), but the organization is an effective approach to drinking cessation in some individuals. As there is no accepted cure for alcoholism, AA meetings may provide you with the social support you need for not drinking.

Perhaps you do not want to quit drinking entirely, but only consume a set amount of alcohol at given times. You may not want to drink during the week, for example, but would like to go out with your friends on the weekend. If this is your decision, it is imperative that you set and adhere to any limits you establish.

Self-Assessment

At the beginning, establish your baseline of drinking. This entails that you jot down information regarding places, situations, and events related to your use of alcohol. These circumstances provide triggers for your drinking; by identifying triggers before initiating your program, you will know what action to take to avoid them. You will likely identify what seem to be the consequences that lead to and maintain your use of alcohol. This knowledge can be invaluable in helping you not only avoid consequences, but in developing alternatives to drinking.

Commitment

The steps of the model for behavior change, developed by Prochaska, Norcross, and DiClemente (1994) and outlined in Chapter 16, should be used in developing a commitment to controlling alcohol consumption. The initial three steps—precontemplation, contemplation, and preparation—are particularly important in helping individuals decide whether they are prepared to undertake a program designed to curb their drinking. Without this preparation, any program developed to change behavior may be predestined to fail.

External Environment

Williams and Long (1991) note that self-assessment is apt to reveal two types of external events that serve as setting events for your drinking: physical and social stimuli. You can attempt to control these setting events by avoiding, limiting, or neutralizing them. You can quit buying alcoholic beverages; in addition, Williams and Long suggest that you should: (a) avoid drinking alone; (b) wait until the evening before having a drink; (c) drink alcoholic beverages only at mealtime or at parties; (d) drink beverages lower in alcoholic content than distilled liquor (although it is possible to become an alcoholic by drinking only beer); and (e) only drink distilled liquor before a meal or at a party. As the consumption of distilled liquor is declining in the United States, there are a number of options for you to take as an alternative to these products.

Self-Statements

The instruction you provide yourself via self-statements will direct and maintain your abstinence from alcohol. Use all the strategies suggested in earlier chapters to be certain self-statements help you achieve your goal. Eventually, the effective use of self-statements, included in any self-monitoring procedure, will determine how successful you are at halting your consumption of alcohol.

Maintenance

Once you have achieved your goal, you must establish procedures to maintain your abstinence. Prochaska, Norcross, and DiClemente have a number of proven suggestions for maintaining alcohol abstinence; you may wish to consult their book. Careful self-monitoring, coupled with the performance of a variety of alternative activities, is the best choice for helping you maintain your change. Keeping in contact with the local AA chapter may also be of assistance. In addition, the local AA chapter can provide help if you slip and again begin drinking to excess. As noted, there is no cure for alcoholism. All you can achieve is to control your drinking. Only you can decide upon the procedures to use in managing your drinking.

Self-Management Procedures for Control of Alcohol Use

A number of techniques can be used to help control your consumption of alcoholic beverages. These include:

1. Stimulus control. Both environmental and cognitive procedures can be used to change the stimuli that promote drinking and help you halt consuming such beverages when you wish.

Environmental control. You can change the environmental stimuli that may lead you to drink. Avoiding or escaping situations where you tend to drink, such as avoiding bars or parties where alcoholic beverages are served, illustrates how you might achieve this aim. You can also establish discriminative stimuli for not drinking alcoholic beverages, such as seeking nonalcoholic beverages instead of those that contain alcohol. Once you develop a history of not drinking alcoholic beverages, you will have developed a number of discriminative stimuli for not drinking. It is important that you avoid peer pressure and the modeling of others if you are around others who drink. It is difficult to abstain from drinking if surrounded by peers who drink and who attempt to have you join them in engaging in such behavior.

Cognitive stimulus change. There are a number of ways you can change cognitive stimuli to help you refrain from the consumption of alcohol. Methods include using: (a) self-instructions and self-statements; (b) refocusing your thinking and adopting alternative strategies to drinking; (c) rehearsing the behaviors you can perform in situations where you formerly drank; (d) using imagery to imagine yourself behaving differently in circumstances where you formerly drank; (e) stopping thoughts that concern drinking; and (f) becoming assertive and refusing alcoholic beverages.

2. Self-monitoring. Improving and refining how you monitor your consumption of alcoholic beverages can help you reduce drinking. The data you plot concerning your behavior can serve as a discriminative stimulus to help promote and maintain your goals concerning alcohol consumption. The levels of blood alcohol produced by a specific number of drinks, as well as the amount of time it takes the alcohol to leave your body, are depicted in Table 17–2. As noted, you only need to consume three 12-ounce bottles or cans of beer to be considered as legally drunk in many states.

3. Self-reinforcement. You should reinforce yourself when you refrain from drinking in situations where you formerly drank. Reinforce yourself when you refrain from drinking or when you control your drinking by performing thought stopping or engaging in alternative activities (e.g., drinking seltzer water).

4. Alternative activities. There are a number of alternative activities you can engage in instead of drinking. This is reflected in the success of the so-called "designated driver." Drinking soda or mineral water is an alternative activity; when you consume these products instead of drinking alcoholic beverages, reinforce yourself for your responses.

5. Problem solving. When you want to quit drinking alcoholic beverages in any situation, it is important that you use problem-solving skills. These include those tactics described throughout the book, including: (a) planning ahead; (b) considering what alternatives you have to

TABLE 17-2 Number of Drinks Required to Produce Levels of Blood Alcohol in Body and the Amount of Time it Takes to Rid Body of the Alcohol

Number of Drinks	Percentage of Blood Alcohol Level	Time for Alcohol to Leave Body
5 whiskey cocktails (1 1/4 oz. each) 25 oz. wine 5 12 oz. beers	0.15 (legally drunk in all states)	10 hours
4 cocktails 20 oz. wine 4 12 oz. beers	0.12 (legally drunk in most states)	8 hours
3 cocktails 10 oz. wine 3 12 oz. beers	0.09 (legally drunk in many states)	6 hours
2 cocktails	0.06	4 hours
1 cocktail 5 oz. wine 1 12 oz. beer	0.03	2 hours

drinking; (c) rehearsing beforehand what approach you are going to take; (d) acting on your developed plan; (e) evaluating the results of your performance; (f) preparing for any potential setbacks; and (g) considering other options that you have instead of drinking.

SELF-MANAGEMENT PROJECTS

One student attempted to control the number of times he drove while drinking. The results of his program are shown in Figure 17–1. He used self-monitoring to control his behavior. As depicted, he decreased his drinking and driving in the weeks following baseline; however, the number of times he drank and drove then rebounded. He finally decided that he could not control his drinking; thereafter, he abandoned the thoughts of attempting to control the number of times he drove while drinking and selected a designated driver. Thus, the program was not a total failure.

The program developed and followed by a second student was a failure. His results are depicted in Figure 17–2. Some success was achieved in the program, particularly in weeks 2, 4, 5, 6, and 9. However, it is doubtful that the student was committed to his self-management program. Based upon his comments, he never accepted that drinking was under his control; rather, he repeatedly stated that the drinking was a function of his relationship with his girlfriend. Prior to his attempt to quit drinking, the student should have followed the steps outlined by Prochaska and colleagues (1994).

196 Chap. 17 Alcohol Abuse

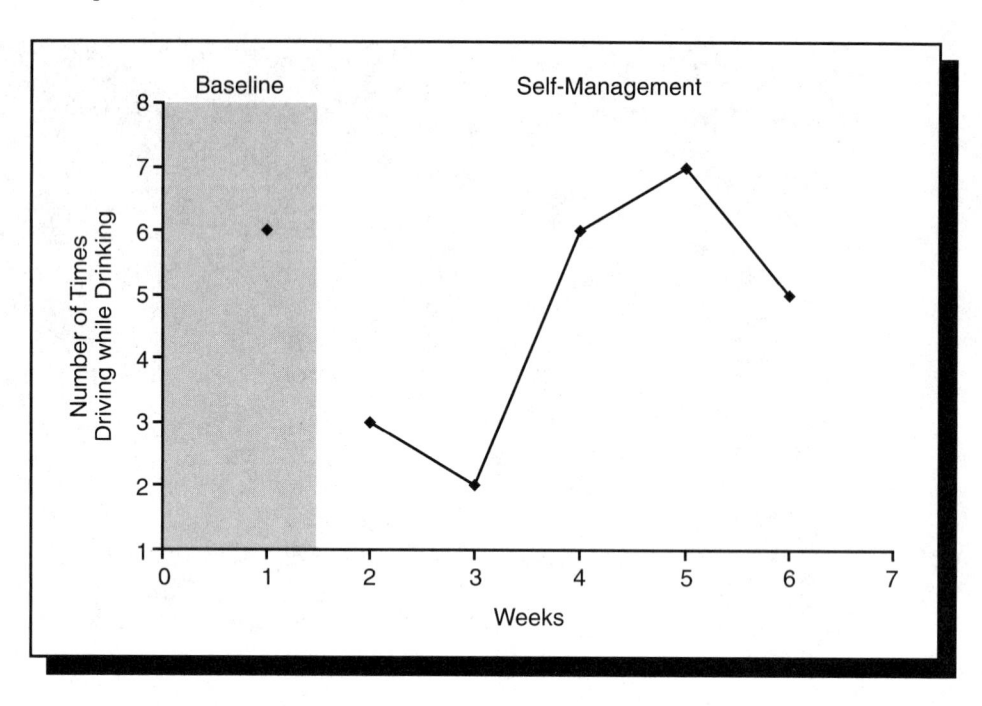

FIGURE 17–1
Use of self-monitoring to decrease number of times driving while drinking.

FIGURE 17–2
Reduce consumption of alcohol.

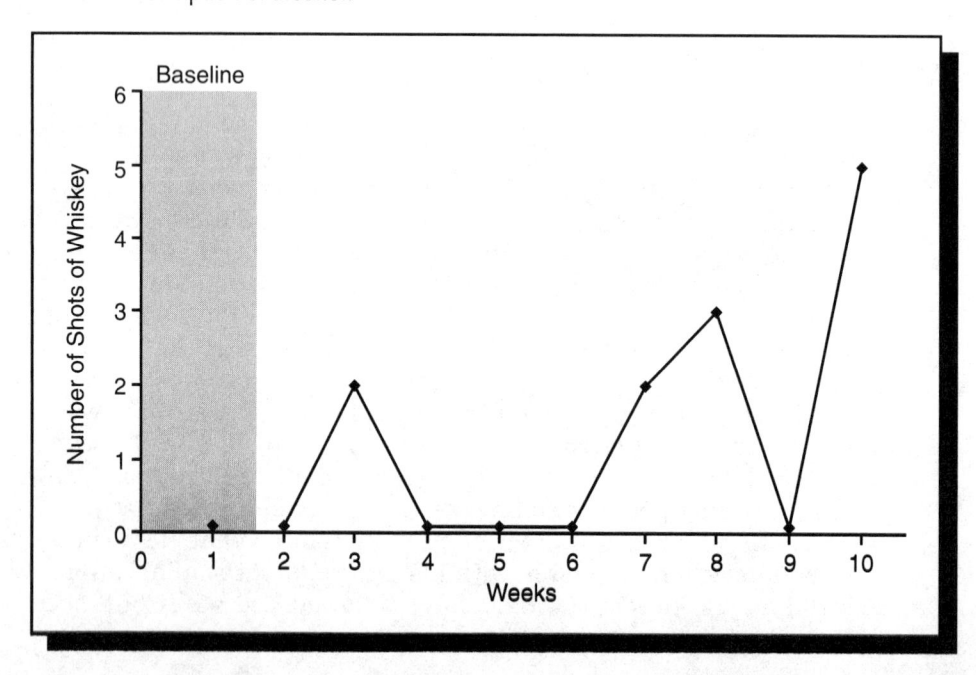

EXERCISE

Do you abuse alcohol?

If you do, under what circumstances?

What should be the goal of a self-management program if you decide to establish one for alcohol abuse?

What will be the criteria that will indicate you achieved your goal?

How will you maintain abstinence from alcohol?

REVIEW TERMS

External environment   Self-assessment

QUESTIONS

Describe five methods that can protect you against alcohol abuse.

Describe six general ways of practicing self-management with respect to alcohol abuse.

CHAPTER 18

Sexual Behavior

"When you are young, you think that sex is the culmination of intimacy. Later you discover that it's barely the beginning."
— Peter Hoeg, *Smila's Sense of Snow*

"I know girls in the dorm who think they have no chance of getting any kind of sexually transmitted disease like AIDS. They think if you're careful, you can't get anything. Some think the thing about AIDS has been overblown by the press. There are others in the dorm who think differently. A couple have herpes. As it's my decision when and where I will have sex, I would rather be safe than sorry."
—Pat, a freshman

Self-management is significant for most sexual behaviors in that consequences of your behavior may affect not only you, but also your partner. There is no such thing as an uninvolved partner in a sexual relationship. For this reason, it is imperative that you always consider potential outcomes of sexual behavior before a consequence occurs that can greatly alter your life, perhaps in a negative way. For some of you, the discussion that follows may be of little relevance; for others, it could be very important. With this as an introduction, we will consider three topics: overcoming sexual problems, sexually transmitted diseases, and safe sex practices.

OVERCOMING SEXUAL PROBLEMS

In a recent book, Dr. Miriam Stoppard (1991) listed common complaints made about sex by couples. Contrary to what you might believe, most were not due to physical causes, but included: (a) fear of sex; (b) discomfort with intimacy; (c) pressure to be a sexual athlete; (d) lack of sexual knowledge; (e) lack of effective communication; (f) lack of consensus on sexual activity; and (g) problems with distasteful and boring sex. These problems, argues Stoppard, can "best be solved between a couple by an open attitude to sex and communication" (p. 192). Stoppard went on to describe problems that were common to men and women. These include, for each sex, the following:

Women

Sexual problems common to women are unresponsiveness, lack of orgasm, painful intercourse, and vaginismus.

1. Unresponsiveness. Stoppard suggests that a woman who is unresponsive may feel little need to be satisfied by a man when making love. There may be a number of factors for such feelings, many of which are rooted in the woman's past. To overcome the problem of unresponsiveness, a couple should allow enough time and privacy for sexual activities. Self-management techniques, particularly relaxation and systematic self-desensitization, should be considered. Sensate focus is widely recommended as a way to overcome unresponsiveness in either partner (Stoppard, 1991). This is a relaxation technique that promotes attention to stimulation of various parts of the body. Sensate focus allows couples to give and receive pleasure through touch alone with the agreement that sexual intercourse will be delayed for a period. There are three stages to sensate focus. First, you should concentrate on your feelings. You want to awaken sensual feelings by learning what is arousing to you. This may involve the use of massage. Second, begin to involve your partner. This involves mutual massaging, sometimes nothing more than a back massage. You should be expressive about what gives you pleasure. Third, when both of you agree on the timing, you can move on to touching the more sexually sensitive parts of each other's bodies. Proceed at your own pace, but be certain to convey to your partner what you find pleasurable and what you wish to avoid. Expect your partner to do the same. The successful use of sensate focus may take several weeks or months. However, the result of employing the technique should be that both you and your partner are comfortable about sexual activity.

2. Lack of orgasm. Few women, notes Stoppard (1991), suffer from physical problems that could lead to orgasmic impairment. Rather, women often suffer from an impaired partner. Such techniques as sensate focus can assist women to have orgasms. Some sex therapists suggest that women who have never had an orgasm try to have one through masturbation; more often, however, sex therapists focus on a couple's relationship rather than on sexual functioning. If women expect to attain orgasm each time they make love, warns Stoppard, they have unrealistic expectations.

3. Painful intercourse. It is common, suggests Stoppard, for women occasionally to experience painful intercourse. This may be due to a number of factors including physical problems, but the most common factor is a clumsy or unsophisticated partner. In these instances, you and your partner both may want to review your sexual relationship and see if it can be gradually changed to prevent painful intercourse in the future.

4. Vaginismus. Vaginismus is painful spasmodic contractions of the lower third of the vagina, which can prevent sexual intercourse. Because the reasons for this problem can be psychological, a woman may wish to

use relaxation, systematic self-desensitization, or sensate focus to overcome the problem. It is also important that her partner work with her to solve this barrier to their happiness.

Men

Three problems are commonly reported by men: premature ejaculation, difficulty with erection, and impotence.

1. Premature ejaculation. This is a more common problem than generally assumed, particularly among younger men. Approximately one-third of men report they experience premature ejaculation. Ways to avoid the problem are to limit foreplay, avoid unnecessary stimulation, occasionally pause during intercourse, and utilize self-management techniques, such as thought stopping or imagining an activity other than sex. Other techniques such as Seaman's focus, whereby the male masturbates almost to the point of ejaculation, halts, and repeats the process; nondemands intromission, whereby the penis is inserted into the vagina with no action by either partner; and the squeeze technique, whereby the glands of the penis are squeezed to delay ejaculation, are also recommended. The problem of premature ejaculation often disappears with age and experience.

2. Difficulties with erection. Difficulties with maintaining an erection are common in men after the age of fifty. An understanding partner can often overcome the problem. If attaining and holding an erection becomes a prolonged difficulty, the male should see a physician or sex therapist. There are techniques that can assist most men, including penile implants or injections.

3. Impotence. From time to time, impotence is common in many men. A number of conditions, many of them temporary, can contribute to impotence. Commonly cited factors include anxiety, depression, fatigue, arguments between partners, and too much alcohol consumption. If impotence becomes a recurring problem, it is suggested that a male contact his physician or a sex therapist. There are techniques, including those described above, for resolving erection problems that may be of value in improving the sexual relationship of couples.

Sex is a natural part of life. However, mutually satisfying sexual relationships are the result of learning and experience. You can learn what your partner expects from the relationship; at the same time, you should be able to convey to him or her your expectations. Open communication with your partner and the enjoyment of sexual fantasies are recommended by other authors on sexuality (Crooks and Baur, 1990; Hyde, 1990). In addition, a book such as *The Magic of Sex* (Stoppard, 1991) is recommended.

In their guide to assertive learning, Alberti and Emmons (1990) propose that women learn to be assertive in responding to situations where they might feel coerced into unwanted sex. They suggest that women practice learning to "say no" in a variety of situations, especially those that could involve them in situations they would like to avoid. Men, continue Alberti and Emmons, should consider their attitudes toward sexuality, the rights of each person to self-determination, and respect for each other. Coercive tactics, including those that are a part of a "macho mode," should be avoided. Alberti and Emmons emphasize the need for commitment that can grow out of active engagement and open communication with one's partner. Commitment, to these authors, is not: (a) silent, (b) doggedly accepting, (c) a matter of blind faith, (d) ignorant, (e) passive, nor (f) naive. Rather, commitment is: (a) active, (b) communicating, (c) growing, (d) encountering, (e) joyfully alive, and (f) a matter of shared responsibility. As Alberti and Emmons conclude: "Commitment is intolerant of one-sided sexual idiosyncrasies, of sadistic treatment, of emotional traumatization. Commitment does not allow, and summarily curbs, physical or sexual abuse or assault. There are times to speak out forcefully and draw the line. Commitment does have limits" (p. 194). More on assertiveness will be discussed further in Chapter 21.

SEXUALLY TRANSMITTED DISEASES

It was pointed out earlier that you must always consider the consequences of your action if involved in a sexual relationship. This point must be emphasized because of the tremendous increase in sexually transmitted diseases in the past few decades. These diseases, particularly Acquired Immune Deficiency Syndrome (AIDS), will be discussed in this section.

Chlamydia

Close to 5 million new cases of chlamydia are reported each year. This disease is caused by *Chlamydia trachomatis*, a bacteria that can affect various mucus membranes of the body cavities. Symptoms of the disease in women are vaginal discharge, abdominal discomfort, and pain during urination; in men, symptoms of the disease are pain during urination and a discharge from the penis. These problems usually occur one to two weeks after a person is infected. Diagnosis is made, for women, by a cervical smear; for men, it involves an analysis of discharge of fluids from the penis. Treatment involves a ten- to fourteen-day course of tetracycline or erythromycin.

Gonorrhea

Almost 2 million new cases of gonorrhea are reported each year. Gonorrhea is caused by *Neisseria gonorrhoeae,* a bacterium. Symptoms are similar to those described for chlamydia in both men and women; they appear two to ten days after infection. Depending upon the type of intercourse that took place when gonorrhea was contracted, diagnosis of the disease is made from cultures of secretions from the cervix, throat, or rectum. Treatment involves the administration of penicillin, although new strains of gonorrhea are proving difficult to treat with the drug.

Genital Warts

Approximately a million new cases of genital warts, caused by the human papilloma virus, occur each year. Symptoms are growths in the genital and rectal areas; they occur three months to one year after infection. Diagnosis is made though a visual examination or, for internal warts, a viral culture. Genital warts may be removed through use of a caustic solution, electrosurgery, or surgery.

Herpes

Brody (1992) noted that nearly 30 million Americans—16 percent of people between the ages of fifteen and seventy-four—are thought to harbor the herpes virus. Each year, approximately half a million new cases of genital herpes are reported, caused by the Herpes Simplex Virus I and II. Symptoms include painful blisters on the genitalia of both men and women; these symptoms can occur two weeks to several years after contact. Diagnosis is achieved through visual examination and/or a viral culture. There is no known cure for herpes, although the disease can be controlled.

Syphilis

Approximately 100,000 new cases of syphilis are reported each year. It is caused by *Treponema pallidum*, an organism transmitted by contact with an open sore. Symptoms are the same for men and women. They first include reddish-brown sores on the mouth and/or genitalia; these sores may disappear, although the bacteria remains. In the second, more infectious stage of syphilis, a widespread skin rash may appear. Diagnosis of syphilis is made through blood tests. It is treated by penicillin or other appropriate antibiotics.

AIDS

AIDS is an immunodeficiency disease. This means that the normal checks and balances that permit us to coexist with microbes are disrupted in the body (Grief and Golden, 1994). The human immunodeficiency virus (HIV) is thought to cause AIDS. There is a two-step process in confirming the diagnosis of HIV, as presented in Table 18–1. As noted, blood serum from a person suspected of HIV is mixed with HIV viral antigens in the ELISA test. If there is a positive reaction, the patient receives the Western Blot test. A positive reaction on this test is considered the positive indicator for HIV. T-Cell Subsets are examined to determine if a patient has advanced from being HIV-positive to having AIDS. As noted, one indicator examines a patient's blood to determine if there has been a decreased T4-T8 ratio. The decrease in the number of T4 or helper cells or an increase in T8 or suppressor cells determines the clinical state of the individual. The second indicator examines the number of CD4 counts. Certain cells in the body contain a compatible protein on their surfaces called CD4. "Specifically," point out Grief and Golden (1994), "the cells that contain the surface antigen CD4, and thus become infected with AIDS, include many of the cells of the immune system as well as those of the brain, lungs, and intestinal tract" (p. 19).

There are also specific indicator diseases that help define AIDS. Those described by the Centers of Disease Control (1992) for adults and adolescents are depicted in Table 18–2. As noted, there are a number of types of diseases that may afflict a person with AIDS. Different diseases can strike almost every part of the body, including the respiratory system, the brain, and the intestinal tract.

TABLE 18–1 Four Tests Used to Determine the Presence of Human Immunodeficiency Virus (HIV) and Acquired Immune Deficiency Syndrome (AIDS)

HIV TESTS
1. **Enzyme-Linked Immunoabsorbent Assay (ELISA).** In this test, blood serum is mixed with HIV viral antigens (proteins). If antibodies to HIV are present in the blood, the sample turns yellow. Although the test is 99% accurate, another ELISA test is performed if the blood tests positive. If both tests are positive, a second and more specific test, the Western Blot, is performed.

2. **Western Blot.** This test relies on an electrophoresis technique. Blood serum is placed in contact with strips of paper that have been treated with antigens from two structures on the virus—the core and the envelope. When a dark line appears on the paper at specific locations, it indicates an antigen-antibody reaction between the blood and the viral antigens. The reaction is considered a positive test for HIV.

T CELL SUBSETS
The test requires two tubes of blood be drawn from a patient. Changes in the proportions of various subsets of T lymphocytes is an early indicator of advancement from being HIV positive to AIDS. Two indicators are:
1. **Decreased T4-T8 Ratio.** This test indicates a decrease in the numbers of T4 (CD4 or T helper) cells, an increase in the numbers of T8 (or T suppressor) cells, and overall reversal of the ratio of T4 to T8 lymphocytes. The lower the overall numbers of T4 cells and the lower the ratio of the T cell subsets, the more severe the clinical state of the patient.

2. **CD4 Test.** Healthy individuals have CD4 counts that average 1,100 per cubic millimeter. HIV-positive individuals lose 85 to 100 cells/mm^3 per year; thus, T cell reduction to critical levels may take an average of 10 years. A CD4 count of 200/mm^3 or less is an indicator that some manifestation of AIDS may soon occur.

TABLE 18–2 Indicator Diseases of AIDS

1. Candidiasis (fungal infection) of the esophagus, trachea, bronchi, or lungs.
2. Cryptococcosis (fungal infection) outside the lungs.
3. Cryptosporidiosis (parasitic infection) with diarrhea persisting more than a month.
4. Cytomegalovirus (virul infection) disease of an organ other than the liver, spleen, or lymph nodes.
5. Herpes simplex virus infection causing a mucocutaneous ulcer that persists longer than 1 month; or bronchitis, or esophagitis (inflammations of the lungs or esophagus) for any duration affecting anyone older than 1 month of age.
6. Kaposi's sarcoma (rare form of cancer) affecting anyone less than 60 years of age.
7. Lymphoma (cancer of the lymphatic tissue or lymph glands) of the brain affecting anyone less than 60 years of age.
8. Mycobacterium avium complex or M. kansaii disease that spreads to a site other than or in addition to lungs, skin, cervical or lung lymph nodes.
9. Pneumocystis carinii pneumonia.
10. Progressive multifocal leukoencephalopathy (a rare and rapidly progressive disease of the central nervous system caused by an infection). It is usually fatal.
11. Toxoplasmosis (protozoan carried by cats) of the brain affecting anyone more than 1 month of age.
12. Pulmonary tuberculosis.
13. Recurrent pneumonia.
14. Invasive cervical cancer.

An estimated 284,830 cases of AIDS have been reported to the Centers for Disease Control in the United States since 1981; it is thought that approximately one million Americans are infected with HIV. The new and expanded definition of AIDS, based upon three additional indicator diseases—tuberculosis of the lungs, recurring pneumonia, and invasive cervical cancer—and an additional test—the CD-4 cells test—resulted in a 204 percent increase in the number of new cases of AIDS in the first quarter of 1993, compared to a similar period in 1992. Overall, a 75 percent increase in the number of new cases of AIDS in the United States was anticipated in 1993. Despite the alarming increase in reported cases of AIDS in the United States, however, the data pales against reports from Africa. The World Health Organization reported that two million more people were infected with the HIV virus in 1993, with the highest increase occurring among teenagers and young adults.

As noted in Table 18–3, we are uncertain how many people are infected with AIDS, let alone how many individuals are infected with HIV each year. It is thought to be caused by the HTLV-III virus, although there is considerable debate about the exact nature of the virus. Initial symptoms are the same for both men and women, and include fatigue, fever, swollen lymph nodes, weight loss, diarrhea, night sweats, and susceptibility to infections. Symptoms may appear six months to eight years after infection. Treatment is through experimental drugs such as AZT. There is, however, no known cure for AIDS and the result is inevitably death.

TABLE 18–3 Recent Information Regarding AIDS, 1992

1. It is estimated that 10 to 12 million adults in the world are infected with HIV.
2. The World Health Organization (WHO) believes 30 million people in the world will be infected with the AIDS virus by the year 2000. Other experts believe the number could reach 110 million.
3. The infection rate of AIDS among women is rising and will pass the rate in men by the year 2000.
4. By the year 2000, AIDS could become the largest epidemic of the century, eclipsing the influenza scourge of 1918. That disaster killed 20 million people, or 1% of the world's population.
5. In the United States, needle sharing and homosexual sex account for 81% of AIDS in adults over 24, but only 77% of cases among 13- to 24-year-old individuals.
6. Heterosexual contact, accounting for 6% of U.S. adult AIDS cases, accounts for 12% of AIDS cases among young people.
7. AIDS strikes 9 times as many men as women in the U.S., but among 13- to 24-year-olds, the male/female ratio is 4 to 1.

There are two parts to Figure 18–1, which illustrates recent data from the Centers for Disease Control. The top graph indicates AIDS cases by geographical region. As noted, the United States is second—fortunately a distant second—to Africa in reported cases of AIDS. With respect to AIDS cases by type of transmission, homosexual sex accounts for the highest number of AIDS cases. However, the number of cases due to intravenous drug use and heterosexual contact is on the rise. This is reflected in Table 18–3, which also notes current data regarding the AIDS epidemic. As emphasized in Table 18–3, there is more and more ominous information emerging regarding AIDS and young people.

SAFE-SEX PRACTICES

Two types of information are presented in this section. Guidelines for the prevention of sexually transmitted disease, suggested in part by Hafen, Thygerson, and Frandsen (1988), are shown in Table 18–4. Safe- and unsafe-sex practices, suggested in the manual by Moffatt, Spiegel, Parrish, and Helquist (1987) and the AIDS Project Los Angeles, are depicted in Table 18–5. No additional explanation is needed for either table. They provide what should be blunt, commonsense guidelines for the prevention of sexually transmitted diseases, including AIDS.

SELF-MANAGEMENT PROJECT

A married student observed that he was having marital difficulties because of premature ejaculation. He elected to use a self-management strategy that consisted of self-monitoring and what he referred to as a

206 Chap. 18 Sexual Behavior

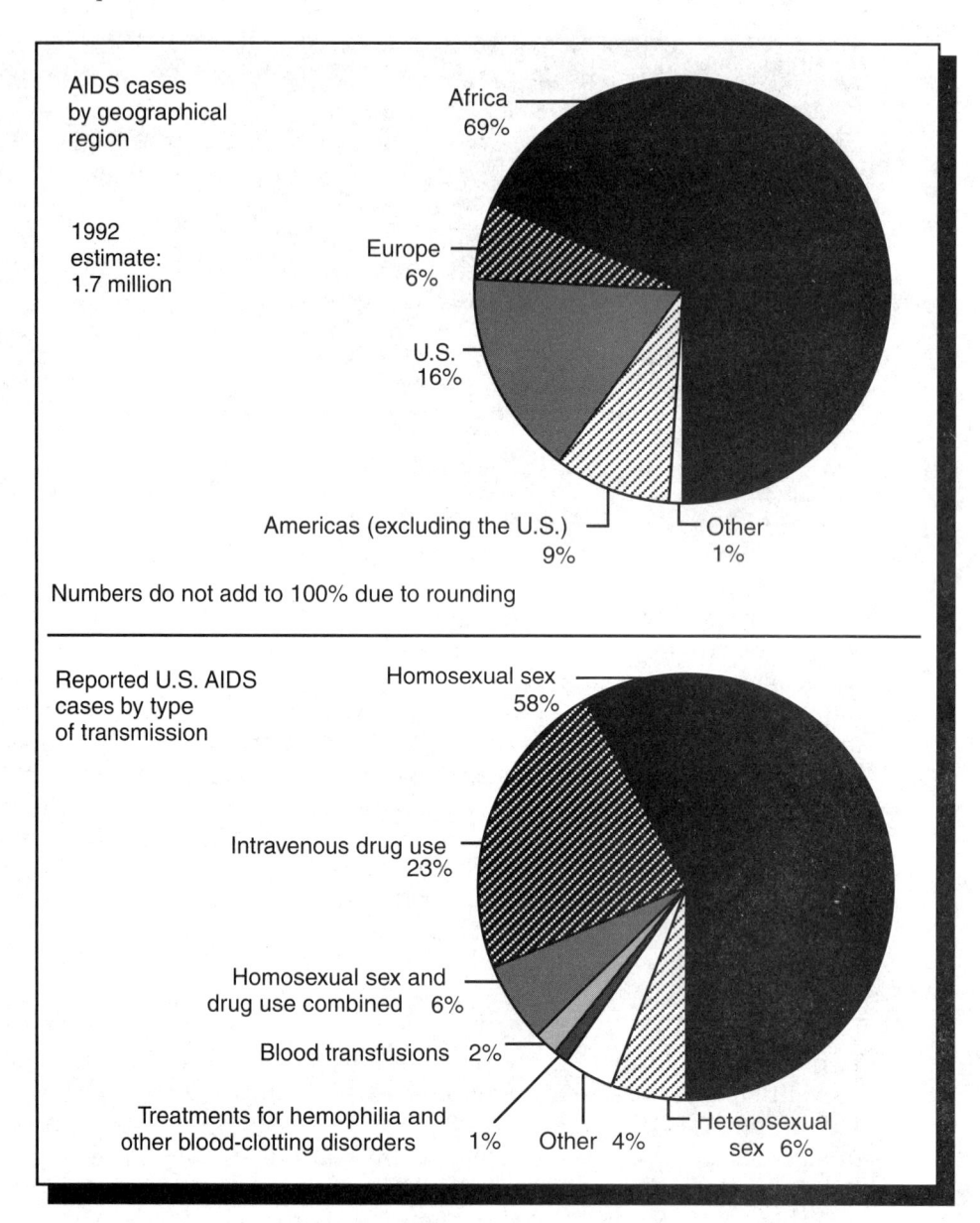

AIDS cases by geographical region

1992 estimate: 1.7 million

- Africa 69%
- Europe 6%
- U.S. 16%
- Americas (excluding the U.S.) 9%
- Other 1%

Numbers do not add to 100% due to rounding

Reported U.S. AIDS cases by type of transmission

- Homosexual sex 58%
- Intravenous drug use 23%
- Homosexual sex and drug use combined 6%
- Blood transfusions 2%
- Treatments for hemophilia and other blood-clotting disorders 1%
- Other 4%
- Heterosexual sex 6%

FIGURE 18–1
Recent information concerning AIDS.

TABLE 18–4   Guidelines for Prevention of Sexually Transmitted Diseases (adapted in part from Hafen, Thygerson, and Frandsen, 1988)

1. Be abstinent.
2. Know your partner.
3. Limit your number of sexual partners.
4. If you are sexually promiscuous, receive periodic checkups from your physician.
5. Use barrier methods of contraception, particularly latex condoms (avoid lambskin/sheepskin condoms).
6. Be certain condoms do not leak, and use them properly to avoid spillage.
7. Abstain from sexual activity if you know you have an infection.
8. Urinate immediately following sexual intercourse.
9. Wash thoroughly immediately following sexual activity.
10. If you suspect your partner is infected, ask.
11. Abstain from sexual relations if you have an illness or disease, since these conditions increase your susceptibility to other infections.
12. Wear loose-fitting clothes made of natural fibers. Tight-fitting clothing can create conditions that encourage growth of bacteria and aggravate sexually transmitted diseases.

TABLE 18–5   Guidelines for Safe Sex (adapted from Moffatt, Spiegel, Parrish, and Helquist, 1987)

Safest Practice
  Abstinence

Safe-Sex Practices
  Massage, hugging, body-to-body rubbing
  Dry social kissing
  Masturbation
  Acting out sexual fantasies without engaging in unsafe-sex practices
  Using own vibrators or other sex toys

Low-Risk Sex Practices (not considered completely safe)
  French (wet) kissing (if neither partner has mouth sores)
  Mutual masturbating or touching each other's genitals (risk may be further reduced by using disposable latex gloves)
  Vaginal or anal intercourse using a condom (use latex, not lambskin condom)
  Oral sex, male (fellatio) using latex condom
  Oral sex, female (cunnilingus) using thin piece of latex between mouth and female organ
  External contact with semen or urine provided there are no breaks in skin

Unsafe-Sex Practices
  Vaginal or anal intercourse without condom
  Semen, urine, or feces in mouth or vagina
  Unprotected oral sex
  Unprotected penetration of vagina or anus with hand or finger
  Oral-anal contact (rimming) or anal penetration with fist (fisting)
  Blood contact of any kind
  Sharing sex toys or needles

208 Chap. 18 *Sexual Behavior*

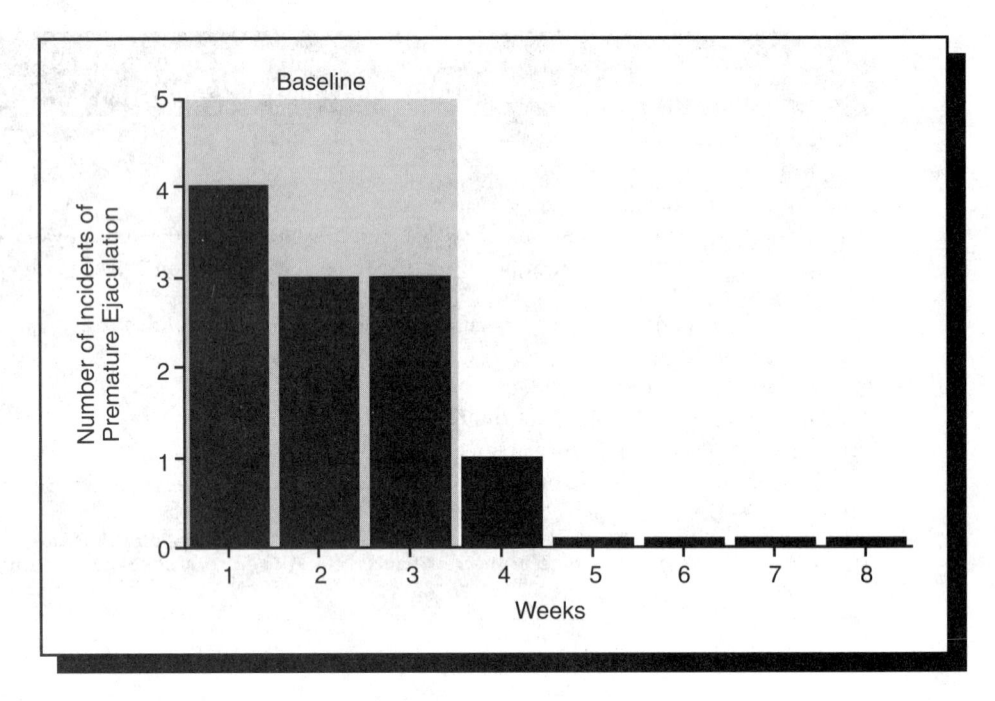

FIGURE 18–2
Controlling premature ejaculation.

combination of thought stopping and distracting thoughts. The results of his project are depicted in Figure 18–2. The strategy he took overcame his problem. He later noted that overcoming his problem of premature ejaculation had strengthened his marriage.

EXERCISE

For almost all of you, sex is or will become a natural part of your life. It should be. At the same time, however, it is important to reaffirm the significance of the consequences of your activity and the role of self-control in guiding your behavior. Thus, the exercise is to ask yourself whether there is any potentially aversive consequence that could occur as a result of any sexually active behavior that involves you.

REVIEW TERMS

Chlamydia
Gonorrhea
Herpes

Seaman's focus
Sensate focus
Vaginismus

QUESTIONS

Describe the two tests used to diagnose HIV.

Describe the two immunological indicators of AIDS.

List twelve guidelines for the prevention of sexually-transmitted diseases.

CHAPTER 19

Sexual Violence

"Rape remains the only crime in which the victims—most often women, but frequently men and children—are stigmatized by others for their victimization and blamed for their participation in an act committed by forcible compulsion."

—Linda A. Fairstein, *Sexual Violence: Our War Against Rape*

"Frank seemed like such a nice guy. Friendly and good looking, you know? My big mistake was dating him. We went to a party at his fraternity. Big mistake. I hardly knew anyone there. The next mistake I made was that I drank too much. I usually don't drink, but Frank told me that I was drinking watered down punch. After a while, I thought I was going to be sick and vomit. Frank said he'd drive me home. The next thing I know, he said he wanted sex. I told him I didn't. It made no difference to him. He came on like an animal, even tearing off part of my dress. I've never been so scared in my life. Afterward, he lightened up and thanked me for agreeing to have sex with him. I never did. Is there anything I can do about this?"

—Debbie, a sophomore

Recently, the National Women's Study estimated that 12.1 million American women had been victims of forcible rape at least once in their life; in addition, it was noted that 61 percent of the victims said they had been raped as minors. There were 683,000 adult women raped in 1990, a figure five times higher than the number of sexual assaults reported for the same year by the Justice Department. Only 22 percent of the women reported they had been raped by strangers; 9 percent said they had been raped by a boyfriend or a former boyfriend. Unfortunately, the data for 1991 are even more alarming: the Justice Department reported a 59 percent increase in rape and attempted rape over 1990 figures. No reliable data is kept concerning the number of men raped each year. Many think men who rape other men are always homosexual, but this is not the case. Most male rapists consider themselves heterosexual. Young boys are not the only victims of rape; the average age of male victims is twenty-four. It is also reported that as many men are raped outside of jail as are raped in jail. Such attacks are simply not reported. Roiphe (1993) noted that according to statistics reported by Harvard University in 1992, a man walking home in Cambridge was more likely to be attacked than a woman.

No one can deny that rape is a reality in today's world. A problem increasingly scrutinized is what is referred to as acquaintance or date rape. This means a woman is raped by a male acquaintance, often someone she thinks she knows and trusts. Acquaintance rape comprises a large number of rapes that occur on all college campuses. How large a problem date rape presents is debatable (Roiphe, 1993). On one hand, it is doubtful that one in four college women, an estimate of some experts, has been the victim of rape or attempted rape. Data that is accumulated and described each year in the *Chronicles of Higher Education*—colleges and universities are required to gather and report this information—fail to support this claim. On the other hand, it is likely that date rape comprises a large number of rapes that do occur on college campuses. This finding would not be unexpected as developing social skills, such as those acquired through dating, is an important aspect of college. The increase in acquaintance rape is probably also higher for freshmen and sophomore students, who, perhaps because they are away from home for the first time, are naive and less sophisticated about how to prevent rape.

Those who discuss the topic, including Roiphe (1993), suggest that women and men have a role in the prevention of rape. What follows are suggestions on how women might avoid becoming a rape statistic. This discussion will be followed by suggestions for men on ways to avoid being raped or being involved with rape.

STRATEGIES FOR WOMEN

There is no sure method to prevent rape. However, unpleasant as the thought may be, it is a wise woman who knows beforehand how she might avoid being raped. Most rape crises and college counseling centers have developed pamphlets and brochures. A number of common suggestions are usually contained in these printed materials. They include:

Know your personality. Know your own personality and your style of responding to a physical assault. Are you self-assured when around men? Can you be assertive if you must? Would you be able to hurt someone if they were trying to hurt you? Only you can answer these questions.

Avoid the wrong kind of men. Many acquaintances or date rapists give off clues or signals about themselves. You should run, not walk, from any man who displays any of the following characteristics:

1. Classic stereotypes. Beware of men who believe they should be dominant and you should be submissive. If a man insists on calling all the shots regarding what you are going to do on dates or eat at restaurants, he is apt to do the same thing when it comes to sex.

2. Emotionally abuses you. If a person abuses you through insults, belittling comments, or ignoring your opinions, drop him. Some experts believe intimidation is a necessary precondition to rape. Emotional abuse is strong evidence of intimidation.

3. Attempts to pressure you. Be wary of a man who pressures you into activities you don't want to engage in while on a date, such as drinking beer or smoking pot. If you go along with what he wants, he may feel that you like the way he treats you.

4. Negative about women. Men who are rapists do not like women. They rape less for sexual satisfaction than because they hate women in general. Avoid such individuals.

5. Easily jealous. Men who attempt to dominate women often become jealous with little reason. Seeing you talk to another man may provoke emotional outbursts. If these occur, it is time to look elsewhere.

6. Drinks heavily or uses drugs. The man who drinks heavily or uses drugs will often attempt to get you under the influence of alcohol or other substances. These are men you should avoid. As described in Chapter 18, avoid binge drinkers.

7. Berates you for not participating in different activities. Men who are potential acquaintance rapists may berate you for not drinking, getting high, having sex, or refusing to go to a personal or isolated place. Most women quickly drop such men.

8. Anger over money. Some men become angry if you offer to share the expenses of a date or offer to pay your way. As these men may attempt to be domineering in other ways, they have zero potential to you.

9. Physically violent to others. If your boyfriend is physically violent to others, even if its just grabbing and pushing you to get his way, you should seriously evaluate the relationship.

10. Acts in intimidating way. Intimidation is a signal given by many potential rapists. If a male friend acts in an intimidating way, such as using his body to block your way or touching when you tell him not to, you will likely want to end the relationship.

11. Can't handle frustration without anger. All of us are frustrated from time to time; frustration can lead to anger. If your male friend is unable to handle sexual or emotional frustration in an appropriate manner, it's time to terminate the relationship.

12. Does not view you as an equal. Dominating men often do not perceive women as equals. They see themselves as smarter or socially superior to you. If your boyfriend does not accept you as an equal, there is no future for you with him.

13. Fascination with weapons. Men who are potential rapists often show a strong fascination with weapons, particularly guns and knives. Be aware of these characteristics and escape from men who exhibit them at your earliest convenience.

14. Cruel to others. It is wise to avoid men who seem to enjoy being cruel to animals, children, or others they can bully.

Wrong places. There are certain settings you want to avoid, since assaults are more likely to occur in isolated spots, such as parked cars, nighttime bars, or the "upstairs" room of a fraternity house. If you don't know your date well, insist on going only to public places, such as restaurants and movie houses.

The following list, offered by rape experts, suggests how you can avoid rape when out alone or at home. When out alone:

1. Be aware of yourself and your surroundings.
2. Know where you are going by planning your route.
3. Walk briskly and confidently, and don't look lost.
4. Vary your routine and walk different routes home, especially at night.
5. If alone, walk in middle of sidewalk and stay on well-lighted streets with pedestrian traffic.
6. If you suspect you are being followed, cross the street, walk in a different direction, and vary your speed.
7. If you are being followed, go to the nearest well-lighted home or business and call a friend, a taxi, or the police.
8. If a car pulls up beside you, stay more than an arm's length away and don't become involved in a long conversation.
9. If a driver persists, record the license number and call the police from the nearest business.
10. Keep a purse, a newspaper, or an umbrella tucked under your arm.
11. Wrap a whistle around your wrist and use it if necessary.
12. If you fear danger, yell "Fire!" or "Police!" and run to nearest lighted place and get in quickly.

When at home, to reduce both rape and other violent crimes:

1. Make certain all entrances are well-lighted.
2. Install dead-bolt locks on all doors.
3. Have locks, shades, blinds, or curtains on all windows.
4. Use only first initial on mailbox and in telephone book.
5. Know your neighbors.
6. Know who is at your door before you open it.
7. When returning home, have your keys in hand.
8. If someone wants to use your telephone, make the call for him or her.
9. If there is a person on the elevator displaying suspicious behavior, push the emergency button and all floor buttons so you can get off as quickly as possible.
10. Hang up on an obscene telephone caller.
11. Notify the telephone company if obscene calls continue.
12. Don't give out personal information over the phone.
13. Avoid using basement laundry rooms when alone, especially at night.
14. Memorize emergency numbers.
15. Teach children caution in answering the phone or the door.

Reduce your risk for rape. There are a number of ways you can reduce your risk of rape including:

1. Set sexual limits and communicate them clearly to your date. Let men know your limits, in no uncertain manner. You don't need to sacrifice your own beliefs to appease anyone.

2. Be assertive. Avoid misleading messages. If a date ignores your limits, act immediately and tell him what you object to. You should ask to go home if he does not abide by your comments.

3. Talk openly about your sexual expectations if appropriate. If you don't want sex at the outset of a relationship, say so. Inform your date of your expectations. Clearly state your feelings and fears.

4. Stay sober. You must stay sober if you suspect your date is attempting to get you drunk. If you believe this is what is occurring, terminate the date and return home. As asked by Roiphe (1993), whose fault is it if you have sexual intercourse while intoxicated? Every woman has some responsibility to prevent becoming intoxicated. In the study by Wechsler and colleagues (1994), described in Chapter 17, 20 percent of the infrequent binge drinkers reported they engaged in unplanned sexual activity; 8 percent of the group reported they did not use protection when having sex. Of the frequent binge drinkers, 42 percent reported they engaged in unplanned sexual activity; 22 percent of the group reported they did not use protection when having sex. Wechsler and colleagues indicated that men and women reported similar frequencies of these problems.

5. Learn about a new date. You should learn as much as you can about someone you are dating for the first time. You may want to double date with friends the first few times you date a particular individual. You should never leave a party alone with someone you don't know.

6. Remain in control. Think and plan what you must do. Take enough money so that you can go home in a cab by yourself if necessary; you should also carry a credit card so that you will not need change to make a call to summon help.

7. Take care of yourself. Self-defense courses are becoming increasingly popular. It is estimated that one in four American women may face the prospect of being raped, so a self-defense course is a worthwhile investment.

8. Trust your feelings. If you notice aspects of a man's behavior that you don't like, trust your instincts and end the date.

Confrontation with a rapist. A self-defense course will help you prepare for confrontation. There are certain suggestions that you should consider if attacked; these include:

1. Stay calm. Try to calm your assailant or persuade him not to attack you by suggesting you go for a drink or a similar activity. Buy time;

Strategies for Women **215**

there is the possibility that you may distract him or that some type of assistance, such as a passing car, can come to your aid.

2. Appraise your situation and act quickly. When confronted with an attacker, think quickly of how you can escape from the situation. The better prepared you are, the more apt you are to be successful.

3. Try to escape. This would be difficult in an isolated area, but if you are around others, you can scream or yell. If in a car, you may attract attention by driving in an illegal or erratic manner. Go down the wrong way of a one-way street, honk the horn and turn on the flashers, or drive up on someone's lawn.

4. Destroy a man's idea of seduction. Cry hysterically, pretend to faint, act insane, or do something disgusting like gagging yourself in order to vomit on the individual; urinate on him if you must.

5. Use whistles or weapons to defend yourself. Many women carry whistles, mace, guns, or knives to protect themselves. Whistles may be of use, but are of little value in an isolated place; the same caveat should be noted with respect to mace. If you are going to use a weapon, it is imperative that you be skillful at using it. Otherwise, the experts caution, the weapon is apt to be used on you.

6. Use physical resistance. Most experts on rape suggest that these behaviors, acquired in a self-defense course, can help you protect yourself. You should go for the man's most vulnerable body parts, including his eyes, ears, nose, mouth, Adam's apple, or groin. The aim is to hurt him enough to give yourself a chance to escape. You can hit a man's ears, chin, or nose as hard as you can with the palm of your hand, you can strike the middle of his throat in a karate chop, stab your fingers into his eyes, or tear at his ears, nose, fingers, throat, or any other body part you can reach. You can kick him hard in the groin; however, if you attempt this tactic, be certain the man is unable to grab your leg and knock you down. If you are grabbed from behind, you may kick back hard on his shins or knees, step hard on his instep, or ram the back of your hand into his nose. If he grabs your arms, rotate them backward and squeeze his thumbs by pressing them against your rib cage. The guiding rule is that whatever type of self-defense you use, you must think it out beforehand and practice it if it is to become effective.

7. Safety comes first. If you believe you will be hurt, such as may occur if the attacker has a knife at your throat, experts suggest that you do not resist. There is agreement among experts that it is better to be raped than to risk being permanently injured or killed. You should not feel guilty for failure to resist; submission does not make the rape any less of a crime.

8. If you are raped, tell someone. Ask for a medical examination as soon as possible. Talk to a female counselor or police officer, if possible, about what occurred.

9. If you have been raped in the past and scarred by the experience, seek professional help.

STRATEGIES FOR MEN

Men may want to change some of their behaviors in order not to become involved in a rape situation. Suggestions include:

1. Don't force a woman to have sex. Even though a woman may initially say she would like sex but later changes her mind, don't force yourself on her. Believe that she has changed her mind.

2. Don't pressure women. Men often see their verbal pressure as more persuasive than do women. Verbal pressure is not a viable method for forcing women to go along with your plans of seduction.

3. Don't buy the myth about drunk women. There is a myth that a drunk woman deserves to be seduced. Don't buy it; it could result in rape charges against you.

4. Stay sober. Stay sober and be in command of your responses.

5. Don't join in a sexual encounter. If a friend or friends invite you to participate in questionable sexual activities, ignore them. Remember that you are as culpable as they are for any aversive consequences.

6. Don't misunderstand scoring. Don't confuse scoring with having a successful sexual encounter. Scoring means that you had a successful social relationship.

7. Don't assume you can read a woman's mind. Never assume that you know what a woman wants (and vice versa). If you want to be involved sexually with a woman, ask her in an unpressured atmosphere. Permit her time to say yes or no.

8. Remember that no means no. Regardless of what you have heard from others, no means no, not yes. You must go on what the woman tells you, not what you or others may think women mean.

9. Speak up. If you feel you are getting a double message from a woman, ask her what she wants. Be direct in making such a request; request a clear and unambiguous answer.

10. Communicate with women. Learn to talk with women about what they want. As noted in Chapter 18, communication is a relevant component in any sexual relationship.

11. Communicate with other men. Most of you have learned about sex from other men. It is important that you continue to communicate with men about sex and women. It is a lifelong process for women to learn about men and for men to learn about women.

12. Take action to avoid male rape. Reduce the chances that you might be raped by another man by reading and following many of the guidelines listed in the previous section.

SELF-MANAGEMENT PROCEDURES FOR AVOIDING RAPE

Preceding sections have described methods for avoiding rape. To repeat these suggestions within the framework of self-management, the following is offered.

1. Stimulus control. The importance of stimulus control was noted in earlier suggestions. Again, both environmental and cognitive stimuli may be involved.

Environmental stimuli. The importance of altering the stimulus, such as avoiding people or contexts where rape could occur, was repeatedly noted. This point probably cannot be overemphasized.

Cognitive stimuli. When there is the potential of rape occurring, consider such strategies as using self-instruction and self-statements, refocusing thinking, and rehearsing what to do if faced with a rape attempt.

2. Self-monitoring. If the potential for rape becomes pronounced, observe your behavior and that of your date carefully. Calmly take action on the basis of your observations. Change your behavior by becoming more assertive. You definitely want to remain in control by keeping sober.

3. Self-defense skills. It was noted that taking a self-defense course was a good investment. The use of a whistle or mace is recommended, provided that you are skilled in the use of mace. Periodic rehearsal of any self-defense technique is also recommended.

4. Problem solving. These skills are useful in preventing rape. Particular skills include: (a) planning ahead, such as by taking a self-defense course; (b) considering all options you might want to take if attacked; (c) rehearsing the plans you are apt to use; (d) acting out plans if required; (e) evaluating your performance in avoiding or escape from a dangerous situation; and (f) considering other alternatives if you believe they are required.

SELF-MANAGEMENT PROJECTS

Two students selected rape-related behavioral problems for self-management. Before starting their projects, they discussed their topics with the instructor. It was suggested that they could be referred to a student counseling center if they wished. However, both reported they had been in counseling two years or more because of the sexual violence perpetuated on them. They concluded that they could learn to control the problems they selected through self-management.

Figure 19–1 depicts the program developed by a woman who had been sexually molested by a family member. Although she had been in therapy for a period, she found she tended to be manipulative toward male friends. This behavior, she concluded, jeopardized her chances of having a deep and long-term relationship. After gathering baseline data, she used a combination of approaches, centered around self-monitoring

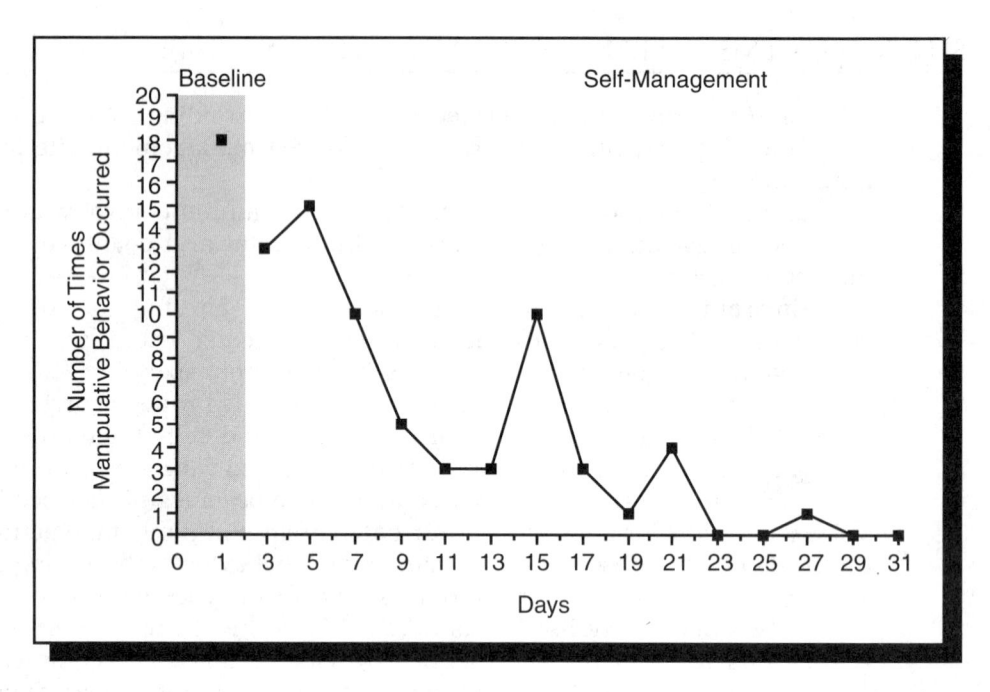

FIGURE 19–1
Self-management to eliminate manipulative behavior.

and cognitive restructuring, to change her behavior. As noted, her program was a major success.

The student whose data are shown in Figure 19–2 had also been a victim of sexual abuse. After undergoing counseling, she appeared to recover from the situation. However, she noted that she had recently began experiencing nightmares, a situation she linked to the trauma of sexual abuse. Her reactions are not uncommon: it is increasingly recognized that victims of rape may experience posttraumatic stress disorder (PTSD), an anxiety disorder characterized by instrusive memories of the traumatic incident, emotional withdrawal, and increased anxiety and arousal levels. PTSD may occur anytime following the traumatic incident, including years later. In this case, the student noted that she experienced a number of nightmares each week. After baseline data was gathered, she used self-management skills, including relaxation and self-monitoring, in an attempt to decrease the nightmares she experienced. She also altered environmental stimuli by listening to soft music while trying to go to sleep at night. The student concluded that her program was neither a success nor failure. She noted that she had performed self-management skills for only 6 weeks, and the program would require more time to be a success. Months later, she reported that she no longer experienced nightmares. She credited her success to a continuation of her self-management program and to a serious relationship that was developing with her boyfriend.

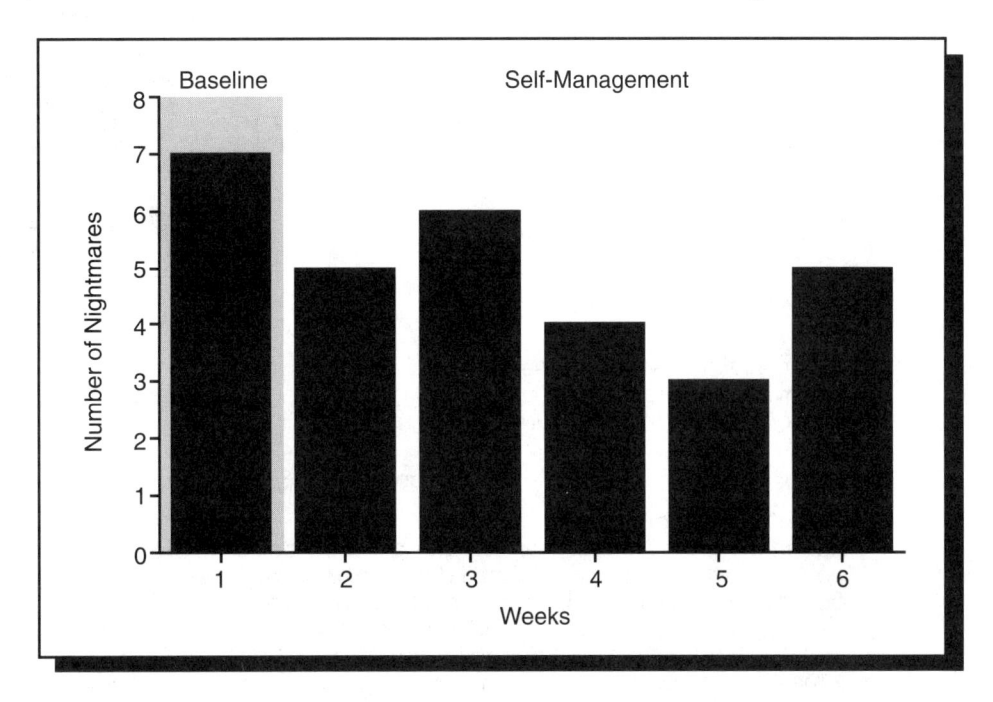

FIGURE 19-2
Self-management to decrease number of nightmares.

EXERCISE

Are you a woman who is involved in a relationship that could result in acquaintance rape? If you believe you are, consider how to terminate this relationship.

Are you a man who has been in situations where you have thought you might have been sexually attacked by another male? If this is the case, prepare to avoid the possibility of such attacks occurring in future situations.

Whether you are a man or woman, seriously consider taking a self-defense course.

REVIEW TERMS

Acquaintance rape
Myth of drunken women
PTSD

QUESTIONS

List seven suggestions of what to do if confronted with a rapist.
List twelve suggestions for men of how not to be involved in a rape situation.

Sexual Harassment

CHAPTER 20

> "Since Christianity upped the ante and concentrated on sexual behavior as the root of virtue, everything pertaining to sex has been a 'special case' in our culture, evoking peculiarly inconsistent attitudes."
>
> —Susan Sontag, *Styles of Radical Will*

> "I don't have a great deal of interest in the feminism movement. Hell, many feminists think that just having a man look at you in a certain way is sexual harassment. I disagree. However, I really couldn't put up with my boss's crap. I told him to knock it off when he kept making comments about my body and wanting to go to a motel with me. When he pinched me on the rear, I'd had it. I just turned around and belted him across the face. His boss had come around the corner and saw the whole episode. I would have eventually brought sexual harassment charges against the dummy had he kept it up, but he was fired when his boss saw what happened. I work for a woman now."
>
> —Sondra, an office worker

Many Americans sat spellbound through part of the confirmation hearings of Clarence Thomas. They were particularly interested in the testimony of Anita Hill and her comments about Thomas. The episode became a sideshow in what were otherwise dull hearings. However, many people learned about what constitutes sexual harassment in these hearings. Most viewers of the confirmation hearings concluded that they did not know who to believe, Clarence Thomas or his accuser, Anita Hill. They discovered that sexual harassment is generally one person's word against another's.

Sexual harassment is any unwelcome sexual advance or conduct that creates an intimidating, hostile, or offensive working environment (Petrocelli and Repa, 1992). It results from a misuse of power, not from sexual attraction. Factors such as violence, economics, and discrimination as a form of control fuel harassment. There are a number of myths about sexual harassment.

Myth 1. Some people ask to be sexually harassed. Myths such as "she or he wore provocative clothing" and "he or she enjoyed it" are neither accurate nor acceptable. It is doubtful if any of you dress in a certain way to provoke sexual harassment; it is certainly not an experience that anyone enjoys, with the possible exception of whoever is doing the harassing.

Myth 2. If a person wanted to discourage sexual harassment, she or he could. As many who harass are in a position of authority and can punish someone by withholding a promotion or pay raise, it may be difficult for you to confront or discourage the harasser.

Myth 3. Most charges of sexual harassment are false. Charges of sexual harassment may occasionally be false. You might think you could "get back" at someone by accusations of harassment. What would you gain, however, from filing false charges? Confronting the harasser can be both physically and financially draining to you. In addition, those who file false charges often endure greater risk to themselves and their careers when their charges are disproven.

Myth 4. Sexual harassment is inevitable when men and women are working together. As most of you have worked at different jobs where women and men work together, you know this statement is a myth.

Myth 5. If you ignore sexual harassment, it will go away. This approach generally does little; if anything, ignoring sexual harassment encourages the harasser to continue his or her attempts to harass you. Confronting the person tends to make things better in the majority of cases.

The legal definition of sexual harassment is found in Table 20-1. As

TABLE 20-1 What Is Sexual Harassment?

The Equal Employment Opportunity Commission guidelines define two types of sexual harassment. Both are illegal under Title VII of the Civil Rights Act of 1964. The types are:

1. **Quid Pro Quo** (Something given or received for something else).
   This occurs when an employee is subject to unwelcome sexual advances and submission to them is made the basis for hiring, advancement, firing, and the like.
2. **Environment**
   This occurs when any type of unwelcome sexual behavior creates a hostile work environment.

Examples of Sexual Harassment

1. Unsolicited and unwelcome flirtations, advances, or propositions
2. Graphic or degrading comments about employee's appearance, dress, and anatomy
3. Display of sexually suggestive objects or pictures
4. Sexual or intrusive questions about employee's personal life
5. Explicit description of the harasser's own sexual experiences
6. Abuse of familiarities such as "honey," "baby," or "dear"
7. Unnecessary and unwanted physical contact such as touching, hugging, pinching, patting, and kissing
8. Whistling or catcalls
9. Leering
10. Exposing genitalia
11. Physical or sexual assault
12. Rape

noted, it is contained within the Civil Rights Act of 1964. Ironically, the clause was added because opponents of the Civil Rights Act thought the clause would derail the law. It did not. In fact, as noted in Table 20–2, the legal definition of the law has continued to evolve.

As sexual harassment is an all too common phenomenon in the United States for both women and men, you need to perform self-management skills if you believe you are being discriminated against because of sex. Despite recent decisions of the U.S. Supreme Court that have liberalized making complaints regarding harassment, you may want to consider the following advice for making your case. The advice includes suggestions by Petrocelli and Repa (1992).

Observe the situation. If you believe you are being harassed, make careful observations of the behavior you think constitutes the harassment. Use the guidelines provided in Table 20–1 to assist you.

Record observations. Perhaps the most important part of proving a case of sexual harassment is keeping detailed and accurate notes of what you think is occurring. A detailed journal of your observations is particularly useful. Petrocelli and Repa suggest that you save any offensive letters, photographs, or notes you receive. If you feel uncomfortable because of posted jokes or pinups, confiscate or make copies of them. If your employer has evaluations of your work, be certain you have copies. You will want your entire personnel file if you are considering making formal charges. Remember that the more reliable and valid your data, the greater the probability you can prove sexual harassment.

Obtain collaborating evidence. If you think you are being harassed, obtain evidence from others to support your case. You may wish to consult with friends and coworkers. If the harassment is pervasive, organize

TABLE 20–2 The Evolution of the Legal Definition of Sexual Harassment (adapted from *Time*, June 6, 1994)

1964	Civil Rights Act of 1964 is enacted.
1975	First reported sexual-harassment decision under the Civil Rights Act of 1964. A federal court in Arizona rules that the law does not cover a suit brought by two women who claimed they suffered verbal and physical abuse from a supervisor.
1977	Federal appeals court in Washington rules that sexual harassment is discrimination under the act in the case of a woman who claimed her job was abolished because she refused her supervisor's sexual advances.
1980	U.S. Equal Employment Opportunities Commission (EEOC) issues landmark sexual harassment guidelines.
1986	U.S. Supreme Court upholds validity of the EEOC guidelines that sexual harassment that leads to a hostile or abusive work environment is a violation of the law.
1991	Florida federal district court rules nude pinups in the workplace can create an atmosphere that constitutes sexual harassment.
1993	U.S. Supreme Court rules that a hostile work environment need not be psychologically injurious but only reasonably perceived as abusive.

a group. Several simultaneous complaints of harassment are more effective than a single complaint. Any information that will independently support the data you gather through self-monitoring will improve your chances of resolving the harassment you experience.

Put evidence together. Before making any charges, be certain that you have all of your evidence assembled in an orderly manner. This will later help you in presenting your case.

Go through established channels. Most organizations have established channels you should go through if you wish to make formal sexual harassment charges. Learn what these channels are and follow prescribed procedures. Usually, this process will expedite the resolution of your complaint; if it does not, you may seek another recourse.

Be resolute. At the beginning, remember that any chances of your complaint succeeding ultimately depend upon you and no one else. You alone have suffered what you consider sexual harassment. Accordingly, only you can put together the evidence to support the case you may bring against an individual or organization. Before expending what may be considerable time and effort in making your case, be certain that you want to follow through with your formal complaint.

WAYS TO END SEXUAL HARASSMENT

William Petrocelli and Barbara Kate Repa are both attorneys. In their book, *Sexual Harassment on the Job* (1992), they list the following approaches you can take to end what you perceive to be sexual harassment:

Confronting the harasser. The best strategy for you is to confront the harasser and persuade him or her to stop. This may not be appropriate in all cases, however, particularly if you have suffered injuries or are in some danger. The approach does work in the majority of cases.

Using company complaint procedure. An increasing number of companies have policies against sexual harassment. Petrocelli and Repa point out that you may file a complaint under the company procedure immediately, or you can use the procedure as the next step if your confrontation of the harasser does not produce satisfactory results.

Filing a complaint with a government agency. If sexual harassment does not end with implementation of either of the above approaches, you may file a complaint under the U.S. Civil Rights Act with the U.S. Equal Employment Opportunities Commission (EEOC) or under similar state law with a state or local fair employment practice (FEP) agency. In some cases, these agencies can resolve a dispute between you and a harasser with no cost to you, and with relatively little legal involvement on your part.

Filing a lawsuit under the Civil Rights Act or FEP laws. If all attempts fail to produce satisfactory results, you may wish to file a lawsuit for damages under the Civil Rights Act or under one of the state FEP statutes.

Even if you intend from the beginning to file a lawsuit, you often must first file a claim with a government agency.

Filing a common law tort suit. Petrocelli and Repa note that if sexual harassment has resulted in severe injuries, you should consult an attorney. You can then skip all of the above steps and file a lawsuit for damages based on the basis of intentional infliction of emotional harm or wrongful discharge. Common law torts are generally best suited for those who have been seriously injured because you must not only prove the harasser's conduct was truly outrageous, but because such action is costly in time and money.

SELF-MANAGEMENT OF SEXUAL HARASSMENT

There are individuals who, for whatever reason, would prefer to consider other options rather than bring sexual harassment charges against another person. If you include yourself in this category, consider the following:

1. Stimulus change. There are both environmental and cognitive changes that you can make with respect to stimuli surrounding the setting where harassment occurs.

Environmental changes. You might consider avoiding or escaping from the individual you believe is harassing you. Request working in another section of a firm or with someone else if it is an employer. If you believe that bringing charges is not worth the hassle, you might consider another career option.

Cognitive changes. You should always keep calm when harassed, even if it is difficult to do so. Use self-instruction and self-statements to achieve this aim. Become more assertive when confronted with the person you believe is harassing you. Plan beforehand how you might handle a situation and rehearse your strategy. Finally, learn and keep abreast of governmental and company policies regarding sexual harassment in the event that you do seek a legal remedy.

2. Self-monitoring. As it is apt to be your word against that of another, it is imperative that you observe and record aspects of the harassment and your responses to the situation. Be certain to: (a) record detailed information; (b) secure collaborating evidence if possible; (c) record and maintain the evidence in an orderly fashion; and (d) go through the proper channels as outlined by your organization.

3. Problem solving. As harassment can be a major problem, it is important to consider how to solve it. Consider: (a) planning your strategy out beforehand; (b) gathering accurate information; (c) rehearsing your plan; (d) acting on the tactics you have decided to employ; (e) evaluating the effectiveness of your strategy; and (f) preparing for any setbacks. Despite recent rulings of the U.S. Supreme Court, the burden of proof is

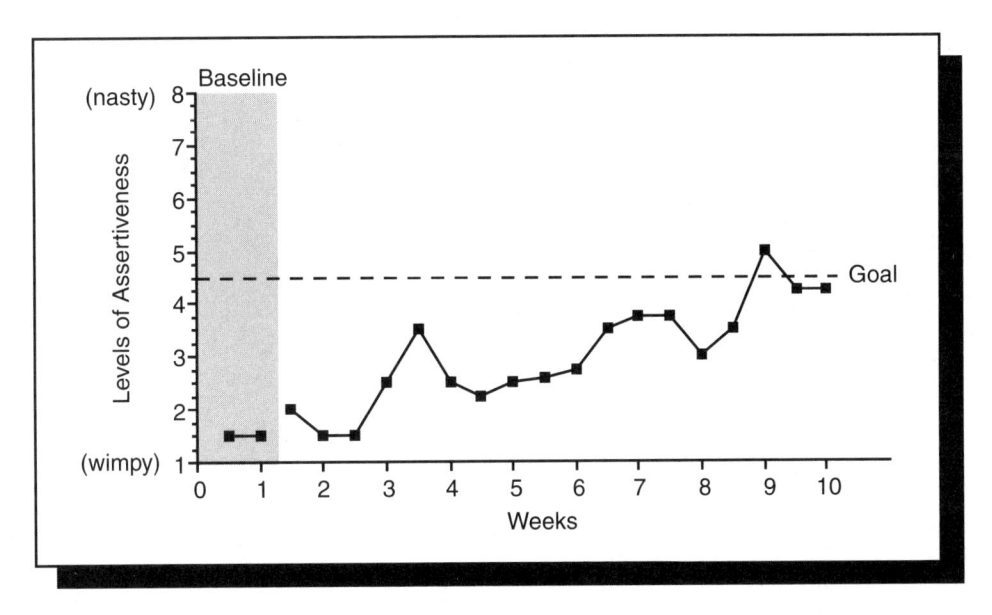

FIGURE 20–1
Performing self-management skills to increase assertiveness and reduce harassment.

likely to be on you. The better prepared you are, the greater the probability of success. At all times, however, remain resolute.

SELF-MANAGEMENT PROJECT

A student was concerned because she was not assertive around people she thought were constantly harassing her, including employers. After she collected baseline data, she increased her assertiveness by performing a combination of self-management skills including self-monitoring, positive self-statements, and negative reinforcement. As depicted in Figure 20–1, the program proved highly effective at improving the woman's assertiveness. The increase in assertiveness was accompanied by a decrease in harassment on the job.

EXERCISE

If you believe that you are experiencing sexual harassment, define the problem as precisely as you can.

Initiate self-monitoring procedures.

Assemble additional evidence to support the data you gathered through self-monitoring.

Proceed through formal channels to make your case.

REVIEW TERMS

Civil Rights Act of 1964　　　　　FEP
EEOC　　　　　　　　　　　　　　Quid pro quo

QUESTIONS

List twelve examples of sexual harassment.
Discuss six myths regarding sexual harassment.
Describe six guidelines for determining if sexual harassment has occurred to you.

CHAPTER 21

Shyness and Assertiveness

"As if it harm'd me, giving others the same chances and rights as myself—as if it were not indispensable to my own rights that others possess the same."

—Walt Whitman, *Thoughts*

"I hate my roommates. They leave the place looking like a dump. They never pick up anything or vacuum. There are always dirty dishes scattered around the house. They take the food that I buy from the refrigerator and never tell me until I find it gone. I wish I could tell them how I feel, but I just can't."

—Paula, a junior

How many times do you wish you had said something when someone crowded ahead of you in a theater line or blamed you for something that was not your fault? All of us have had these experiences. We may later become angry at ourselves or those around us because we did not express ourselves when we were in the right. In these situations, we showed a lack of assertiveness. You do not want to be overly aggressive in expressing your views, as you are bound to discover if you ride with New York cabdrivers a few times; at the same time, you have a perfect right to express your views in any situation. Assertiveness involves your acting in your best interests by directly and honestly expressing your thoughts and feelings without violating the rights of others. It is verbal behavior that expresses your rights without generating feelings of aggression. It is preferable to submissive behavior, where you consistently give in to others, or aggressive behavior where you act to harm someone. A more comprehensive definition was proposed by Alberti and Emmons (1990):

> "Assertive behavior promotes equality in human relationships, enabling us to act in our own best interests, to stand up for ourselves without undue anxiety, to express honest feelings comfortably, to exercise personal rights without denying the rights of others" (p. 7).

All of us like to believe we can be assertive when we need to be. We recognize that being assertive is the right of each of us. It permits us to express

TABLE 21-1 Signs and Symptoms of Inferiority
1. Too sensitive to criticism
2. Overreact to praise and flattery
3. Overly critical of self
4. Tendency to blame others for own shortcomings
5. Negative feelings towards competition
6. Easily influenced and persuaded
7. Seclusive, timid, and shy
8. Feelings of persecution
9. Neurotic need for perfection

ourselves in an appropriate and positive way while respecting the rights of others.

REASONS FOR LACK OF ASSERTIVENESS

Many of us have never learned to be assertive, although we can acquire this pattern of behavior through learning and practice. Some of us may lack assertiveness because of other factors. Perhaps we have strong feelings of inferiority. Signs and symptoms of inferiority are listed in Table 21-1. If any of these factors pertain to you, take one factor at a time and attempt to change it through self-management. If your program fails to work, you might seek professional counseling or assistance. Some of you may be extremely shy. You may wish to overcome your shyness before embarking on a self-management program to increase assertiveness. Or, you may design a self-management program to decrease shyness and increase assertiveness.

SHYNESS

Shyness refers to discomfort, inhibition, and extreme caution in interpersonal relations (Zimbardo, 1977). Shy people tend to be timid about expressing themselves, overly self-conscious, and easily embarrassed, and occasionally to experience physiological symptoms of anxiety. Studies by Zimbardo indicate that 80 percent of respondents indicate they have been shy sometime in their life; over 40 percent indicated they were presently troubled by their shyness.

Dealing with Shyness

If shyness is a major impediment to your attaining the goals you seek in life, you might consider the following strategies.

Analyze your shyness. Zimbardo suggests that you analyze why you are shy and attempt to pinpoint what situations make you shy. He thought a number of reasons or combinations of reasons could contribute to shyness. He cited eight reasons as contributing to shyness: (1) concern about negative evaluation, (2) fear of rejection, (3) lack of self-confidence, (4) lack of social skills, (5) fear of intimacy, (6) preference for being alone, (7) emphasis on and enjoyment of nonsocial activities, and (8) personal inadequacy.

Build your self-esteem. Zimbardo speculates that shy people lack self-confidence or self-esteem. He suggests fifteen steps that could make you more confident, as enumerated in Table 21–2. They are useful suggestions for decreasing shyness and increasing assertiveness.

Improve your social skills. A number of procedures can be introduced to overcome shyness. These include:

1. Rehearse positive behaviors. Using strategies suggested in the book, rehearse how you want to act or what you want to say in a given situation. Write a description of the behaviors you want to rehearse. You can rehearse your script by yourself in front of a mirror or a friend.

TABLE 21–2 Fifteen Suggestions for Becoming More Confident (adapted from Zimbardo, 1977)

1. Recognize your strengths and weaknesses; set your goals accordingly.
2. Decide what you value, what you believe in, and what you realistically would like your life to be like.
3. Determine your roots and build on past successes.
4. Don't allow guilt and shame to shape your behavior.
5. Look for the causes of your behavior in the present and not as a personality defect in yourself.
6. Remind yourself that there are alternative views to every event.
7. Never say bad things about yourself.
8. Don't allow others to criticize you as a person; only your specific actions are open to evaluation.
9. Remind yourself that failure and disappointment are sometimes blessings in disguise.
10. Don't tolerate people, jobs, or situations that make you feel inadequate.
11. Give yourself time to relax, to meditate, to listen to yourself, and to enjoy activities that you can do alone.
12. Practice being a social animal.
13. Stop being overprotective of your ego; it is tougher and more resilient than you think.
14. Develop long-range goals in life with highly specific short-range subgoals.
15. You are not an object to which bad things just happen. You are a unique person who makes things happen. You can change your life if you wish to. With self-confidence, obstacles turn into challenges and challenges into accomplishments. Shyness recedes, and you become absorbed in the living of your life.

2. Focus on strong points. Attempt to emphasize your strong points. Don't dwell on what you or others perceive as your weaknesses or failures, but concentrate on turning flaws into stepping stones for stronger, more positive responses.

3. Practice smiling and making eye contact. You can learn to develop these behaviors by performing before a mirror, then practicing with friends and acquaintances, and finally, by initiating interactions with strangers.

4. Work on speech. A tape recorder will permit you to record samples of your voice. After listening to the recorded tapes, you can develop and practice new ways of talking to others. You can monitor your progress through additional tape recordings.

5. Observe others. You can watch how others are assertive in different situations. They can serve as a model for you. Imitate those who seem particularly appropriate at obtaining their wishes without becoming obnoxious. You will notice they are able to laugh at themselves when they make errors, rather than make self-deprecating comments about their behavior.

6. You are not alone. As noted, surveys indicate that at least four out of every five people have been or are shy. You may want to join other shy people with whom you can develop and practice a program; together, you can rehearse your strategies for overcoming shyness (Zimbardo, 1977).

7. Be your "true self." Don't try to hide your true self; accept who you are. Think of the characteristics and peculiarities as special traits that make you distinctive.

8. When with others, focus on them. Listen to what others are saying instead of attending to what you may be thinking about them, or what they may be thinking of you.

9. Use imagery. Use imagery to visualize yourself doing what you want to do and being successful.

10. Practice relaxation and other self-management techniques to enhance your ability to manage stress.

11. Avoid relying on alcohol or drugs to relax.

These are a few suggestions for overcoming shyness. Other exercises are found in the excellent book *Shyness* (Zimbardo, 1977), which presents a number of proven methods for becoming less shy and more assertive.

BECOMING ASSERTIVE

Robert Alberti and Michael Emmons published *Your Perfect Right* in 1970. It has since undergone several revisions and sold millions of copies; it has become something of a bible for learning to become more assertive. In a recent edition of their book, Alberti and Emmons (1990) describe seventeen steps for increasing assertiveness. These are similar to many of the self-management techniques you have learned:

1. Observe your behavior. Observation has been repeatedly cited as the cornerstone of self-management. It is required if you decide to increase your assertiveness.

2. Keep track of your assertiveness. Recording information on your behavior is, along with self-observation, the other part of self-monitoring.

3. Set realistic goals. If you decide to increase your assertiveness, be realistic in the goals that you set. You can't expect to become assertive overnight; it takes time and an effective program.

4. Concentrate on a particular situation. It will help you develop assertive behaviors if you concentrate on performing such behaviors in a given situation or context. Use imagery to rehearse how you want to react assertively in given circumstances.

5. Review responses. Regular review of the progress you record on your graph provides you with feedback as to where you are toward achieving your goals.

6. Observe an effective model. Whenever you attempt to acquire a new behavior, it is helpful to observe someone skilled at performing the competencies you wish to acquire. With assertiveness, you want to imitate the actions of an individual you think is especially appropriate and effective in being assertive.

7. Consider alternative responses. If the particular method you select does not produce the behavioral change you anticipate, think of alternatives you might introduce to achieve your goals. If you have these alternatives developed beforehand, you can quickly shift to an alternate plan without becoming frustrated and giving up your efforts.

8. Imagine your handling of situations. You usually know in advance those situations that require assertiveness. Perhaps you are going to see an instructor to protest a grade or an employer to seek a pay raise. You should plan, imagine, and rehearse the tactics you plan on using before these situations occur.

9. Practice positive thoughts. In earlier chapters, it was noted that thoughts, either negative or positive, guide your performance. If you expect to become assertive, you must think positively about the steps you will perform in order to be successful.

10. Get help if needed. You can bounce any ideas you have off friends or roommates. They may help you rehearse the strategies you are considering. If these approaches don't work, there are alternatives, such as courses on learning to become assertive or brief problem-solving counseling.

11. Try it out. You have nothing to lose in trying out a strategy or technique. If you planned carefully, the approach you take will likely succeed; if it does not, you can drop back and use one of the alternative plans you have developed. Failure is better than not doing anything.

12. Get feedback. You should obtain feedback not only from regular perusal of your graphs, but from your friends and roommates.

13. Shape your behavior. Remember that you did not become nonassertive overnight; it took years for you to reach this state. Thus, you cannot expect to become assertive in a rapid manner. You need to take one step at a time and gradually shape your behavior to the point where you perceive yourself as assertive.

14. The real test. The real test comes when you are actually assertive when confronting someone, such as a boss, a bullying roommate, or an instructor. Remember that you merely want to exercise your right as a human being by being assertive.

15. Evaluate the test. Analyze your performance to determine if you performed assertively in the test you selected. You may use a recorder to record your performance or receive feedback from a friend who observed your behavior.

16. Further reading. If you would like to read more on learning to become assertive, the best place to start is with a number of other books on assertiveness, aimed at people such as you, available at any bookstore.

17. Social reinforcement. By being responsibly assertive, you will gain the respect of those around you. This, in itself, will be reinforcing to you. Equally important is the fact that you will begin to realize that you can cope with more and more situations in an assertive manner.

SELF-MANAGEMENT AND ASSERTIVENESS

Davis, Eshelman, and McKay (1982) recommended use of what they refer to as the LADDER approach. (LADDER is an acronym formed by the first letter of each step.) This approach is an excellent method to use for increasing assertiveness in specific situations. The procedure is as follows:

Look at the situation. You need to be specific in describing your rights and goals in a situation. Martin and Osborne (1989) suggest that you be certain *who* the interaction is with, *when* it typically occurs, *what* the subject matter is, *how* you usually respond, your *fears* of what will happen if you are assertive, and your *goal*.

Arrange a time. Rehearse the approach you are going to take in managing a situation. Then arrange a time when you can discuss your problem with the appropriate individual. You should be prepared for any outcome that may arise before you arrange the time where you will need to be assertive.

Define the problem. Before you are assertive, be certain to specify the problem as precisely as you can. This will not only provide you with increased confidence, but it will enhance your abilities to communicate with the other person.

Describe your feelings. Be certain that you describe your feelings in your own words. Use personal pronouns in presenting your case.

Express your request. You should plan beforehand to use only one or two simple and specific questions to express your request. This will accentuate the impact of your message.

Reinforce. Reinforce your listener. Let him or her know the good that may come from complying with the request. If the individual agrees with you, thank him or her in a simple and sincere manner.

For most individuals, the LADDER approach should be effective in helping you be assertive in a situation that requires responsible assertiveness. Even if you elect not to choose assertion as a project, you may still find that this exercise can be of value to you in the future.

SELF-MANAGEMENT PROCEDURES FOR CONTROLLING SHYNESS AND INCREASING ASSERTIVENESS

Procedures used to increase assertiveness can also be used to decrease shyness. In addition, the following steps might be considered:

1. Stimulus control. Both enviromental and cognitive stimuli can be changed to decrease shyness and increase assertiveness.

Environmental changes. If you want to reduce the shyness you experience, it is imperative that you be around people. Consider the social activities you enjoy and begin to engage in them. You may also think of other things that you have always wanted to do but thought yourself too shy to do. College is an excellent time not only to be involved in a number of activities, many of which you may never have had a time to pursue, but to expose yourself to others. Careful analysis and consideration of your goals will likely lead you to alter the environment in some manner to take advantage of college and decrease your shyness.

Cognitive changes. There are a number of cognitive changes you can take to decrease shyness. These include: (a) using self-instruction, including self-statements, when in a situation that induces shyness on your part; (b) focusing your thinking so that you begin to become less shy in situations that formerly produced such a reaction; (c) using relaxation when in social situations; (d) using self-desensitization to overcome the feelings you consider as reflective of shyness; (e) rehearsing how you will interact with others before you do so; and (f) modeling those who do not seem to be shy around others.

2. Self-monitoring. Attempt to evaluate honestly your performance when around others. Don't be too critical of yourself; remember that everyone is shy in different situations. Look at how you respond to different stimuli and different situations. The aim here is to promote generation of your behavior across settings.

3. Self-reinforcement. Reinforce yourself when you behave in a more outgoing and assertive manner in contexts where you were usually shy.

4. Problem solving. Problem-solving skills are useful in planning how you will defeat your feelings of being shy. These skills include: (a) planning on how you will respond to stimuli that generate shyness; (b) considering the options that you have in a given situation; (c) rehearsing the strategy you have selected, possibly with your friends or roommates; (d) acting on plans; (e) evaluating your performance; (f) preparing for any setbacks; (g) considering other alternatives you might pursue; and (h) asking others for feedback on your efforts.

SELF-MANAGEMENT PROJECTS

A number of students have selected increased assertiveness as a project. Unfortunately, a few give up on their projects because they do not quickly achieve the success they wish. Those who have followed their projects through to fruition were all proud of the change they produced in themselves. Figure 21–1 indicates the success made by a student

FIGURE 21–1
Use of self-monitoring in different situations to increase assertiveness.

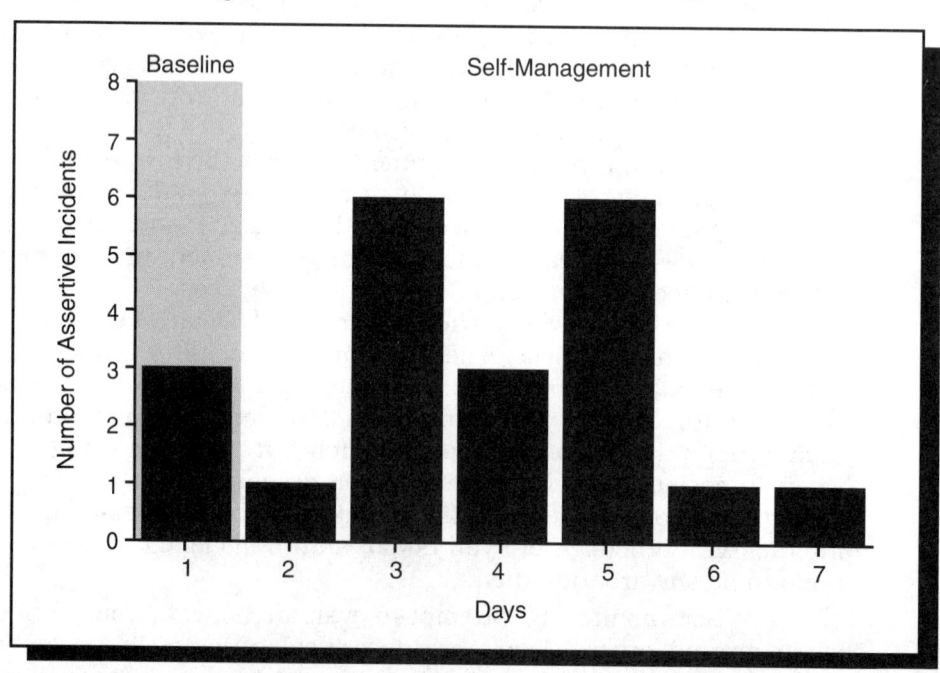

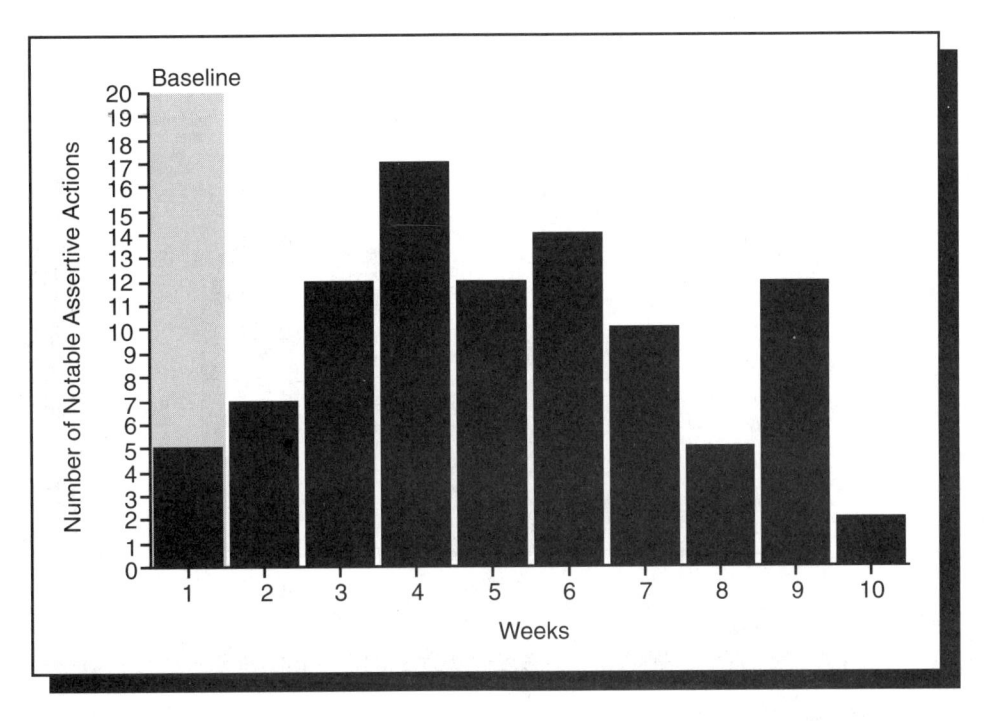

FIGURE 21–2
Use of self-monitoring to increase assertiveness.

who attempted to be more assertive by using self-monitoring in different situations. She kept a diary and noted each time she was responsibly assertive. She found a number of good things happened to her each time she was assertive. She not only began to control her life vis-à-vis her friends, particularly by learning to say no to activities in which she did not want to participate, but she acquired a job and improved her grades. Figure 21–2 depicts similar success experienced by a student who utilized self-monitoring. He improved his assertiveness in the classroom, on the job, and in various activities in which he was involved. The results shown in Figure 21–3 were reported by a student who used the LADDER approach to increase her assertiveness. As indicated, she attained the goal she set for herself at the beginning of the program. Figures 21–1, 21–2, and 21–3 do not show continuous change over time as there were only so many opportunities for the students to practice being assertive; thus, their data indicate that assertiveness is, in part, a function of the number of settings that occur where the behavior was required. This accounts for the variability reflected in the students' behavior.

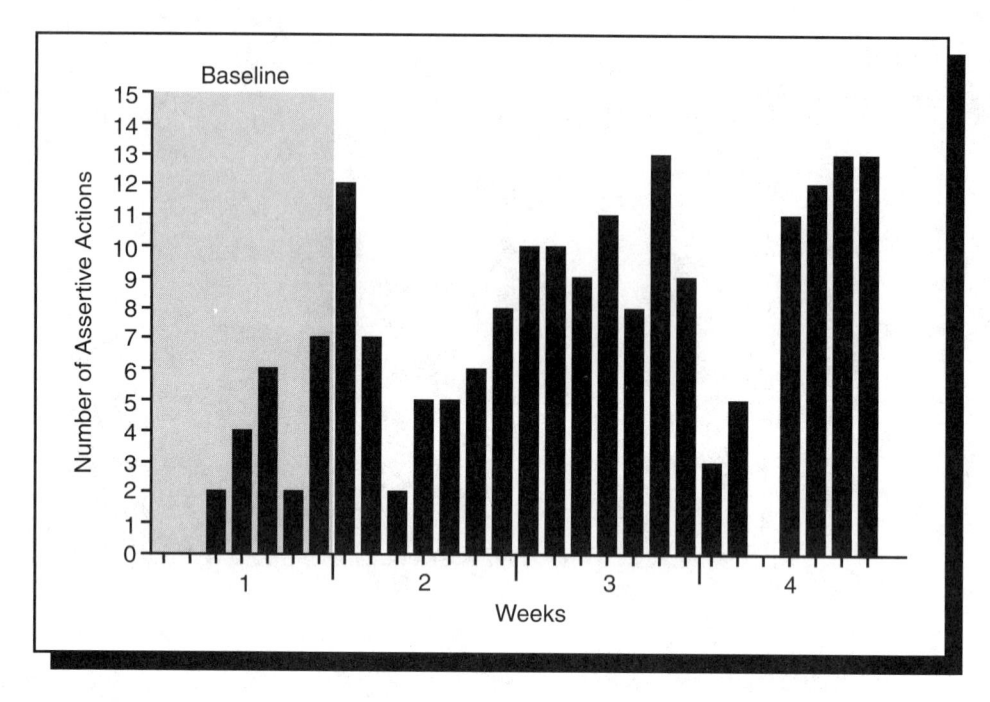

FIGURE 21-3
Use of LADDER technique to increase assertiveness.

EXERCISE

Use the LADDER technique to analyze a situation where you might become more assertive:

Look at the situation:
Arrange a time:
Define the problem as precisely as you can:
Describe your feelings:
Express your request:
Reinforce yourself and others:

REVIEW TERMS

Assertive behavior
Assertiveness

Shyness
Your Perfect Right

QUESTIONS

List fifteen suggestions for becoming more confident.
Describe fifteen steps for increasing assertiveness.
Discuss the LADDER method of increasing assertiveness through self-management.

CHAPTER 22

Friends

"Each friend represents a world in us, a world possibly not born until they arrive, and it is only by this meeting that a new world is born."
—Anaïs Nin, *The Diary of Anaïs Nin*

"My friends have always meant a great deal to me. I still meet monthly with friends I have had since grade school. They have always been there for me. I hope I have always been there when they have needed me. I really valued my friends when my husband, George, died. They gave me support when I needed it most. I don't know what I would have done without them."
—Grace, an elderly widow

Entering college is a shock to many students. They are used to living with only a few people and, sometimes, having a room to themselves. Many students relish the space they have in such environments. When arriving at college, however, they are put into contact with a number of people with diverse behaviors. Students constantly share living space with others; they quickly learn about others' habits whether it be in music or personal hygiene. Most students are malleable and adapt to changes in their life. The privacy and personal space many enjoyed may become nothing more than a fond memory.

A function of college experiences is to provide you with opportunities to learn about others. Perhaps more important, you are able to develop new friendships. Many of the friendships you develop are special relationships that will endure for the remainder of your life. This aspect of college is reaffirmed each year during Homecoming Week when aging friends joyously greet each other with fondness and affection. They reminisce about events that occurred many years ago, but are recalled in vivid detail as if they occurred only yesterday. Each year, it is like renewing a relationship that ended only a few hours ago, much like seeing a close friend for the first time each day. They have formed friendships where people attempt to interact frequently and to engage in a variety of mutually satisfying activities. Friends are one of the strongest and most significant parts of the lives of most of us.

QUALITIES OF POSITIVE RELATIONSHIPS

What qualities make a good friend? In descending order, qualities frequently cited by 40,000 people were compiled in a study by Parlee and the editors of *Psychology Today* (1979); they are listed in Table 22–1. It is doubtful any of us would disagree with these qualities, although we might rank them in a different order than did the informants in the survey. We would be more apt to agree with the findings of a cross-cultural study by Argyle and Henderson (1984), who identified six rules of friendship:

1. Share news of success with a friend. You often are more interested in sharing the news that you scored high on a test or received an A in a course with a friend than with anyone else. You know the friend will be as excited as you for your success.

2. Show emotional support. When you need emotional support, a friend is usually the first person to whom you turn. You know that not only will they provide support, but that they will do so in an open and nonjudgmental manner. Friends also show support by agreeing with you regarding whatever wrong you may attach to an incident, such as breaking up romantically with someone.

3. Volunteer help in time of need. If you want someone to help you review your studies or listen to you rehearse a speech, your friend is the most likely candidate. You can expect a friend not only to assist you, but to provide accurate feedback. Because he or she is your friend, you are more likely to accept such advice.

4. Strive to make a friend happy when in each other's company. A friend will attempt to make you happy when you are together. You usually feel the same way about a friend and reciprocate by attempting to make the friend happy. The result is the mutual enjoyment of each other and an enhancement of your friendship.

TABLE 22–1 Qualities of Good Friends (adapted from Parlee et al., 1979)

1. Maintains confidence
2. Loyal
3. Warm and affectionate
4. Supportive
5. Frank
6. Sense of humor
7. Willing to take time for you
8. Independent
9. Good conversationalist
10. Intelligent
11. Socially oriented

5. Trust and confide in each other. Friends are those you trust in your life. You know you can tell a friend anything you want without feeling guilty or fearful that the person will tell others. Friends you trust maintain your confidence.

6. Stand up for a friend in his or her absence. A friend will stand up for you when you are not present. Friends know you best. They therefore know how you might respond to a situation and can defend you when you are absent.

QUALITIES OF A GOOD FRIENDSHIP

How can you become a friend to someone else? Fortunately, most of you know how to form and maintain friendships. However, there are aspects of you, potential friends, and the situation that contribute to forming friendships.

Personal Characteristics

Personal characteristics that lead to friendship include:

1. Attributions. Attributions are the inferences you make about the causes of events, your behavior, and the behavior of others. You may attribute the causes of behavior to internal factors such as personality, traits, or abilities; these are referred to as internal attributions. Or you may attribute the causes of behavior to situational factors, contextual variables, or the like; these are referred to as external attributions. How you attribute events can influence a friendship. You may blame the breakup of a relationship as due to the other person or to situational factors and not to the personal characteristics of a friend. On the other hand, you may attribute some misfortune to internal factors of someone who you don't like.

2. Self-esteem. Self-esteem is the perception you have of your worth as a person. It refers to the overall evaluation you make that includes many separate evaluations you have of yourself as a worker, a student, or whatever is relevant to you. Self-esteem can influence how you react to others. Individuals with low self-esteem are often shy and awkward in social situations. They may tend to react in a more positive manner to a favorable evaluation and more negatively to an unfavorable evaluation than people with high self-esteem. To increase your self-esteem you can use the guidelines suggested in Chapter 21 for overcoming shyness and increasing assertiveness.

Baumeister, Heatherton, and Tice (1994) have conducted numerous investigations of self-esteem. Based upon their own studies and the research of others, Baumeister and his colleagues (1994) found that people with high self-esteem performed better at self-management than did people with low self-esteem. The findings indicated that self-management depends heavily on self-esteem. People with high self-esteem tended to be more proficient at self-management. They could set appropriate goals and manage their behavior to attain these goals. The conclusion of Baumeister and colleagues are that threats to a person's self-esteem can result in self-management failure. There also seems to be an empirical basis for these findings, as will be discussed in Chapter 34.

3. Self-perception. Self-perception is the theory that states that when we are uncertain of our beliefs, we try to understand ourselves by inferring our attitudes from others' behavior. This places us in a peculiar situation in that instead of examining our own behavior, we become dependent upon the behavior of others to tell us what we believe. This could easily result in misinterpretation of ourselves and our beliefs. For example, if your friend seems to be ignoring you, you may think that it is because he or she is losing interest in you. In reality, however, your friend is preoccupied with an upcoming test and the studying that he or she should be doing to pass the test. As we are all prone to make self-perceptions, a long-range goal of self-management would be to reduce your reliance upon self-perception.

4. Impression management. Impression management refers to an overt effort on our part, with or without our awareness, to present ourselves in a particular way to others. We use impression management in many ways, whether it involves how we dress or how we behave when around others. All of us use impression management when meeting someone for the first time. If you have a job interview, for example, you will probably make every effort to dress appropriately, be neat and clean, and polite. You want to make every effort you can to impress the person who is interviewing you. We believe first impressions are important, although they often lack the impact we attribute to them.

5. Attractiveness. Studies have indicated that physical attractiveness can be important in forming friendships, particularly with members of the opposite sex. Fortunately, what constitutes attractiveness is a decision made by individuals. Thus a person attractive to one individual may not be attractive to someone else; we all form our own perceptions and beliefs. Whether or not we perceive a person as possessing physical beauty is influenced by three factors: desirable personality characteristics, intelligence and competence, and social status.

6. Personality characteristics. We find that certain personality characteristics are desirable. A partial listing of desirable behaviors and personality characteristics, suggested by Anderson (1968), is presented in Table 22–2. We are all apt to want friends who exhibit these behaviors and personality characteristics.

7. Intelligence and competence. We would like friends who are intelligent and competent. However, we sometimes dislike highly intelligent and competent people because they seem threatening to us. These people often recognize the perceptions others have of them, however, and intentionally make mistakes to look more human to us.

8. Social status. The person's social status may be a factor that decides whether we want to become a friend with an individual. Also, it may

TABLE 22–2 Desirable Personality Characteristics (adapted from Anderson, 1968)

1. Sincere	11. Reliable
2. Honest	12. Warm
3. Understanding	13. Kind
4. Loyal	14. Friendly
5. Truthful	15. Happy
6. Trustworthy	16. Unselfish
7. Intelligent	17. Humorous
8. Dependable	18. Responsible
9. Thoughtful	19. Cheerful
10. Considerate	20. Trustful

have an impact on whom you are exposed to, or what kinds of people you are apt to meet. Hopefully, social status will be less of a factor in influencing the development of friendships than other considerations.

9. Warmth, genuineness, and empathy. We tend to like individuals who appear warm, genuine, and empathetic to us. They have the personal characteristics everyone seeks in friends.

Situation

In addition to the personal characteristics described above, contextual variables can determine if you form friendships with others. These variables include:

1. Proximity. You generally form friendships among individuals who are spatially close to you. Many people report their best friends were former roommates. Sharing the same space can bring people together (just as proximity can sometimes serve to drive other people apart).

2. Similarity. You are more likely to make friends with those who share interests similar to yours. Other common characteristics, such as intelligence, race, age, religion, physical attractiveness, and attitudes, can influence with whom you make friends.

3. Reciprocity. Reciprocity entails liking those who indicate they like us. If someone indicates that he or she wants to be with us, we often share the desire to be with that person. This reciprocity can be the foundation of friendships.

4. Social exchange theory. This theory proposes that we form friendships on the basis of our perceptions of the rewards and costs involved in the friendship. We are likely to be friends with someone with whom we share many common characteristics and with whom we enjoy a number of experiences. We develop friendships because we see the rewards we obtain through such interactions. At the same time, other people may have little interest to us or we believe that the friendship involves a cost we don't wish to assume. A person who is constantly argumentative and contentious represents someone who carries around a baggage of potential costs to others. We may avoid making friends with such individuals.

These are but a few of the factors that help us form friendships with other people. Once we have formed friendships, it is often natural for us to want to maintain the interactions we have formed. We can do these through continuing the performance of the qualities of friendship discussed earlier.

SELF-MANAGEMENT APPROACH

If you want to make friends, the following suggestions are offered:

Be with people. If you want to make friends, go where people are. You should see what events or activities occur that are of interest to you. This will permit you to be with individuals who share similar interests. College offers a rich array of social opportunities for you. You can join social, political, or religious groups; you can also get together with others with a common interest to you whether it be a hobby, such as photography, or something related to your career, such as a business group.

Open up. You can use impression management by permitting others to see your positive qualities. You want to look and feel good about yourself. This sense of self-esteem will be picked up by others. Express yourself as you normally do. This will permit others to know the "true" you.

Develop qualities of warmth, genuineness, and empathy with respect to others. Some people seem to be born with these qualities. If you lack them, you can attempt to acquire them through goal setting and self-monitoring.

SOFTEN up. Wassmer (1978) suggests you use six behaviors to help others view you more positively. These qualities form the acronym of SOFTEN:

Smile. This communicates that you are interested in others.

Open posture. An open posture reduces the constraints you may impose so others do not attempt to become friends. Crossed arms and legs suggest to a person that he or she should stay away.

Forward lean. A forward lean communicates interest because you are leaning forward to hear better what the speaker is saying.

Touch. Touching others, such as through a firm handshake, not only conveys information about yourself to others, but it suggests you are interested in them.

Eye contact. Eye contact is crucial. It signals not only that you are interested in what the other person is saying, but that you are confident in yourself.

Nod. A nod is not only a simple signal that we understand what the other person is saying to us, but it reinforces the speaker.

Use self-management techniques. You might use relaxation, systematic self-desensitization, imagery, or rehearsal to help you improve the ability you have to attract and maintain friends.

DEVELOPING FRIENDSHIPS

A number of self-management techniques can be used to develop and enhance friendships. These include:

1. Stimulus control. Both environmental and cognitive stimuli may be introduced or changed to develop friendships.

Environmental stimuli. If you want to become friends with others, it is necessary that you go where you both meet others and others have an opportunity to meet you. Look for the characteristics and qualities that you want to cultivate in a friendship. Develop qualities or characteristics that you think will appeal to others, such as those qualities that comprise the acronym of SOFTEN.

Cognitive stimuli. Use self-instruction and self-statements to guide you in the process of cultivating and maintaining friends. If you find you're uncomfortable around someone you would like to have as a friend, use proven methods of self-control to diffuse these feelings. The techniques would include: (a) thought stopping; (b) self-desensitization; (c) modeling; (d) cognitive methods suggested by Ellis (1973) or Beck and colleagues (1979); (e) imagery; and (f) rehearsal of strategies to take to develop friends. Methods to overcome shyness and develop assertiveness, described in detail in Chapter 20, should be considered. The fifteen steps suggested by Zimbardo (1977) for increasing self-confidence or the fifteen steps outlined by Alberti and Emmons (1986) for increasing assertiveness are excellent starting points for you.

2. Self-monitoring. Honestly observe and record your own progress toward making friends with others. This may help you change your behavior to take advantage of future opportunities to make friends.

3. Self-reinforcement. Reinforce yourself when you have behaved in what you believe is an appropriate manner when attempting to make a friend.

4. Problem solving. Problem-solving skills can be used to guide your performance. Specific steps include: (a) planning on how you can form friendships; (b) considering the various options you have to be in situations where you can meet others; (c) rehearsing potential plans beforehand; (d) acting on your plan; (e) evaluating, perhaps with the help of a friend, your progress; and (f) considering other alternatives if they appear necessary.

MAINTAINING FRIENDS

Friends are valuable to us. Maintaining friendships requires attention and effort on your part. Suggestions for keeping your friends include the following:

1. Continue to open up. Once you have a friend, you should continue to open up and share your feelings. Opening up permits you to form strong friendships.

2. Be sensitive. Friends are sensitive to one another's feelings and needs. You need to be aware that the needs and goals of your friends may be different from yours. Friendship helps you be aware of differences between others and yourself.

3. Express appreciation. We all like to be complimented. Your friends are no different than you in this respect. It is important, therefore, for you to provide acknowledgement of acts you consider as deserving of praise and appreciation.

4. Realistically perceive friends. Everyone has faults, including your friends. A friend clearly sees and accepts the faults of others. You are likely to be far more diplomatic in pointing out a friend's flaws than is anyone else.

5. Enjoy friendships. Friends are not only people we confide in, but people we enjoy in both good and bad times. Friends provide us with joy and happiness.

6. Know that friends can be disappointing. We occasionally disappoint ourselves. Friends are no different in that they sometimes can disappoint you. These occasional disappointments should not undermine your friendship, however.

7. Talk about your friendships. Talking about the friendship you have with others can serve to clear up misunderstandings and strengthen your relationships.

8. Stay in touch. Finally, it is important that you remain in touch with your friends and constantly work to strengthen your friendships. Many of us make friends in college and hope we will have them throughout the remainder of our lives. These are years when many changes occur in our lives, however, and we are apt to lose track of some of our current friends. Years from now, you may wonder why you failed to make the effort to remain friends with someone whose company you once enjoyed. Don't lose track of friends, but constantly make the effort to cement friendships you hope you have throughout your life.

SELF-MANAGEMENT PROJECTS

A number of students have been concerned about their friends. As a result, they have elected to change behaviors that they believed could threaten their friendships. A number of projects have been concerned with reducing bad language. The data in Figure 22–1 were obtained by a student who thought his language was repulsive not only to himself, but to his friends. He used an approach involving self-monitoring, self-statements, and church attendance to decrease his rate of cursing each day. Figure 22–2 depicts results reported by a student who used an imaginative program involving self-monitoring, peer support, goal setting, stimulus change, and response cost (she forfeited her pillow when she swore, something she said she *hated* to do) to decrease swearing. She was happy to achieve her goals.

The student whose data are shown in Figure 22–3 reported, "Over the years I have developed the act of complaining into a fine art—I can find fault with anything." However, she continued, the "art" was beginning to influence her friends in a negative manner. She developed a program that involved self-monitoring, stimulus change, thought stopping,

FIGURE 22–1
Use of self-monitoring, self-statements, and church attendance to reduce rate of cursing each day.

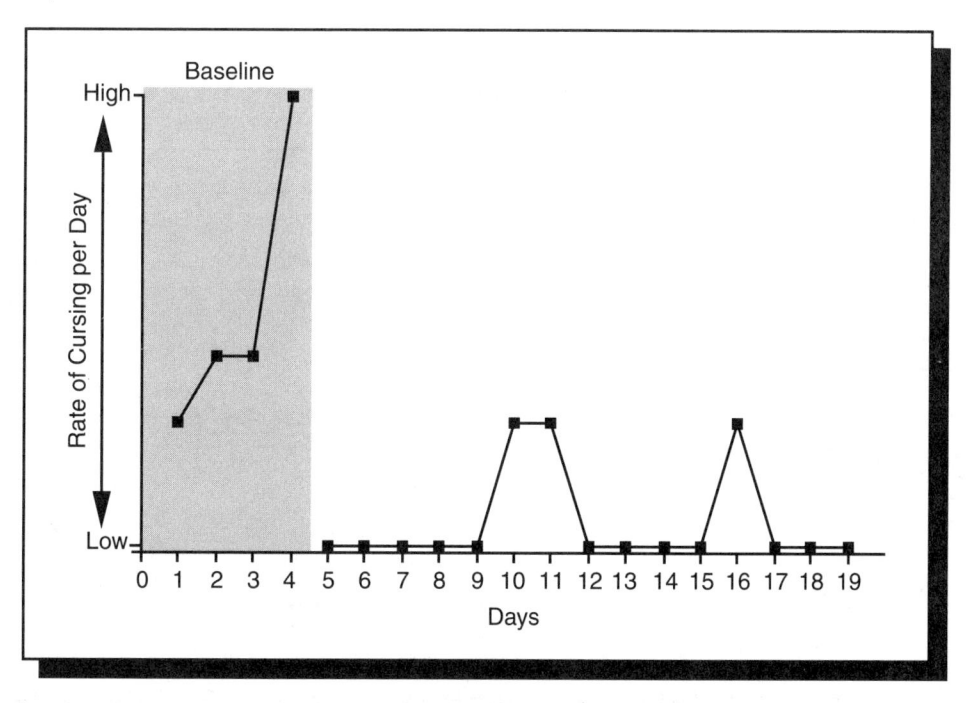

246 Chap. 22 Friends

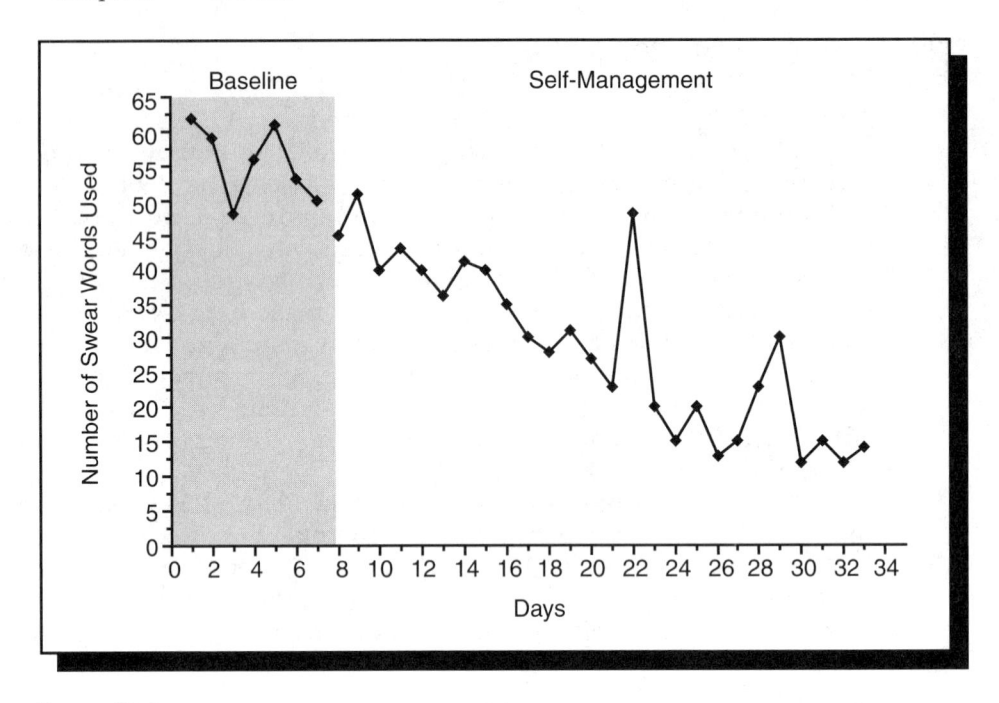

FIGURE 22–2
Use of self-monitoring, peer support, goal setting, stimulus change, and response cost to decrease swearing.

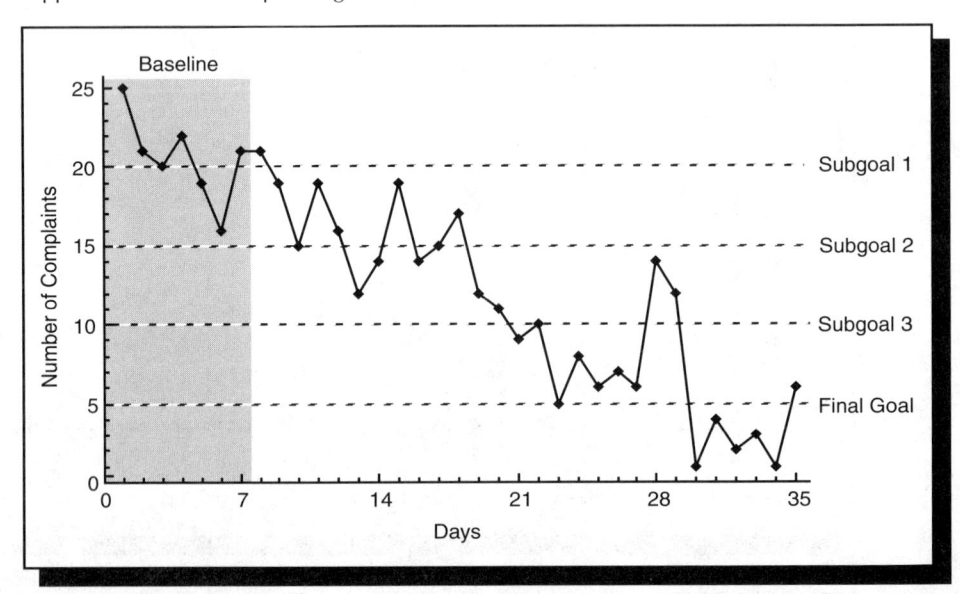

FIGURE 22–3
Use of self-monitoring, stimulus change, thought stopping, positive self-instruction, and peer support to decrease complaining.

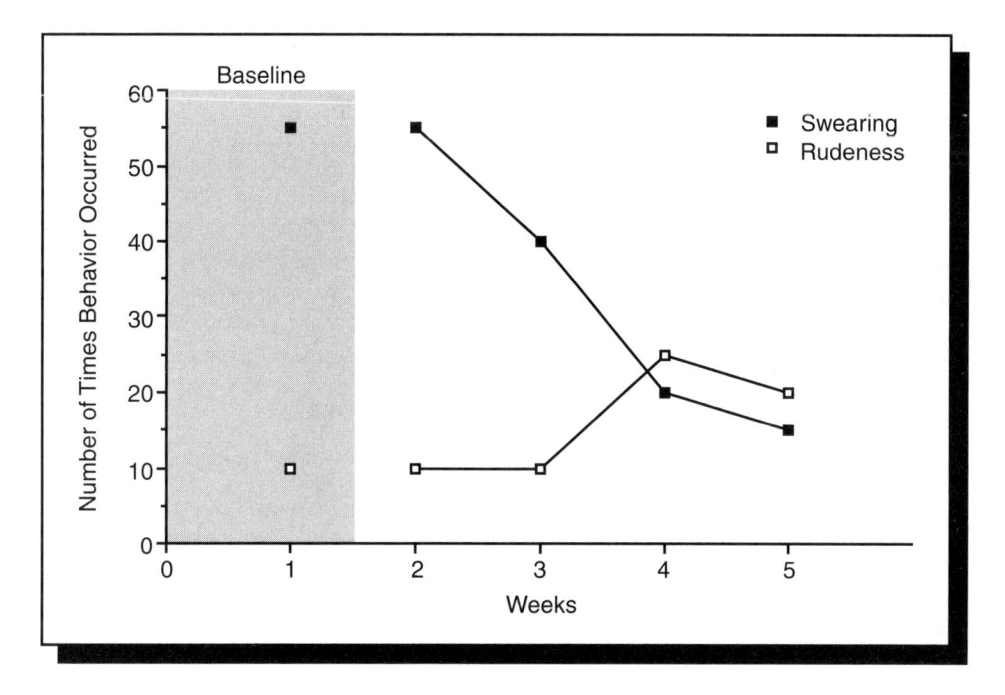

FIGURE 22–4
Use of self-monitoring, stimulus change, and prayer to decrease swearing and attempt to reduce rudeness.

positive self-instruction, and peer support to help her reduce complaining. She concluded by saying that both she and her friends were pleased with the results. Figure 22–4 shows the results obtained by a student who attempted to decrease her rudeness and swearing when around friends. She used self-monitoring, stimulus change, and prayer in her program. The results show that while she reduced her swearing, she became more rude to her friends. She attributed the latter change to a particularly rough quarter, and concluded that she had begun to reduce rudeness when the quarter ended.

EXERCISE

Have you been able to make friends?
Evaluate the skills and behaviors you have to make friends.
Consider the strategies you can use to make more friends.
Apply and evaluate your success.

REVIEW TERMS

Impression management
Proximity
Reciprocity

Self-esteem
Self-perception
Social exchange theory

QUESTIONS

Describe six rules of friendship.
Discuss what is meant by SOFTEN.
List eight suggestions for maintaining your friends.

CHAPTER 23

Dating

"Youth is wholly experimental."
—Robert Louis Stevenson, *Letter to a Young Gentleman*

"I didn't date in high school, but I thought I would when I got to college. I haven't. I wish I did. It bothers me when my roommates go out on dates and come back and tell their stories. I know I've got to do something about dating, but I don't know how to go about it."
—Mark, a sophomore

Most of you date while in college. You practice what is referred to as free dating in that you will feel able to ask anyone for a date without fear of social sanction. In asking for a date, you are performing what has been an American phenomenon for decades. You may directly ask someone for a date or you may indirectly ask for a date by having a mutual friend make the request for you. You may also have a date with someone you don't know, commonly referred to as a blind date.

Overall, most of your dates will be successful. This does not mean that you will enjoy all the dates you have. Many college students—as many as 64 percent of students in a study summarized by Grossman and McNamara (1991)—report that they are anxious when around members of the opposite sex. Other college students have reported that they are anxious in dating or that they perceive social inadequacies in asking others for dates. Many tend to use negative self-thoughts such as, "Boy, am I a turkey. No one will ever go out with me after this date," "I know she thinks I'm a total klutz," or "Wait until he tells his roommates about the dog he went out with." These self-statements are not only self-defeating, but they suggest that you are overly concerned about your self-perceptions and how others respond to you. This is not the purpose of dating. Dating is a way for you to meet a number of people in an attempt to develop a more lasting relationship with a particular person who shares common interests and goals with you. It is unlikely that you will find such a person on your first date; rather, the probability is that you will need to have a broader sample of dating experiences with different individuals before you not only decide the type of person you like, but find someone to fit your description of Mr. or Ms. Right.

A number of suggestions have been offered to help you attain greater satisfaction from dates. These include the following:

Asking for a date. Grossman and McNamara (1991) suggest you follow the following steps in asking for a date: (a) plan ahead in that you know exactly what you are going to say to a potential partner; (b) be direct; (c) be prepared for rejection; and (d) decide beforehand if you want to ask for the date on the telephone, face to face, or indirectly through someone else. Never be discouraged by rejection; it is a part of dating for everyone. Reward yourself for asking for a date in an appropriate manner, no matter the outcome.

Rehearse. If you are uncertain how to act on a date, write a brief scenario and rehearse it. Use imagery in preparing such a script. It is useful if you first rehearse by yourself in front of a mirror. In this way, you can rewrite the scenario if necessary. Do not be too harsh on yourself in rehearsal; remember that it is only a date and not anything heavier, such as a wedding or an appearance on a national television program. You can later rehearse with your roommates the scenario you have prepared. Listen to all feedback and accept that which is helpful.

Date anxiety. If you are anxious when dating, you can use such tried-and-true self-management procedures as relaxation, systematic self-desensitization, imagery, and rehearsal. Modify negative self-statements so they become positive outcomes. Alter any inappropriate cognitive responses so that you are realistic and not overly concerned about the outcomes of any given date. Going on a date with a group or engaging in an activity, such as skating, are also good ways to deal with date anxiety. Remember you are involved in a sampling process to determine which individuals are most likely to share your interests and offer the prospect of a meaningful relationship. Under these circumstances, you may hope that a number of your dates are less than thrilling or exciting. If they were all thrilling, you would never be able to determine the qualities of the person you seek.

Eliminate self-defeating habits. You may find that you have difficulty in maintaining eye contact with others; for this reason, you will likely want to rehearse the behaviors you intend to perform before a date. In addition, you may have difficulties in initiating a conversation. Think of a few potential questions you might ask before dating (e.g., what is your major, where are you from, what are your plans for the future).

Develop conversational skills. Most people like to talk about themselves. This knowledge should help you through any date, as well as permit you to use the questions you have prepared to break any long pauses or lulls in a conversation. A number of other approaches can be taken in learning how to be a good conversationalist, including:

1. Be a good listener. You should focus on what your date says. Be an active listener by paraphrasing what is being said or by asking questions. If your date starts discussing career options, listen and ask questions when appropriate. Periodically, you may wish to paraphrase and summarize what is being said to you. This will improve communication between you and your date. It is also a good social reinforcer for your date to continue describing future plans. Nod your head if you agree with what your date is saying; nodding is an excellent social reinforcer.

2. Watch body language. Attend to your partner's facial expressions, body postures, and movements. These signals communicate emotions and attitudes. You can be particularly skillful at interpreting another's body language the more you date.

3. Ask open-ended questions. Rarely ask questions that can be answered with a simple yes or no. Rather, ask questions that stimulate talk. Open-ended questions are apt to open a lengthy and enjoyable discussion.

4. Give sincere approval. If you like the comments of your date, express your feelings by approving them in a sincere manner. Individuals who are highly skilled at dating often report that they find dating to be natural to them. These are the same individuals who are likely to be successful in any social encounter. To almost any person, they are the type of individuals who exude warmth, openness, and genuineness. You simply like listening to and being around such people.

5. Self-disclosure. The basic rule is that you tell someone about yourself at the same ratio that your partner tells about himself or herself. This permits the conversation to be shared equally by you and your partner. At the same time, it prevents you from later berating yourself for dominating the conversation, often with irrelevant information.

Reinforce your date. If you enjoy your partner, let him or her know by reinforcing the behavior. This is likely to increase the probability that further dates will follow. In addition, you should practice reciprocal reinforcement by reinforcing those who reinforce your behavior. Reciprocal reinforcement is the basis for most enduring relationships; it is good to learn to use such reinforcement when dating.

Evaluate your progress. Following a date, review it to yourself. Don't do so in a critical manner, but look for highlights of the date both in yourself and in your partner. This may lead you not only to ask for another date with your partner, but may help you crystallize the qualities you are seeking in a partner. You can record your observations, particularly as you may want to review them before future dates.

IMPROVING COMMUNICATION WITH YOUR DATES

In her book *You Just Don't Understand: Women and Men in Conversation*, Deborah Tannen (1990) suggests ways men and women can communicate more effectively. The hints she offers should improve the dating behaviors of both men and women.

Communication Hints for Men

Men generally need to listen more effectively when conversing with women. In addition, Tannen suggests:

1. Observe whether you have a tendency to interrupt women. If you do have this tendency, apologize and ask the woman to continue with her conversation. This habit may take diligent effort on your part to correct.

2. Avoid responding in monosyllables. Earlier, it was noted that you should not ask questions that can be answered with a yes or a no. If you are a man, it is also important that you avoid answering with a monosyllable, such as "Uh-huh." If you answer yes or no, explain your answer. The explanation might lead to a stimulating conversation.

3. Learn the art of give and take. Ask your dates questions about themselves. Listen to what they say. Be prepared that your dates may ask you similar questions in return. This is not only a good way to learn conversational give and take, but it can provide many interesting discussions.

4. Don't be demanding or order women around. No one likes to be ordered around, including your date. If you ask your date to do something for you, do so in the polite manner you hope someone would use in requesting something from you.

5. Don't be a space hog. Be aware of whether you take up too much space and make your date uncomfortable by intruding into her space. No one likes to feel like they are being crowded out.

6. Be open. As noted in earlier sections, talk about your feelings, hopes, and interests. Sharing personal feelings and concerns often causes your date to open up to you.

7. Be enthusiastic. Conveying your enthusiasm about events can excite your date to share your excitement. This can be an effective method for establishing rapport with a date.

8. Ask for help if needed. If you need help, such as financial assistance to pay an unexpectedly large dinner bill, don't be afraid to ask your date. She will likely not only be understanding, but appreciate your predicament. It is another way to establish a bond with your date.

Communication Hints for Women

Women often need to be more assertive in communicating with their dates. In addition, Tannen suggests that you:

1. Redirect conversation when interrupted. As men often may interrupt you, politely but firmly redirect the conversation back to you. You can do this by saying something such as, "Excuse me, but I haven't finished." Your date will not only be apologetic, but appreciate your assertiveness.

2. Establish and maintain eye contact. This is essential in conversing for both women and men.

3. Keep voice pitched low. A higher-pitched voice may cause your listener to associate you with young girls. For this reason, use your abdominal muscles and speak in a lower pitch.

4. Claim and maintain space. Don't be crowded into an uncomfortable position by lack of space. Excuse yourself and request more space if uncomfortable.

5. Talk about yourself and your accomplishments. Rather than being a passive listener who learns more about your date than you ever wanted to know, enter into the conversation by talking about yourself. This can serve as a springboard for more detailed discussions with your date. Your date will undoubtedly appreciate your participation, as well as learning more about you. You will also enjoy sharing your knowledge and expertise about various topics of conversation.

6. Keep up with current events. If you keep up with current events, you always have an opening in any discussion. You can always ask your date his opinion about a current event. This may not only prompt more conversation, but convey to him that you are an interesting person. Avoiding politically sensitive subjects is a good approach when on your initial date.

7. Don't be overly apologetic. If something happens that you feel sorry about, simply say, "I'm sorry." You shouldn't get into the trap of being either overly apologetic or explanatory about an event that happens.

SELF-MANAGEMENT PROCEDURES

The techniques discussed throughout the book are useful in promoting dating. They include:

1. Stimulus control. You may alter both environmental and cognitive stimuli to increase the dates you have.

Environmental stimuli. You must be in social situations in order to meet people. If you believe that you do not have the number and quality of dates that you would like, look around to see how you can be involved in various activities to improve your dating behavior. College offers many and varied opportunities to meet others; in fact, there is a greater chance to date in college than is apt to occur elsewhere. Take advantage of these opportunities!

Cognitive stimuli. You can use an array of cognitive tactics to enhance the quantity and quality of your dates. These include: (a) self-instruction and self-statements to guide your performance; (b) imagery; (c) rehearsal of the steps you decide you should perform to date more; and (d) desensitization and thought stopping to manage any anxiety that may accompany dating. Becoming more assertive, as outlined in Chapter 20, will also enhance your dating performance.

2. Self-monitoring. Observe and record aspects of your dating behavior. If you effectively alter your dating behavior, a review of your progress will serve as a discriminative stimulus to further improve your dating habits.

3. Self-reinforcement. Reinforce yourself after a successful date!

4. Problem solving. Problem-solving skills can be a framework for your dating performance. These include: (a) plan on how you can enhance your dating behavior; (b) consider the options available in a date; (c) rehearse how you will behave when on a date; (d) act on your plans; (e) evaluate your performance; (f) prepare for any setbacks (which are normal in dating) that may occur; and (g) consider any other alternatives that may improve your dates.

SELF-MANAGEMENT PROJECTS

Several projects have been taken by students to improve their dating behaviors. Figure 23–1 depicts what happened when a student applied self-monitoring to improve his attitude toward women. The student was not antiwomen; rather, he had been exposed to dormitory talk and it had in-

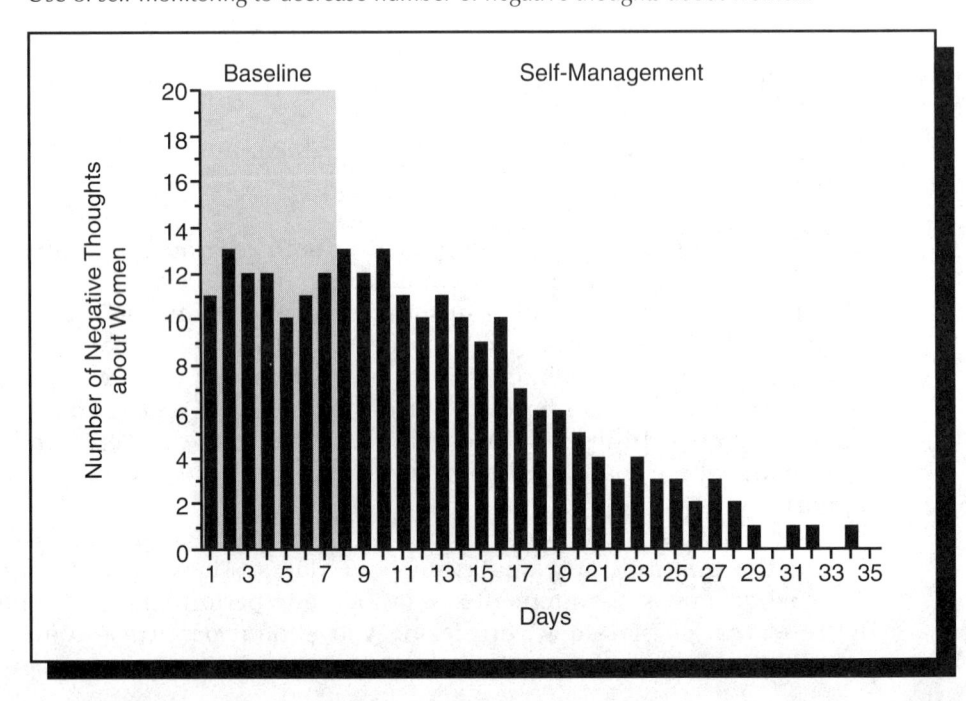

FIGURE 23–1
Use of self-monitoring to decrease number of negative thoughts about women.

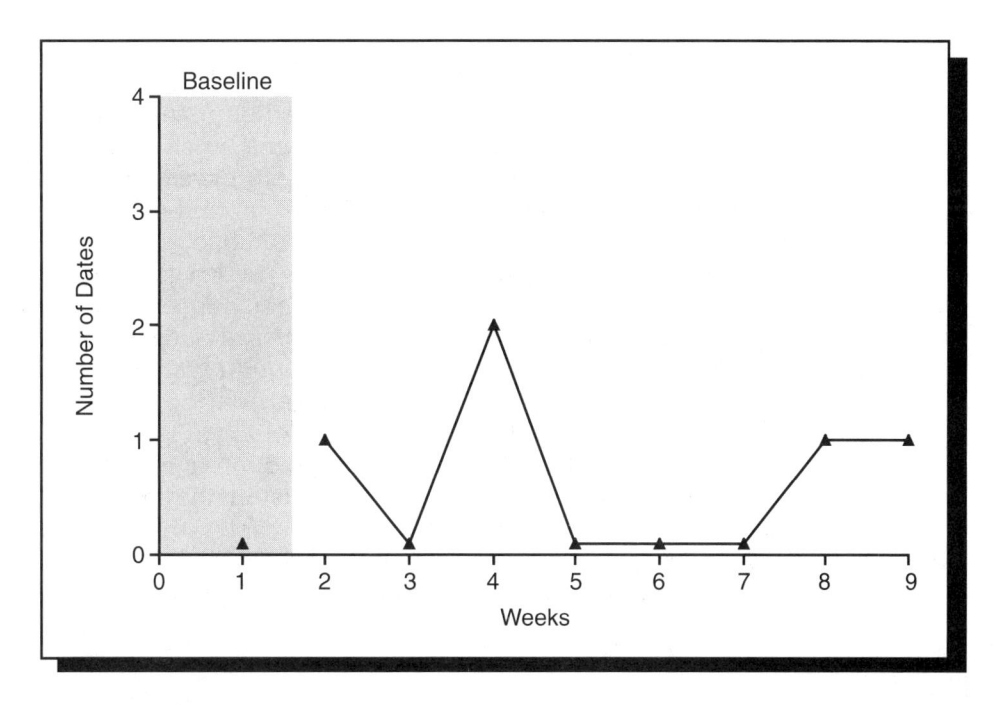

FIGURE 23–2
Use of self-monitoring to increase number of dates.

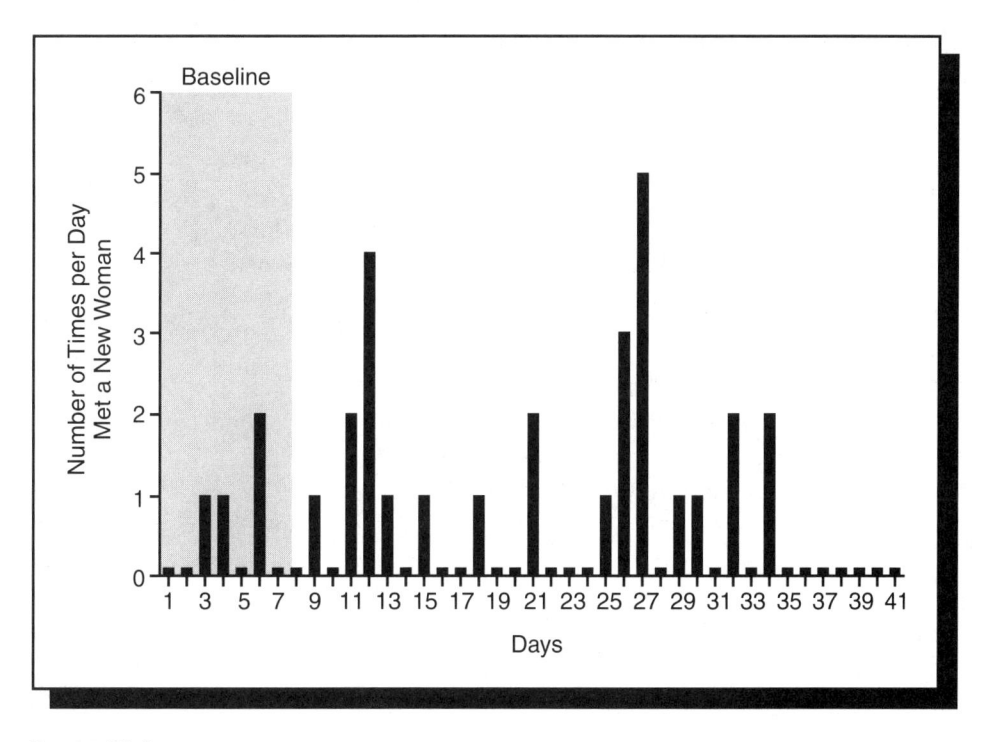

FIGURE 23–3
Self-management to increase social interaction with women.

fluenced him in a negative way. He concentrated on using self-monitoring to filter out what he heard and what he thought he should believe. The result was that he came to realize he was going to have to change a number of negative cognitions he acquired when he entered college. As noted, he decreased the number of negative thoughts he had about women. The self-management was augmented by his dating on a regular basis toward the end of his project. Figure 23–2 depicts what happened when a student used self-monitoring to increase the number of dates he had weekly. He increased the number of dates he had, although his performance was somewhat erratic. Ironically, the student began dating a woman in the class during the last two weeks of his project. Finally, Figure 23–3 depicts the results obtained by a student who attempted to increase the social interactions he had with women. He changed his environment by going to more parties where he could meet women, increasing the self-monitoring of his behavior, and setting a goal of interacting with at least one woman a day. His program proved successful.

EXERCISE

Are you dating regularly? Would you like to increase this activity?
How might you increase the number of dates you have?
How will you monitor your progress?
What criteria will you use to determine if you have attained your goal?

REVIEW TERMS

Blind dates
Four dating suggestions

Free dating
Self-disclosure

QUESTIONS

Discuss five approaches to becoming a good conversationalist.
List eight communication hints for men.
List seven communication hints for women.

CHAPTER 24

Planning a Career

"The more human beings proceed by plan the more effectively they may be hit by accident."
—Fredrich Durrenmatt, *The Physicists*

"I've planned my career since junior high school. I took all the right courses in high school and throughout college. I've been accepted into a good graduate school. I think I'll be highly employable once I receive my doctorate. My roommate, however, hasn't done anything. It has taken him two years longer to graduate than he thought because he couldn't decide on a major. He still doesn't know what he wants to do. He has had no job interviews. Lately, he has talked about going on to graduate school. I don't know how he can because he hasn't prepared for it. His grade point average is barely a two point. The other day, he asked me what the GRE test was. I think he's got some problems."
—Ben, a graduating senior

By now, many of you have decided upon a career. You are taking concrete steps, through your coursework, to prepare for employment. Others of you may be unsure of what you want to do with your life. You may have changed majors several times because of your uncertainty. The good news is that you are not locked into a job for life as were your parents and grandparents. Statistics indicate that you may change jobs an average of seven times during the span of your employment career. The bad news is that economic considerations, such as health insurance and other benefits, may curtail the opportunities you have to change occupations. What follows are suggestions all of you might consider in planning a career.

PREPARING FOR A CAREER

You may try any of the following strategies to assess your progress in planning a career.

General Preparation

Take interest inventory. A number of interest inventories can suggest occupations for which you may have an aptitude and interest. You are familiar with them because you have periodically taken such inventories throughout your academic career. The Strong-Campbell Vocational Interest Inventory is an example of such an instrument. Administration of these inventories usually occurs in counseling offices or employment agencies.

Obtain information. There are number of sources for career information:

1. Visit the library. Libraries, particularly college libraries, have excellent resources. Those that supply career information and are used widely are:

Occupational Outlook Handbook. This handbook is published annually by the Bureau of Labor Statistics. It provides considerable information about jobs and the qualifications required for them.

Occupational Outlook Quarterly. This is also published by the Bureau of Labor Statistics. It contains information similar to the handbook, but is published on a quarterly basis.

Guide for Occupational Exploration. This guide, also available in libraries, permits you to compare your interests and abilities to a variety of occupations.

College Placement Annual. This annual describes characteristics of companies that employ college graduates, as well as the qualities they expect in these graduates.

2. Visit a resource or placement center. Almost all colleges and universities maintain a resource or placement center. You may want to schedule an appointment and meet with one of their staff. They can assist you in both planning your career and obtaining a job. When you graduate, they often maintain materials that can be sent to prospective employers at your request.

3. Visit an academic department. Academic departments often offer an array of materials for those who anticipate majoring in the subject matter of the department. These are often provided to academic departments by various professional organizations. In addition, the department may have prepared information regarding potential job opportunities for graduates of its program. You may also want to talk with professors in your department. They can often offer you their perspective not only about career preparation, but where they see their areas moving in the future.

4. Interview professionals. You may want to visit with those who operate employment agencies. They can inform you of the likelihood that you can find a job with a particular degree.

5. Interview people working in a particular career area. Before you invest considerable time, effort, and money in furthering your education, you may want to talk to someone already working in the career field you are preparing to enter. If you want to teach, you may want to visit your local school and talk about career options with a teacher; if you want to enter law school, you may want to talk with a local attorney.

People at work in a certain area can offer you a unique perspective about your career decision. In addition, they can often suggest what they think will be future openings in your chosen field. You can make appointments and interview these individuals when on vacation in your home communities.

6. Obtain part-time or summer work experience. If you can get hands-on experience at working in a job related to your career choice, it can be a major determinant in helping you decide whether you want to continue your studies in that area. These types of work experiences can either enhance your enthusiasm or dampen your interest in a given career choice. Either possibility is helpful to you.

Prepare a letter. The letter you write to a potential employer will probably be the employer's initial contact with you. Since you want to make a good impression, be certain that: (a) you start with a statement of the purpose of your letter; (b) you describe, in general, how your skills and training have qualified you for the position; (c) the letter has no misspellings or grammatical gaffe; and (d) the letter is neat and clean.

Preparing a Resume

A resume is a summary of your assets, education, skills, experiences, and potential described in a way that will maximize the likelihood that you will be hired for a particular job. As this may be the only opportunity you have to move forward in the hiring process, you want to be certain that you convey what in your background best indicates you can do a job and what are your major selling points. For this reason, you want to devote time to preparing a resume that reflects the impression you wish to give to potential employers. If you have compiled a solid resume, your strengths will leap out at the reader. You want to be certain your resume is relevant, concise, free of typographical and grammatical errors, and has no spelling errors. If any spelling errors are detected by one person, you can anticipate that he or she will circle them so that all readers of the document will know that you either cannot spell or that you did not take the time to prepare your resume carefully.

There are several types of resumes:

1. Chronological resume. In this type of resume, you highlight your work history by date, generally by starting with your most recent experiences and moving back to earlier experiences (as you gain experiences, you may wish to rewrite your resume and go from earlier experiences to the present). It is particularly important that you keep a chronological resume current and have no time gaps.

2. Functional resume. Your skills are highlighted in this format though the categorization of different experiences. Organizing information in this manner permits you to emphasize the functions that are most relevant to the position for which you are applying. The functional resume permits you to avoid problems that might occur if your most recent job experiences do not relate to a position you want in the future.

3. Targeted resume. This type of resume is targeted for a particular position. It focuses on skills and achievements by linking them to the job for which you are applying. With personal computers, you can easily target your resume to any given position and produce a customized resume for a given job opportunity.

4. Combination resume. There are a number of options that you may wish to consider. You might take a functional resume and tailor it toward particular positions, or you might describe how your skills were acquired in a chronological manner.

Cohen and De Oliveira (1987) summarize six basic facts regarding resumes:

1. Resumes are a shorthand for employers. Resumes summarize what you can bring to a potential position. In addition, they permit a potential employer to quickly know who you are.

2. Resumes should be clear and concise. Resumes written in such a manner not only permit potential employers to obtain a picture of you, but they facilitate communication at the company where you are applying for a position.

3. Resumes should make their point quickly. Since an employer may have a large number of resumes to review, you only have a brief window of opportunity to make your case via a resume.

4. Resumes are essential to obtaining management, professional, clerical, or even sales work. For this reason, they are worth an investment on your part.

5. Resumes should contain only relevant information. A resume is not your biography. For this reason, you want to describe only your work experiences, education, and other relevant data. Emphasize the skills you could bring to the position for which you are applying.

6. Resumes should emphasize style and tone. Cohen and De Oliveira note that a resume can as easily be a reason to deny you an interview as a reason to grant you one. Attempt to put yourself into an employer's position and read whatever resume you have prepared.

Martin and Osborne (1989) advise that you add the following information in a resume:

1. Identifying information. This contains your name and address. Be certain that your address is current. In addition, list a telephone number where you can always be reached. Most people do this by listing their telephone numbers both at home and at work. It may be worthwhile to purchase an answering machine to insure that you are contacted.

2. Personal data. You usually list where you are currently working; if such information is not provided, an employer may wonder if you currently have a job. Other personal information, such as your social security number, your marital status, and whether you have children, is optional. If you believe reporting that you have a family may be helpful in gaining employment, note it; if you believe that it may hurt you, it is legal to omit mention of such personal information. As noted earlier, with the advent of personal computers, you can tailor a particular resume for a given job. This permits you to add what you think may or may not be important information for a potential employer to consider.

3. Career objective. Give some consideration to what you list as your career objective. You do not want to list something like, "I have always dreamed of working with your company." While this could be true, it is doubtful that a bored personnel employee will believe you. At the same time, you don't want to say something such as, "I really want to do something else, but this job could tide me over until I find what I am really looking for." This sentence will certainly convey that you are not that interested in the job. List what your long-term objective is and attempt to write how the job you are applying for can assist you in reaching your goal. This is an honest approach to take.

4. Educational background. You will usually want to list all the education you have obtained. If you were only at a school for a brief period and flunked out, you may want to consider whether you should put this information on a resume. If it has nothing to do with the job, it could be safely omitted. You want to put down information about any academic honors and your grade point average, provided the latter is high. If your grade point average is low, don't put it on a resume. Instead, emphasize the skills you do have. If you have specific skills, be certain to list them.

5. Employment experience. Be certain you list all employment you have had that is related to the job for which you are applying. If you think that other jobs you have had while going to school could be of interest to your employer, list them. Many companies are impressed with students who have worked their way through school; if this was the case with you, note it on your resume.

6. Extracurricular activities. Many of you have accumulated a wealth of extracurricular experiences during your academic career. These should be noted. Don't merely note membership in clubs; describe the role you had in such organizations.

7. Honors. Any major honors you attained in school, particularly those indicative of high academic achievement, should be noted. If you attended school on a scholarship or graduated summa cum laude, this should be noted.

8. Languages and foreign travel. As companies become more multinational, they often seek employees who are skilled at languages or who have spent some time abroad. You should try to capitalize on any skills that you have in this area.

9. References. Cohen and De Oliveira suggest that you write "References available upon request." This is sage advice. Lining up references is sometimes tricky. Ask yourself this question: Do I know three professors in my major area who would write letters for me? You should have a minimum of two and preferably three professors who can write letters for you. Any employer is apt to want to see what teachers in your major field of study thought of you both in the classroom and as a potential employee. Before listing anyone on your resume, ask that person if he or she would be willing to write letters for you. Supply a copy of a current resume, as well as a list of the firms to which you are applying. Computers have again simplified what used to be a horrendous undertaking: writing a number of letters of recommendation. A professor may also want to talk to you about potential topics he or she should note in the letter.

In starting out, you do not always know who to ask for letters of recommendation. Besides professors in your major field, you can ask current employers, past employers, and others who know you well. Always be certain that you ask them beforehand if they are willing to write letters of recommendation for you. If they are, you can list them on a resume; if they are unwilling, you are less apt to receive a letter from someone who either does not know you or who is disinterested in writing letters for you. As a general rule, use people you trust as references. A bad letter is tantamount to a kiss of death for the job for which you are applying. To compound the problem, you may not learn that you did not receive the job because someone wrote you a poor letter of recommendation.

Many students are often hesitant to ask someone, particularly their professors, to write letters of recommendation for them. Don't be this way in asking others to be of assistance to you. Always remember that they have others write letters of recommendation for them whether they are seeking employment or advancement in their positions. In addition, most people who know you want to see that you have the opportunity to develop your skills and potential. For this reason, they are usually more than pleased to help you pursue your goals. Writing a letter of recommendation is the least they can do.

Other suggestions for preparing an effective resume are:

1. Be honest. In writing a resume, you want to accentuate your strong points. Don't oversell yourself and describe skills that you do not have. This can become a major problem, particularly if a company hires you believing you can perform that skill. At the same time, don't undersell yourself. Think carefully about your resume before writing it. This will allow you time for thinking of all the activities you should list.

2. Invest in your resume. Besides making certain that your resume has no spelling errors, be certain that all the information you list is accurate. It is worthwhile to take your resume to a copying service and ask them to prepare you a professional-appearing resume. This may impress some employers (and you only need to impress one potential employer).

3. Keep your resume current. If you keep your resume current, you will not omit experiences that you have had since you first wrote the resume. In addition, keeping the resume current will allow you to send it out quickly if an unexpected job opportunity develops.

OBTAINING JOB LEADS

It is becoming increasingly difficult to find suitable employment. Methods for locating a potential employer are:

1. Use personal contacts. You may want to talk to relatives, family members, or friends about potential employment opportunities. A number of students have reported that they heard about a potential job from a friend already working with a company who was familiar with the firm's plans.

2. Ask your instructors. Many teachers often hear about employment opportunities, particularly for those with an advanced degree. In addition, employment notices are posted on the bulletin boards in many departments.

3. Follow up with past employers. You may contact places where you worked in the past to determine if there are any openings at a level for which you are qualified. This means that you need to maintain ties with past employers if you think they may be of value to you in the future.

4. Register with the school placement office. Many graduates find their jobs through college placement offices. Not only do employers contact these facilities, but the personnel in such offices attempt to match the employers' needs with the wishes of a potential employee. In addition, you can remain registered with these offices in the future.

5. Register with the state employment office. You will likely want to register with your local state employment office. They also attempt to meet the needs of employers with individuals registered at their office.

6. Register with a commercial placement office. It may pay you to register with a commercial placement office. They can charge either the employer or you for their services. You may not want to pay any fees for these services, but it could represent a job for you in the long run. For this reason, registration with these agencies is worthwhile.

7. Search newspapers and other periodicals. Companies advertise for college graduates in the newspapers. For this reason, you should

persue the employment ads in a newspaper on a regular basis. In addition, many specialties have professional organizations that publish employment notices. These listings can often be found in the library or in the administrative offices of your major area of study.

8. Temporary help services. Many temporary positions turn into permanent positions. If not, you will have both accumulated additional experiences and provided yourself with an income while searching for a more suitable job.

IMPORTANT FEATURES IN A JOB

When looking for employment, you may want to consider the job features a group of 23,000 people thought were important (Renwick and Lawler, 1978). These are listed, in order of how respondents ranked them, in Table 24–1. A more recent report by the Gallup Poll (1991) shows how important certain job characteristics were to American workers, as depicted in Table 24–2. It is of note that fringe benefits and job security are emerging as two of the most important characteristics of the work place.

TABLE 24–1 Features Thought Important in a Job (adapted from Renwick and Lawler, 1978)

1. Chance to do something that makes you feel good about yourself
2. Chance to accomplish something worthwhile
3. Chance to develop new things
4. Chance to develop your skills and abilities
5. Some freedom on job
6. Chance to do something you do best
7. Resources to do job
8. Respect from fellow employees
9. Feedback on job performance
10. Chance to take part in making decisions
11. Job security
12. Amount of pay
13. Treated in positive manner by fellow employees
14. Friendliness of fellow employees
15. Amount of praise you receive for doing good work
16. Amount of fringe benefits
17. Chance of promotion
18. Physical environment

TABLE 24-2 Factors Important in a Job (Gallup Poll, 1991)

1. Good health insurance and other benefits
2. Interesting work
3. Job security
4. Opportunity to learn new skills
5. Annual vacation of two weeks or more
6. Being able to work independently
7. Recognition from coworkers
8. Having a job in which you can help others
9. Limited job stress
10. Regular hours, no nights or weekends
11. High income
12. Working close to home
13. Work that is important to society
14. Chances for promotion
15. Contact with a lot of people

MYTHS OF JOB SEEKING

There are a number of myths about seeking work that you should consider in planning your career moves, including the following:

1. An academic degree is a ticket to the job market. While this was once the case, many professions are now flooded with potential employees. It is widely thought that approximately one-fourth of college graduates are working at positions that do not require a college degree.

2. Searching for work is a part-time quest. This is a myth unless you are looking for another job while still working. Treat your search for employment as a top priority, particularly as you approach graduation. You can be certain that many of your peers view job hunting in this light.

3. If I cannot find work immediately, I'll switch careers or go to graduate school. Switching careers is often a mistake because you are immediately pitted against others with experience in your new field. Moving on to graduate school may or may not be a good idea. Advanced degrees may not be marketable, particularly for those without equivalent experiences. A good idea is to be flexible while remaining focused at attaining your long-term goals.

4. Lowering my job demands will guarantee employment. This may be the case with some employers. However, employers often are more inclined to hire those who seek an equivalent or better salary then they obtained in their last position.

5. There is no such thing as job security. This seems to be increasingly the case if you desire to work for the same company for your entire career. However, it is not the case if you continue to develop skills that make you marketable in other settings. You must create this type of job security for yourself through your own performance and not be dependent upon given employers.

6. I should request the highest salary possible. This may prove an unfortunate demand. Often the fringe benefits at a position, such as the opportunity to obtain additional training or to have more flexible hours of employment, may be more important than your salary.

7. I should only look at large companies. This is a myth in that, at the current time, most job growth is being experienced by small to medium-sized companies. Some employment experts suggest that you devote 75 percent of your job-seeking time to looking at opportunities in small companies.

8. I should stay away from a certain company because they are laying off employees. This is a myth in that while a company may be laying off some employees with some skills, they may be attempting to hire those with other skills. You may have the background that such a company is searching for as an employee.

9. If I am specialized in a field, I will not be able to work in another area. This is a myth in that most jobs are examined from a functional viewpoint. You may have the skills that can be easily adapted to the needs of another company.

10. I have enough severance pay from my last position to permit me to take it easy for awhile. This would be a mistake; use any severance pay you may receive to obtain additional skills or to conduct a more thorough search for the job you want.

11. The economy is so bad that I'll never obtain work. This is certainly a myth. While the economy has changed in recent years, you should take advantage of the changes rather than wishing for a return to the past. In addition, you should always remember that your career is a marathon, not a sprint.

SELF-MANAGEMENT PROCEDURES

Self-management techniques can be very useful when it comes to seeking a job. These include:

1. Stimulus control. Environmental and cognitive stimuli are both contributing factors to a successful job search.

Environmental stimuli. You must arrange your environment to assist you in seeking a job. As it may be a full-time activity, you may use an alarm clock to remind you to search eight hours a day for your job. Obtain whatever materials you can find, such as want ads, to help spur your job search.

Cognitive stimuli. These are important discriminative stimuli in guiding your search. Only you will know what steps you should take to secure employment. For this reason, you will likely use such methods as: (a) self-instructions and self-statements, (b) imagery, and (c) rehearsal of steps you need to take to find work. Self-instruction using self-statements are particularly important cognitive stimuli.

2. Self-monitoring. This procedure underlies much of your job search. You should keep accurate records of everything you have done in seeking work. This helps you arrange a schedule, as well as serving as a discriminative stimulus to prompt additional efforts.

3. Self-reinforcement. You are apt to be the only person who reinforces you if your job search takes a period of time. Don't give up—reinforce yourself contingent upon positive steps you take to locate suitable employment.

4. Problem solving. These skills are also useful in searching for a job. Of particular importance are the following skills: (a) planning your schedule; (b) considering the employment options that you have; (c) rehearsing your approach to seeking work; (d) acting upon your plans; (e) evaluating your success; (f) preparing for setbacks that are almost invariable in seeking work; and (g) seeking other alternatives if necessary.

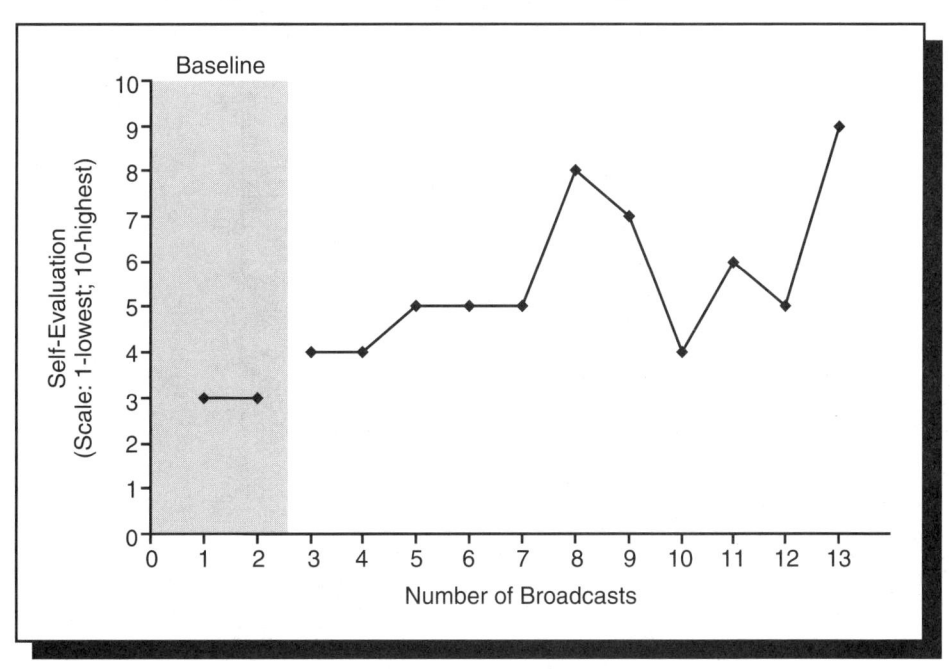

FIGURE 24–1
Use of self-monitoring and rehearsal to improve broadcasting voice.

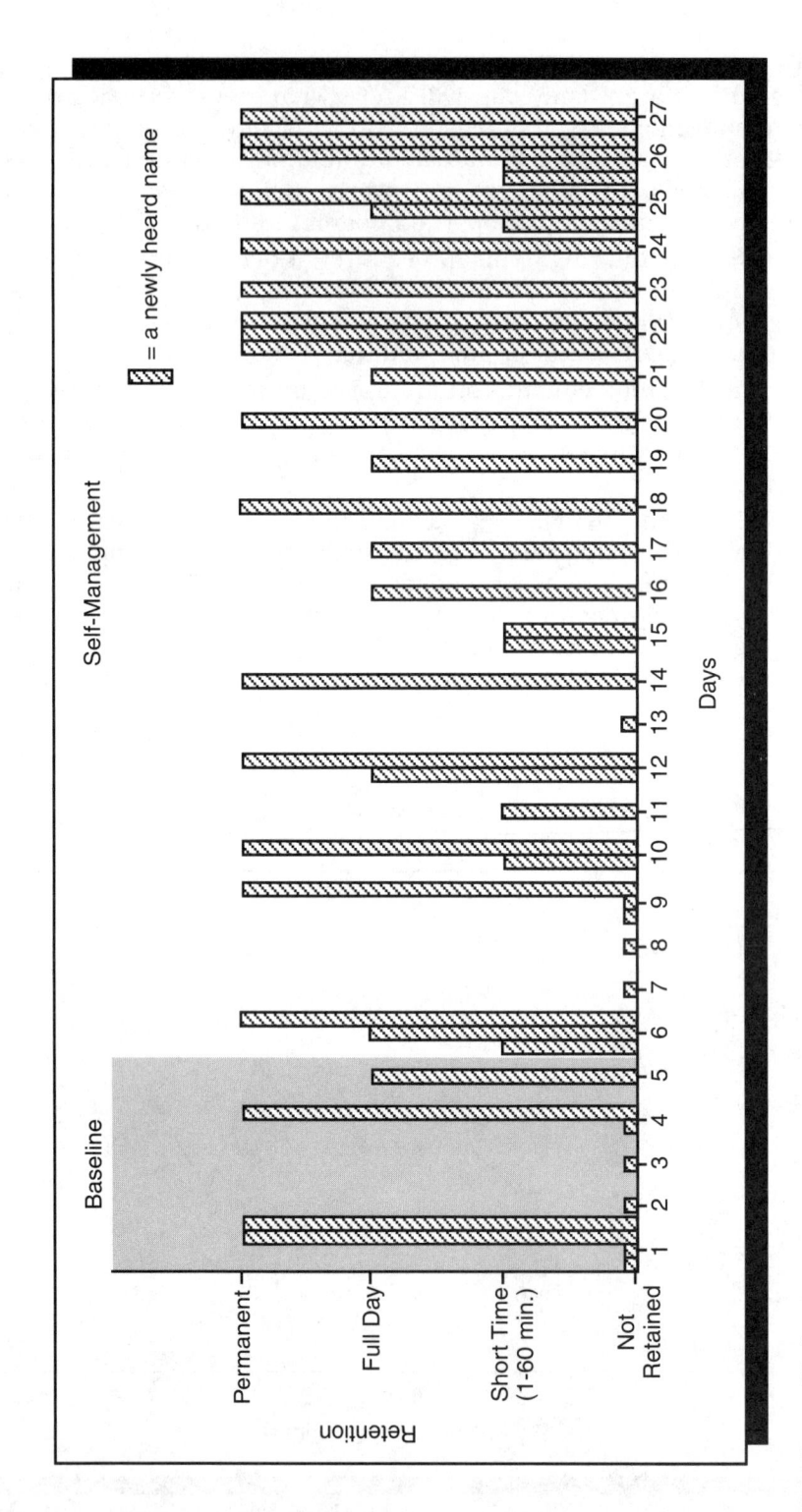

FIGURE 24–2
Use self-management to increase ability to remember names.

SELF-MANAGEMENT PROJECTS

Few students undertake a project designed to help them obtain a job. One student—a telecommunications major—attempted to improve his broadcast voice through self-monitoring and rehearsal. As noted in Figure 24–1, he made progress, particularly toward the end of his project when he attained what seemed to be a natural and effective style of broadcasting. He decided, on the basis of his experience, however, that he was better suited to being a radio producer. He has since taken that career path. Another student, about to start working at a major corporation, took on the project of increasing his ability to remember names. The results of his program are depicted in Figure 24–2. The student used self-monitoring, combined with a mnemonic technique of being certain to hear a new name clearly, associating the name with a feature of the person, and repeating the name to himself, to improve his memory. As noted in Figure 24–2, the student was highly successful at his project.

EXERCISE

Consider how you will prepare to seek a job.
Consider self-management skills you can employ to obtain employment.

REVIEW TERMS

Chronological resume
Functional resume

Occupational Outlook Handbook
Targeted resume

QUESTIONS

Discuss six basic facts regarding resumes.
List nine topics that should be listed on a resume.
List eleven myths concerning a job search.

CHAPTER 25

Obtaining Employment

"Work keeps at bay three great evils: boredom, vice, and need."
—Voltaire, *Candide*

"Most people hate looking for work, but I kind of enjoy it. It not only gives me the chance to see how other organizations operate, but it allows me to see how my skills compare to other positions. I don't see how you can move ahead if you aren't constantly challenging yourself by looking for a better position. I don't think I'm a big risk taker, but you have to take some risks if you want to move ahead."
—Ken, a division manager

You want to be able to apply your knowledge and skills to a job as soon as you graduate. At the same time, you have undoubtedly heard horror stories of the economy and the difficulty of finding a position that is both challenging and rewarding. There is no doubt that the market is tough for college graduates, although the picture is currently brighter than it has been in the past few years. Obtaining the best position for you will require considerable persistence on your part. At the same time, it will require preparation and the use of the self-management procedures presented in the text.

JOB SEARCH TIPS

Chapter 24 highlighted some aspects of seeking work. Suggestions offered in this chapter will amplify what was noted. Seeking work is one of the most difficult jobs that any of us will experience. It is also an activity that occurs repeatedly throughout our work career. For this reason, consider the following suggestions when it comes to seeking work.

Consistency of work-seeking behaviors. When you seek work, you must realize that there are no specific hours or days of operation. Seeking work is a full-time activity, day in and day out, seven days a week. You have no specific office or work site, nor do you have a supervisor. Seeking work is an activity entirely dependent upon self-instruction.

Immediate objective in seeking work. The immediate goal you have is to get as many interviews as possible, even in companies where there may be no openings for anyone with your skills. You cannot achieve this goal without considerable effort on your part. Make up a daily schedule and adhere to it. In the evening, compose your schedule for the next day. If you have no appointments scheduled, you may wish to visit an employment service, the library, or the personnel office of a company. Keeping busy helps maintain your momentum.

Research the companies that interest you. You may conduct part of this research at the library. If you know someone who works at the firm where you are seeking employment, discuss the firm with this person. Employees of a company can provide you with invaluable information. At the same time, such individuals can come to serve as a network of contacts for you.

Line up as many interviews as you can. Aim to have several interviews a week. The research you have conducted will permit you to achieve this goal.

Don't quit. Even if you have several interviews lined up, keep to your basic schedule until you are offered employment. You will find work, even though it may take time.

Maintain a positive attitude. A daily schedule will contribute to your attitude; you can reinforce yourself for trying. You might also plan to do some daily physical exercise and to do something that permits you to escape from the constant grind of job seeking. If you find that you are beginning to worry about whether you will ever find work, intensify your efforts by reading job search materials.

BUILDING CONFIDENCE THROUGH PREPARATION

The better prepared you are, the more confident you are apt to be in seeking employment. The process of looking for work is stressful for everyone. We all realize that obtaining work is not only required for our livelihood, but that we will be unable to use our skills and experiences without relevant employment. To prepare for a position, the following suggestions are offered.

Learn about the company and position. Learn as much as you can about the company where you are seeking employment. This will improve your ability to answer any questions you may be asked.

Consider your skills in relation to the position. Once you have acquired a basic knowledge regarding the company and the position you are seeking, you can consider how your experiences and abilities best fit the employer. You must concentrate on selling yourself as the best person available for the advertised position. At the same time, careful consideration of your abilities will permit you to think of how your personal goals fit the position. If additional knowledge leads you to believe that the position is not compatible with your goals, you may want to consider either how best to make it congruent with these goals or if the position is the best slot for you (don't be too fussy in looking for work, particularly in a tight market).

Delay discussion of salary and benefits until becoming a candidate of choice. If an employer indicates you are the top candidate for the position, you can broach the topic of salary and benefits. In suggesting a salary, give an estimate of what you think you should receive. A thorough review of what others are paid for comparable work in both your area of expertise and the geographical area where you are seeking employment will make this easier for you. If forced into a game of verbal Ping-Pong regarding salary, attempt to keep the ball on the employer's side of the net; this task will become easier with increased knowledge and experience.

Jot down notes. It is important that as you go through the job seeking process, you keep notes regarding your efforts. Note any unexpected questions that you were asked. You can then think of appropriate answers in case the same questions are asked again in the future. Taking notes also permits you to analyze your performance. Because seeking a job is a skill in and of itself, knowing how you performed will allow you to hone and refine your performance. Finally, jot down any questions you may have. You may even want to jot down a list that you can pull out if offered a job. Most employers are impressed with this practice not only because it indicates that you have done your homework, but because it permits them to explain fully the company, the position you are seeking, and the salary and benefit package offered by the company. It also saves employers' time.

Perform self-management skills. Applying self-management skills is, as with other topics, a major theme that runs throughout the job seeking process.

INTERVIEWING FOR A JOB

There are two types of interviews: a screening interview and a job interview. Screening interviews help companies select the candidates they would like to interview in a follow-up meeting. The following are suggestions for doing well in a job interview.

Rehearsal. You will want to rehearse a job interview with a friend before being actually interviewed. A list of potential questions, culled from several sources, is presented in Table 25–1. Review these questions, as well as how you would answer them, before you go to an interview.

Arrival. Dress neatly and conservatively. For men, this means wearing a jacket and tie; for women, it means wearing your favorite dress. Leave the open shirt and gold chain at home. Go alone to the interview. This will convey the impression that you are independent. Be certain you are on time; in fact, it doesn't hurt if you are a few minutes early for an interview. This not only suggests that you are interested in the job, but it may permit the interviewer to have more time with you.

TABLE 25-1 Questions You May be Asked During a Job Interview

1. Why did you decide to apply for this position? Why are you interested in working for our company?
2. What contributions do you feel you can bring to the company?
3. What qualifications do you have to be successful in our company?
4. What previous work experiences do you have?
5. What are your long-term and short-term goals for the future? How do these goals relate to the position for which you are applying?
6. How do you plan on achieving these goals?
7. What are your strong points?
8. Name one or two accomplishments that illustrate these strong points.
9. What are your major weaknesses?
10. Describe a problem you faced and how you resolved it.
11. What have you learned from your mistakes?
12. Have you ever been fired from a job? Why did you quit your previous jobs?
13. If you were hiring someone for this position, what qualities would you look for?
14. How do you perform under pressure?
15. Why should we hire you?

The interview. There are a number of points to keep in mind during the job interview process.

    1. Make a strong impression. First impressions are strongly influenced by a firm handshake, eye contact, and a smile. If these are not natural responses for you, rehearse them until they become natural. You should remain standing until told where and when to sit.

    2. Attempt to project a positive image. Besides your clothing, you can attempt to project a positive image by being attentive during the interview, and by speaking and answering questions in a firm, clear voice. Because communication skills are significant in an interview, this is another reason you should rehearse what you will do when an interview actually occurs.

    3. Keep answers short and to the point. If the interviewer seems to want you to amplify your answer, ask him or her if more information is required. Do not unnecessarily prolong the interview.

    4. Prepare for tough questions. The most difficult questions are those related to your weaknesses, dislikes, or situations where you have failed. You do not have to answer personal questions about age, sex, or marital status. However, you should use your own judgment when considering whether these personal questions are discriminatory. In some situations, for example, an employer may want to know if arrangements should be made to also hire a spouse or to help a spouse find work.

    5. Don't make a bad impression. Don't alienate your interviewer by making excuses, blaming others for your shortcomings, disagreeing with an interviewer, or using poor diction and grammar (Williams and Long,

1991). Suggesting that a company might be run in a better way is also a way to lose points with an interviewer.

6. *Emphasize qualifications.* Emphasize that you have a strong commitment to seeking a career, and that you want to develop your skills. Attempt to convey that the job you are seeking will permit you to enhance the skills you have.

7. *Ask questions.* You may ask questions regarding the possibility of any on-the-job training. You may also ask other questions about company policies as they relate to improving your job skills.

8. *Reinforce the interviewer.* In leaving, you may want to ask the interviewer what the next step is in the hiring process. Be certain to provide reinforcement to the interviewer for his or her time and consideration. You may complement this appreciation by shaking the interviewer's hand upon leaving or by sending the employer a thank-you note.

9. *Body language.* Some experts believe that your body language may be equally as important as how you verbally answer questions. Different behaviors and how they may be interpreted are enumerated in Table 25–2. You may wish to consider these before your next interview.

TABLE 25–2 Body Language in the Interview Situation

Behavior	Possible Interpretation
Talking too fast	Anxiety; urgency to make good impression
Slow, halting speech	Anxiety; lack of preparation; slow thinker
Frequent clearing of throat	Anxiety
Slouching in chair	Fatigue; laziness; disinterest
Poor eye contact	Timidity; fear; hiding something
Limp handshake	Lack of confidence
Leaning forward in chair, eye contact, smiling and nodding agreement	Interest; sincerity; agreement
Peeking at watch or clock	Concern to see interview ended; disinterest
Eyes down or focused away from interviewer	Shyness; self-consciousness; lack of confidence; hiding something
Open hands, unbuttoned jacket, sitting in relaxed position	Openness; interest; confidence
Blank stare or no eye movement	Disinterest; lack of attention
Hand gestures do not cover face; hands appear relaxed	Interest; confidence
Hands on hips, sitting straight in chair	Interest; readiness; ready for action
Occasionally rubbing hands together	Interest; expectancy
Crossed arms, clenched fists, or crossed legs	Defensiveness
Short breaths, fidgeting in chair	Anxiety; frustration
Drumming fingers on table, foot tapping, drooping eyes	Impatience; boredom; indifference

TABLE 25-3 Suggestions for Assessing Your Performance During a Job Interview (adapted from Williams & Long, 1991)

1. Did I appear neat and clean?
2. Was I on time for my interview?
3. Did I speak clearly, concisely, and directly?
4. Did I appear to be listening actively during the interview?
5. Was I prepared for the questions I was asked?
6. Were my questions appropriate?
7. Did I express appreciation for the company's interest in me?

10. Self-assessment. Williams and Long (1991) suggest that you review your peformance after you have had a job interview. An adaptation of the scale you might use is found in Table 25-3. You should rate each item according to scale: 1 = very weak; 2 = moderately weak; 3 = average; 4 = moderately strong; and 5 = very strong. The higher your score, the stronger your performance.

DEALING WITH REJECTION

Almost all of us have had the experience of not obtaining a job that we applied for. There is often disappointment and, sometimes, a certain amount of resentment that we were not hired. However, not obtaining the job you want can be a great learning experience. After you get over any anger engendered by not receiving a job, call and make an appointment with whomever you talked with concerning the position. Prepare a few questions that you may want to ask such as, "Did I interview okay?" or "Did I lack any qualifications that you were looking for?" Dress for the meeting like you did when you interviewed; after all, you still want to make a good impression upon the person you are talking with. Be polite in asking your questions. If the feedback you receive is unclear, don't hesitate to ask further questions. Thank the interviewer for his or her time. The feedback you obtain from these follow-up meetings can be invaluable. It may offer you ways to rewrite your resume, to dress more appropriately, to present suggestions for interviewing better, or to indicate the type of job that best fits your training and interests. In the long run, your failure to obtain a particular job may be the best experience you have in guiding you forward in your career.

FACTORS TO CONSIDER IN DECIDING TO ACCEPT OR REJECT A JOB OFFER

There are certain aspects of a job offer that you may wish to consider before accepting a position.

1. Encouragement of interactions among employees. You would like to work in a position where there is informal and spontaneous conversation among workers. These conversations may or may not be work-related, but should occur across all levels of employees.

2. Established grievance procedures. You would like to work at a position where there are established guidelines for filing a grievance. These should be guidelines that are accepted by both employees and managers.

3. Toleration of individual differences.

4. Feedback provided to employees. All employees would like to know if they are doing a good job. You need such feedback if you are to progress in your career.

5. Possibility of stock ownership plans and profit-sharing. When you work at a company that offers these benefits, you feel that you are somehow partially responsible for the success of the company.

6. Newsletter or bulletins produced by employees. These help you identify with the aims of the company. In addition, they are a source of reinforcement when your work successes are described.

7. Policies and procedures are adjusted to meet the needs of employees.

If these are inadequate guidelines to assist you in deciding whether to accept a job offer, you might also ask: (a) to talk to the employees with whom you will be working; (b) for additional materials regarding pay and benefits; and (c) additional questions of the person who interviews you or who makes you a job offer.

SELF-MANAGEMENT PROCEDURES

Self-management skills are at the core of job seeking. Those you should perform include:

1. Stimulus control. Environmental and cognitive stimuli will guide much of your performance.

Environmental stimuli. You should arrange the environment to help you seek employment. Use a clock to be certain you wake up and go about seeking work much as you would if you were employed. The schedule you jot down should be placed in a prominent place to remind you of what you intend to do during the day. You need access to a telephone where you can discuss job opportunities in private and without interruptions. In short, change the environment any way necessary to help it contribute to your job search.

Cognitive stimuli. Self-instructions will prompt, direct, and maintain your employment search. Self-instructions require the constant use of self-statements to guide your performance. Rehearsal is important in considering how you will manage interviews. You may also want to use relaxation exercises to manage the stress of the job search, and thought stopping to control any negative thoughts that threaten to disrupt your quest for employment.

2. Self-monitoring. Only you will know if you actually sought work. Observing and recording aspects of your behavior permits you to determine if any additional steps are required. In addition, an accurate record can serve as both a discriminative stimulus and a reinforcement to you.

3. Self-reinforcement. You should reinforce yourself for your job-seeking performance. During the early stages when you may not obtain any job leads, only the reinforcement you provide yourself may maintain your behavior.

4. Problem solving. Problem-solving skills underlie much of what you do when seeking work. Particular skills include: (a) planning what you are going to do; (b) considering the options you have; (c) rehearsing your selected strategy; (d) acting on your plan; (e) evaluating your progress; (f) preparing for any setbacks that are apt to occur in looking for work; and (g) considering additional alternatives in seeking work.

EXERCISE

Consider how you might improve your job search.
Recall your last job interview. Could you have made a stronger impression?
Consider the factors you want to consider before accepting your next position.

REVIEW TERMS

Screening interview
Self-monitoring and job search
Self-reinforcement and job search

QUESTIONS

List seven aspects regarding the job search.
List seven suggestions for assessing your performance during a job search.
List seven factors to consider in deciding whether to accept a job offer.

CHAPTER 26

The Workplace

"I don't like work—no man does—but I like what is in the work—the chance to find yourself."
—Joseph Conrad, *Heart of Darkness*

"It's not that I hate to work. Most days, it doesn't bother me to get up and go to work. What I don't like is to be told what to do, you know? I've been told I have problems with authority, whatever the hell that means. I like doing things my way. If I feel like working hard, I work hard. If I feel like taking a break, I'll take a break. Since my ideas aren't always the same as those I work for, I've had many jobs. Too many, according to my wife. Someday, I'll find the right job."
—Roger, an unemployed factory worker

Many of you have held at least one job. You have already tasted what it is like to be in the workplace. In most cases, you worked because you wanted to earn money to help with school expenses or to purchase items you wanted, such as clothes or a car. You recognized you were not locking yourself into a long-term commitment with a given employer when you accepted employment, but wanted to work until you had achieved your short-term goals. Knowing your employment was apt to be of relatively brief duration, you probably cared little about policies, long-term benefits, or chances for advancement within the company. You were likely concerned only with whether you could survive your immediate supervisor, work as many hours as you could while maintaining your studies, and, hopefully, make more than the minimum wage.

The experiences you have had in working will prove useful to you during your college education and when you launch your career. There are a number of ways you can use self-management procedures to forge ahead in the workplace. Approaches you might consider are addressed in this chapter.

STARTING A NEW JOB

Deutsch (1984) listed six tips for starting a new job:

1. Dress for success. When starting a job, you want to prepare as much as you did when you interviewed for the position. Be clean, neat, and dress conservatively. You may overdress at first, but you can later change your dress to fit the policy of the company. The employees in most companies dress more casually than they did a decade or so ago; whether this trend will be maintained in the future is unknown.

2. Capitalize on employee orientation program. Most companies offer pamphlets or orientation sessions for new employees. Take advantage of them. They will explain not only the goals of the company in more detail, but what is expected of you. In addition, you will learn about company benefits and how to utilize them. During the first weeks you hold a new job, you also are involved in an informal orientation to the company. You must attach names to faces, acquire knowledge of the chain of command within the firm, and learn new procedures. Your success at mastering these tasks will depend upon your memory.

3. Determine the company's style. Some firms are formal. Not only will you be expected to dress in a conservative manner, but interactions between and among employees are very formal. Other organizations, particularly small or newer firms, often tend to be informal. You must adapt your behavior to fit the style of the company.

4. Develop friendly relations with your coworkers. Deutsch suggests that you make friends, but do so carefully. Remember the rule of thumb about disclosure and only disclose as much about yourself as others disclose about themselves. Sometimes you may be so anxious that you talk too much about yourself; self-management procedures, particularly relaxation, can help you control this behavior. There are usually factions of employees in any organization. A potential problem in starting at a new job is that you may become involved in a faction without wishing to do so. There always seem to be malcontents in any office who actively seek recruits to their cause. Avoid cliques, at least at first. Later, you may find that belonging to a particular group can be advantageous not only to your success within the company, but to attaining your overall goals.

5. Self-monitor your performance. Monitoring your progress in fulfilling assignments is a key part of any employment. Suggestions on performing such self-management duties will be described later.

6. Go all out. You want to do your best when you start a job. Despite what may be indifference or a lack of productivity by your coworkers, you want to demonstrate to the company that they made the right choice in selecting you. What is more important, however, is that you must perform tasks to achieve your personal career goals, and not be swayed by the work habits of others. You can only achieve your goals through the monitoring of your behavior.

SELF-MANAGEMENT AND JOB PERFORMANCE

A number of suggestions are offered by Williams and Long (1991) for improving your job effectiveness and satisfaction. All have potential for enhancement through self-management.

Develop priorities. You may feel overwhelmed with work during your initial days with a company. In order to achieve all that is expected of you, review the material on setting priorities presented in Chapter 11. Keep an ongoing record that states: (a) what work is expected of you, (b) the importance of different tasks, and (c) the dates certain work is due. Based on this information, you can prioritize your work assignments. You can use the same principles that were discussed with respect to time management and studying behaviors to develop both a short-term and a long-term schedule of when you will accomplish given tasks. Such schedules also allow you to better plan your personal time.

Complete work on time. Williams and Long (1991) point out that there are two reasons for completing your work on time. First, others' work may depend upon what you are doing, and second, you achieve personal satisfaction in completing assigned tasks on time. In achieving a deadline, you should remember that completing your work is usually less significant than the quality of your effort. No time is saved if you have to redo shoddy work. In addition, poor-quality work does little for your overall reputation within a company.

Once you have completed work, ask for feedback. This is especially important during the first few weeks you are on a job. After a few months, such feedback is often unnecessary; you know if your work is of high quality or not. If you find that you have free time upon completion of a task, ask for other tasks or develop other skills that will be useful to you in your career.

Contribute to company goals. You want the company you work for to achieve their goals. In business, this means that they prosper. If your company achieves its goals, you will be reinforced; at the same time, you will have taken a step toward fulfilling your career goals. If, after a period of working for a company, you find that the goals of your company seem to be on a course for collision with your personal goals or you see little chance for personal advancement, reevaluate your position and consider other options. It is unwise to make this decision when only working for a company for a few weeks or months; however, at the same time, you don't want to wait until you have too much invested in the company, particularly their benefits and retirement package, that you feel locked in and unable to change jobs.

Function effectively in meetings. Much of your time will be spent in planning or other types of organizational meetings. It is wise to prepare for any meeting, even if it involves nothing more than jotting down a few notes you would like to make at the meeting. If you want to be critical of company policies, avoid doing so at public meetings. Such comments are apt to be perceived as a personal criticism by your supervisors. It is better to emphasize how existing policies might be improved. If you approach the matter in this way, you are likely to rally support among your coworkers. A basic skill you should achieve in any meeting is when to talk and when to listen. Acquiring this skill can guide you through the remainder of your employment career.

Overall, most meetings you will attend are a drag. As some administrators in the company think they are necessary, you can alleviate your

TABLE 26–1 Assessing Your Job Performance (adapted from Williams and Long, 1991)

1. I balance my work and personal life.
2. I have defined my priorities at work.
3. I usually complete work assignments on time.
4. My work is generally of high quality.
5. My personal work goals benefit my organization.
6. My recommendations in meetings are usually accepted.
7. I know the most respected workers in my organization.
8. I have good rapport with most of my coworkers and supervisors.
9. I frequently acknowledge and reinforce the accomplishments of coworkers.

boredom by actively listening and participating in any meeting. While you may not be converted to the necessity of such meetings, you will learn points about how you would run a company when you are in a supervisory position.

Use informal structure. All companies, no matter how large, have a formal and informal structure. The formal structure consists of written policies, procedures, and lines of supervision. You will be told during your orientation how you are to function within this structure. The informal structure represents how the company really operates. Your success within a company will depend not only upon your knowledge of informal procedures, but of the contacts you have with others in the company. For this reason, you should make every effort not only to learn how a company operates, but to build constructive contacts within the organization. Your ability to use the informal structure may ultimately determine your success in a company.

Develop constructive relationships. To repeat a point made earlier, you should take a cautious approach in developing relationships. If you don't, you could find yourself allied with a clique that can cause you more harm than good. If you can establish friendly relations with everyone in the company, it will alleviate any personal stress and permit you to concentrate on your work. Being perceived by your coworkers and management as an independent person is generally a plus in every company.

Assess effectiveness. Williams and Long (1991) provide a checklist that you might consider in evaluating your work performance. An adaptation of this checklist is provided in Table 26–1.

DEALING WITH DIFFICULT COWORKERS

Brinkman and Kirschner (1994) describe ten types of difficult coworkers you are apt to encounter in any office or work environment. They represent normal people at their worst. The people are:

1. The tank. These people are confrontational, pointed, and angry. Their aggressive actions are intimidating to many of their coworkers.
2. The sniper. These people are sarcastic, make rude comments, and perform gestures, like rolling their eyes, that are intended to make you look foolish.
3. The grenade. These people are generally calm, but they can explode into undirected and unfocused ranting and raving about things that have no relevance to the stimulus or event that sets them off.
4. The know-it-all. These people are seldom in doubt that they know best. They have a low tolerance for frustration and contradiction. When something goes wrong, they always speak out to say who is at fault. It is never them.
5. The think-he (she)-knows-it-all. These people can't fool all the people all the time, but they can fool some of the people enough of the time to gain attention. These people can often be effective with people, particularly supervisors, who have only recently joined your unit.
6. The yes person. These people always want to please everyone; as a result, they say yes without thinking of other commitments they may have.
7. The maybe person. These people procrastinate on even the most mundane decisions. While they wait for a better decision to present itself, the problem often solves itself.
8. The nothing person. These people essentially do or say nothing.
9. The no person. These people find a never-ending battle of futility and despair.
10. The whiner. These people feel overwhelmed by an unfair world. As a result, they whine about everything.

Brinkman and Kirschner point out that there are four ways of dealing with these difficult people:

Do nothing. You can basically do nothing and suffer whatever consequences occur because of your inaction.

Walk away. This is sometimes a viable option. Walking away and escaping from these people is certainly an alternative choice that you sometimes may want to take.

Change your attitude. This solution has value. You can listen to what the person says, and either change or do not change your attitude toward them. Difficult people occasionally present a different perspective; for this reason, you may not want to ignore automatically what they say or do. Listen and make your own judgment.

Change your behavior. Since this approach will involve the performance of self-management skills, this is the best solution. If the problem will not go away unless you take action, be certain to focus on the behavior and not the personality of the individual. Choose a private moment and confront the person about the problem. Don't insult the individual, but express your concern about what you perceive as the problem. Ask the person not to do it again. Refuse to take any of these problems personally; they will consume more of your time and thought than they are worth. Taking the problem personally will not permit you to change what you see as a difficult situation. Other suggestions for dealing with difficult people are offered both in this chapter and throughout the book.

SELF-MANAGEMENT SKILLS

Besides specific duties that you may be asked to discharge, there are general characteristics of a job that may be of value to you. These concern communicating effectively, listening, receiving criticism, managing stress, and providing reinforcement.

Communicating effectively. No skill is more important than being able to communicate either orally or in writing. Work on these skills; your success in any career is apt to be a function of your being able to communicate effectively. Guidelines for effective communication have been offered by Verderber and Verderber (1989). These include:

1. Consider frame of reference of listener. In talking to others, you should consider their background, intelligence, attitudes, and way of responding to your talk. Don't speak in a manner that the listener does not understand; equally ineffective is to talk in a manner that a listener may see as an insult to his or her intelligence. Don't be perceived as condescending.

2. Be specific and concrete. Think beforehand about how you are going to communicate your message. Being specific and direct is most apt to convey your message. If time limits are involved, spell them out in a concrete manner.

3. Avoid "loaded" words. There are certain words that can trigger emotional reactions in individuals. For example, referring to female coworkers as "girls" can understandably provoke an emotional reaction.

4. Be certain verbal and nonverbal messages are congruent. If there is a lack of consistency between your verbal and nonverbal message, the result will be confusion on the part of your listener. An example is attempting to provide constructive criticism while not attending to the person and performing another task.

You should be aware that most people are poor listeners, so you may want to repeat a message or ask people if they have questions. Encouraging them, in a positive manner, to paraphrase what you told them permits you to determine if they understood your message.

Suggestions for improving communication are offered by Unisys, a major computer company (Martin and Osborne, 1989). These steps, some of which reiterate those noted above, are presented in Table 26–2.

Listening effectively. Earlier chapters described methods for improving listening habits. You will recall these habits when considering that effective

> **TABLE 26–2 Ways to Insure Effective Communication (adapted from Martin and Osborne, 1989)**
>
> 1. Insure you have the attention of your listener.
> 2. Select setting to minimize distraction.
> 3. Be certain spoken language is consistent with body language.
> 4. Give instructions with an erect but relaxed posture.
> 5. Maintain eye contact.
> 6. Project voice energetically.
> 7. Don't end sentences so they sound like questions.
> 8. Be specific and provide clear description of problem.
> 9. Put expectations in measurable and observable terms.
> 10. Know goal of instructions.
> 11. Ask for feedback.

listening skills in the work place include: (a) physically attending to the speaker; (b) making eye contact with the speaker; (c) remaining still and refraining from making distracting and impatient signals; (d) maintaining appropriate facial expression; (e) actively attending to and processing the verbal message; (f) attending to nonverbal signals; (g) nodding frequently to show you understand the message; (h) asking pertinent questions; and (i) reflecting back the content of the speaker's statements in your own words. Above all, be certain you understand the message being delivered to you.

Receiving criticism. No matter how high you go in a company, even if you become the Chief Executive Officer, you will receive some form of criticism. Rather than becoming angry when receiving such rebukes, attempt to consider the criticism as a way you can improve your performance and learn new skills. Ways you can learn to manage criticism, including some suggestions by Martin and Osborne (1989) and Williams and Long (1991), are:

1. Distinguish between constructive criticism and destructive attempts to manipulate you. Most criticism is well-meaning; the person providing it wants to help you do a better job. Attempt to accept it this way. This means that you will occasionally need to look for the idea the person wants to convey to you and overlook such personal characteristics as sarcasm, biting remarks, overgeneralizations, and sexist or hostile remarks meant to intimidate you.
2. Listen attentively to relevant criticism until fully expressed.
3. Maintain eye contact and a relaxed posture; avoid confrontational body language.
4. Use self-statements and relaxation strategies to cope with a situation if you begin to feel angry or emotional. Keep cool.
5. When criticism is finished, ask nonthreatening questions to clarify your understanding of the speaker's concern.

6. Paraphrase what has been said to you so that you fully understand the criticism.
7. Once you understand the criticism, recognize the mistake and make every effort to correct it.
8. Discuss alternative ways of resolving the problem.
9. Avoid lengthy explanations or justifications for your behavior.
10. If you feel you were unjustly criticized, permit a passage of time to elapse before you respond. This will allow you to respond in a calm and reasoned manner to your concern.
11. Look at criticism in a positive manner as a way for you to learn. As noted earlier, we often only learn through making mistakes.

Managing stress. You have been taught a number of self-management techniques for managing stress. These can be used to control common stressors in the workplace (Williams and Long, 1991): (a) being underchallenged; (b) being overworked by having either too much work (quantitative work overload) or work that is too difficult (qualitative work overload); (c) working for someone who regularly ignores or criticizes your work; (d) working under adverse organizational or environmental conditions; and (e) becoming an informal spokesperson for others' complaints.

Reinforcing effectively. You want to have good relations with your supervisors and coworkers. This can be achieved by regular reinforcement. You can use general praise or specific praise as reinforcers.

SELF-MANAGEMENT PROCEDURES

Self-management techniques can be indispensable in helping you survive the workplace. These would include:

1. Stimulus control. Environmental and cognitive stimuli can be manipulated to enhance stimulus control of work habits.

Environmental stimuli. If you work in the same area each day, you can arrange stimuli to prompt and maintain good work habits. At the same time, you might design your work area to be reinforcing to you. Add photographs, pictures, or plants. As you spend a major portion of your life at work, it behooves you to take advantage of any opportunity to arrange stimuli in a manner designed to make your work more pleasant.

Cognitive stimuli. Cognitive stimuli can be established through self-instruction and self-statements, refocused thinking, imagery, rehearsal of your job functions, and relaxation exercises.

2. Self-monitoring. You will certainly want to establish a way to monitor your performance. Using self-monitoring will permit you to determine if you are reaching the work goals established for you.

3. Self-reinforcement. There are usually gaps between the types of reinforcement provided to you. You can bridge these gaps through the use of self-reinforcement.

4. Problem solving. Working at any job occasionally requires that you solve problems that may occur. You can rely on the following strategies: (a) planning ahead to establish the schedule on which you work; (b) considering the options you have in solving a problem; (c) rehearsing the tactics you decide to employ; (d) acting upon your decision; (e) evaluating the success of your selected strategy; (f) preparing for any setbacks if they occur; and (g) considering other alternatives to solve job-related problems.

EXERCISE

Think of problems you have encountered in the work place.
List the problems.
Think of self-management procedures applicable to changing the behaviors.

REVIEW TERMS

Employee orientation Formal structure
Informal structure Loaded words

QUESTIONS

List ten types of difficult coworkers.
Discuss four guidelines for effective communication.
List eleven methods for managing criticism.

CHAPTER 27
Changing Jobs

"Is any man afraid of change? Why, what can take place without change? What then is more pleasing or more suitable to the universal nature?"
—Marcus Aurelius, *Meditations*

"I have always looked at what changes would be best for me. I had certain long-term goals that I wanted to achieve, namely being the president of a company. I have made seven major job changes. Many were excellent positions. In fact, I think a couple were the most enjoyable jobs I've had during my career. However, I would reach a point where there was nowhere to go at a company. Job satisfaction was just not enough of an incentive for me. I needed change. A couple of the jobs I had did not last. It didn't take long to realize that I had made a horizontal move rather than one that could help me advance. Overall, however, I think I learned something at every place I worked. The knowledge has all come in handy in my current position."
—Pete, president and CEO of a health organization

The first job you have is unlikely to be the only job you will have in your work career. Some experts estimate you will change jobs at least six or seven times during the span of your work life. In addition, there is increasing evidence that many people change their careers two or three times over the course of their lives. Those who change jobs fall along a spectrum. One end of the spectrum is anchored by those individuals who actively plan on changing their careers once or twice during their lifetime. Most of you, for example, know someone who quit a steady job working for someone else in order to start his or her own small business. This practice is far more common than it was a couple of decades ago. Many individuals work at a job for a period before deciding that it is time to do something they have planned on doing in their lives. The other end of the spectrum is anchored by those workers who have been forced to consider other career alternatives. These are workers who often took jobs with the expectation that they would remain with a given company for their entire career. Corporate downsizing, restructuring, and layoffs have led a growing number of people to reexamine their job choices. Along the spectrum are a growing number of workers who are discontented with their jobs. Whether they make any attempt to move will depend upon how willing they are to make the commitment to change jobs or careers.

Massive changes in a broad number of industries indicate that job stability that relies upon a firm or company is fast becoming obsolete. A different sort of job stability has begun to emerge: the shift toward job or career stability being placed upon the skills and competencies of individual workers rather than a company or corporation. Experts suggest that this trend will be accelerated over the course of your work career. Before exploring strategies that you can take to plan a job or career change, this chapter will describe reasons individuals want to change their jobs.

REASONS TO CHANGE A JOB OR CAREER

A variety of factors contribute to the desire to change jobs. These include:

Organizational factors. People may wish to change careers because of factors existing within the company or organization for which they work. Organizational factors include:

1. Lack of financial incentives. When you work at a job for a period, you often become aware of the salaries others within your company and in your specialty are being paid. If you are not making a salary comparable to those performing the same job as yours, this usually leads to job discontent.

2. Lack of career development. In accepting a position, you expect that it will serve as a stepping stone to a more challenging and higher-paying position. When it does not, there is often the feeling that you are stuck in a rut with respect to your job. You begin to desire an opportunity to reach the career goals you had when you started.

3. Work overload. You may feel that you are being overloaded with work. Some individuals thrive under these circumstances. Many others, however, begin to wonder if it is all worthwhile. The time urgency surrounding the completion of tasks or the increasing complexity of a position may also lead you to consider other options. You may also feel that you are becoming overspecialized in a particular job and yearn to broaden the number of skills you can develop and use.

4. Decision making in organization. When you work for others, you are usually excluded from the decision-making process. The locus of control for what occurs in the company rests entirely with others, although the consequences of the decisions are apt to have a greater impact upon you and your fellow workers than anyone else. For example, automobile workers at one company complained to their supervisors that the firm was producing a product that would be a lemon and not sell. Company officials, however, were enamored with their new product and ordered production of the new model. Unfortunately, the workers were right: the model of the automobile not only failed to sell, but the automobile plant itself was closed.

Individual factors. A number of factors can contribute to the desire to change jobs. These include:

1. Job frustration and stress. It is difficult to continue working at a position if you feel frustrated with working conditions, supervision, or other factors. After a period of frustration, you may begin to feel stress. Seven out of ten American workers say job stress causes frequent problems, and 46 percent rate their jobs as highly stressful. According to a study by the Northwestern National Life Insurance Company (1991), 34 percent of surveyed workers thought about quitting and 14 percent actually did. Characteristics of stress are described in Table 27-1. When stress consistently occurs, it may be time to consider other job and career opportunities. If you cannot leave a company or do not wish to move, review the options you have within the company. They may provide you training if you decide to seek another opportunity within the organization. If such an opportunity is not available, you might seek professional counseling to assist you in reducing job-related stress.

2. Job ambiguity. You may be unsure of what you should be doing at your job. Job ambiguity can be created by one or more of the following factors: (a) unclear policies and objectives surrounding your job; (b) confusion regarding your responsibilities; (c) ambiguous working procedures; (d) unclear expectations regarding what you should be doing; and (e) limited feedback with respect to your performance.

Environmental factors. A number of factors in your work environment may contribute to your desire to seek other positions, including:

1. Supervisors. This is one of the major factors leading to worker discontent and, in some cases, worker stress. You simply may not get along well with your immediate supervisor, despite every effort on your part to do so. If the situation worsens and becomes untenable, it is time

TABLE 27-1 Conditions Commonly Indicative of Stress

Lack of initiative or interest
Reduced initiative or interest
Physical changes, including high blood pressure, unexplained perspiration, fatigue, headaches, stomachaches, weight loss, troubled sleep, or respiratory disturbances
Mood changes, including frustration, anger, or feelings of worthlessness
Excessive criticism of self and others
Inflexibility and lack of spontaneity
Lack of sense of humor
Perception that you are working more but achieving less

to consider seeking another position or career. More on bosses will be described in Chapter 28.

2. Work changes. You may be asked to do a task that you feel you either do not want to perform or lack the skills to perform in an adequate manner. Unless you receive additional training, you may wish to consider a change in jobs.

3. Reorganization of the company. A reorganization of a company may change your job description or the opportunity you have for advancement. When this occurs, it may be a signal to consider changing jobs.

4. Work schedule. Many jobs call for employees to work different times of the day. This is no problem for many workers; they seem to do well whether working a day or a night shift. Others, however, find it difficult to work at night. Despite every effort on their part, they find that they cannot adjust to working at any time other than days. Since their biological rhythms may contribute to this difficulty, it is more than just their expressed desire. A senior pilot of a major airline once confided that although his peers thought he had the best route of his airline—the New York to Paris run—he had given it up. He could not adjust to the change in time zones despite his considerable experience as a pilot. If you have difficulty adjusting to time changes, it is time to consider a change in jobs.

5. Relocation. Some workers have no problems moving to other areas of the country if asked to do so by their firm. Others, particularly older workers, find such moves are disruptive. Other workers do not wish to move because they believe that they are living in a desirable geographical area. You may have no choice but to look for other work if you decline a move when asked to do so.

6. Physical environment. A number of factors can contribute to worker dissatisfaction including excessive noise, inadequate lighting, temperature fluctuations, and the physical posture required to do a task. Those who work at computers most of the time, for example, complain of physical difficulties ranging from vision to hand and wrist problems.

Burnout. Burnout is another factor creating the desire to make a job change. You may be like an increasing number of employees are experiencing burnout at their positions. Burnout is attributed to a number of factors, including: (a) lack of challenge, (b) personality conflicts, (c) lack of opportunities for advancement or to achieve personal goals, (d) corporate policies and politics, and (e) ambiguous working conditions. If you experience burnout at your position, it may be time to seek another position.

PLANNING A JOB CHANGE

Whether a job change is expected or unexpected, there are a number of tactics you may take in planning for it, including the following suggestions:

Develop a positive outlook. If you are considering a change of jobs or careers, it is imperative that you adopt a positive outlook toward the process. This should not be difficult to attain if you have decided to change jobs or careers without any external pressures. It may be more difficult if you find that you are terminated, particularly after working at a job that you enjoyed. A company takeover and the changes that ensue can be difficult for many employees. As Bing (1992) noted, "A takeover is the ultimate career disaster for the dedicated employee. The more loyal and emotionally tied to the existing company you have been, the bleaker the future looms" (p. 63). Whatever the circumstances prompting your job quest, a positive outlook incorporates the following five components:

1. Positive expectations. You need to be positive in expecting that change will present new opportunities for success. Even if unexpectedly thrown out of a job, you should believe that your next position will be better than the one you held. Expectations have a way of being self-fulfilling; if you believe that circumstances will improve with a new job, they are likely to do so.

2. Goal orientation. You should consider the goals you would like to achieve in a new position and then set about to achieve the goals. Any setback should be regarded as a temporary impediment to the attaining of your goals.

3. Flexibility. You need to be flexible in attempting to achieve your aims. One of the few abilities we all have is the potential for creativity. Be creative in the approach you take toward attaining career goals. You may find that you have to alter the expectations that you start out with, but the change may prove better than your original objectives.

4. Organization. Any job or career change requires that you be organized. As was emphasized in Chapter 25, a successful job search is based upon solid organization on your part. In turbulent economic times, you will flourish better if you are well organized.

5. Proactiveness. Always take the initiative in seeking to change your job or career. Being proactive is necessary if you are to use self-management techniques successfully in your job search. Don't wait for change to occur; take action to induce positive change.

Self-assessment. Preparatory to a job or career change, you should perform an objective self-assessment of yourself. Ask yourself the following questions: What are my strengths? How can I best convey these strengths to others? What are my weaknesses? How can I best change them into strengths? What has been the most satisfying aspect of my previous work history? How can I best translate this aspect into another job or career? What are the major accomplishments I have achieved in my career? Honest self-assessment may be the determining factor in guiding you toward a new and satisfying career.

Financial support. If you are going to look for work, you will want to determine how you can support yourself while you search. If you have received severance pay from a previous employer, this may tide you over until you have made a job or career change. If not, you might want to consider the following suggestions by Stern (1993):

1. Determine budget priorities. Start with rent or mortgage payments to keep a roof over your head. Then, in descending order, you should pay utilities, bank cards, and local store or gasoline credit cards. Stern suggests that you make minimum payments on cards to conserve cash. You might negotiate other debts with dentists, physicians, and other professionals. If you have carefully planned your job or career switch, you may not need to make such arrangements.
2. Restructure your debt. This is a particularly solid strategy in periods when interest rates are low.
3. Obtain health insurance. You might consider an HMO or a short-term health policy.
4. Sell some belongings. Have a garage sale and sell anything you have that you no longer use or need. This may provide you with enough to pay for printing a new resume, postage stamps, and gasoline.
5. Seek temporary employment. You might consider doing such tasks as being a waiter, clerk, or cab driver as a stop-gap measure to support you while searching for work.
6. Forgo unnecessary luxuries. You can always cancel such luxuries as TV cable service, magazine subscriptions, or going out to dinner.

If you are planning a major midlife career change that requires more formal education, you might consider these options:

1. Obtain financial support. Financial support is attainable for midlife students. The financial officer of a college or university can tell you what aid is available and how to apply for it.
2. Determine what schools have midcareer programs. Discuss your goals with career counselors or admission officers at a nearby college or university. If they do not have programs available for your needs—and most of them do—they can suggest options for you.
3. Talk to professional groups. A number of professional groups can provide assistance to those seeking a midlife career change.
4. Conduct your own research. You can always look at what is available through research in a library or a university.

Targeted search. The second time around, it is particularly important to target your job search carefully. By now, you have a good idea of the goals you want to attain in a job or career. You can talk to placement officials at your university to receive pointers on conducting a targeted search for a new position. There are also a number of support programs, particularly for older employees, that can be of assistance in planning and conducting a targeted search for a new position.

Information interview. It is good to interview someone in the area where you are seeking work. Even if a company has no jobs available, a member of the personnel staff may discuss the pros and cons of your job or career selection. You may also want to discuss this topic with personnel in an employment office. They are generally very knowledgeable about which areas are hot and which are not.

Resume. Chapter 24 offered a comprehensive discussion of the importance of a resume. A resume assumes even greater importance when you seek to change jobs or careers. As you accumulate more experiences and training, you want to emphasize your accomplishments to enhance your attractiveness to a potential employer. The use of a personal computer will permit you to highlight aspects of your resume in order to tailor it for a given company or firm.

Emotional support. Being terminated from a position is one of the most difficult crises that a person can undergo. People go through many of the processes that are characteristic of death (Chapter 31) in that they deny what is happening to them, become angry, attempt to bargain with fate over their circumstances, become depressed, and finally accept the inevitable. You need the support of others to overcome these problems. For this reason, it is important that you become involved in networking by establishing contacts with people who will support you as you attempt to find work. A network may be formal or informal. Employment experts suggest that you should attempt to contact as many people as possible in an attempt to recruit assistance in the job search. Many experts even go so far as to suggest that the more people who know you are seeking work, the greater is the likelihood that you will find job prospects.

SELF-MANAGEMENT PROCEDURES

Self-management methods should be the foundation of any job or career change. Techniques useful in this regard include:

1. Stimulus control. Environmental and cognitive stimuli can induce employment change.

Environmental stimuli. As much as possible, you should arrange your environment to generate and maintain your career opportunities. Ways to achieve this aim were described in Chapter 24.

Cognitive stimuli. Such cognitive procedures as self-instructions and self-statements, imagery, rehearsal, relaxation, and thought stopping have a role in changing jobs or careers. Becoming more assertive, as outlined in Chapter 21, may also be necessary.

2. Self-monitoring. Keeping accurate records of your behavior can serve both to prompt and to maintain your job or career change. The data can also serve as a discriminative stimulus to maintain your focus.

3. Self-reinforcement. During all stages of changing a job or career, you will need to provide reinforcement to yourself. This is particularly needed when there are no other sources of reinforcement.

4. Problem solving. Problem solving should serve as a framework for job change. Relevant methods include: (a) planning and establishing your goals; (b) considering if there are other equally attractive options available to you; (c) rehearsing the strategies you want to follow as you seek to change employment; (d) acting on your plans; (e) evaluating the success of the tactics you have applied; (f) preparing for the setbacks that invariably accompany a job search; and (g) considering other alternatives to the ones you have taken.

EXERCISE

Consider how you might arrive at a decision to seek another job or career.
Consider the self-management techniques you might use to change jobs or careers.

REVIEW TERMS

Burnout	Networking
Job ambiguity	Proactive

QUESTIONS

List seven characteristics of stress.
Discuss five components involved in developing a positive outlook.
Discuss six suggestions for reducing expenses while searching for a job.

CHAPTER 28

Directing Others

"Organizational sanity becomes quite simple to define: the sane person is the one who fulfills his title, consistently doing what people expect him to do. Indeed, doing what people expect defines more than sanity; it defines something even more important, in the long run: success."

—Stanley Bing, *Crazy Bosses*

"I've had every kind of boss there is. Some have been excellent, others have been bastards. Some really care about you and want to see you do the job as best you can. Others really don't give a damn about you. As long as they get ahead, that's all that counts. I used to wonder why middle-aged workers started looking forward to retirement. I don't any more."

—Mary, an office manager

All of you, if you wish, will likely have the opportunity to supervise others in the future, for two reasons. First, by virtue of your education, you will have a broader array of skills than many individuals. This will permit you opportunities that others do not have. Second, there are not always candidates for supervisory positions. This statement may sound strange, but the majority of American workers do not wish to direct others either because they lack confidence in their ability or they are afraid they will make mistakes. The problem becomes acute because those who do seek leadership positions often are not qualified because they lack either the appropriate experience or, more importantly, the personality for the position. Most would agree with Townsend (1984), who lamented that we are not producing leaders like we used to.

Considering the above comments, how can you best prepare yourself for a leadership role if you desire such a position? There are several comments that can be made here.

First, acquire all the experience you can both in school and in the workplace. The broader the array of experiences you have, the more likely you are to experience success as a leader.

Second, work constantly to improve your communication skills. As was noted in Chapter 26, communication is at the backbone of most organizations. The better you can communicate, both orally and in writing, the greater will be your ability to communicate. Becoming a good listener is equally important.

Third, avail yourself of every opportunity to develop and refine your leadership skills. Even if this involves nothing more than becoming a supervisor of one other person, it is a start. Don't set your sights too high at first, especially as you can always move up the ladder.

Fourth, you can't lead others if you don't know the directions they will go with you as their leader. As the Chinese philosopher Lao-Tzu exclaimed, "To lead the people, walk behind them." Robert Townsend added, "True leadership must be for the benefit of the followers, not the enrichment of the leaders" (1984, p. 122). While you ultimately may make the decision as to the direction in leadership, you must be certain that your staff will go with you. Strive to achieve the qualities of leadership expressed by Lao-Tzu:

> As for the best leaders, the people do not notice their existence. The next best, the people honor and praise. The next, the people fear; and the next, the people hate. . . . When the best leader's work is done the people say, "We did it ourselves!"

Fifth, always remember the experiences you had working for someone else. You may harbor some bitterness toward previous bosses. Rather than let this influence you as a supervisor, remember the Golden Rule and treat others as you would like to be treated. To do this, you must acquire and practice all of the skills described in Chapter 26.

Finally, remember that the opportunity to lead others is not an end in and of itself; it is the chance for you to see that the people in the group you supervise are successful at their jobs. If they are, you will be a success as a supervisor. If you take a supervisory position strictly to advance your career, it likely will not happen. You should accept these roles both because you think you can be an excellent boss and because you think you can learn from your experiences. With this attitude, you should do well.

MANAGING PEOPLE

Robert Townsend was a highly successful CEO of Avis. Following his retirement, he wrote two books on his perceptions regarding management. *Further Up the Organization* (1984) contains a number of characteristics that he sees as important in leadership.

Traits of leadership. Townsend proclaimed that he would employ the following criteria in picking the best person as a CEO. These characteristics would be important to anyone in a supervisory position in that the person would:

1. Be used to making people decisions. The person should be skilled at making decisions that concern the workers he or she supervises. The leader should base decisions about people on performance, not friendship or some other factor.

2. Have a high energy level. The person in a leadership role has considerable energy that he or she is able to direct toward performing a job in the most effective manner.

3. The common touch. The good leader is comfortable listening to others. It also helps if the person has served in the trenches in positions similar to those he or she supervises.

4. Be a good listener. In short, the individual would have mastered most of the listening skills described as important in Chapter 26.

5. Have strong and uncomplicated views on company values. The leader should know where the company is going and why. In addition, he or she should be able to communicate these views to those he or she supervises.

6. Be dissatisfied with the current state or direction of the company. This would be less important to someone in middle management, but it certainly would be important to someone who is being appointed as the president or CEO of a company or organization.

Townsend also believes that a good leader exhibits ten other characteristics, as depicted in Table 28–1. Townsend asks that you rate your boss as a leader by scoring each characteristic from 0 to 10. If your boss scores less than 50, Townsend suggests that you look for another job. He

TABLE 28–1 Form for Rating Boss as a Leader (adapted from Townsend, 1984)

_____	1. Person is available. If you have a problem, he or she is there. The person is forceful in making you do your best to generate solutions, not problems.
_____	2. Person is inclusive. He or she is quick to let you in on information or people who are useful and stimulating to you.
_____	3. Person is humorous. He or she has a great sense of humor, particularly when the joke's on that person.
_____	4. Person is fair. He or she is concerned about you and gives credit where credit is due. The person also holds you to your promises.
_____	5. Person is decisive. He or she is determined to get at those unresolved decisions that can tie up an organization for days.
_____	6. Person is humble. He or she admits to own mistakes openly. The person learns from mistakes and expects others to do the same.
_____	7. Person is objective. He or she can distinguish the seemingly important from the truly important and goes where needed.
_____	8. Person is tough. He or she won't let top management or others waste time. The person is more jealous of others' time than of his or her own.
_____	9. Person is effective. He or she teaches you to describe your mistakes, what you have learned, and how you have corrected them.
_____	10. Person is patient. He or she knows when to bite the bullet until you solve your own problem.

also suggests you ask anyone you supervise to rate you and compare your ratings against those of your boss. You may not only be surprised, but you will certainly know the areas of leadership you should work to improve.

Meetings. Townsend believes that regularly scheduled meetings are unnecessary. He suggests only holding problem-oriented meetings when required. This not only saves others' time, but it permits them to focus on resolving a problem when you do have a meeting.

Mistakes. Everyone makes mistakes. Townsend claims that two out of three of his decisions were wrong; nevertheless, he believes that a .333 batting average is good. He also suggests that a supervisor should admit his or her mistakes openly. As noted in an earlier chapter, he or she may even do so with a sense of humor. Townsend offers the opinion that you should beware the boss who walks on water and never makes a mistake; if you have such a boss, you can save yourself considerable grief by seeking employment elsewhere.

Comments about work. Townsend makes the following comments regarding work:

1. People don't hate work. It is as natural as any other activity for them.
2. People don't have to be forced or threatened to work. If they are committed to a given objective, they'll drive themselves more efficiently than anyone can drive them.
3. People will commit themselves only to the extent that they see that the work will satisfy their needs, whatever these needs may be.

It is difficult to argue with these comments.

Policy manual. Townsend believes that you do not need policy manuals in order to be successful as a manager. If one is needed, he recommends the Ten Commandments.

Promises. Townsend believes that if you make promises, you should keep them. Don't make promises that may not be kept.

Thanks. This is a highly neglected form of compensation according to Townsend. It is certainly an underused method of reinforcing others, including those workers you may supervise.

SUPERVISORS

Stanley Bing, a business executive as well as a business columnist for *Esquire* and the *Wall Street Journal*, wrote an insightful book on supervisors, *Crazy Bosses* (1992). He provided profiles on five types of crazy bosses. If you are fortunate, you may encounter only one of these types during your working career. If you are a typical employee or manager, you are likely to encounter two or more. If you are unfortunate or otherwise hexed, you could encounter all five.

The Five Types of Bad Bosses

THE BULLY "The guy always wants you to know that he's the boss. He expects me to be at his beck and call whenever he wants me. One weekend, he'll ask me to come in and prepare a report that isn't due for a couple of weeks. The next week, he may call me in one day and tell me he wants me to make up a fresh pot of coffee. Even though the coffee is fine for everyone else, he says it isn't fresh enough. He'll often thank me for what I do, and then turn around and ask me to do something else that he could do, like checking whether we have enough stationary with his name on the letterhead. The bastard's a control freak. He hasn't any friends, but who wants to be friends with him? He'll just figure out a way to screw you even more than he does now."

—Helen, an executive secretary

Bing pointed out that management by terror is a time-honored technique because it works, at least in the short run. Mediocre men or women suddenly seem dynamic or fearful by passing anxiety and hatred down the managerial line until it infects all who work for them. Bullies expect loyalty from those who work under them; they only wonder what you have done for them lately. Above all, bullies want control, in part because of tremendous and immature needs they think you can fulfill. As Bing concludes: "The complex of behaviors that characterize the bully—brutality, the demand for control, the thirst for loyalty that need not be returned—floats on a sea of insecurity that is as deep and ancient as the life of the bully itself" (p. 129).

THE PARANOID "I don't think the woman trusts anyone. She locks herself in her office and communicates by memo. She only comes out to blow up and criticize someone. She is never satisfied with what we do. She'll ask that perfectly written memos be done over and over until they suit her. No one knows what criteria she uses to judge whether something is what she wants. No one ever does. She's always looking to see what we are doing. I know she thinks we are all out to get her. I tell you, she's a basket case if there ever was one."

—Max, a midlevel manager

Bing suggests these individuals lose their regulators and implode. They suddenly become fearful, anxious, and suspicious of all around them. They can be dangerous to work for because they are constantly searching for proof that their subordinates and superiors are out to get them. Bing points out that they are always on edge because: (a) it's hard to live in continual fear; (b) henchmen make lousy allies; and (c) they are atrocious managers. He concludes by warning: "Cut off, incapable of analyzing situations and formulating strategies, the paranoid is, more than any other form of crazy boss, doomed to destruction. The trick is not to get swallowed up in his conflagration" (p. 132).

THE NARCISSIST   "This woman was something. I have never been around anyone who was so self-centered and good at manipulating everyone, including me. She could come on as the most pleasant person in the world. When she did, you'd do anything for her. There were times when I even did things that were probably illegal, like help her load up a PC that she took home. But I never thought anything about it at the time. She was so convincing in saying that her boss and she thought she needed to work more at home. It was never returned. I don't think she ever thought, or cared for that matter, that I could have gotten into trouble. All she cared about was getting what she wanted. She did."

—Bernie, an office manager

Bing notes that we had many narcissists, including many convicted of insider trading, on the prowl in the 1980s. They seemed to be everyone's hero, at least before their worlds collapsed around them. Narcissists have no concept of you; they only care about themselves. They see what they do or want as far more important than anything you may want. You are there to help them see that they achieve their goals, nothing more. Bing points out that narcissists can be dynamic, charming, and pleasantly ruthless in pursuit of their goals. He notes: "In his mind, he's the Great One who created the business, knows it better than any tiny mortal, and will brook no contradiction about what's best for it. He's also not too good about listening to advice" (p. 168).

THE BUREAUCRAZY   "This PR guy was an absolute fruitcake. He operated totally by the policy and procedures manual of the place where I worked. He never deviated from the manual unless directly told to do so. The memos he wrote were hilarious. He once wrote one on giving talks that said you shouldn't pick your nose or scratch your butt while speaking. That caused more laughs than anything I ever read. When his bosses started to be uncomfortable, they would call him in for conferences. He'd come in with a briefcase that included not only the latest policy and procedure manual and a stack of memos, but a pistol. No one ever knew if the pistol was loaded. They certainly didn't ask him. After each conference, he'd just become more rigid in sticking to the policies and procedure manual. Finally, they fired him. They didn't do it directly. After all, no one knew if the pistol was loaded. They waited for him to go on vacation, packed all his belongings, and sent them to his house. I think he got a good severance package because no one wanted to mess with him."

—Dan, a former employee of a medical center

This person would fit Bing's characterization of a supervisor who was a timid worm unable to provide leadership, but dependent upon the exercise of official authority. The formality of a company is a wimp's best hope. Bureaucrazies can cover their trail with paper and protocol, no matter how trivial. They are fearful of the personal implications of the authority they wield and seek to spread responsibility for their every action so thin that blame can never be placed on them. Unfortunately, the bureaucracy of companies creates such people in that they provide a system where following orders is the highest good, and responsibility is spread so thin that no person need worry about his or her personal share.

A loathing for responsibility, notes Bing, "creates two separate managerial phenomena: the pure wimp and the organizational fascist" (p. 197). Both types depend upon the structure to confer power and to eliminate. The wimp views personal action as fearful and difficult; the organizational fascist finds comfort within the exercise of his or her function.

THE DISASTER HUNTER   "He was some president. We never knew if we were going to have a job come each Monday. He was constantly overspending. You never knew if you were going to be paid or if the check would bounce. Somehow, probably because he owed the bank so much money, they'd increase the loans of the company. The guy was constantly freezing and unfreezing our accounts. You never knew whether you should be purchasing needed supplies or not. If you did go ahead and order something, you never knew if the supplier would be paid or not. He liked to be on the edge with our customers. They liked our products, but never knew if we would deliver. To be honest, we never knew either. The company was finally gobbled up and the president sacked. Most of the employees were also fired. Those who remained do have better job security."

—Marty, a sales representative

Bing notes that you can identify the disaster hunter by the following actions: he or she (a) is hysterical, (b) is depressed, (c) is addicted to alcohol, to drugs, to work, and to power over others; (d) will lie when necessary, (e) has no insight into his or her own problems, and (f) sees any problems as yours until he or she finds the disaster he seeks.

Managing Crazy Bosses

Bing suggests ways of managing each of the five types of bosses he describes in his book. You may wish to review his suggestions if you are working for any of the bosses he describes. He also suggests general techniques for managing strange supervisors; these rely upon self-management.

Break the cord. A crazy boss relies upon your emotional dependence for his or her authority. If you do not form this dependence or if you eliminate its need, the boss becomes simply one more work obstacle to you.

Do the job. Competence is always the best defense in managing strange supervisors. Constantly developing and refining your personal skills remains the single best strategy to help you with bizarre bosses.

Stay frosty. Always keep cool around crazy bosses. As Bing pointed out, the saner you are, the crazier your boss will appear. And when the fruits of that craziness come to pass, you're less likely to be associated with it.

Be prepared. The crazy boss eventually falls. When that happens, Bing suggests that you already have established the kind of relations with his or her superiors that will insure your existence after he or she is gone. This may involve some duplicity on your part but, as Bing points out, duplicity is not the sole province of senior management.

Practice self-management techniques. In the epilogue to his book, Bing suggests:

> The only true solution is to take matters into your own hands and manage. No, you may not solve things. Yes, you may be thrown out on your ear. But at least you'll be alive! Taking risks! In short, you'll be in business. The greatest power you have is your sanity. Not only madness confers strength. Rational thought and action, pursued with boldness and, when necessary, ruthlessness is a mighty banner (pp. 267–268).

CHARACTERISTICS OF SUCCESSFUL COMPANIES

In an influential book, *In Search of Excellence,* Thomas Peters and Robert Waterman (1982) described what they found to be lessons from America's best-run companies. The book sold five million copies in ten years. It sparked a revolution in management, particularly in medium and small companies. Peters and Waterman explained characteristics of successful companies:

A bias for action. Well-managed companies show an action orientation or a bias for getting things done. They don't simply respond to whatever may occur, but initiate action on their own. Their policy is to try something and, if necessary, fix it. They experiment by doing something, rather than endlessly debating what they should do.

Close to customers. Excellent companies are close to their customers, permitting them a wide extent and intensity of intrusion into the business. As a result of listening to their customers, these companies understand what their customers want and can cater to their needs.

Autonomy and entrepreneurship. Successful companies have the ability to be big, yet they can act small. They encourage the entrepreneurial spirit among their people far down the line. By breaking the company into independent units, they encourage risk taking. The result is not only many new products, but what companies view as a reasonable number of mistakes. A good example of this approach is the 3M Company. They give many of their employees free reign to create and develop new products. While not all attempts prove successful, the 3M Company has been innovative in developing and introducing new products ranging from furnace filters to more effective medications.

Productivity through people. Excellent companies have respect for the individual. They respect each worker and reward them for using their heads, not just their hands. This belief is omnipresent throughout entire companies.

Hands-on, value driven. Some companies attend to values, as well as creating exciting work environments through personal attention, persistence, and direct intervention far down the line. Executives of these companies wander around plants and talk with employees. The executives are visible and stay in touch with employees to solicit ideas on how to improve companies and their productivity. The behavior of the executives promotes a strong company culture built on basic values.

Stick to the knitting. Organizations that branch out but stick close to their knitting outperform other organizations. The most successful are those diversified around a single skill. The basic credo of these companies is that you do what you know best and don't do something that you don't know how to do well.

Simple form, lean staff. Things need to be kept simple if a company is to pull together. Most successful companies have a fairly stable, unchanging form that provides the essential touchstones that everyone understands, and from which the complexity of day-to-day life can be approached. They create a simple organizational structure by eliminating management layers. Beyond the simplicity in structure, it was found that excellent companies were flexible in responding to fast-changing environmental conditions and in dealing with issues as they arose.

Simultaneous loose–tight properties. These properties foster a climate where employees are dedicated to the company's core values yet are freed from working under strict rules or structures. It is in essence the coexistence of firm central direction and maximum individual autonomy—what Peters and Waterman called "having one's cake and eating it too."

EXERCISE

Assess yourself to determine if you want to be a manager or supervisor.
What skills could you bring to such a leadership position?
What skills should you acquire before accepting a leadership role?

REVIEW TERMS

Bias for action
Close to customers
Hands-on, value-driven
Simple form, lean staff
Simultaneous loose–tight property

QUESTIONS

Discuss six ways you can prepare for a leadership role.
Discuss three comments Townsend (1984) had about work.
List six ways for managing crazy bosses.
List eight characteristics of successful companies.

Marriage

CHAPTER 29

"Marriage has many pains, but celibacy has no pleasures."
—Samuel Johnson, *Rasselas*

"We've been married for over sixty years. There were some tough times when we started out, what with the Depression and such. However, we've both tried. I guess that's the secret—we both tried to make the marriage work. We guess it has."
—Ethyl and George, an elderly couple

Most of you will marry at least once. Data indicate that more people are marrying than ever before. Because nowadays many couples are older when they tie the knot, they are more mature and prepared for marriage. This hopefully will reduce the rate of divorce, which is increasing each year. Goleman (1995) recently noted that couples wed in 1970 had a fifty-fifty chance of splitting up or staying together. However, for married couples starting out in 1990, the likelihood that the marriage would end in divorce was projected to be a staggering 67 percent (Gottman, 1993). Considering the potential for divorce, it is important to consider the factors that distinguish a stable marriage and those that can result in divorce.

Three topics will be explored: myths about love, important characteristics in selecting a mate, and determining your readiness for marriage.

MYTHS ABOUT LOVE

Many of you may hold what Weitan, Lloyd, and Lashley (1991) characterize as the myths of love.

Myth 1. When you fall in love, you will know it. Songs exclaim that when we fall in love, we hear bells, our heart flutters, and the sky is always blue. This is mythical. In reality, love grows gradually. Because of its slow process of nurturing, many people wonder if they are actually in love. Time allows them to decide.

Myth 2. When love strikes, you have no control over your behavior. Love is supposedly so powerful that we cannot manage our affairs. This is not only false, but it is a dangerous belief. The myth encourages people to avoid taking responsibility for significant actions that can have a lasting impact on their lives.

Myth 3. Love is a purely positive experience. This is an illusion. In reality, love can bring a variety of negative emotions. We may suffer great pain as we attempt to resolve the conflict as to how we can love and hate a person at the same time.

Myth 4. True love lasts forever. While almost everyone who marries is at first certain that his or her marriage is going to last forever, at least four out of ten will be wrong. The disillusioned person may then adopt the thought that he or she just didn't find the "right person," as if there is a person out there who is exactly the one and only for that individual. This is a fable.

Myth 5. Love conquers all problems. Weitan and colleagues cite this myth as the basis for many unsuccessful marriages. People who are encountering problems during courtship often marry with the belief that taking the wedding vows will solve their interpersonal problems. Nothing could be further from the truth; marriage merely exacerbates the differences that exist between partners.

SELECTING A MATE

What characteristics do many people look for in choosing a mate? Buss and Barnes (1985) found that, in descending order, the ideal person: (a) is kind and considerate; (b) likes children; (c) is easygoing and adaptable; (d) is socially exciting; (e) is artistic and intelligent; (f) is domestic; (g) has a professional status; (h) is religious; and (i) is politically conservative. The factors listed, at least through professional status, were judged as highly important; the latter two factors, religiosity and politically conservative, were regarded by many as irrelevant to a marriage. The significance of any factor would ultimately be a function of each individual; furthermore, while the subjects in this study rated religious factors as low, they do become significant variables in contributing to divorce.

READINESS FOR MARRIAGE

Kirkendall and Adams (1971) described important factors to consider in deciding if you are ready for marriage. An adaptation of the questionnaire listing these factors is presented in Table 29–1. Answer each question and carefully consider why you responded as you did. Be certain you have resolved any personal doubts induced by a given question before you make the commitment to marriage.

TABLE 29–1 Marriage Readiness Test (adapted from Kirkendall and Adams, 1971)

1. While you accept advice from your parents, do you make important decisions yourself?
2. Are you often homesick?
3. Do you feel embarrassed or uneasy in giving or receiving affection?
4. Are your feelings easily hurt by criticism?
5. Do you enjoy small children?
6. Do conversations about sex embarass you when they are with older persons or those of the opposite sex?
7. Do you have a clear understanding of sexual intercourse and reproduction?
8. Do you understand the psychological factors that determine good sexual adjustment?
9. Have you used some of your earnings to meet expenses of others?
10. Do you lose your temper easily in an argument?
11. Have you and your fiancé(e) ever worked through disagreements to your mutual satisfaction?
12. Can you postpone having something you want for the sake of later enjoyment?
13. Are you normally free of jealousy?
14. Have you thought about the goals you will set for marriage?
15. Do you sometimes feel rebellious with respect to the responsibilities of marriage, occupation, or family life?
16. Have you been able to give up something that you wanted very much?
17. Do you think of sexual intercourse as mainly a pleasurable experience?
18. Do you find it difficult to differ from others on matters of conduct or dress, even though you disagree with what they think?
19. Do you often have to fight to get your way?
20. Do you find yourself strongly emphasizing the glamorous aspects of marriage, particularly with respect to the ceremony itself?
21. Do you find yourself making biting remarks or being sarcastic toward others?
22. Have you and your fiancé(e) been with each other in a variety of situations?
23. Have you and your fiancé(e) discussed matters that might cause marital conflict?

EXPECTATIONS OF MARRIAGE

Most couples believe that they are different: their marriage will be one that lasts. To make a marriage a success, there are a number of daily activities in which you can expect either to change or to have a conflict with your spouse. Those noted by newly married couples include:

1. Changes in housekeeping. When single, you may have been a slob and tossed around your clothes, never made your bed, and rarely picked up items around your apartment. These habits will change, particularly if you marry a person who is neat and tidy. And, more than likely, you will be the one who changes.

2. Changes in budget. When single, you may have worried little about household expenses. After paying your rent and your share of a food bill, you could pretty well do what you wanted to with your money. If you ran short, you may have been able to ask your parents for assistance. All this changes in a marriage: you have to plan and budget the money you and your spouse have to spend. This often means that you cannot purchase items you formerly bought with little forethought. In a marriage, you have to concentrate on how you, as a couple, will survive on your shared income.

3. Change in sleep patterns. When single, you may have been used to going to bed late and getting up around noon. This habit will undoubtedly change as you and your spouse adjust to marriage. Early in your marriage, both of you are apt to work. When this occurs, you have to make adjustments in your sleep patterns to accommodate one another.

4. Changes in television and listening habits. When single, you could watch what you wanted to watch or listen to whatever music you wished. When married, however, you have to change your television and listening habits to adapt to those of your spouse.

5. Changes in closet space. When single, you probably had enough space to put your belongings—assuming you hung up your clothing. The apartment or house that you share with your spouse will likely have little closet space. Thus, both you and your mate need to change to utilize the limited space you have most effectively.

6. Changes in social habits. When single, you probably spent considerable time visiting with your roommates or friends. You also may have hung out at bars or other social establishments. When you are married, you hope to find activities that both you and your partner enjoy. This may mean that you totally revamp your social schedule to find interests that both of you share.

7. Changes in eating habits. When single, you may have been used to wolfing down a hamburger at the nearest fast food restaurant. You ate when you wanted to. When you are married, however, you need to adjust your eating habits to fit with those of your spouse. Since you will probably begin on a limited budget, meal planning becomes of central concern in your relationship.

8. Changes in privacy. When single, you may have come home, turned on your stereo, and gone to bed. Once married, every aspect of your life is shared with someone else. You and your spouse have to accommodate your perceptions of privacy to fit the marriage.

9. Changes in pet ownership. When single, you may have cared little for cats or dogs. If your spouse has had a cat or a dog for a number of years, prepare to welcome it into the household.

10. Changes in sharing. When single, you did not have to share personal belongings, such as a stereo, a computer, or a car. When married, you share just about everything, including T-shirts and toilet articles. Be prepared to share what were your personal belongings and possessions.

FACTORS IN A GOOD MARRIAGE

Despite the increase in divorce rates, many couples have long and happy marriages. Each couple would probably offer a different reason why their marriage has been successful. However, factors that contribute to long and happy marriages include:

Trust. Couples who are married for a length of time say they trust each another. In many instances, trust is noted more by couples than is love as a factor that cements a marriage.

Commitment. A shared commitment to making a marriage work seems to be one of the most commonly cited reasons why some marriages last while others fail.

Living with spouse's shortcomings. Many couples are keenly aware of the shortcomings of a spouse. These flaws may be changed over the course of a marriage. When they are not, the ability to live with the flaws is a hallmark of a solid marriage. Couples in successful marriages are less than brutally honest; they think before they talk. Overall, they are able to focus on what's right with a spouse.

Ability to live with change. Happy couples note that they are able to adapt to changes as they occur. The challenges and changes required in a marriage strengthen the relationship.

Shared history and enjoyment of one another. Couples married for a length of time have a history shared only by them. They relish this common history. Shared interests and values are a key ingredient to many marriages.

Effective resolution of conflicts. Conflicts between spouses occur in all marriages. To have a successful marriage, you need to learn to negotiate for what you want. Couples with a solid marriage tend not to argue over trivial matters, but to analyze an argument to determine if the source of the conflict is some other reason than a seemingly insignificant incident. You always need to keep your perspective if your marriage is to succeed.

There are a number of ground rules to resolving conflicts. While they do not guarantee success in resolving a conflict, they are effective methods of conflict resolution in any relationship, including marriage. Those cited by a number of experts include:

1. Start sentences with "I," not "you." Instead of starting with an attacking statement, start out by explaining your position.
2. Argue about the right issue. When discussing a situation, stay focused and don't broaden the argument. If you can't resolve the issue, agree to disagree or to further discuss the problem at a later time.
3. Don't embarrass your mate by fighting in public or around others.
4. Think before you talk.
5. Listen to your spouse.

6. Avoid generalizations as much as possible. Don't bring up past issues that have led to conflict.
7. Provide feedback that will not result in either you or your spouse becoming defensive.
8. Specify behaviors that should be changed to resolve conflict. Focus on the actions both you and your spouse can take to improve your marriage.

Effective communication with each other. Couples with a strong marriage tend to talk to each other more regarding a variety of subjects. They convey that they understand what is being said and show sensitivity to each other's feelings. They make certain that communication channels, both verbal and nonverbal, remain open. Other approaches to communicating effectively in a marriage include:

1. Be certain of your own feelings before communicating with your spouse.
2. Make and maintain eye contact when saying something important.
3. Remember your point of view is not the only one.
4. If you are uncertain what your spouse is saying, paraphrase back what you think was said.
5. Try to describe a negative situation in positive terms whenever possible.
6. Be specific about your aims.
7. Don't expect your partner to be able to read your mind.
8. After you make your point, be quiet so you can listen to your partner's response.

Balance of power. Couples with enduring marriages maintain a balance of power with respect to decisions. Each partner has a feeling of personal authority and equality.

Being best friends with your spouse. Good marriages are characterized by partners who are best friends. Couples in a good marriage take pleasure in each other. They listen to and confide in each other by constantly communicating their thoughts and feelings. They are tuned in to each other's feelings and are able to deal with negative emotions when they do occur.

FACTORS IN MARITAL DISCORD

A large number of factors contribute to the rising rate of divorce. These vary from couple to couple; it is likely that several of the problems may lead to conflict in many marriages. Important factors include:

Money. Many couples lack the money to purchase what each partner would like. This is particularly a factor in financially distressed times. In addition, many couples quickly incur debt when they are married. The pressures of debt add fuel to marital conflicts.

Sex. Partners may not only lack information about sex, but they may have differing expectations about the role of sex in a marriage. In many instances, these problems could be corrected with a solid sex manual or counseling; in other cases, the problems eventually prove irreconcilable. Suggestions for enhancing a sexual relationship were offered in Chapter 18.

In-Laws. Most people laugh when they hear in-law jokes. However, in-laws can generate marital conflict. Despite well-meaning intentions of many parents to remain aloof from their children's marriage, many parents succumb to the temptation of attempting to help their children. The result is often marital discord.

Recreation. Many partners in a marriage have different expectations about how free time should be spent. If a male is used to bowling once a week, he will probably continue this behavior. His wife, however, may have differing thoughts about how he should spend his time. The result is another potential source of marital problems.

Friends. When a couple is courting, there is often nothing said concerning the attitudes a partner may have about the other's friends. When the couple is married, however, attitudes about the other's friends are apt to emerge during the course of arguments.

Drug and alcohol use. Drug and alcohol use by a partner is a major source of marital conflict. The use of such substances can become a factor around which all other characteristics of the marriage come to revolve.

Religion. When courting, partners may give little thought to religion. It is a topic that always lurks beneath the surface, however, and can quickly rise to become a source of marital conflict.

TABLE 29–2 Behaviors that Distinguish Happy from Unhappy Marriages (adapted from Mathews and Mihanovich, 1963)

1. We don't think alike on many things.
2. My spouse has little insight into my feelings.
3. We say things that hurt each other.
4. I often feel unloved.
5. My spouse takes me for granted.
6. I need someone to confide in.
7. My spouse rarely compliments me.
8. I have to give in more than my spouse does.
9. I desire more affection.
10. I can't talk to my spouse.
11. My spouse does not enjoy many things I enjoy.
12. I often feel neglected.
13. I keep things to myself.
14. I can't please my spouse.
15. We don't confide in each other.
16. My spouse is not open to suggestion.
17. I can't discuss anything with my spouse.
18. My spouse is stubborn.
19. My spouse can't accept criticism.
20. My spouse magnifies my faults.

Children. Couples often do not talk about children when they are courting. Many partners do not even know what the beliefs of their mate are with respect to having and raising children. The prospect of children creates problems; the raising of youngsters leads to additional difficulties.

Attitudes. Mathews and Mihanovich (1963) describe a number of attitudes that distinguish happy from unhappy marriages, as depicted in Table 29–2.

Communication. Some marriage experts claim your marriage faces difficulty if any of the following occur: (a) you or your spouse avoids talking to one another about important issues; (b) you or your spouse turns routine discussions into arguments; (c) you or your partner takes something the other says and turns it into a negative; and (d) you or your spouse routinely disregards the other's opinions and feelings.

DIVORCE

McGoldrick and Carter (1982) compiled a list of risk factors that make marital adjustment difficult and that could eventually result in divorce, as depicted in Table 29–3. It is suggested that you use this list of factors as guidelines to improve your marriage. Reasons couples divorce include:

Infidelity. This is probably the main reason for divorce.

Emotional problems. A spouse may bring unresolved emotional problems to a marriage or the marriage itself can induce these responses. Divorce may occur if the problems remain unresolved.

TABLE 29–3 Risk Factors for Divorce (adapted from McGoldrick and Carter, 1982)

1. Couple meets or marries shortly after a significant loss to one or both partner(s).
2. Family backgrounds of each spouse are significantly different with respect to social class, religion, education, ethnicity, and so on.
3. Couple resides either extremely close to or at great distance from either family.
4. Couple is dependent upon either extended family financially, emotionally, or physically.
5. Couple marries before age twenty and after age thirty.
6. Couple marries after being acquainted less than six months or after being engaged three years or longer.
7. Wedding occurs without family or friends present.
8. Wife becomes pregnant before or within first year or marriage.
9. Either spouse has a poor relationship with parents or siblings.
10. Either spouse believes he or she had an unhappy childhood or adolescence.
11. Marital partners were unstable in either extended family.

Financial problems. A couple may incur too much debt. Often a spouse blames the other person for the mountain of bills the couple faces; again, the outcome may be a divorce.

Physical abuse. One spouse, usually the husband, may be physically abusive. To escape from such battering, the other spouse seeks a divorce.

Alcohol or substance abuse. The stability of a marriage can be undermined by alcohol or substance abuse. Escaping from the marriage may be the only solution for one of the spouses.

Sexual problems. Unresolved sexual problems can eventually result in divorce.

In-laws. In-laws can, sometimes without any intent, lead to the dissolution of a marriage.

Neglect of children. A spouse not helping to raise children may undermine a marriage.

Communication problems. Couples who divorce often complain that they were never able to communicate with each other.

Falling out of love. Some spouses say they obtained a divorce simply because they ceased to love their partner. In these instances, one wonders if they ever did truly love the other individual.

Other factors. All the risk factors enumerated in Table 29–3, can help destroy a marriage.

A divorce is usually far more complicated than a marriage. Besides the legal aspects of divorce, there may be economic considerations, child-custody decisions, and emotional scars that can be healed through the passage of time (and, in some cases, psychotherapy).

SELF-MANAGEMENT PROCEDURES

Self-management techniques have a role in the success or failure of a marriage. Methods you might use include:

1. Stimulus control. Environmental and cognitive stimuli can be used to enhance a marriage.

Environmental stimuli. There are a number of ways to arrange environmental stimuli in a manner designed to improve your marriage. These range from attempting to arrange stimuli to create a more romantic ambience to helping keep an environment livable by sharing household duties. You can undoubtedly think of any number of ways to rearrange your environment to help enhance your marriage.

Cognitive stimuli. A number of cognitive stimuli lend themselves to use in strengthening a marriage. Self-instructions and self-statements are extremely important in that they can guide you into considering what behaviors to perform and what behaviors not to perform. Refocusing your thoughts can help improve your marriage. Using relaxation to remain calm when you might otherwise lose your cool is a solid strategy. You can also exercise thought stopping to avoid saying something that you may later regret, and responsible assertiveness to insure that your marriage is truly a shared arrangement.

    2. Self-monitoring. Observing and monitoring aspects of your performance can improve a marriage. Marriage is a two-way street; anything that you can do to improve the relationship, from your point of view, is worthwhile. Self-monitoring is an activity that readily lends itself to use in a marriage.

    3. Self-reinforcement. When you have performed an act to improve your marital relationship, you may or may not obtain immediate reinforcement from your spouse. For this reason, you want to use self-reinforcement as a bridge between the reinforcers provided by your marital mate.

    4. Problem solving. It is doubtful that there are any arrangements where you will need to use problem-solving skills more than in a marriage, often in a manner similar to that of a diplomat, to resolve a conflict. Be prepared to use the following skills: (a) planning on how to cope with a situation, often before it becomes a problem; (b) considering the options you have to resolve a problem or potential problem; (c) rehearsing the strategy you have decided to follow; (d) acting on your selected solution; (e) evaluating the success of your plan; (f) preparing for any setbacks that may occur in your resolution of marital conflicts; and (g) considering other alternatives you have to solving a problem. Since problems occur in every marriage, be persistent in using problem-solving and other self-management techniques.

SELF-MANAGEMENT PROJECTS

Occasionally, students design and execute self-management programs to correct what they believe could become a marital problem. Figure 29–1 depicts the results obtained by a student who used self-monitoring to open up more with his girlfriend. He reported that his inability to express his feelings had led to difficulties between himself and his girlfriend. The student stated that he hoped he could continue his self-monitoring to be more open in his relationship in the future. Figure 29–2 shows what happened when a student decided to decrease the number of times she nagged at her boyfriend. She used self-monitoring and self-reinforcement to reduce nagging. The student commented that she did not realize that she nagged as much as she did until she collected baseline data. She found that systematic self-monitoring initially decreased the behavior, but that it began to increase when she did not monitor herself consistently. The student returned to employing self-management skills to alter her behavior.

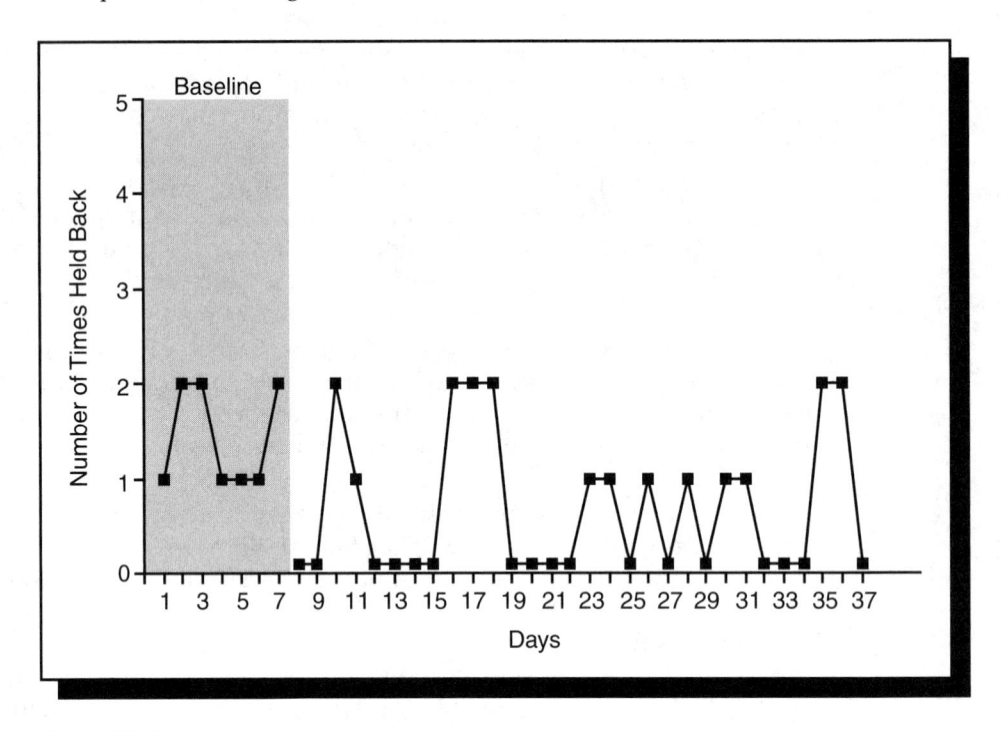

FIGURE 29–1
Self-management to open up more in relationship.

FIGURE 29–2
Self-management to decrease nagging behavior.

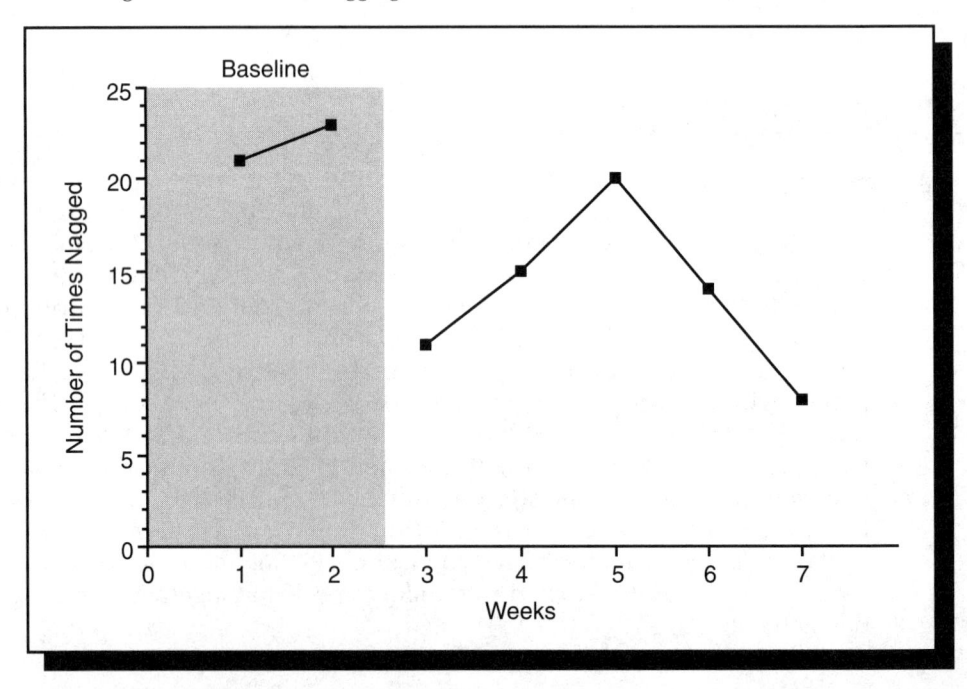

EXERCISE

Analyze the factors that are important to you in a marriage.

Think of how you might achieve your goals.

Think of ways self-management procedures can be used to strengthen a marriage.

REVIEW TERMS

Attitudes   Readiness to marry

QUESTIONS

Discuss five myths about love.
List ten changes that can occur in a marriage.
List eight ways to communicate effectively in a marriage.
List ten factors that contribute to marital discord.

Raising Children

CHAPTER 30

"Children have never been very good at listening to their elders, but they have never failed to imitate them."
—James Baldwin, *Nobody Knows My Name*

"My husband and I were lousy parents. We were too young and totally unprepared for our first child. Since we got married just before he was born, we were supposed to adjust to marriage and raising Timmy, our son, at the same time. We didn't. Looking back, I wish we had done better. It's funny, but you get no training for doing the thing that is the greatest responsibility in your life—raising a child."
—Jane, a middle-aged homemaker

It is doubtful any of you will ever have a task more difficult, or more rewarding, than raising children. Your parents will verify this statement. We all want to raise children who are socially competent in that they are happy and experience good peer relationships. Social competence is characterized by other children responding positively to your youngster, the friendliness of your child to others, his or her being able to obtain group attention in a positive way, and your youngster being liked by others. Socially competent children are independent, and ask for the help of you or others only when unable to solve a problem. Your child is well on the road toward being a highly productive, moral, and socially responsible adult.

There are two dimensions to being a parent. The first dimension is parental acceptance. The degree of acceptance of parents of their children ranges along a dimension from total acceptance to total rejection. Fortunately for us, most of our parents showed some degree of acceptance. The second dimension is parental control. The degree of strictness exhibited by parents ranges from being highly demanding and controlling of their children, referred to as authoritarian parenting, to permissiveness parenting, where few or no demands are placed by parents on their children. Children raised by authoritarian parents are said to be fearful, moody, passively hostile, aimless, and unhappy; children raised by permissive parents are said to be rebellious, impulsive, aggressive, and aimless. The way most of us achieve positive results with our children is by being an authoritative parent. This means we are warm and responsive to our children, while setting high standards for their responsibility and maturity. We hope to raise children who are energetic, friendly, self-reliant, curious, and cooperative. We try to be a good model because we recognize that our children are imitating us. We also practice what most experts believe to be positive and nurturing child management practices. These practices include:

1. We help our children establish reasonable standards appropriate to their age.
2. We consistently reward positive behaviors when we see them.
3. We explain our reasons for asking children to perform specific tasks or to behave in a particular manner.
4. We consistently reinforce whatever rules we have established with our children.
5. We encourage children always to consider the perspective of others, including their siblings and parents.

EFFECTIVE CHILD-REARING PRACTICES

You have learned specific techniques that can be used to raise socially competent children; these are the learning and social learning techniques described earlier in the book. The use of these principles and techniques in teaching children new skills and behaviors (Creer, Backial, Ullman, and Leung, 1986) includes:

Positive reinforcement. This operation helps your child learn while encouraging him or her to try new things. Examples of positive reinforcers are smiles, a pat on the back, attention, an encouraging word or look, and praise. We all need and thrive on positive reinforcement. Following are some suggestions for using positive reinforcement in raising children.

1. Find what stimuli reinforce the child. Children are like us in that we each respond uniquely to different stimuli. Anything that makes your child feel genuinely good can be a reinforcer. We often think this has to be a tangible stimulus, such as candy, but our physical and verbal responses, such as hugging, touching, and praising, are often the most effective reinforcers to use with others, particularly children. Attending to your child, particularly when you pay sole attention to the youngster, is a potent social reinforcer.

2. Reinforce immediately. Positive reinforcement is most effective when given immediately after the desired behavior has occurred. The desired behavior will then be more likely to be repeated. However, if reinforcement cannot be immediately provided, it is better to offer it at a later time than not at all.

3. Be specific. It is important that your child is reinforced for performing specific behaviors. Reinforcing specific behaviors is most effec-

tive when you have established simple rules for the child. If the child then adheres to or violates the rules, he or she knows why reinforcement is or is not provided. If you use reinforcement, be consistent. Consistent use of reinforcement communicates to the child how he or she should behave.

4. Reinforce often with a variety of reinforcers. A general guideline is to provide reinforcement, in the form of attention, praise, hugs, or touching, as often as you can. It is particularly effective when applied contingent upon a desired response, but reinforcement at any time can set the stage for the acquisition of behavior. If your child is trying to learn a new behavior or skill, he or she needs frequent encouragement, especially at first, to build confidence and pride as he or she learns. As the new skill or behavior becomes a habit, the amount of positive reinforcement can be reduced. It can always be stepped up if the desired behavior begins to weaken.

Small steps. Each skill is made up of small steps. You learn to crawl before you walk. Use shaping to teach a child by rewarding the youngster for achieving small steps that will lead him or her toward a terminal behavior. If the process doesn't work, analyze your approach. The steps may be too large; if so, go back and make each step easier to reach. The reinforcers may not be potent enough or they may not be given promptly or consistently. You must analyze a child's behavior to determine the effectiveness of any stimulus as a potential reinforcer. Use social reinforcers as much as possible.

Specific goals. Describe the final goal in detail. A small child may not be able to understand what you mean by the thundering cry "Clean up your room!" "Clean" is a very general term and each of us is likely to have different meanings for that demand. To your child, a clean room may mean toys out of the middle of the floor and the bedspread pulled up over the pillow. But if you make up a list of what you mean, either with pictures or in words, to give your child specific reminders to go by, you are more likely to understand each other.

Punishment. Two procedures that can be used with children are time-out and response cost. Time-out, described in Chapter 6, is especially effective with children. If you use time-out, be certain that you: (a) have explained to your child the procedure before you introduce it; (b) use a short duration, usually two to five minutes; (c) pick a place that is dull and nonreinforcing; and (d) remain calm when using time-out, no matter how difficult it may be for you. Response cost can be used with older children, particularly if you use withdrawal of set amounts of a child's allowance contingent upon specific behaviors. Physical punishment, such as a spanking, should only be used when you want to apply an immediate contingency to prevent a child from engaging in behavior dangerous to the youngster, such as touching a hot stove or running into the street. Avoid physical punishment since it is not only imitated by your child, but it can provoke unwanted behaviors such as aggression.

STEPS IN INSTITUTING BEHAVIORAL CHANGES

The following steps are suggested for instituting behavioral changes (Creer et al., 1986).

1. Specify end goal or problem behaviors. Pinpoint the behaviors you want to change. The behaviors to be changed must be observable and countable. For example, "Being messy" needs to be defined by observable behaviors such as leaving toys on the floor or not combing hair, and "Being neat" may mean having all the toys put away by a specific time and having hair combed.

2. Track the behavior. You need to observe and count each time the target behavior occurs. If you want to initiate a self-management program, gradually transfer responsibility for tracking or monitoring behavior to your child.

3. Plan a program to reward desired behavior and discourage undesired behavior. A program is a plan of action for specific behavior change that usually involves some kind of contract or agreement about what is to be changed and what the reward will be for achieving behavioral change. When planning your program, make all steps small and attainable. In the beginning, it is important for your child to achieve success with the program. Later, the program can be revised and increased performance of the desired behaviors will be required to achieve a reinforcer. Include both social and nonsocial reinforcers in your program. Social reinforcers include praise, a hug, and a smile; nonsocial reinforcers include a point system, a star chart, allowance, or a food treat. Be certain reinforcers are items your child really wants; don't hesitate to change reinforcers if they are no longer effective. Reinforce as soon as possible after the desired behavior occurs and, in the beginning, after each time the desired behavior is performed. Later, you may want to use an intermittent schedule because it makes the desired behavior more resistant to extinction.

4. Institute the program, making certain that each person involved understands and agrees to all elements of the program. You will likely wish to negotiate rules and consequences with your child, particularly with an adolescent. Suggestions for negotiating with children are presented in Table 30–1.

5. Continue to use shaping to achieve the desired goal. Use the principles of shaping described earlier and in Chapter 6.

HELPFUL HINTS AND POSSIBLE PITFALLS

Described by Creer and colleagues (1986), these include:

1. Whenever possible, ignore a behavior you do not like. An undesirable alternative is nagging, which is not only miserable for all involved, but is unsuccessful at helping someone learn a new skill or behavior. Small and irritating behaviors can trap you.

TABLE 30–1 Rules for Negotiation

1. Establish context. You want to negotiate at a time appropriate for both you and your child. Be aware of the goals you have before you start the negotiation process.
2. Negotiation process. There are several steps involved in negotiation, including:
    a. Create a pleasant atmosphere for you and your child.
    b. Clearly and logically state your goals. Talk in terms that the child can understand. At the same time, you want to assess your child's understanding and perspective of your goals, as well as the decision-making ability of the child in performing all aspects of your agreement.
    c. Determine your child's goals. Negotiation implies give-and-take on the part of both you and your child. You want to determine the expectations of your child; in addition, it is helpful to clear up any misunderstandings of your youngster.
    d. Appraise positions of both you and child. Consider all perspectives regarding a goal. There are times when you may be wrong and your child is right. For this reason, you need to be flexible in negotiation with children.
    e. Generate acceptable alternatives. Think of potential alternatives, even if you need to brainstorm with your child. You often want to show that other choices are worse than your suggestion, but don't hesitate to ask for your child's input if it will improve the outcome. Negotiate to arrive at a suitable reinforcer for the child that is attainable for his or her adherence to the final agreement. Integrate the child's concerns into an agreement, even if they are minor and subtle. Always be optimistic and provide encouragement throughout the negotiation process.
3. Draw up a contract. Clearly state the terms and conditions of the contract you have negotiated with your child. Be certain that you explain the agreement fully to your child so that you both understand the terms of the agreement. You and your child should then sign the contract.
4. General points to negotiation with children:
    a. Don't demand compliance.
    b. Don't become discouraged; successful negotiation requires patience.
    c. Don't take anything personally that is said during negotiation.
    d. Use common sense.
    e. Provide reinforcement to child for adhering to agreement.
    f. Be certain to keep your commitment.

2. Do not debate or argue with your child about what you expect or what will be the consequences if these expectations are not met. This turns into a power play between you and the child. The result is usually anger, not change.

3. Discuss with your child what you are trying to do and why. Be certain that each step along the way is explained so that your child will know what to expect, as well as what is expected of him or her. It is easy to let yourself be caught up in an argument at this point. If one begins to develop, say what you mean and drop it.

4. Provide natural consequences whenever possible. We all feel free to learn and try new things if we know what to expect.

5. Recognize that change is slow. Try not to become impatient if the desired behavior is a long time coming. It has taken a long time for your child's inappropriate habits to develop; it will take time for new behaviors to take their place.

TABLE 30–2 Checklist to Determine If You are Consistently Using Behavioral Principles in Teaching Your Child New Skills (adapted from Creer et al., 1986)

1. State clearly and specifically to your child what your expectations are.
2. Give positive reinforcement immediately after and often for desired behavior.
3. Use reinforcers that are meaningful to your child.
4. Set up small steps to reach the final goal.
5. Provide natural consequences for the final goal.
6. Follow through with consequences when the desired behavior is not achieved.
7. Ignore undesirable behavior as much as possible.
8. Be consistent about what you expect of your child.
9. Apply contingencies on a consistent basis.

6. For small children in particular, provide a certain amount of time for them to prepare when you want something done. If you want them to go to bed when they are playing, give them time to wrap up their game.

7. Be consistent when setting up and enforcing rules and expectations. Your child is apt to be more successful when he or she knows what to expect and you are consistent in applying contingencies.

8. Reinforcers besides social reinforcers should be used. These reinforcers may include treats, later bedtime, food, TV time, money, and so on. Do not use these tangible reinforcers without pairing them with social reinforcers. Social reinforcers are the most powerful reinforcers over time; there is no substitution for them.

9. Be certain the reinforcers you use are meaningful for your child. If you think they are great reinforcers but your child does not respond to them, pick new ones.

10. It is often easier and faster for you to do something yourself than teaching your child to do it. Fight this urge. The more chances your child gets to practice a behavior, the faster he or she will learn.

11. Think about something you enjoyed learning. See if you can pick out the factors that made the learning experience a positive one for you; apply these concepts when helping your child learn.

Table 30–2 contains a checklist you might review to be certain you perform each of the described guidelines consistently. In addition, a number of excellent references on child management are available. These include books by Dreikurs and Stolz (1964), Becker (1970), and Patterson (1977).

SELF-MANAGEMENT AND CHILD-MANAGEMENT PROJECT

As her project, a mother sought to improve her son's performance at school. The problem was that the youngster did not pay attention to his teacher; consequently, he did not complete his homework assignments as

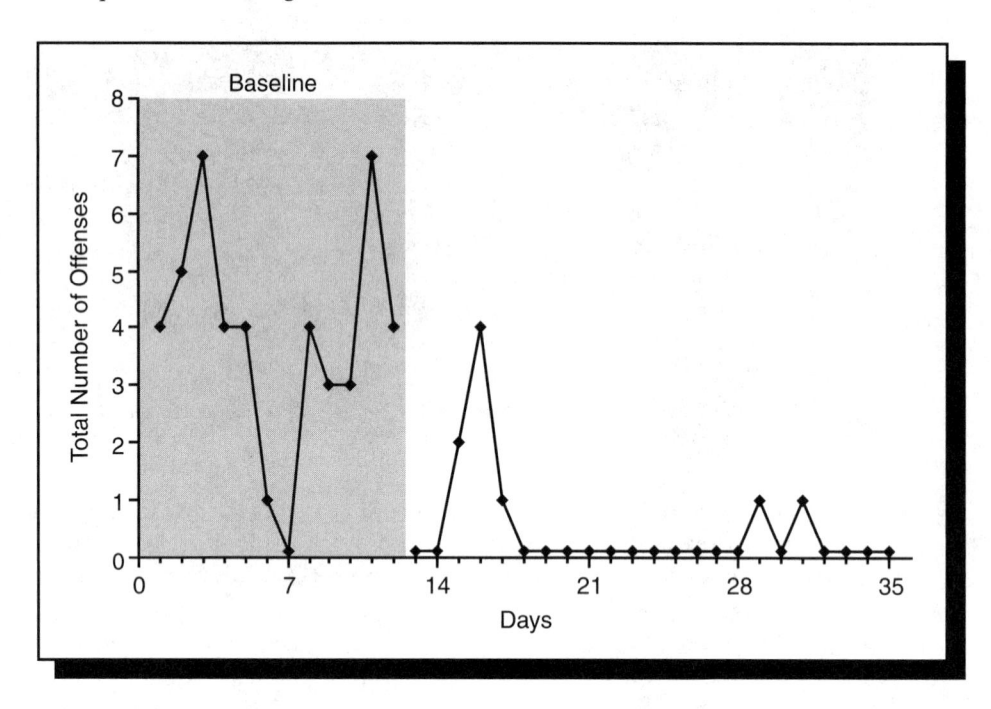

FIGURE 30–1
Help son reduce daily classroom offenses.

directed. Specific target behaviors were to decrease the number of classroom problems the child encountered and to increase his completion of assignments. Negotiation took place between the mother and her son. It was agreed that he would receive $10.00 to spend at a video arcade if his classroom performance improved over the course of the project. Figure 30–1 shows that the boy's performance was variable during the baseline period, a trend that continued at the beginning of self-management. After four days of the program, it was decided to add a daily report card system whereby the boy's teacher checked off if the youngster had turned in all assignments and had not received any check marks for disciplinary reasons that day. The boy took the report card home to his parents. Closer monitoring by the teacher and parents of the boy, as well as the negotiated contingencies, brought about the dramatic change noted over the course of the program.

EXERCISE

Think of what seemed to be effective procedures used by your parents to teach you new skills.

Think of how your skills in self-management might be used in teaching your child appropriate skills.

REVIEW TERMS

Authoritative parenting
Positive reinforcement
Punishment
Response cost
Social competence
Time-out

QUESTIONS

List five positive child management practices.

Discuss five steps for promoting behavioral change in children.

List a nine-point checklist that can be used to determine if you are consistently using behavioral principles to teach your child new skills.

Aging and Death

CHAPTER 31

"The problem of self-identity is not just a problem of the young. It is a problem all the time. Perhaps the problem. It should haunt old age, and when it no longer does it should tell you that you are dead."
—Norman Maclean, *Young Men and Fire*

"I remember when I was young. It really seemed that old people were really old. They constantly complained about losing their memory and about their aches and pains. I used to think it kind of funny. It won't happen to me, I said. Well, it did. I got old. Rather than worry about what I can or cannot do, I have made every effort to adjust to my age. I continue exercising, mainly by walking several miles a day, I eat properly, try and sleep each night, and keep myself as alert as I can by continuing to work crossword puzzles, write letters, and read the newspaper. Old age requires a lot of adjustment, but so far I've enjoyed it."
—Ted, an elderly retiree

Regardless of our wishes to the contrary, we all age and die. Worldwide, the number of adults aged sixty-five years and older is increasing faster than the global population as a whole. Factors accounting for this change are fertility and, in particular, longevity. A time that clearly calls for adjustment is the midlife period between the ages of forty to sixty-five years. During this period, both men and women experience physical changes. Women may gain weight and feel less attractive. They begin experiencing menopause where their reproductive system slows and finally halts as menstruation ceases. Men often undergo what is called the "midlife crisis" in that they become dissatisfied with their life and how they have lived it. They may search for their lost youth by divorcing and remarrying someone much younger than they. Whatever their sex, however, everyone has to learn to change with the physical alterations they undergo.

PHYSICAL AND PSYCHOLOGICAL CHANGES WITH AGING

Two different theories have been proposed to account for aging: genetic and environmental.

1. Genetic theory. The genetic theory of aging hypothesizes that the mechanism of aging is inherited. It assumes that how fast we age is con-

trolled by a genetically based program that controls the life span of cells in our body. After we reach a biological limit on the number of times cells can divide and multiply, cells begin to die and we start to age. The biological clock begins with our birth; it continues until our death.

2. Environmental theory. The environmental theory of aging assumes we age because of the "wear or tear" on our bodies. According to this theory, changes in our body are due to our living long enough to wear out body parts. These changes may include an interference in the functioning of cells, a breakdown in the immune system, or increased errors in the genetic mechanism, which interferes with cell structure and function. This process, in turn, may be accelerated by "good life" diseases, or physical changes related to living too rich a life-style, such as consuming too much fat or not exercising regularly.

Regardless of which theory is correct—and it can be argued that aging is the result of the interaction of both theories—men and women experience physical and psychological changes. These include:

Physical changes. Women undergo menopause during their middle years. They may become depressed over their changing appearance and feel themselves psychologically unprepared for older age. Men may experience a similar reaction, although they do not undergo the menopause process. Both men and women may find that their hair has begun to turn gray, a process based upon inherited factors; they may also experience aging of the skin, a process that may be influenced by exposure to the sun. Other changes occur with respect to the skeletal, cardiovascular, and visual systems. With respect to vision, for example, almost half of the people between the ages of seventy-five and eighty-five years suffer from cataracts. Other physical changes that occur with age are shown in Table 31–1.

Psychological changes. At one time, it was thought that our intelligence began to decrease after our teenage years. There is no evidence to support this view. The intelligence of many continues to increase with aging. Experts describe three types of memory: sensory, short-term, and long-term.

1. Sensory memory. Sensory memory refers to the large-capacity memory system that briefly holds sensory information from an instant to several seconds. There is some evidence that sensory memory may begin to decline beginning around sixty years of age.

2. Short-term memory. Short-term memory refers to a memory system that retains information for brief periods. It has a limited capacity to store seven to eight items for two to thirty seconds. There is evidence that short-term memory may be unchanged with age, particularly with continued practice of cognitive tasks.

3. Long-term memory. Long-term memory refers to a memory system involved in the process of storing what, theoretically, are unlimited amounts of information over a long period of time.

There is considerable variation among older individuals with respect to memory. The memory of many elderly people remains strong; the mem-

TABLE 31–1   Physical Changes that Occur with Age

Pituitary gland and hypothalamus. The secretion of growth hormone begins to decline at age 50; this causes muscles to shrink and fat to increase.

Sight. There is decreased difficulty in seeing nearby objects beginning at age 40 or older. The ability to see fine detail, however, does not deteriorate until we are in our 70s.

Hearing. Hearing loss may begin to occur when we reach 50.

Smell. Our ability to smell declines slowly beginning at age 45 and declines rapidly after age 65.

Thymus. The thymus begins to shrink at puberty. The immune response associated with the thymus declines slowly, however.

Heart. No decline occurs in output of the heart while resting. However, a 20 percent decline in maximum rate during exercise occurs after age 40 because the heart becomes less responsive to stimulation from the nervous system.

Lungs. A 40 percent drop in maximum breathing capacity occurs between 20 and 70 years of age.

Bones. Bones begin to weaken after age 40 through osteoporosis, especially in women.

Skin. Changes in collagen, a connective tissue, causes skin to lose elasticity in later years. Exposure to sun also increases skin damage.

Muscles. There is a 20 percent to 40 percent muscle mass loss between ages 20 and 90 without exercise. Exercise may prevent most loss, however.

Adrenal glands. After age 30, the secretion of a hormone that slows cancer growth and boosts immunity begins to decline. After age 70, production of the stress hormone, cortisol, soars.

Ovaries. There is a dramatic reduction of estrogen after age 50.

Prostate. After age 45, the prostate begins to enlarge. It may continue to grow for the remainder of a man's life, usually in a benign fashion. The result may be pressure on the urethra, which may result in frequent urination, especially at night, weak or interrupted urine stream, and difficulty in starting urination.

Blood vessels. The diameter of vessels narrows, arterial walls stiffen, and there is a 20 percent to 25 percent increase in systolic blood pressure.

Nerves. The speed of message transmission along nerves drops 10 percent between the ages of 40 and 80.

---

ory of others, particularly certain aspects of their memory, may decline. Age appears to affect the speed at which we perform intellectual tasks, the retrieval of information, our success at performing some tasks, and the quality of our work. Men tend to show little decline in spatial orientation, such as reading a map correctly; the most enduring mental skill for women is inductive reasoning. The sharpest declines in the memory of both men and women are in the area of basic mathematics. Total intelligence generally does not decline with age; although ability in a number of intellectual functions (such as vocabulary recall) increases, other functions (such as our ability to detect patterns in a novel situation) may increase. A caveat to the latter comment is that there is evidence of decline in intelligence in the period before a person dies. In addition, between 20 and 47 percent of people have enough symptoms to warrant a diagnosis of Alzheimer's Disease by age eighty-five.

There are a number of ways to enhance your memory as you age. Suggestions from experts in gerontology include:

1. Remain mentally active. Just as you need physical exercise for your body, you need to exercise your brain regularly. Intellectual and other cognitive exercises help prevent deterioration of your memory. This step is probably the single most important action you can take as you age.

2. Push memory limits. There are a number of ways you can adjust to age, including: (a) attaching names to information you have stored in your memory; (b) studying and organizing new materials you learn; and (c) concentrating better by reducing distraction.

3. Give yourself more time to learn. If you take more time and use distributed practice, you should be able to keep your memory skills as you grow older.

4. Monitor your memory. Many older people probably pay too much attention to what they see as declining memory; others see a decline in memory as a natural consequence of aging. However, if you notice a dramatic and swift change in your memory as you grow older, you may wish to consult your physician.

Knowledge regarding memory continues to change. In a recent review, Goleman (1994) noted that extensive practice can break through barriers in mental capacities, particularly short-term memory. This was demonstrated in a study where college students were taught to listen to a list of as many as 102 random digits and then recite it correctly. Acquiring this ability required 400 hours of practice. The capability to increase memory in particular domains, through the chunking of information, is at the heart of high-level performance of everyone. Dr. Herbert Simon, a professor of psychology and a Nobel laureate at Carnegie-Mellon University, noted that every expert has attained a high level of memory through practice and performance. The experts have acquired an index in that they have approximately 50,000 chunks of familiar units of information they recognize. The new research on memory suggests that through practice, many older adults can retain and even improve their cognitive abilities despite increasing age.

It is generally thought that there are few changes in a person's personality after age thirty, except that which occurs through psychotherapy or dementing illness. Many experts believe in what is referred to as the Big Five, as given in Table 31–2. These dimensions of personality are bipolar. Terms similar in meaning are listed under the poles at both the left and right sides of the table. The Big Five are not accepted by all personality theorists, but they do provide a comprehensive system for description. Perhaps you may wish to consider which dimensions currently describe your personality and which you would like to be used in describing you. Now would be the time for you to attempt to change personality characteristics, not when you grow older.

TABLE 31–2 Dimensions of the Big Five Personality Characteristics

I. **Extroversion**	*versus*	**Introversion**
Talkative		Quiet
Energetic		Reserved
Assertive		Shy
Bold		Timid
Friendly		Aloof
Spontaneous		Inhibited
II. **Emotional stability**	*versus*	**Neuroticism**
Stable		Anxious
Calm		Worried
Contented		Temperamental
Unemotional		Emotional
Secure		Insecure
Not envious		Jealous
III. **Conscientious**	*versus*	**Undirectedness**
Organized		Careless
Responsible		Frivolous
Cautious		Irresponsible
Self-reliant		Helpless
Scrupulous		Lax
Knowledgeable		Ignorant
IV. **Agreeableness**	*versus*	**Antagonism**
Good natured		Irritable
Helpful		Uncooperative
Trusting		Suspicious
Lenient		Critical
Sympathetic		Cold
Kind		Quarrelsome
V. **Openness to experience**	*versus*	**Closed-mindedness**
Creative		Simple
Intellectual		Shallow
Open-minded		Unintelligent
Daring		Unadventurous
Original		Conventional
Artistic		Unartistic

HEALTHY AGING

Whereas many middle-aged adults may feel their life was misspent, older adults are often pleased with the life they have led. They are accepting of themselves, even though they may believe they made a number of incorrect choices in life. Approximately two-thirds of these older adults are pleased with their personal lives compared to half of the adults between the ages of eighteen and forty-nine years.

Individuals who are able to age gracefully demonstrate a number of characteristics. They:

Maintain social relationships. Those who establish and maintain warm social relationships show healthy aging. These interactions can boost your immune system and lower your risk of dying.

Are calm and patient. Being impulsive, antagonistic, or hostile can lead to unhappiness at any time in your life. When you are older, these patterns contribute to physical difficulties.

Are conscientious. This pattern, initiated at an early age, enhances a person's chances for longevity.

Seek help for depression. Several federal agencies, particularly the National Institute of Aging (1995), described the clinical depression that occurs in some elderly adults. Symptoms include: (a) an "empty" feeling; (b) tiredness and lack of energy; (c) loss of interest or pleasure in ordinary activities; (d) sleep problems; (e) problems with eating and large gains or losses of weight; (f) crying a lot; (g) aches or pains that won't go away; (h) difficulty concentrating or making decisions; (i) lack of positive feelings toward the future; (j) feelings of extreme guilt, helplessness, or worthlessness; (k) irritability; and (l) thoughts of death or suicide. If an older person is depressed, he or she may seek professional counseling or use self-management techniques. Techniques that can be used to help alleviate mild depression are presented in Table 31–3.

Maintain autonomy. Maintaining some autonomy is an important contributor to a longer life, even if the person is in a nursing home.

Enhance personality variables. The Big Five important personality characteristics tend not to change with time. If these can be maintained in a positive manner, longevity is increased. If not, professional help should be sought.

Establish regular exercise routines. Regular exercise programs should be established when you are young. If the regimens can be main-

TABLE 31–3   Self-Management Tactics for Use with Depression (adapted from Goleman, 1992)

Most effective procedures
   Taking action by doing something to change the problem causing depression
   Bolstering self-esteem by considering your achievements
   Self-reinforcement
   Resolving and acting to do better
   Downward comparison by telling yourself that you are not as bad off as many others

Partially effective procedures
   Socializing with others
   Avoiding alcohol, drugs, and desserts
   Exercising

Ineffective procedures
   Distraction by watching too much TV, or reading too many magazines
   Blaming your moods on others
   Being alone
   Fatalistic approach in accepting depression
   Venting bad feelings on others

tained as you age, exercise improves your chances of a happy and longer life.

Remain sexually active. A part of healthy aging is to maintain healthy and responsible sexual activity.

Become involved. Being involved in various activities, including those you may not have had time to participate in when younger, can lead to happy and healthy aging.

Attempt to remain physically healthy. There are a number of steps all of us can take in an attempt to remain healthy. These are more applicable to older individuals than to those in any other age group and include: (a) watching weight; (b) eating a low-fat and balanced diet; (c) not smoking; (d) drinking one alcoholic drink or less a day; (e) keeping high blood pressure and other chronic conditions under control; and (f) obtaining regular medical checkups.

DEATH AND DYING

Elisabeth Kubler-Ross (1969) proposed that we evolve through a series of five stages as we confront our own death. These stages may coexist and often overlap.

Stage 1: Denial. If informed of a life-threatening disease, the initial reactions of individuals are denial, shock, and disbelief. Patients may seek opinions from others. Few patients, according to Kubler-Ross, maintain this stance to the end.

Stage 2: Anger. In this stage, people may become angry, demanding, difficult, and hostile. They may direct their anger at physicians and other medical personnel. They repeatedly ask themselves, "Why me?"

Stage 3: Bargaining. Here, the individual asks for favors to postpone death. While such bargaining may take place with medical personnel, it is often with God. A person promises good behavior and says something like, "I'll go to church every day if you let me live!"

Stage 4: Depression. Patients experience sadness at what is past and of impending losses. This is actually a signal that the individual is beginning to accept his or her fate. Kubler-Ross referred to the stage as preparatory grief, the sadness of anticipating an inevitable and impending doom.

Stage 5: Acceptance. The final stage occurs when the individual accepts his or her fate. The person has taken care of any unfinished business and is ready to die. Patients may show little emotion and become disinterested in their outside world. They often want to be with someone they are close to during this final stage.

Coping with the impending death of a loved one can be difficult for most people. Suggestions are that you treat the person, not his or her disease. This seems to have been especially beneficial for those families called upon to care for patients afflicted with AIDS during the final weeks and days of their life. Be open with individuals who are dying. Ask them what they need. At the same time, begin to prepare yourself for feelings of grief, guilt, distress, and anger that may occur when they die.

EXERCISE

This exercise is different from the rest in that you are asked to perceive how self-management procedures might help you with elderly relatives, perhaps parents, that you might interact with on a regular basis. Consider the following exercises:

1. How can self-management skills help seniors adjust to the aging process?
2. How can self-management techniques help older adults cope with physical changes that occur with aging?
3. How can self-management processes help seniors maintain their cognitive abilities?
4. How can self-management skills help older adults cope with psychological problems, such as depression, that can occur in seniors?
5. How can self-management techniques help seniors adapt to the death of a loved one?
6. How can I get involved in working with senior citizens in my family or community?

There are ample opportunities for all of us to work with older adults either through a formal community program or through informal interactions. Our involvement will not only brighten the lives of the seniors we know, but will better prepare us for stages of aging that we will pass through during the course of our lives.

REVIEW TERMS

Blood vessels and aging
Collagen
Environmental theory of aging
Genetic theory of aging
Lungs and aging
Short-term memory

QUESTIONS

Describe the Big Five personality characteristics.
List ten characteristics of healthy aging.
Discuss the five stages of death and dying.

CHAPTER 32

Self-Efficacy

"They can because they think they can."

—Virgil, *Aeneid*

"I don't know what happens. I learn things more thoroughly than other students. I'm always studying. I practice and rehearse what I am going to do. Finally, the time comes when I have to act. And that's when I fail. No matter how skilled I am at everything from playing basketball to taking courses, I don't do well when I try to act on what I know."

—Carol, a junior

Effective functioning requires that we develop competencies and skills. The purpose of this book is to teach you how to use self-management techniques to adjust to potential problems you are apt to encounter in life. This has been the theme of the text. Albert Bandura (1977, 1986), however, has proclaimed that we must not only be able successfully to perform the skills and competencies we have acquired, but that we must have a strong self-belief in our efficacy in using these skills. Bandura proposed the term *self-efficacy* to account for the belief that you can perform adequately in a given situation. More specifically, Bandura (1986) indicated:

> Perceived self-efficacy is defined as people's judgments of their capabilities to organize and execute courses of action required to attain designated types of performances. It is concerned not with the skills one has but with judgments of what one can do with whatever skills one possesses. (p. 391)

Perceived self-efficacy is your judgment that you are capable of attaining a certain level of performance. It differs from your expectations of what will occur when you consider the likely outcome of your behavior.

INFLUENCE OF SELF-EFFICACY

The distinction between efficacy and outcome expectations is illustrated in Figure 32–1. As Bandura (1977) pointed out, an outcome expectation is our belief that a given behavior will lead to a certain outcome; efficacy expectations, on the other hand, are our convictions that we can successfully execute the behavior required to produce the outcome. Bandura distinguished outcome and efficacy expectations because while we believe that particular actions will produce certain outcomes, we may question whether we can perform these actions. The strength of our convictions regarding our effectiveness determines whether we even try to cope with difficult situations. We tend to fear and avoid threatening situations when we believe ourselves unable to handle them, but behave in a positive manner when we judge ourselves capable of successfully managing the situations.

In discussing his concepts and ideas with Evans (1989), Bandura added that skills are not fixed, but have the capability of being developed and refined. Self-efficacy plays a critical role in determining whether we use the skills and competencies we have in a well, poor, or extraordinary manner. Bandura described how self-efficacy can influence three aspects of our lives: choices, motivation, and thinking.

Choices. Each day, we make decisions about what courses of action to take and how long to continue the actions we pursue. Anything that influences choice behavior can have a profound effect on your life. Self-efficacy influences the choices you make with respect to which of your abilities or capabilities you attempt to cultivate and which will remain uncultivated. Reasonably accurate appraisal of your own capabilities, points out Bandura (1986), is of considerable value in your ability to function successfully.

Motivation. Self-efficacy exerts a powerful influence on motivation. Judgments of efficacy will determine how much effort you will expend and how long you will persist in the face of obstacles or aversive experiences (Bandura, 1986). A high sense of efficacy may lead you to mobilize greater levels of effort in the activities you undertake. You are likely to persevere in working toward achieving your goals despite obstacles and difficulties.

FIGURE 32–1
The difference between efficacy and outcome expectations (adapted from Bandura, 1977).

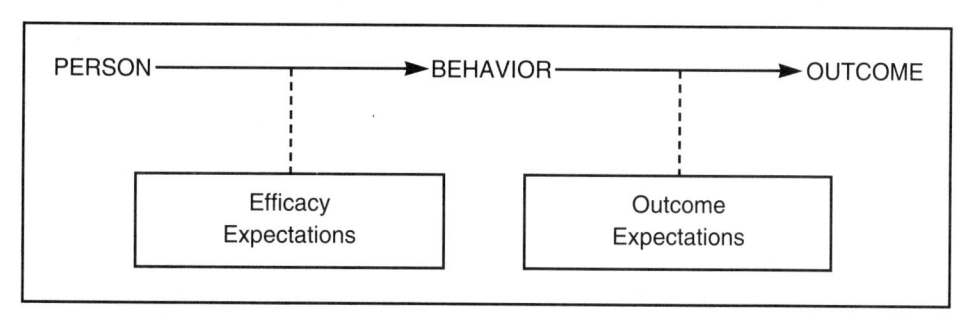

PERSON ──────► BEHAVIOR ──────► OUTCOME

Efficacy Expectations

Outcome Expectations

Thinking. Perceived self-efficacy affects your thinking processes. When you encounter problems, the way you think may help or hinder you. If you have a developed sense of self-efficacy, you tend to devote your attention and cognitive resources to overcoming and mastering the problems. If you lack self-efficacy, you are plagued by self-doubts and ruminate over all the things that might go wrong.

A robust sense of self-efficacy is required for your well-being and achievement. Bandura noted that the reality we face is, in essence, pretty lousy. To succeed in life, you must have a robust sense of your efficacy in order to display the perseverance needed to succeed. Most successes do not come early, but only occur through consistent effort in the face of repeated failures. A resistant sense of personal efficacy, Bandura commented, provides the necessary staying power to you.

DEVELOPING SELF-EFFICACY

Bandura noted that there are four ways of building self-efficacy: through modeling, social persuasion, judgments of physiological indicants, and mastery.

Modeling. The appraisal of our self-efficacy is partly influenced by watching others. Seeing or visualizing those similar to us experiencing success can create and increase our self-efficacy beliefs that we are capable of mastering comparable activities. We persuade ourselves that if others can do it, so can we. By the same token, observing others of comparable abilities fail, despite high effort, can lower our judgments of our capability and, ultimately, undermine our efforts.

Social persuasion. We use self-statements widely to tell ourselves that we can achieve the goals we seek. While social persuasion alone may be limited in its power to create enduring increases in self-efficacy, it can contribute to successful performance if the increased appraisal is realistic (Bandura, 1986). As Bandura explained:

> People who are persuaded verbally that they possess the capabilities to master given tasks are likely to mobilize greater sustained effort than if they harbor self-doubts and dwell on personal deficiencies when difficulties arise. To the extent that persuasive boosts in self-efficacy lead people to try hard enough to succeed, they promote development of skills and a sense of personal efficacy. Persuasory efficacy attributions, therefore, have their greatest impact on people who have some reason to believe that they can produce effects through their actions. (1986, p. 400)

Judgment of physiological indicants. We all rely on information from the physiological states of our bodies to judge our abilities. We observe whether physical arousal in response to stress is a situation we can manage or a sign of vulnerability and potential dysfunction. In some instances, we may believe that we have the resources to control the stress; in other situations, however, we can perceive that we lack whatever it will take to control the stress. Our interpretation of whether we can or cannot manage the situation is based upon our competencies and self-efficacy beliefs. Learning and performing the self-management procedures for controlling stress increases the skills we need to master the stimuli that are producing stress; the repeated performance of these self-management skills in a wide array of contexts should enhance our self-efficacy beliefs that our self-management competencies will permit us to control stress in other situations.

Mastery. We must develop the skills and self-efficacy required to succeed at a given task. To do so entails that you have mastered the self-management techniques you have been taught. If you have mastered these procedures, you have also acquired self-efficacy beliefs. You can then set about applying self-management techniques to other problems. To master a situation requires a recapitulation of what you have already done, including:

1. Setting goals. A project should have realistic goals, yet be challenging to you. You need to: (a) make a commitment to make every effort to achieve the goal; (b) consider all the self-management skills you have acquired; (c) visualize yourself succeeding at your project; (d) make a list of specific situations where you anticipate problems with your program; and (e) consider how you could change the program if required.

2. Performing self-management skills. The more you have mastered the performance of given techniques, the more success you can expect. Discriminate between your past performance and your current program. Consider any obstacles that occurred in the past and how you will control them if they occur with this program.

3. Monitoring progress. Self-observation and recording of information is always the single most significant component of self-management.

4. Evaluating progress. Good data gathered through self-monitoring can assist you in deciding whether you are succeeding with your program. If it appears as if the outcome of your program is a success, you can continue with your efforts. Evaluation also permits you to make any changes in your program or to start the process over again.

EXERCISE

Review the self-management procedures you believe you have mastered.

Consider other problems that may be changed through application of these procedures.

Consider your self-efficacy beliefs with respect to the performance of self-management competencies.

REVIEW TERMS

Perceived self-efficacy
Self-efficacy
Social persuasion

QUESTIONS

Define and distinguish efficacy and outcome expectations.
Discuss three aspects of life influenced by self-efficacy.
Discuss four ways to build self-efficacy.

CHAPTER 33
Why Self-Management Fails

"Success is relative: It is what we can make of the mess we have made of things."

—T.S. Eliot, *Family Reunion*

"I can't say that I can't lose weight. I can. I can put myself on a diet and lose thirty to forty pounds. The problem is that I don't keep the weight off. I not only gain the weight back, but each time I do, I add another two or three pounds to where I was when I started. So, my problem is not starting a diet or losing weight. My problem comes in keeping the pounds off once I lose them. How can I solve my problem?"

—Betty, a homemaker

When we develop and implement a self-management program, we are usually enthusiastic about what we anticipate will be the success of our efforts. We believe we are finally going to get a handle on whatever problem we face. In many cases, we are successful. A number of you have demonstrated that you can select a problem behavior and institute a self-management program to bring about change. Many of you will not only experience success, but you will maintain the gains you have made. For most of us, however, we attain goals for but a fleeting moment; without our awareness, our successes may begin to evaporate and, before long, we are back at the point where we started. What happened? Why do some behaviors seemingly resist permanent change?

The barrier we have hit up against in maintaining behavioral change over time or across settings has been referred by Kirschenbaum and Tomarken (1982) as "the generalization problem" (p. 120). This means that we fail to perform the behavior we have acquired across settings or over time. In other words, though you may lose weight while at college, you may regain it once you return home. Or, you may find that the pounds you have lost gradually return as, over time, you pay less attention to your eating habits. Kirschenbaum and Tomarken refer to the relapse we experience as *self-regulatory failure*. This term "describes all processes by which individuals fail to generalize desired behavior changes over time and across settings, in the relative absence of immediate external constraints" (p. 137). The study of self-regulatory or self-management failure, they continue, is a search for self-managed components that prevent or inhibit generalization of behavior change.

THREE MODELS OF SELF-MANAGEMENT FAILURE

Daniel Kirschenbaum has been a pioneer in investigating why self-management programs fail. Kirschenbaum and Tomarken (1982) summarize three models that provide suggestions of why self-management fails. Critical elements of these models are shown in Table 33–1.

Closed Loop Model

This behavioral model, proposed by Kanfer and Karoly (1972), emphasizes that self-regulation or self-management includes those processes by which we alter or maintain behavioral change in the absence of some sort of external support. While the model does not explicitly describe self-

TABLE 33–1 Three Models that Describe Elements of Self-Management Failure (adapted from Kirschenbaum and Tomarken, 1982)

Closed Loop Model
Failure to discriminate reemergence of the problem
Discontinuation of self-monitoring
Discontinuation of self-evaluation
Discontinuation of self-reinforcement or self-punishment

Self-Efficacy Theory
Lowered perceived self-efficacy
Observation of failure in others
Reinforcement for failure
Attribution of physiological arousal to personal inadequacies
Observing a decline in rate of improvement
Perception of coping skills as inadequate for situation

Cognitive-Behavioral Relapse Model
Exposure to high-risk situation
Failure to initiate coping responses
Lowered self-efficacy expectations
Expectation of favorable outcomes from relapsing
Initial relapse
Attributions to personal weaknesses for initial relapse
Experiences of pleasant consequences from relapsing

management failure, four elements of the model could account for such a result:

1. Failure to discriminate reemergence of the problem. The self-management program you developed likely resulted in a positive change in your behavior. If you fail to maintain the program, you may be unaware that the problem once controlled with your program is returning. You fail to note that the behavior once managed is insidiously creeping back into your life as a potential problem. A good example is failure to note that, in a weight control program, you have unknowingly gained back a few pounds.

2. Discontinuation of self-monitoring. Self-monitoring is emerging as the key ingredient to a successful self-management program (Baker and Kirschenbaum, 1993; Kanfer, 1972). If you fail to monitor your behavior, it is likely that what may have been a successful self-management program will cease to be effective.

3. Discontinuation of self-evaluation. You constantly need to evaluate the data you gather about yourself. This information is unavailable if you fail to monitor your behavior. If you continue to collect data on your behavior, it is meaningless unless you evaluate the information and make whatever changes are needed in your behavior. You display what Baumeister, Heatherton, and Tice (1994) refer to as underregulation of self-control.

4. Discontinuation of self-reinforcement or self-punishment. If you continue to perform the self-management behaviors you acquired, reinforce yourself through self-statements or in some other manner. Or, if you have established a system of self-punishment, such as not viewing your favorite television program if you haven't completed your homework, continue applying that consequence to maintain your studies. Discontinuing either type of consequence may result in a weakening of the effective self-management behaviors you developed.

Self-Efficacy Model

Bandura (1977) suggested that the success of any behavioral program was a joint function of self-efficacy and outcome expectations. Self-efficacy expectations have been discussed throughout the text, particularly in Chapter 32. Outcome expectations are the judgments you make that a particular behavior, when performed, will result in certain outcomes. These types of expectancies alone do not produce desired outcomes, but they can influence your motivation. Self-efficacy factors that could result in self-management failure include:

1. Lowered self-efficacy. If you do not have strong self-efficacy beliefs that your performance will result in a particular outcome, you may not experience success in taking certain action. Failure at performing a task may result in lowered self-efficacy beliefs that you can successfully perform the task in the future.

2. Observation of failure in others. If you observe that a friend fails in changing the behavior you also want to change through the application of self-management procedures, you may conclude that you will also be unsuccessful. You base your judgment not on your performance, but on the failure you witness in someone else.

3. Reinforcement for failure. You may have established a time-management program that has strengthened your studying behavior. However, it could fail if you receive reinforcement from others, such as spending more time with a girlfriend or boyfriend, for engaging in some other activity. Such activities reinforce the failure of your program.

4. Attribution of physiological arousal to personal inadequacies. In the past, you may have used relaxation techniques to manage anxiety. If relaxation techniques fail to alleviate future bouts of anxiety, you may conclude that you possess an inner weakness that prohibits these procedures from being effective with all the forms of anxiety you experience. This conclusion may reduce the probability that you will continue to use relaxation techniques to manage these emotional responses.

5. Observing a declining rate of improvement. Self-efficacy beliefs can weaken if you observe a declining rate of improvement in the behavior you targeted for change. If your weight or grades plateau, you may experience a concomitant decline in your self-efficacy beliefs that you can manage and control your behavior.

6. Perception of coping skills as inadequate for situation. You may find that you have developed a number of ways to cope with stress. Toward the end of a school term, however, you may have been overwhelmed with the intense stress that frequently accompanies a time when you are busy taking tests, completing assignments, and the like. You may attribute what you perceive as an inability to reduce the stress as a lack of coping skills on your part and not to the fact that you did not manage your time effectively throughout the term.

Cognitive-Behavioral Relapse Model

The model that has received the most attention with respect to self-management failure has been the cognitive-behavioral model of the relapse described by Marlatt and Gordon (1980). Seven stages or factors of our behavior increase the probability of relapse:

1. Exposure to high-risk situations. If you select alcohol abstinence as a problem, you are apt to be successful as long as alcoholic beverages are not in your immediate environment. If you resume going to bars or taverns, however, you expose yourself to a high-risk situation. In these settings, you might experience a relapse.

2. Failure to initiate coping responses. If you are in a high-risk situation, you may fail to initiate responses required to cope successfully with the stimuli in the setting. This occurs either because you fail to detect the need for coping responses or you lack whatever coping skills are required to manage the situation.

3. Lowered efficacy expectations. If you fail to control a high-risk situation, there is apt to be a reduction in the self-efficacy expectations you have regarding your ability to use self-management techniques successfully to manage similar situations in the future. Although you may know what skills to perform, you begin to question whether the performance of these skills will permit you to cope with high-risk stimuli.

4. Expectations of favorable outcomes from relapsing. You may have developed alternative sources of reinforcement when away from a high-risk situation. If alcohol abstinence is your target behavior, however, you may return to an environment that includes past experiences you perceived as enjoyable. Ordering a beer and drinking it with your friends may be an expectation of a favorable outcome if you relapse and again start drinking alcoholic beverages.

5. Initial relapse. The initial incident you experience as a setback in self-management is a crucial factor in relapse according to Marlatt and Gordon (1980). It can not only alter your coping behaviors, but it can have a profound effect on the expectancies you have regarding your ability to manage a high-risk situation. Initial relapse does not automatically lead to a decrease in the performance of self-management skills, or what Baumeister, Heatherton, and Tice (1994) refer to as a "snowballing" effect. Much depends upon the factor that led to the initial relapse and your ability to manage these factors and the relapse they generate.

6. Attributions to personal weakness for initial relapse. The violation of abstinence or any other self-imposed rule, coupled with perceived attributions of your failure to a personal defect, greatly increases the likelihood of further relapse in the future.

7. Experiences of pleasant consequences from relapsing. You may think that you will violate your self-imposed self-management rule only once. According to the model by Marlatt and Gordon (1980), pleasant sensations or effects resulting from the relapse become strong reinforcers for both your weakened self-efficacy expectations and your attributions of personal weakness. At the same time, you may discover that you are again trapped in a situation where the contingencies available though drinking (e.g., your friends, or the ambiance of a tavern) reinforce the behavior.

ELEMENTS OF SELF-MANAGEMENT FAILURE

Kirschenbaum and Tomarken (1982) reviewed the literature in four areas—successful versus unsuccessful self-managers, the relapse process, self-monitoring, and self-attention. From the research in each area, elements thought to contribute to self-regulatory failure were extracted. These are listed in Table 33–2. Note elements that are common across the four areas of research; these common elements will be described in the next section. Knowledge of these elements may provide you with suggestions as to why your self-management program may not be as successful as you wish and how it might be improved.

In 1987, Kirschenbaum published an article in which he analyzed the experimental literature from three areas—success at self-management, the relapse process, and attention in self-regulation—in an attempt to determine what factors contributed to self-management failure. Eight components were identified in the three types of research; these are shown, according to the three types of research, in Table 33–3.

TABLE 33–2 Elements of Self-Regulatory Failure (as suggested by Kirschenbaum and Tomarken, 1982)

Successful versus Unsuccessful Self-Managers
Use of overly specific goals or standards
Infrequent self-reinforcement
Weak outcome expectations
Weak self-efficacy expectations
Inadequate use of self-management and coping skills
Exposure to stressful situations

Relapse Theory
Initial relapse episode
Negative emotional states
Positive emotional states
Interpersonal conflicts and pressure
Biological cravings
Coping skills deficits
Low self-efficacy expectations
Exposure to high-risk situations

Self-Monitoring
Discontinuation
Positive self-monitoring of well-mastered behaviors
Negative self-monitoring of poorly-mastered behaviors

Self-Attention
Discontinuation of self-attention
Self-attention plus failure plus perception that failure is unchangeable
Attention direct to non-individual aspects of environment
Repeated engagement in well-mastered behaviors
Self-attention plus low self-efficacy and outcome expectations
Self-attention plus sustained performance of well-mastered behaviors

TABLE 33-3 Components of Self-Regulatory Failure (as described by Kirschenbaum, 1987)

Successful versus Unsuccessful Self-Management
  Depressogenic cognitions
  Difficulties coping with emotional stressors
  Decreased use of habit change techniques, especially self-monitoring

The Relapse Process
  Initial relapse episode
  Social pressure
  Physiological pressures

Attention in Self-Management
  Problematic attentional focusing
  Disengagement from self-monitoring

Successful versus Unsuccessful Self-Management

Kirschenbaum (1987) pointed out that the strategies employed in the research varied widely in methodological rigor (i.e., some studies were experimentally stronger than others). He also noted that these factors should be regarded as correlates, not causes, of self-management failure. At this point, it is also impossible to say whether the components are the essential or active agents that differentiate those who are successful at self-management from those who are not.

The relevance of each of the three components that distinguished successful from unsuccessful self-manager is as follows:

Depressogenic cognitions. Kirschenbaum (1987) labeled certain cognitions as depressogenic because they were typical of those made by depressed individuals. Cognitions described as depressogenic included expectancies, attributions, self-evaluation, and self-reinforcement. Kirschenbaum (1987) pointed out that those unsuccessful at self-management were also apt to show weak self-efficacy and outcome expectations. In addition, data indicated that individuals unsuccessful at self-management often had a lower initial commitment to changing their behavior, rewarded themselves less and punished themselves more, and reportedly made negative self-statements about themselves and their performance.

Difficulties coping with emotional stressors. With a number of problems, particularly weight loss, smoking cessation, and alcohol abuse, Kirschenbaum (1987) found that stress decreased the use of self-management and coping skills. Emotional stressors, in fact, prompted an increase in eating, smoking, and drinking in many individuals. Eighty-two percent of those unsuccessful at maintaining their weight reported they ate in response to emotional stressors as compared to zero percent in individuals successful at maintaining their weight (Gormally and Rardin, 1981).

Decreased use of habit change techniques, especially self-monitoring. Kirschenbaum (1987) emphasized that in most studies of successful and unsuccessful self-management, regardless of the problem, one pattern clearly emerged: unsuccessful self-managers showed less consistent self-monitoring of target behaviors than successful self-managers. The consistency of this finding, he continued, was remarkable. It indicated that disengagement from a variety of habit change techniques, particularly self-monitoring, is strongly associated with self-management failure.

The Relapse Process

Relapse is defined as a violation of rules governing the rate or pattern of self-management behaviors (Marlatt and Gordon, 1980). As noted by Kirschenbaum (1987), rule violation concerns the failure to generalize the performance of goal-directed behaviors in the absence of external constraints or boundaries. Marlatt and his colleagues have conducted a number of studies where they interviewed several hundred smokers, alcoholics, heroin addicts, compulsive gamblers, and dieters (e.g., Marlatt and Gordon, 1980). They found they could reliably classify relapse episodes into specific categories of emotional and situational precipitants. Three factors—initial relapse, social conflicts and pressures, and physiological pressures—contribute to what Kirschenbaum referred to as a "relapse crisis." The role of each of these factors in creating a relapse crisis is as follows:

Initial relapse episode. Data by Marlatt and Gordon (1980) found that the vast majority of former smokers and drinkers they interviewed resumed their habits following either the first or second relapse episode. Irrational thinking, lowered self-efficacy expectations, and cognitive styles reminiscent of depressogenic cognitions contributed to the relapse of these individuals.

Social conflicts and pressure. Interpersonal conflicts and social pressures were prominent in the data collected in the United States by Marlatt and Gordon (1980) and in data collected in a series of studies conducted in Sweden by Sjoberg and colleagues. A report by Sjoberg and Persson (1979) noted:

> Conflicts may create demands on mental energy which in turn is taken from the resources available to the cognitive system. When the cognitive system is drained of these resources, it becomes much weaker and more primitive, thus giving rise to distorted and low quality reasoning and judgments. . . . The theory thus predicts that breakdowns will occur under emotional

stress and that they will be preceded by distorted reasonings and a narrow perspective. (p. 349)

Kirschenbaum (1987) concluded that stress arising from interpersonal conflicts may represent a particularly difficult challenge to successful coping. As these conflicts may involve people significant to those using self-management techniques, social support that might facilitate coping is weakened or withdrawn. This outcome, in turn, could increase the likelihood of self-management failure.

Physiological pressures. Many problems, including smoking or alcohol cessation and weight reduction, are often a function, in part, of physiological factors. Kirschenbaum, for example, summarized data that indicated physical cravings for a cigarette, a drink, or food often contributed to relapse and self-management failure. The degree of physiological involvement for addictive disorders, including alcoholism, smoking, and eating problems, and exercise or medication adherence is more prominent than it might be for other target behaviors. Research on relapse processes also underscores the roles of depressogenic cognitions, difficulty in coping with emotional stressors, and disengagement from self-monitoring in self-management failure.

Attention in Self-Management

Two facets of attentional phenomena—depressogenic cognitions and failure to self-monitor—have been described as contributing to self-management failure. Two other factors are problematic attentional focusing and disengagement from self-monitoring.

Problematic attentional focusing. Attention has often defied an unambiguous definition. However, it is assumed that attention consists of two major parameters: intensity and selectivity. Intensity refers to the person's full awareness of what he or she is observing; it assumes that the individual is in a vigilant state. Selectivity refers to the focus of our attention on particular stimuli or their properties; it assumes we focus on only certain stimuli at any given time. Attention is important in self-management because it concerns both the intensity and selectivity we direct toward both the behaviors we attempt to control through self-management and the stimuli that influence control over these behaviors. It becomes of paramount importance when considering the role played by self-monitoring in self-management.

Disengagement from self-monitoring. Self-monitoring has been described throughout the text. Kirschenbaum (1987) formally defines it as the "systematic gathering of information about target behaviors" (p. 91). It means we attend to and record information regarding the occurrence of target behaviors. Self-management occurs when self-monitoring occurs; self-management fails when self-monitoring fails to occur. Kirschenbaum suggests that while self-monitoring is necessary for self-management, it is often insufficient. We usually need to add more, such as environmental manipulation, to produce the change we seek in a particular target behavior.

The complexity of self-monitoring is revealed in searching for the conditions under which self-monitoring increases or decreases self-management failure. The most replicated finding, according to Kirschenbaum, is that positive self-monitoring improves self-management of poorly mastered tasks. Positive self-monitoring can, however, promote self-management failure when tasks are well-mastered, and negative self-monitoring can promote self-management failure when tasks are poorly mastered. These are but a few examples of what is emerging as the empirical basis for problematic attentional focusing.

AVOIDING SELF-MANAGEMENT FAILURE

Avoiding or altering the components of self-management failure permits you to experience success in using self-management techniques to alter target behaviors. Kirschenbaum (1987) pointed out that a common thread running throughout the self-management literature was that some type of systematic attention to the self-managed behavior must be sustained to avoid self-management failure. To achieve this goal, Kirschenbaum and Tomarken (1982) proposed that the term obsessive-compulsive self-regulation be used to describe the complex process of maintaining successful self-management and preventing self-management failure. They noted that their definition of obsessive-compulsive differed from the clinical definition of the term. Obsessions, for example, are often defined as repetitive thoughts, impulses, or images that are both unwanted and difficult to control; compulsions are usually defined as persistent, stereotyped, and unwanted behaviors. Kirschenbaum and Tomarken, however, eschewed the pathological aspects of the term and stressed that obsessive-compulsive was the best term to use in describing the intensity of involvement required to be successful with self-management and to avoid self-management failure.

Many of you would concur that an obsession with changing your target behavior is necessary if self-management is to produce a positive change. You would no doubt agree with Kirschenbaum (1994) that when those who are dieting "find their usual routines about eating, exercising, and monitoring disrupted, they get testy. These individuals have developed a healthy obsession with weight control. They rely on a certain approach to eating and exercising and observing themselves in order to feel comfortable. Disruptions are greeted with annoyance, irritability, and dissatisfaction. This is the state you want to be in if you want to become a successful, persistent weight controller" (p. 208). No doubt, many of you have developed a healthy obsession about changing your target behavior through self-management.

EXERCISE

Review the three models of self-management failure.
Note the components of self-management failure you might encounter with your self-management program.

REVIEW TERMS

Depressogenic cognitions
Generalization problem
Healthy obsession
Initial relapse episode
Obsessive-compulsive self-regulation
Self-regulatory failure

QUESTIONS

Briefly describe three models of self-management failure.
List the eight key elements to self-management failure.

CHAPTER 34

Relapse Prevention and Management

"It is only the wisest and the very stupidest who cannot change."
—Confucius, *Analects*

"My efforts to study fell to pieces. After midterms, I spaced out for a few weeks in front of the TV. About all I did was go out and get more food to pig out on. After a couple of weeks, I heard from a roommate that I was going to get an F in econ if I didn't start going to class. I didn't want the F. So, I looked over the program I had developed and started it up again. It was hard getting it going. Monitoring my behavior was probably what pulled me through the term by the skin of my teeth. The next term, I kept on the program and got the best grades I've received in college."
—Burke, a sophomore

Once we have changed a behavior through self-management, we hope to maintain the change. We have invested too much time and effort in our program to watch the gains we made slip away. Unfortunately, there are often problems, particularly with such behaviors as weight loss, smoking cessation, alcohol use, and exercise, where the progress we achieve disappears and our behavior returns to where it was during baseline. To avoid this fate, we can use proven strategies for preventing and managing relapse.

RELAPSE PREVENTION AND MANAGEMENT STRATEGIES

Marlatt (1982) proposed a relapse prevention model as a paradigm for coping with behavioral relapse. Relapse refers to a violation of self-imposed rules or sets of results that have governed the rate or pattern of a selected target behavior or set of behaviors. The model was proposed to account for failure of programs designed to modify addictive or habitual behavioral patterns. It soon became apparent that the relapse prevention model advocated by Marlatt (1982) had implications for any self-regulatory or self-management program (Bandura, 1986; Creer, Kotses, and Wigal, 1992). A number of steps have been suggested for coping with relapse prevention (George and Marlatt, 1986; Creer, Kotses, and Wigal, 1992). An adaptation of these strategies is presented in Table 34–1. These steps include:

TABLE 34–1 Steps for Preventing Relapse of Self-Management Program (adapted from Creer et al., 1992)

Avoid high-risk situations.
    Minimize quality of situations.

Escape from high-risk situations.
    Use distraction.

Master the performance of self-management skills.
    Make commitment.
    Establish and pursue goals.

Rehearse self-management skills.
    Monitor behavior.
    Reduce reliance on memory.

Avoid factors that weaken self-management.
    Negative emotions, including discouragement.
    Interpersonal conflict or situations.
    Social pressure or situations.

Take remedial steps.
    Review coping and self-management strategies.
    Remind yourself of delayed aversive consequences.
    Use reminders from others.

Introduce new coping strategies.

Avoid high-risk situations. A number of strategies have been suggested for teaching you to avoid situations where you are at a high risk to abandon your self-management efforts. To prevent relapse, you must avoid these situations, even after you have controlled a target behavior through self-management. In addition, you can minimize the quality of contexts where known stimuli could trigger a relapse. If you are attempting to avoid drinking alcohol, immediately ask for a soft drink or mineral water when you go to a party. Not only will this allow you to continue your self-management program, but it will permit you to avoid accepting offers of drinks from others.

Escape from high-risk situations. If you are in an environment where you believe you are going to experience difficulties in avoiding entrapping stimuli, you might distract yourself by performing other tasks or by concentrating on something else. If you believe you will be unable to withstand a known stimuli, leave. This will permit you to escape from high-risk situations and their attendant stimuli.

Master the performance of self-management skills. Mastery of self-management skills is necessary not only for the skills to be effective, but for you to acquire self-efficacy beliefs regarding your ability to perform them in a given situation (Bandura, 1986). It is important that you make the commitment to change and establish goals for your change program.

These goals should be periodically reviewed to permit you to evaluate where you are with respect to their achievement, and to motivate you to continue performing positive change behaviors.

Rehearse self-management skills. Rehearsal of behaviors was an approach to self-management emphasized in Chapter 7. Reread this chapter and consider how rehearsal can help you prevent a relapse in your efforts to achieve your goals. Reviewing Chapter 7 will also refresh your memory of how to incorporate rehearsal techniques into your self-change program. Refocus your efforts if you believe you are not using self-monitoring in the most effective manner.

Avoid factors that weaken self-management. Marlatt and Gordon (1980) reported that 71 percent of all relapses were precipitated by one or more of three determinants: (a) negative emotional states, where you might experience unpleasant emotions or feelings such as anger or discouragement; (b) interpersonal conflicts where you might repeatedly argue with a significant person in your life, such as a fiancé(e) or spouse, over whether you should chuck your self-management program; and (c) social pressure or situations, where you experience pressure from others, particularly peers, to scrap self-management performance.

Take remedial steps. As noted in Chapter 33, self-management skills are never static or firmly established. Rather they represent a dynamic set of competencies that must be adapted to the changing exigencies of your life (Creer et al., 1992). For self-management to remain viable, you may need to take remedial steps, including reviewing the coping and self-management skills you can perform, reminding yourself of your goals, and considering the delayed consequences that may occur if you desert this goal. You may find it necessary to ask others for assistance to help you attain your goals.

Introduce new coping strategies. As you develop self-management skills, as well as acquire self-efficacy beliefs regarding your performance of these competencies, you may think of how you can improve your basic program. The self-control or self-management of our behavior is a never-ending quest in adjusting to various problems that occur throughout our lives. As you enhance your skills and self-efficacy beliefs, you will develop more effective and efficient ways of controlling your life.

Other Strategies for Preventing Relapse

A number of factors that contributed to self-management failure were described in Chapter 33. Changing these factors offers other strategies you can use to prevent relapse. In particular, the alteration of components noted by Kirschenbaum (1987) is imperative. These include:

Changing depressogenic cognitions. Any depressogenic cognitions, including expectancies, personal attributions, self-evaluation, and self-reinforcement, that interfere with self-management should be changed. First, it is important that you detect these cognitions when they occur.

The earlier their detection, the more likely you are to alter them. Second, use any approach that you can, including positive self-statements, to alter these cognitions. Reviewing your program and making any changes, developing better coping skills, rehearsing and refining the coping skills you have, and improving self-monitoring are all steps you can take to decrease the damaging role played by depressogenic cognitions.

Coping with emotional stressors. We all experience emotional stressors; we will continue to do so in the future. If you refine or develop more effective tactics for coping with these stressors, you will be prepared to deal with them. Self-management skills are constantly being developed; refining these skills so as to manage the emotional stressors we face is a lifetime goal.

Decreasing use of habit change techniques. We must constantly practice any self-management skill to perform it effectively. All self-management skills are important in one situation or another. If you use relaxation to manage stress, you need to perform these skills constantly so they will be available to you when needed. If distraction is a method you use, this skill also requires repetition to be of future value. Any self-management skill we develop requires continued rehearsal if it is to be useful in situations where the skill must be performed.

Managing the initial relapse episode. Marlatt and Gordon (1980) emphasize that many people who use self-management techniques to manage problem behaviors resume their habits after one or two relapse episodes. This is a major finding in that it suggests that despite our best intentions, we are prone to discard new and more appropriate self-management habits following a single relapse episode. For this reason, attention must be directed at managing and controlling the initial relapse. Augmenting the significance of the initial relapse episode is the finding that we are not always aware of the reemergence of our problem. For example, we may not realize that we are gaining weight or studying less until the problem behavior is again established.

Avoiding conflicts and pressure. Social conflicts and pressure can be a difficult challenge to any self-management program. Not only can they intensify the problem we are trying to control, but they can reduce the likelihood of our receiving social reinforcement for any gains we make. Avoiding interpersonal conflicts and social pressure by adhering to a program or by developing new coping strategies offers a way to manage these pressures.

Resisting physiological pressures. We all experience cravings for many of the stimuli that we wish to control. Anyone who is on a diet knows how difficult it is to pass up the tempting offer of a luscious sundae or a piece of chocolate. Or, if attempting to quit drinking alcoholic beverages, you may think of gulping a cold beer on a hot summer day. These pressures must be resisted if they are to be controlled. Use methods of self-management described in earlier chapters to resist these physical pressures. It is difficult, but some of you do control similar pressures in your daily lives.

Change problematic attention focusing. We all select the stimuli or responses we attend to at any time; we must if self-management is to be successful. The intensity of attention we direct toward certain stimuli or responses is equally important. We need not only attend to the factors that help us manage a situation or problem behavior, but the factors that may lead our attention to waver from the goals we have set. This would include the observations we make of others. If we witness failure in others, for example, we cannot discard our self-management strategies and imitate the inappropriate behaviors we observe.

Continue self-monitoring. Self-monitoring is undoubtedly the most significant self-management skill you can perform. Most readers, particularly those who have created and conducted their own self-management program, will concur with this finding. Self-monitoring, by itself, frequently can be used to produce positive change in our behavior.

DECISION-MAKING STRATEGIES

A number of decision-making strategies have been proposed for effective self-management (Arkes, 1981; Gambrill, 1993). Creer (1990) compared self-reported information gathered from a large number of asthmatic children and their families to data collected from a number of medical students and physicians. The purpose of the analysis was to determine how expert physicians and patients skilled at self-management controlled asthma. A number of common strategies were generated by these two groups. The strategies, depicted in Table 34–2, are similar to those rec-

TABLE 34–2 Twelve Rules for Making Decisions in Self-Management (adapted from Creer, 1990)

1. Be thoughtful and cautious.
2. Avoid preconceived notions.
3. Show awareness of self-management strategies and outcomes.
4. Generate a number of management alternatives.
5. Consider separately each situation in which you need to perform **self-management skills**.
6. Do not misperceive the severity of the situation.
7. Adjust self-management to fit the perceived problem.
8. Refer to your personal data base.
9. Regard events as correlated and not causative.
10. Think in terms of probabilities.
11. Do not rely on memory.
12. Do not be overconfident.

ommended by Arkes (1981) for making decisions. Applying these decision-making strategies to self-management, they can be stated as follows:

1. Be thoughtful and cautious. This means you avoid reacting to a problem in an automatic manner and consider possible outcomes of your behavior before acting. You attempt to balance your personal data base of how you normally manage a situation against the possibility that you may need to generate and apply an innovative approach to solve a problem.

2. Avoid preconceived notions. Avoid preconceived notions about how you will manage all situations. You cannot assume that the experiences you have in one environment, such as with your roommates, are representative of all your experiences across a broader array of settings. By developing a base of knowledge about how self-management skills can be applied in a number of contexts, you hope to react in a manner required to fit the needs of any given situation.

3. Show awareness of self-management strategies and outcomes. By now, you have acquired and, in most cases, performed self-management skills. You have acquired a personal history regarding use of these techniques. The development and refinement of self-management skills is a lifetime pursuit; those who are consistently successful at controlling their behavior make a long-term commitment to learn and refine their performance of these skills.

4. Generate a number of management alternatives. Before taking action in a particular situation, you may want more information. This involves your recalling how you managed similar situations in the past. Additional information may help you generate a number of management alternatives in a search for the self-management skills that could maximize your performance.

5. Consider separately each situation in which you need to perform self-management skills. If you are on a diet, you may need to think of the strategy you will use to avoid overeating when invited out for dinner. This tactic is apt to be different from the one you would take if surrounded by snacks while watching TV with your roommates. It is essential that you make whatever decisions you need in order to perform self-management skills optimally over time and across different situations.

6. Do not misperceive the severity of the situation. If you are attempting to quit smoking, you may not encounter any problems in your apartment, particularly if you have roommates who do not smoke. If you go to a party where others smoke, how will you handle the situation? Being around stimuli that led to smoking in the past may result in a relapse. This might be avoided if you consider the potential severity of the situation before it occurs and prepare yourself with a supply of gum or engage in a distracting activity.

7. Adjust self-management to fit the perceived problem. In a given situation, you may find that the self-management skills you normally use are insufficient or ineffective. For example, you may find that you are tempted to drink alcohol when at a party. If you are trying to abstain from alcoholic beverages, this can pose a problem. If nonalcoholic beverages don't curb the cravings you have for a drink, you may want to escape from the situation by leaving the party.

8. Refer to your personal data base. All of us have accumulated experiences that serve as a personal data base, which can be useful in helping to perform self-management skills in an effective and efficient manner. A personal data base does not insure perfect decisions because, as described earlier, the unique characteristics of a particular situation may require that you generate additional strategies for managing the situation. Thus, while a personal and expanding data base is a necessary condition of using self-management techniques, it is not a sufficient condition for success.

9. Regard events as correlated and not causative. We all take a shorthand approach in organizing events in our life in that we tend to see that stimulus A leads to response B and so forth. This is effective with simple behaviors (e.g., drinking water may quench your thirst). In reality, however, many behaviors are far more complicated than can be accounted for under this simple formula. If you analyze why you behaved in a particular manner in a given situation, you may come up with a number of reasons to explain your behavior. Under these circumstances, you don't know what caused what; all you can say is that certain events were correlated with the action you took.

10. Think in terms of probabilities. When you use self-management skills in a certain way, you think it will result in a particular outcome. It probably will. We are never certain, however, that our behavior will produce the outcome we think it will produce. For this reason, it is more realistic for you to think that certain of your actions are likely to result in a certain outcome. Thinking in terms of probabilities is essential when considering the outcomes of any of your behaviors.

11. Do not rely on memory. You may use self-management skills every day to help manage a problem. Under these circumstances, memory may not be a factor that influences your performance. If the behavior you are trying to change occurs on a more intermittent basis, such as test-taking, you may forget the strategies you use from test to test. This is normal. What you should do is not rely upon your memory, but keep a diary or notes on how you managed similar situations in the past. Such a written record can be invaluable in the future.

12. Do not be overconfident. This is good advice in any situation, including the performance of self-management skills. If you are overconfident, you may be less accurate in making decisions and, ultimately, in managing your behaviors.

EXERCISE

Consider whether you are experiencing any problems in achieving the goals of your self-management program.

Consider any techniques of relapse prevention that might allow you to get back on track with your program.

REVIEW TERMS

Depressogenic cognitions
Initial relapse

Relapse
Relapse prevention

QUESTIONS

List seven steps for preventing relapse of self-management.
List twelve steps for making decisions.

Self-Management Redux

CHAPTER 35

"There is always an easy solution to every human problem—neat, plausible, and wrong."

—H.L. Mencken, *Prejudices*

"The thing about studying is that you have to develop and improve your study skills each term. You have just figured out how to study for one teacher or class, and the term is over. When the next term starts, you begin all over again and have to figure out how you're going to study for your new classes and different teachers. I learned a lot of ways to study in the time I was in college. They all came in handy. Still, there was never a term when I was completely prepared for my classes. Learning how to study was something I had to do throughout my time in college."

—Loren, a graduating senior

Continuously learning and performing self-management skills consumes much of our lives. The older we become—or until we may be unable to take care of ourselves—we gradually learn to be responsible for our actions. Most of us master the basic self-management skills needed to perform functions required in our daily lives. We adjust to the ever-changing boundaries and demands that comprise our existence. Some individuals learn self-management skills better than others. Those skilled at self-management are able to pursue goals that may be unattainable to those less skilled. They use self-management competencies to achieve more of their potential than do other people, although it is doubtful that anyone achieves his or her maximum potential. There may remain barriers that are impossible to overcome with self-management skills. Although a plethora of self-help books promises riches and perfect health if we take certain actions, we all operate within certain parameters, many unique to each of us, that limit our growth and progress.

INDIVIDUAL SELF-MANAGEMENT

There are boundaries within which all of us operate. These dictate where we go as a society. The greatest concern of each of us, however, is our ability to use self-management techniques in a manner that promotes our personal growth and development. In the long run, the only life you may control is your own. This is not easy given the number and variety of self-management behaviors we are asked to perform across time and over settings. We can only echo the hardened manager in *A League of Our Own*, who exclaimed about learning to become a good baseball player, "It's supposed to be hard. If it wasn't hard, anyone could do it." Most of you are personally familiar with the difficulties encountered in altering a behavior and, in particular, in maintaining the self-induced changes you generated. While you may have encountered few problems in initially controlling a problem behavior through self-management, you find it is difficult to keep your hard work from slipping away. This is not unusual. With many instances, behavioral change proves temporary; a reversal of gains can almost always be expected.

Weight loss and control. Maintaining behavioral change is difficult with many behaviors, but none is more resistant to permanent change than weight management. There is no doubt that obesity is a major health problem in the United States (NIH Technology Assessment Conference Panel, 1993). Kuczmarski, Flegal, Campbell, and Johnson (1994) examined four separate national surveys, conducted at four different times extending from 1960 to 1962 through 1988 to 1991, to determine trends in the prevalence of overweight individuals in the United States. In the period 1988 to 1991, it was found that 33.4 percent of adults in the country, twenty years and older were overweight. The estimates showed a dramatic increase in overweight individuals in all race and sex groups. In addition, the prevalence of those overweight in the United States was found to have increased 8 percent between the 1976–1980 and the 1988–1991 surveys. Increasing obesity is associated with greater morbidity and higher mortality. For example, a rise in disease incidence linked to increasing weight includes diabetes mellitus, hypertension, dyslipidemeria, stroke, cardiovascular disease, gout, sleep apnea, osteoarthritis, and some types of cancer (Pi-Sunyer, 1993; 1994). Based on 1986 costs, economic costs of obesity were estimated at $11.3 billion for diabetes, $22.2 billion for cardiovascular disease, $2.4 billion for gall bladder disease, $1.5 billion for hypertension, and $1.9 billion for breast and colon cancer (Colditz, 1992). A conservative estimate of the economic costs of obesity was $39.3 billion, or 5.5 percent of the costs of illness, in 1986. Adding costs due to musculoskeletal disorders, continued Colditz, could raise the estimate to 7.8 percent of the costs of illness in 1986. Severe obesity is associated with approximately a twofold increase in total mortality, and a several-fold increase in mortality due to diabetes, cerebrovascular and cardiovascular disease, and certain forms of cancer (Sjostrom, 1992).

As many as 40 percent of women and 24 percent of men in the United States are trying to lose weight at any given time; many have tried a number of methods, such as diets, exercise, behavior modification, and drugs (NIH Technology Assessment Conference Panel, 1993). In controlled studies, those who remain in weight-loss programs usually lose approximately 10 percent of their weight. However, according to the NIH Panel, one-third to two-thirds of the weight is regained within one year, and almost all weight is regained within five years. The data on weight loss and weight control is so bleak that Seligman (1993) concluded that diets: (a) don't work; (b) may make being overweight a worse problem; and (c) may be bad for your health. Are these conclusions warranted? Considering each conclusion separately, the answer is, at best, equivocal. First, Seligman (1993) argues that diets don't work. This is often the case, but not always: diets work for some individuals, particularly those who see weight control, much like abstinence from alcohol or illicit drugs, as a lifetime challenge. If you have a physical condition, such as diabetes mellitus, you must make a lifelong commitment to keeping your weight at a certain level. Your commitment to weight maintenance would be equal to that of other patients with diabetes mellitus who must take daily insulin shots to remain alive. This point was the emphatic conclusion made both by Manson and colleagues (1995) and Byers (1995). Second, Seligman (1993) suggests that diets may make being overweight a worse problem. The truth to this statement is that you may gain back more weight and be heavier than you were when you started, or you may launch yourself on the roller coaster of yo-yo dieting described earlier. Losing weight, however, is beneficial for you both in terms of physical health (Manson et al., 1995; Byers, 1995) and in psychological perspective toward yourself (Stunkard and Wadden, 1992). The latter may be characterized by an increase in self-esteem and positive emotions. Third, Seligman (1993) warns that diets may be bad for your health. This was thought to be true with people who exhibited a true yo-yo pattern of losing and regaining weight, although there is no compelling evidence to suggest that this pattern, commonly referred to as weight cycling, overrides the benefits of moderate weight loss in significantly obese individuals (National Task Force on the Prevention and Treatment of Obesity, 1994; Wing, Jeffrey, and Hellerstedt, 1995; Iribarren, Sharp, Burchfiel, and Petrovich, 1995). A diet may be harmful if you are not overweight (Brownell and Rodin, 1994). Dieting when you should not reflects a health paradox in modern America: "On the one hand, many people who do not need to lose weight are trying to. On the other hand, most who do need to lose weight are not succeeding" (NIH Panel, 1993, p. 764). A particularly harmful aspect of dieting occurs with younger people, particularly women, if it leads to eating disorders such as bulimia nervosa (binge eating accompanied by the overuse of laxatives or induced vomiting) or anorexia nervosa (extreme weight loss accompanied by a disturbance of body image and an intense fear of becoming obese). The conclusion may be false, however, in that health risks are often a function of your initial weight baseline. If you were obese when you started your diet, you were at risk for a number of health-related problems (Pi-Sunyer, 1993). Losing weight lowers these risks; regaining the weight, however, would increase your risk of poor health (Manson et al., 1995; Byers, 1995).

COMPONENTS OF SELF-MANAGEMENT

The accumulated data presents both the pros and cons of dieting. How should you interpret this information if you are contemplating a diet? The answer is that you consider it as a reference point in helping you decide to diet or not to diet. Deciding to diet is a decision that only you can make; even with social support, how much progress you make toward this goal and maintaining any weight loss is, in part, a function of your behavior. Before rearranging your life in an attempt to diet, you should again consider the suggestions, offered initially in Chapters 2 and 3, depicted in Figure 35–1. These are:

Goal selection. As pointed out in Chapters 2 and 3, goal selection is not always easy. We do not always know what behavior we want to change. Using weight loss as an illustration, you may believe that what you perceive as an inadequate social life is related to your weight. Is it? If you are not obese—defined as approximately 124 percent of desirable weight for men and 120 percent of desirable weight for women (Kucz-

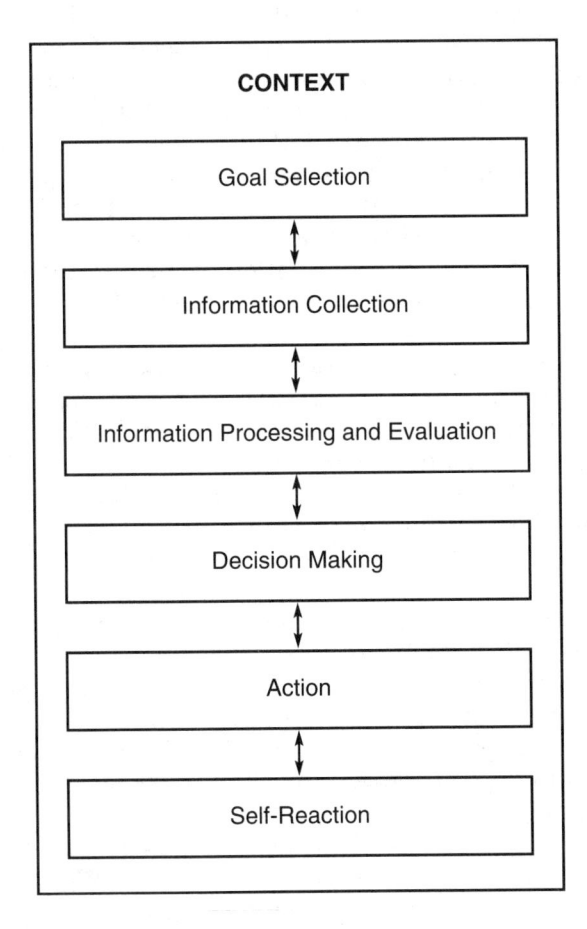

FIGURE 35–1
A model of self-management.

marski et al., 1994)—your lack of social life is probably not due to your weight. It is more likely correlated with some other factor, such as your not being involved in a variety of social activities. Before selecting an inappropriate goal, consider factors related to change, contingencies of behavior, and aspects of the behavioral goal you want to pursue. If you go through the steps outlined in Chapters 2 and 3, you are more apt to pick not only an appropriate goal, but one that you are likely to attain.

Information collection. The backbone of successful self-management is self-monitoring. Not that you need any reminders, but self-monitoring was defined as the systematic observation and recording of the behaviors you want to change. Self-monitoring is not only necessary for self-management, but it must be sustained to maintain effective self-management and to avoid self-regulatory failure (Kirschenbaum, 1987). If weight loss was the goal you selected, you must gather data on your weight as well as on such activities as the number of calories you consume, your expenditure of energy, etc.

Information processing and evaluation. You must constantly process and evaluate the information you collect about yourself. Chapter 2 pointed out that information processing and evaluation consists of five steps: (a) detecting any changes in your behavior; (b) establishing any changes against which to compare any changes that occur; (c) evaluating and making judgments based upon such comparisons; (d) evaluating any changes according to antecedents, behaviors, and consequences of the behavior; and (e) considering the context within which a particular behavior occurred. You need to consider these steps in processing and evaluating any information you collect about yourself, including the data that would be gathered in a self-management weight-loss program.

Decision making. Based upon your evaluation of the information you have collected regarding your target behavior, you must make certain decisions. As stated in Chapter 4, a number of variables are included in this process, including your knowledge, experience, and the context within which you make a decision. Decision making is a dynamic process whereby alternative solutions may be generated and tested. Different solutions may be required according to whether there are changes in the goal of the program, the settings where it is applied, or failure of the program to achieve its aims. If weight loss were your goal, you would have to decide whether your strategies are working or whether any modifications should be made in your program.

Action. After deciding the direction you want to take, you must perform whatever self-management skills are required to change your behavior. This means you consider the contingencies, antecedents, behaviors, and consequences of whatever action you may contemplate. As suggested in Chapter 3, there are a large number and variety of behavioral strategies that you can take in this respect. Any or all of these strategies may be relevant to your weight loss program.

Self-reaction. We need to direct attention constantly toward reviewing and evaluating our performance in a given situation. This permits us to set realistic standards, and to judge how our behavior compares to these standards or expectations. Positive self-reaction to our performance can assist us by allowing us to master whatever self-management skills are required to be performed in a given situation. Negative self-reaction to our performance, however, may have an impact not only on whether we acquire and master self-management skills, but whether we will persist in performing these skills. Self-reaction to whether we lose any weight would be a major factor in determining whether we acquire and later execute weight-loss strategies.

A significant factor in self-reaction is self-efficacy. We have repeatedly noted that this is our belief that we can perform adequately in a given situation. With weight loss, we must have both a potentially effective weight reduction program and the beliefs that we can translate what we know into the self-management skills required to lose weight.

PARTING COMMENT

In conclusion, the basic observables in psychology are stimuli and responses (Kimble, 1994). These events comprise the psychology of behavior. With self-management, this means that all anyone else can observe are the stimuli that may influence you and the responses you make. Only you know what you actually do; the systematic use of your personal observations, as occurs through self-monitoring, will be necessary, but not sufficient, for any success you may experience with the performance of self-management skills and competencies. Perhaps the best advice you can take is that offered by Rich Hall (1994):

> "It's the journey, not the destination." Perhaps the single most important piece of advice ever imparted are in these simple words. But don't forget sometimes it's a weird destination, like when someone has a near-death experience and travels through that tunnel with the blinding white light at the end and there's an angel with her arms outstretched. I don't need to tell you, it's the person who bounces through that tunnel whooping and turning somersaults and singing, "Ahooooooooo! Werewolves of London . . ." who truly understands the meaning of, "It's the journey, not the destination" (p. 118).

That's self-management!

EXERCISE

By now, you should be able to take any behavior you want to change and consider it from the following perspectives:

What is the goal of my program?
What information do I wish to collect?

How will I process and evaluate this information?
How will I make decisions concerning this information?
What action can I take to manage my behavior?
What self-reaction procedures will I use to evaluate my performance?

REVIEW

Develop a self-management program for any problem behavior using the six components.

REFERENCES

ADER, R.; FELTON, D. L.; and COHEN, N., Eds. (1991). *Psychoneuroimmunology* (2nd edition). New York: Academic Press.

ALBERTI, R. E., and EMMONS, M. L. (1990). *Your Perfect Right: A Guide to Assertive Living* (6th edition). San Luis Obispo, CA: Impact Publishers.

AMERICAN PSYCHIATRIC ASSOCIATION (1994). *Diagnostic and Statistical Manual of Mental Disorders* (fourth edition). Washington, DC: American Psychiatric Association.

ANDERSON, N. H. (1968). Likableness ratings of 555 personality trait words. *Journal of Personality and Social Psychology* 9: 272–279.

ARGYLE, M., and HENDERSON, M. (1984). The rules of friendship. *Journal of Social and Personal Relationships* 1: 211–237.

ARKES, H. R. (1981). Impediments to accurate clinical judgment and possible ways to minimize their impact. *Journal of Consulting and Clinical Psychology* 49: 323–330.

BAKER, R. C., and KIRSCHENBAUM, D. S. (1993). Self-monitoring may be necessary for successful weight control. *Behavior Therapy* 24: 377–394.

BANDURA, A. (1986). *Social Foundations of Thought and Action: A Social Cognitive Theory*. Englewood Cliffs, NJ: Prentice-Hall.

BANDURA, A. (1977). Self-efficacy: Toward a unifying theory of behavioral change. *Psychological Review* 84: 191–215.

BARTECCHI, C. E.; MACKENZIE, T. D.; and SCHRIER, R. W. (1994). The human costs of tobacco use. *New England Journal of Medicine* 330: 907–912.

BAUMEISTER, R. F.; HEATHERTON, T. F.; and TICE, D. M. (1994). *Losing Control: How and Why People Fail at Self-Regulation*. San Diego: Academic Press.

BECK, A.; RUSH, J.; SHAW, B.; and EMERY, G. (1979). *Cognitive Therapy of Depression*. New York: Guilford Press.

BECKER, W. C. (1970). *Parents Are Teachers: A Child Management Program*. Champaign, IL: Research Press.

BING, S. (1992). *Crazy Bosses: Spotting Them, Serving Them, Surviving Them*. New York: Pocket Books.

BOOTZIN, R. R. (1972). Stimulus control treatment for insomnia. *Proceedings of the 80th Annual Convention of the American Psychological Association* 7: 395–396.

BRANSFORD, J. D., and STEIN, B. S. (1984). *The IDEAL Problem Solver*. New York: W.H. Freeman.

BRESLOW, L., and BRESLOW, N. (1993). Health practices and disability: Some evidence from Alameda County. *Preventive Medicine* 22: 86–95.

BRINKMAN, R., and KIRSCHNER, R. (1994). *Dealing with People You Can't Stand: How to Bring out the Best in People at Their Worst.* New York: McGraw-Hill.

BRODY, J. E. (1992). Personal health. *New York Times*, August 12, p. B6.

BROWNELL, K. D., and RODIN, J. (1994). The dieting maelstrom: Is it possible and advisable to lose weight? *American Psychologist* 49: 781–791.

BUSS, D. M., and BARNES, M. (1986). Preferences in human mate selection. *Journal of Personality and Social Psychology* 50: 59–70.

BYERS, T. (1995). Body weight and mortality. *New England Journal of Medicine* 333: 723–724.

CASH, T. F.; WINSTEAD, B. A.; and JANDA, L. H. (1986). The great American shape-up. *Psychology Today* 20: 30–37.

CENTERS FOR DISEASE CONTROL (1992). 1993 revised classification system for HIV infection and expanded surveillance case definition for AIDS among adolescents and adults. *Morbidity and Mortality Weekly Reports* 41, No. RR-17: 1–19.

COHEN, S., and DEOLIEVERA, P. (1987). *Getting to the Right Job.* New York: Workman Publishing.

COLDITZ, G. A. (1992). Economic costs of obesity. *American Journal of Clinical Nutrition* 55: 503S–507S.

COOPER, K. H. (1982). *The Aerobics Program for Total Well-Being: Exercise, Diet, Emotional Balance.* New York: Bantam.

CREER, T. L. (1979). *Asthma Therapy: A Behavioral Health Care System for Respiratory Disorders.* New York: Springer Publishing.

CREER, T. L. (1990). Strategies for judgment and decision-making in the management of childhood asthma. *Pediatric Asthma, Allergy and Immunology* 4: 253–264.

CREER, T. L. (1991). The application of behavioral procedures to childhood asthma: Current and future perspectives. *Patient Education and Counseling* 17: 9–22.

CREER, T. L.; BACKIAL, M.; BURNS, K. L.; LEUNG, P.; MARION, R. J.; MIKLICH, D. R.; MORRILL, C.; TAPLIN, P. S.; and ULLMAN, S. (1988). Living with asthma: Part 1. Genesis and development of a self-management program for childhood asthma. *Journal of Asthma* 25: 335–362.

CREER, T. L.; BACKIAL, M.; ULLMAN, S.; and LEUNG, P. (1986). *Living with Asthma: Part 1. Manual for Teaching Parents the Self-Management of Childhood Asthma.* Washington, DC: U.S. Government Printing Office.

CREER, T. L.; BACKIAL, M.; ULLMAN, S.; and LEUNG, P. (1986). *Living with Asthma. Part II. Manual for Teaching Children the Self-Management of Asthma* (NIH Publication 87-2364). Washington, DC: U.S. Printing Office.

CREER, T. L., and CHRISTIAN, W. P. (1976). *Chronically Ill and Handicapped Children: Their Management and Rehabilitation.* Champaign, IL: Research Press.

CREER, T. L.; and HOLROYD, K. A. (In press). Self-management. In A. Baum, C. McManus, S. Newman, J. Weinman, & R. West, Eds., *Cambridge Handbook of Psychology, Health, and Medicine.* New York: Cambridge University Press.

CREER, T. L.; IPACS, J.; and CREER, P. P. (1983). Changing behavioral and social variables at a residential treatment facility for childhood asthma. *Journal of Asthma* 20: 11–15.

CREER, T. L.; KOTSES, H.; and REYNOLDS, R. V. C. (1991). *A Handbook for Asthma Self-Management: A Group Leader's Guide to Living with Asthma for Adults.* Athens, OH: Ohio University Press.

CREER, T. L.; KOTSES, H.; and WIGAL, J. K. (1992). A second-generation model of asthma self-management. *Pediatric Asthma, Allergy, and Immunology* 6: 143–165.

CROOKS, R., and BAUR, K. (1990). *Our Sexuality* (2nd edition). Menlo Park, CA: Benjamin/Cummings.

DAVIS, M.; ESHELMAN, E. R.; and MCKAY, M. (1982). *The Relaxation and Stress Reduction Workbook* (2nd edition). Oakland, CA: New Harbinger Publications.

DEUTSCH, A. R. (1984). *How to Hold Your Job: Gaining Skills and Becoming Promotable in Difficult Times.* Englewood Cliffs, NJ: Prentice Hall.

DISHMAN, R. K. (1985). Medical psychology in exercise and sport. *Medical Clinics of North America* 69: 123–143.

DREIKURS, R., and STOLZ, V. (1964). *Children: the Challenge.* New York: Duell, Sloan, and Pearce.

D'ZURILLA, T. J., and GOLDFRIED, M. R. (1971). Problem solving and behavior modification. *Journal of Abnormal Psychology* 78: 107–126.

ELLIS, A. (1973). *Humanistic Psychotherapy.* New York: McGraw-Hill.

ELLIS, A.; SICHEL, J. L.; YEAGER, R. J.; DIMATTIA, D. J.; and DIGIUSEPPE, D. (1989). *Rational-Emotive Couples Therapy.* Elmsford, NY: Pergamon.

EVANS, R. I. (1989). *Albert Bandura: The Man and His Ideas—A Dialogue.* New York: Praeger.

FAIRSTEIN, L. A. (1993). *Sexual Violence: Our War against Rape.* New York: William Morrow and Company.

FORD, D. H. (1987). *Humans as Self-Constructing Living Systems: A Developmental Perspective on Behavior and Personality.* Hillsdale, NJ: Lawrence Erlbaum.

FRIES, J. F.; KOOP, C. E.; BEADLE, C. E.; COOPER, P. P.; ENGLAND, M. J.; GREAVES, R. F.; SOKOLOV, J. J.; WRIGHT, D.; and THE HEALTH PROJECT CONSORTIUM (1993). Reducing health care costs by reducing the need and demand for medical services. *New England Journal of Medicine* 329: 321–325.

GALLUP POLL (1991). *Factors Important to Employees.* New York: Gallup Corporation.

GAMBRILL, E. (1993). What critical thinking offers to clinicians and clients. *Behavior Therapist* 16: 141–147.

GEORGE, W. H., and MARLATT, G. A. (1986). Problem drinking. In K. A. Holroyd and T. L. Creer, Eds., *Self-Management of Chronic Disease: Handbook of Clinical Interventions and Research.* Orlando, FL: Academic Press.

GERGEN, P. J., and WEISS, K. B. (1990). Changing patterns of asthma hospitalization among children: 1979 to 1987. *Journal of the American Medical Association* 264: 1688–1692.

GOLEMAN, D. (1994). Peak performance: Why records fall. *New York Times*, October 11, pp. B5, B7.

GOLEMAN, D. (1992). Strategies for shaking off gloom are emerging from new studies. *New York Times*, December 29, p. B6.

GOLEMAN, D. (1995). *Emotional Intelligence.* New York: Bantam Books.

GORMALLY, J., and RARDIN, D. (1981). Weight loss maintenance and changes in diet and exercise for behavioral counseling and nutrition education. *Journal of Counseling Psychology* 28: 295–304.

GOTTMANN, J. (1993). *What Predicts Divorce: The Relationship Between Marital Processes and Marital Outcomes.* Hillsdale, NJ: Lawrence Erlbaum Associates.

GRIEF, J., and GOLDEN, B. A. (1994). *AIDS Care at Home.* New York: John Wiley and Sons.

GROSSMAN, K. S., and MCNAMARA J. R. (1991). *Overcoming Dating Anxiety: A Self-Help Approach.* Kansas City, MO: Westport Publishers.

HAFEN, B. Q.; THYGERSON, A. L.; and FRANDSEN, K. J. (1988). *Behavioral Guidelines for Health and Wellness.* Englewood, CO: Morton Publishing.

HALL, R. (1994). *Self-Help for the Bleak.* New York: Price Stern Sloan.

HAMILL, P. (1994). *A Drinking Life: A Memoir.* New York: Little, Brown, and Company.

HAYNES, R. B.; TAYLOR, D. W.; and SACKETT, D. L. (1979*). Compliance with Therapeutic Regimens.* Baltimore, MD: Johns Hopkins Press.

HOLROYD, K. A. and CREER, T. L. (1986). *Self-Management of Chronic Disease: Handbook of Clinical Interventions and Research.* Orlando, FL: Academic Press.

HYDE, J. S. (1990). *Understanding Human Sexuality* (4th edition). New York: McGraw-Hill.

INLANDER, C. B., and WEINER, E. (1992). *Take This Book to the Hospital with You: A Consumer's Guide to Surviving Your Hospital Stay.* New York: Random House.

IRIBARREN, C.; SHARP, D. S.; BURCHFIEL, C. M.; and PETROVITCH, H. (1995). Association of weight loss and weight fluctuation with mortality among Japanese American men. *New England Journal of Medicine* 333: 686–692.

JACOBSON, E. (1938). *Progressive Relaxation.* Chicago: University of Chicago Press.

KANFER, F. H. (1972). Self-monitoring: Methodological limitations and clinical applications. *Journal of Consulting and Clinical Psychology* 35: 148–152.

KANFER, F. H., and KAROLY, P. (1972). Self-control: A behavioristic excursion into the lion's den. *Behavior Therapy* 3: 392–416.

KANFER, F. H., and SCHEFFT, B. K. (1988). *Guiding the Process of Therapeutic Change.* Champaign, IL: Research Press.

KAROLY, P. (1993). Mechanisms of self-regulation: a systems view. *Annual Review of Psychology* 44: 23–52.

KAYE, H. (1992). *Decision Power: How to Make Successful Decisions with Confidence.* Englewood Cliffs NJ: Prentice Hall.

KAZDIN, A. E. (1984). Covert modeling. In P. C. Kendall, Ed., *Advances in Cognitive Behavioral Research and Therapy,* Volume 3. New York: Academic Press.

KIECOLT-GLASER, J. K.; MALARKEY, W. B.; CHEE, M.; NEWTON, T.; CACIOPPO, J. T.; MAO, H.; and GLASER, R. (1993). Negative behavior during marital conflict is associated with immunological down-regulation. *Psychosomatic Medicine* 55: 245–409.

KIMBLE, G. A. (1994). A new formula for behaviorism. *Psychological Review* 101: 254–258.

KIRKENDALL, L. A., and ADAMS, W. J. (1971). *A Reading and Study Guide for Students in Marriage and Family Relations.* Dubuque, IA: William C. Brown.

KIRSCHENBAUM, D. S. (1994). *Weight Loss through Persistence: Making Science Work for You.* Oakland, CA: New Harbinger Publications.

KIRSCHENBAUM, D. S. (1987). Self-regulatory failure: A review with clinical implications. *Clinical Psychology Review* 7: 77–104.

KIRSCHENBAUM, D. S., and TOMARKEN, A. J. (1982). On facing the generalization problem: The study of self-regulatory failure. In P. C. Kendall, Ed., *Advances in*

Cognitive Behavioral Research and Therapy, Volume 1. New York: Academic Press.

KLEINGINNA, P. R., and KLEINGINNA, A. M. (1981). A categorized list of emotional definitions with a suggestion for a consensual definition. *Motivation and Emotion* 5: 263–291.

KOBASA, S. C. (1979). Stressful life events, personality, and health: An inquiry into hardiness. *Journal of Personality and Social Psychology* 37: 1–11.

KOTSES, H.; BERNSTEIN, I. L.; BERNSTEIN, D. I.; REYNOLDS, R. V. C.; KORBEE, L.; WIGAL, J. K.; GANSON, E.; STOUT, C.; and CREER, T. L. (1995). A self-management program for adult asthma. Part I. Development and evaluation. *Journal of Allergy and Clinical Immunology* 95: 529–540.

KUBLER-ROSS, E. (1969). *On Death and Dying*. New York: Macmillan.

KUCZMARSKI, R. J.; FLEGAL, K. M.; CAMPBELL, S. M.; and JOHNSON, C. L. (1994). Increasing prevalence of overweight among U.S. adults. The National Health and Nutrition Examination Surveys, 1960 to 1991. *Journal of the American Medical Association* 272: 205–211.

LAKEIN, A. (1973). *How to Get Control of Your Time and Your Life*. New York: Signet.

LAZARUS, R. S. (1991). *Emotion and Adaptation*. New York: Oxford University Press.

MAHONEY, M. J. (1979). *Self-Change*. New York: Norton.

MANSON, J. E.; WILLETT, W. C.; STAMPFER, M. J.; COLDITZ, G. A.; HUNTER, D. J.; HANKINSON, S. E.; HENNEKENS, C. H.; and SPEIZER, F. E. (1995). Body weight and mortality among women. *New England Journal of Medicine* 333: 677–685.

MARLATT, G. A. (1982). Relapse prevention: A self-control program for the treatment of addictive behaviors. In R. B. Stuart, Ed., *Adherence, Compliance and Generalization in Behavioral Medicine*. New York: Brunner/Mazel.

MARLATT, G. A., and GORDON, J. R. (1980). Determinants of relapse: Implications for the maintenance of behavior change. In P. O. Davidson and S. M. Davidson, Eds., *Behavioral Medicine: Changing Health Lifestyles*, New York: Bruner/Mazel.

MARTIN G. L., and OSBORNE, J. G. (1989). *Psychology, Adjustment and Everyday Living*. Englewood Cliffs, NJ: Prentice Hall.

MATHEWS, V. D., and MIHANOVICH, C. S. (1963). New orientations on marital maladjustment. *Marriage and Family Living* 25: 300–304.

MCGINNIS, J. M., and FOEGE, W. H. (1993). Actual causes of death in the United States. *Journal of the American Medical Association* 270: 2207–2212.

MCGOLDRICK, M., and CARTER, E. A. (1982). The family life cycle. In F. Walsh, Ed., *Normal Family Processes*. New York: Guilford Press.

MCKAY, M.; DAVIS, M.; and FANNING, P. (1981). *Thoughts and Feelings: The Art of Cognitive Stress Intervention*. Oakland, CA: New Harbinger.

MEICHENBAUM, D. (1985). *Stress Inoculation Training*. New York: Pergamon.

MELTZER, E. O. (1994). Prevalence, economic, and medical impact of tobacco smoking. *Annals of Allergy* 73: 381–388.

MILLENSON, J. R. (1967). *Principles of Behavioral Analysis*. New York: McMillan.

MISCHEL, W. (1993). *Introduction to Personality* (5th edition). Fort Worth, TX: Holt, Rinehart and Winston.

MISCHEL, W. (1986). *Introduction to Personality: A New Look* (4th edition). New York: Holt, Rinehart and Winston.

MISCHEL, W.; SHODA, Y.; and PEAKE, P. K. (1988). The nature of adolescent competencies predicted by preschool delay of gratification. *Journal of Personality and Social Psychology* 54: 587–694.

MOFFATT, B.; SPIEGEL, J.; PARRISH, S.; and HELQUIST, M. (1987). *AIDS: A Self-Care Manual*. AIDS Project Los Angeles. Los Angeles: AIDS Project.

NATIONAL INSTITUTE OF AGING (1995). *Depression and Aging*. Washington DC: National Institute of Aging.

NATIONAL TASK FORCE ON THE PREVENTION AND TREATMENT OF OBESITY (1994). Weight cycling. *Journal of the American Medical Association* 272: 1196–1202.

NEZU, A. M., and NEZU, C. M., EDS. (1989). *Clinical Decision Making in Behavior Therapy*. Champaign, IL: Research Press.

NIH TECHNOLOGY ASSESSMENT CONFERENCE REPORT (1993). Methods for voluntary weight loss and control. *Annals of Internal Medicine* 119: 764–770.

NORTHWESTERN NATIONAL LIFE INSURANCE COMPANY (1991). *Stress in the Workplace*. New York.

NOSSITER, A. (1995). Asthma common and on rise in the crowded South Bronx. *New York Times*, September 5, pp. A1, A14.

PARLEE, M. B., and the editors of *Psychology Today* (1979). The friendship bond: PT's survey report on friendship in America. *Psychology Today* 13: 43–54, 113.

PATTERSON, G. R. (1977). *Families: Applications of Social Learning to Family Life*. Champaign, IL: Research Press.

PAVLOV, I. P. (1927). *Conditioned Reflexes: An Investigation of the Physiological Activity of the Cerebral Cortex*. London: Oxford University Press.

PEAR, R. (1993). $1 trillion in health costs is predicted. *New York Times*, December 29, A12.

PETERS, T. J., and WATERMAN, R. H., JR. (1982). *In Search of Excellence*. New York: Harper and Row.

PETROCELLI, W., and REPA, B. K. (1992). *Sexual Harassment on the Job*. Berkeley, CA: Nolo Press.

PI-SUNYER, F. X. (1994). The fattening of America. *Journal of the American Medical Association* 272: 238–239.

PI-SUNYER, F. X. (1993). Medical hazards of obesity. *Annals of Internal Medicine* 119: 655–660.

POPE, A. M.; PATTERSON, R.; and BURGE, H., EDS. (1993). *Indoor Allergens: Assessing and Controlling Adverse Health Effects*. Washington, DC: National Academy Press.

PREMACK, D. (1959). Toward empirical behavioral laws: Positive reinforcement. *Psychological Review* 66: 219–233.

PROCHASKA, J. O.; NORCROSS, J. C.; and DiCLEMENTE, C. C. (1994). *Changing for Good*. New York: William Morrow and Company.

REED, C. E. (1986). New therapeutic approaches to asthma. *Journal of Allergy and Clinical Immunology* 77: 537–543.

RENWICK, P. A., and LAWLER, E. E. (1978). What you really want from your job. *Psychology Today* 11: 53–65.

ROBINSON, F. P. (1961). *Effective Studying*. New York: Harper and Row.

ROIPHE, K. (1993). *The Morning After: Sex, Fear, and Feminism on Campus*. Boston: Little, Brown and Company.

ROTTER, J. B. (1966). Generalized expectancies for internal versus external control of reinforcement. *Psychological Monographs* 80, No. 609.

RUDESTAM, K. E. (1980). *Methods of Self-Change. An ABC Primer.* Monterey, CA: Brooks/Cole.

SCHACTER, S. (1982). Recidivism and self-cure of smoking and obesity. *American Psychologist* 37: 436–444.

SELIGMAN, M. E. P. (1994). *What You Can Change and What You Can't.* New York: Knopf.

SELYE, H. (1976). *The Stress of Life* (2nd edition). New York: McGraw-Hill.

SHODA, Y.; MISCHEL, W.; and PEAKE, P. K. (1990). Predicting adolescent cognitive and self-regulatory competencies from the preschool delay of gratification: Identifying diagnostic conditions. *Developmental Psychology* 26: 978–986.

SIMON, H. B. (1994). Patient-directed, nonprescription approaches to cardiovascular disease. *Archives of Internal Medicine* 154: 2283–2296.

SJOBERG, L., and PERSSON, L. (1979). A study of attempts by obese patients to regulate eating. *Addictive Behaviors* 4: 349–359.

SJOSTROM, L. V. (1992). Mortality of severely obese subjects. *American Journal of Clinical Nutrition* 55: 516S–523S.

SKINNER, B. F. (1953). *Science and Human Behavior.* New York: Macmillan Company.

SOCKRIDER, M. M., and COULTAS, D. B. (1994). Environmental tobacco smoke: A real and present danger. *Journal of Respiratory Diseases* 15: 715–730.

SONTAG, S. (1978). *Illness as Metaphor.* New York: Farrar, Straus and Giroux.

STADDON, J. (1995). On responsibility and punishment. *Atlantic* 275: (February): 88–94.

STERN, L. (1993). How to find a job: New ways of winning in today's tough market. *Modern Maturity* 36: 24–34.

STOPPARD, M. (1991). *The Magic of Sex.* New York: Dorling Kindersly.

STUNKARD, A. J., and WADDEN, T. A. (1992). Psychological aspects of severe severity. *American Journal of Clinical Nutrition* 55: 524S–532S.

SUINN, R. M. (1986). *Seven Steps to Peak Performance.* Lewiston, NY: Hans Huber Publishers.

SULZER-AZAROFF, B., and MAYER, G. R. (1991). *Behavior Analysis for Lasting Change.* Fort Worth, TX: Holt, Rinehart and Winston.

TAITAL, M. S.; KOTSES, H.; BERNSTEIN, I. L.; BERNSTEIN, D. I.; and CREER, T. L. (1995). A self-management program for adult asthma: Part 2. Cost-benefit analysis. *Journal of Allergy and Clinical Immunology* 95: 672–676.

TANNEN, D. (1990). *You Just Don't Understand: Women and Men in Conversation.* New York: Ballantine.

THOMPSON, J. K. (1986). Larger than life. *Psychology Today* 20: 39–44.

TOWNSEND, R. (1984). *Further Up the Organization.* New York: Harper and Row.

VERDERBER, K. S., and VERDERBER, R. F. (1989). *Inter-act: Using Interpersonal Communication Skills* (2nd edition). Belmont, CA: Wadsworth.

WATSON, D. L., and THARP, R. G. (1989). *Self-Directed Behavior. Self-Modification for Personal Adjustment.* Pacific Grove, CA: Brooks/Cole.

WATSON, D. L., and THARP, R. G. (1993). *Self-Directed Behavior: Self-Modification for Personal Adjustment*, (6th edition). Pacific Grove, CA: Brooks/Cole Publishing.

WASSMER, A. (1978). *Making Contact.* New York: Dial.

WECHSLER, H.; DAVENPORT, A.; DOWDALL, G.; MOEYKENS, B.; and CASTILLO, S. (1994). Health and behavioral consequences of binge drinking in college. *Journal of the American Medical Association* 272: 1672–1677.

WEISS, K. B.; GERGEN, P. J.; and HODGSON, T. A. (1992). An economic evaluation of asthma in the United States. *New England Journal of Medicine* 326: 862–866.

WEITEN, W.; LLOYD, M. A.; and LASHLEY, R. L. (1991). *Psychology Applied to Modern Life: Adjustment in the 90s* (3rd edition). Pacific Grove, CA: Brooks/Cole Publishing.

WHEELER, D. D., and JANIS, I. L. (1980). *A Practical Guide for Making Decisions.* New York: Free Press.

WILLIAMS, R. L., and LONG, J. D. (1991). *Manage Your Life* (4th edition). Boston: Houghton Mifflin.

WING, R. R.; JEFFREY, R. W.; and HELLERSTEDT, W. L. (1995). A prospective study of effects of weight cycling on cardiovascular risk factors. *Archives of Internal Medicine* 155: 1416–1422.

WOLPE, J. (1958). *Psychotherapy by Reciprocal Inhibition.* Stanford, CA: Stanford University Press.

WORLD HEALTH ORGANIZATION AND AMERICAN CANCER SOCIETY. *Mortality from Smoking in Developed Countries: 1950–2000.* London: Imperial Cancer Research Fund.

ZHANG, Y.; PROENCIA, R.; MAFFEI, M.; BARONE, M.; LEOPOLD, L.; and FRIEDMAN, J. M. (1994). Positional cloning of the mouse obese gene and its human homologue. *Nature* 372: 425–432.

ZIMBARDO, P. G. (1977). *Shyness.* Reading, MA: Addison-Wesley Publishing.

ZIMMERMAN, B. J. (1986). Becoming a self-regulated learner: Which are the key subprocesses. *Contemporary Educational Psychology* 11: 307–313.

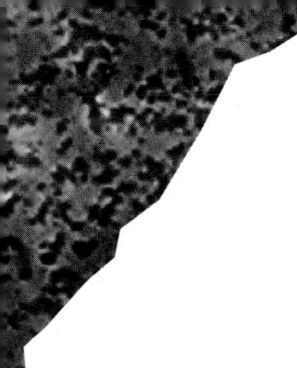

Index

A-B quasi-experimental design, 38–39, 40
Action, 19–26
  antecedents, 19–23
  behavior, 23–24
  consequences, 26
  contingencies, 19
  self-instruction, 24–25
Adams, W. J., 305, 306
Ader, R., 103
Adjustment and self-management, 1–8
  examples of self-management projects, 5
  importance of self-management, 3–5
  limitations of self-management, 5–8
Aging and death, 324–331
  death and dying, 330–331
  healthy aging, 328–330
  physical and psychological changes, 324–238
AIDS, 202–205
Alberti, R. E., 200, 227, 230, 231, 243
Alcohol abuse, 189–197
  definitions of, 189–190
  protection against, 190–191
  self-management of alcohol abuse, 192–195
  self-management projects, 195–196
Alcoholics Anonymous (AA), 192
American Psychiatric Association, 173
Anderson, N. H., 240, 241
Anorexia nervosa, 173
Antecedents, 19–23
  arrange new, 22–23
  identify, 20–21
  modify, 21–22
Argyle, M., 238
Arkes, H. R., 352, 353
Assessment and behavior change, 36–51
  characteristics of successful plans, 47–49
  experimental designs, 37–45
  measurement, 36–37
  observing and recording behavior, 37
  problems, 45–47
Autonomic nervous system, functions of parasympathetic divisions, table, 89

Backial, M., 127, 317, 319
Baker, R. C., 339
Baldwin, James, 316
Bandura, A., 27, 61, 332, 333, 334, 339, 348, 349
Barnes, M., 305
Bartecchi, C. E., 178
Baumeister, R. F., 239, 339, 341
Baur, K., 200
Beck, A., 83
  et al., 243
Becker, W. C., 321
Behavioral change procedures, 52–59
Behavioral deficits or excesses changed, table, 5
  checklist, 29
Behavioral techniques, 52–59
  classical conditioning, 58–59
  operant conditioning, 53–58
Being right, 77
Big Five personality characteristics, table, 328
Bing, S., 291, 295, 298–302
Blaming, 77
Body language, table, 274
Bootzin, R. R., 21
Bransford, J. D., 29, 30, 31
Breslow, L., 136, 137
Breslow, N., 136, 137
Brinkman, R., 281
Brody, J. E., 202
Brownell, K. D., 172, 358
Bulimia, 173
Burchfiel, C. M., 358
Burnout, 290
Buss, D. M., 305
Byers, T., 150, 170, 358

Campbell, S. M., 357
Cannon-Bard theory, 91
Career, planning, 257–269
  important features in job, 264–265
  myths of job seeking, 265–266
  obtaining job leads, 263–264
  preparing for career, 257–263
  self-management procedures, 266–268
  self-management projects, 269
Carter, E. A., 311
Cash, T. F., 170
Catastrophizing, 77
Centers for Disease Control, 203
Chandler, Raymond, 75
Changing criterion design, 41–45
Changing inappropriate emotional responses, 93–98
Changing jobs, 287–294
  planning job change, 290–293
  reasons for, 288–290
  self-management procedures, 293–294

Changing maladaptive thinking, 79–86
  cognitive restructuring, 83–84
  rational-emotive restructuring, 84–86
  thought control, 80–82
  thought stopping, 80
Characteristics of maladaptive thinking, 76–78
  faulty reasoning, 76–78
  illogical ideas, 78
Chekhov, Anton, 18
Children, raising, 316–323
  effective child-rearing practices, 317–318
  helpful hints and possible pitfalls, 319–321
  self-management and child management project, 321–322
  steps in instituting behavioral change, 319
Chlamydia, 201
Christian, W. P., 26
Classical conditioning techniques, 58–59
  systematic desensitization, 58–59
  systematic self-desensitization, 59
Cognitive restructuring, 83–84
Cohen, N., 103
Cohen, S., 260
Colditz, G. A., 357
Components of self-management, 9–17
  additional, 18–27
  context, 10–12
  list, 12–16
Confucius, 348
Context, 10–12
  establishing operations, 11
  establishing stimulus, 12
  setting events, 11
Control fallacies, 77
Cooper, K. H., 151
Coultas, D. B., 179
Creer, T. L., 15, 23, 26, 30, 66, 127, 150, 317, 319, 348, 349, 352
Crooks, R., 200

Dating, 249–256
  improving communication with your dates, 251–253
  self-management procedures, 253–254
  self-management projects, 254–256
Davis, M., 76, 232
Death and dying, 330–331

371

Decision making, 18–19, 28–35
  models of, 28–34
  strategies, 352–354
Delay of gratification, 61
DeOliveira, P., 260
Deutsch, A. R., 278
DiClemente, C. C., 181, 192, 195
Diet and weight control, 161–177
  nutrition basics, 161–164
  principles of weight control, 169–173
  self-management of nutritional needs, 165–168
  self-management procedures for establishing a proper diet, 168–169
  self-management weight loss programs, 174–176
Difficult coworkers, dealing with, 281–283
DiGiuseppe, D., 76
DiMattia, D. J., 76
Directing others, 295–303
  characteristics of successful companies, 302–303
  managing people, 296–298
  supervisors, 298–302
Dishman, R. K., 145
Diseases, sexually transmitted, 201–205
  AIDS, 202–205
  chlamydia, 201
  genital warts, 202
  gonorrhea, 201–202
  herpes, 202
  syphilis, 202
Divorce, 311–312
Dreikurs, R., 321
Durrenmatt, Fredrich, 257
D'Zurilla, T. J., 29

Effective studying, 122–133
  characteristics of successful students, 122–123
  developing effective study habits, 124–127
  strategies for studying, 129–133
  test taking, 127–129
Eliot, George, 60
Eliot, T. S., 337
Ellis, A., 76, 78, 84, 243
Emery, G., 83
Emmons, M. L., 200, 227, 230, 231, 243
Emotional reactions, 87–100
  changing inappropriate responses, 93–98
  feelings, 87–88
  four-stage theory, 91–93
  physiological basis, 88–90
  specific self-management strategies, 98–99
  theories of, 90–91
Emotional reasoning, 77
Emotions, theories of, 90–91
  Cannon-Bard, 91
  James-Lange, 90–91
  Schachter-Singer, 91
Employment, obtaining, 270–277
  accepting or rejecting offer, 275–276
  building confidence, 271–272
  dealing with rejection, 275
  interviewing, 272–275
  job search tips, 270–271

self-management procedures, 276–277
Eschelman, E. R., 232
Evans, R. I., 333
Exercise, 145–160
  general principles of, 152–154
  improved health, 145–149
  longer life span, 150
  lower medical bills, 149–150
  regimens, 155–158
  self-management procedures to enhance, 154–155
  types of, 150–152
Experimental designs, 37–45
  A-B quasi-experimental, 38–39, 40
  changing criterion, 41–45
  multiple baseline, 39–41, 42

Fallacy of change, 77
Fallacy of fairness, 76
Fanning, P., 76
Feelings, 87–88
Felton, D. L., 103
Flegal, K. M., 357
Folge, W. H., 137
Ford, D. H., 5, 6, 7, 14
Four-stage theory, 91–93
Frandsen, K. J., 134, 147, 152, 161, 205
Friends, 237–248
  developing friendships, 243–244
  maintaining, 244
  qualities of a good friendship, 239–242
  qualities of positive relationships, 238–239
  self-management approach, 242–243
  self-management projects, 243–247
Fries, J. F. et al., 139, 150

Gallup Poll, 264
Gambrill, E., 352
Generalization, 57–58
Genital warts, 202
George, W. H., 348
Global labeling, 77
Goal selection, 12–14
  analyze contingencies of behavior, 13
  attend to specific information, 13–14
  behavior change, 12–13
  positive consequences, 14
Golden, B. A., 202, 203
Goldfried, M. R., 29
Goleman, D., 304, 327
Gonorrhea, 201–202
Gordon, J. R., 340, 341, 344, 350, 351
Gottman, J., 304
Grief, J., 202, 203
Grossman, K. S., 249, 250

Hafen, B. Q. et al., 108, 134, 147, 152, 161, 163, 205
Hall, R., 361
Hamill, R., 191
Health and wellness, 134–144
  characteristics of healthy people, 135–136
  characteristics of unhealthy people, 136–137

characteristics of wellness, 138–139
  improving health, 139–141
  self-management projects, 141–144
Health benefits from exercise
  improved health, 145–149
  longer life span, 150
  lower medical bills, 149–150
Health, improving, 138–141
Healthy people, characteristics of, 135–136
Heatherton, T. F., 239, 339
Heaven's reward fallacy, 77
Hellerstedt, W. L., 173, 358
Helquist, M., 205
Henderson, M., 238
Herpes, 202
Hoeg, Peter, 198
Holroyd, K. A., 15, 150
Huxley, Aldous, 1
Hyde, J. S., 200

IDEAL, 29, 30
Imagery, 68
Individual self-management, 356–358
Information collection, 14–15
  self-observation, 14–15
  self-recording, 15
Information processing and evaluation, 15–16
Inlander, C. B., 139
Interviewing, 272–275
Iribarren, C., 358

Jacobson, E., 65
James, William, 36
James-Lange theory, 90–91
Janda, L. H., 170
Janis, I. L., 29, 31, 32, 33
Jeffrey, R. W., 173, 358
Job features, important, tables, 264, 265
Job search tips, 270–271
Job-seeking myths, 265–266
Johnson, C. L., 357
Johnson, Samuel, 304

Kanfer, F., 3, 4, 12, 14, 338, 339
Karoly, P., 1, 14, 338
Kaye, H., 120
Kazdin, A. E., 70
Kiecolt-Glaser, J. K. et al., 103
Kimble, G. A., 361
Kirkendall, C. A., 305, 306
Kirschenbaum, D. S., 15, 173, 337, 338, 339, 341, 342, 343, 344, 345, 346, 350, 360
Kirschner, R., 281
Kleiginna, A. M., 87
Kleiginna, P. R., 87
Kobasa, S. C., 139
Kotses, H., 23, 30, 66, 348, 350
Kubler-Ross, E., 330
Kuczmarski, R. J. et al., 357, 360
Kundera, Milan, 28

LaBruyere, 13
LADDER, 232–233, 236
Lakein, A., 116, 117
Lamb, Charles, 178
Lashley, R. L., 125, 128, 304
Lawler, E. E., 264
Lazarus, R. S., 91–93
Leung, P., 127, 317, 319

Limitations of self-management, 5–8
  environmental boundaries, 6
  individual differences, 6
  organismic boundaries, 5–6
  performance variability, 7
  selective action, 6
  unpredictability of behavior, 7–8
Locus of control, 60
Long, J. D., 48, 49, 182, 193, 273, 275, 279, 280, 281, 284, 285

MacKenzie, T. D., 178
Maclean, Norman, 324
Magnification, 76
Mahoney, M. J., 28, 29
Maladaptive amd dysfunctional thoughts, 75–86
  changing, 79–86
  characteristics of, 76–78
Manson, J. E. et al., 150, 358
Marcus Aurelius, 101, 287
Marlatt, G. A., 340, 341, 344, 348, 350, 351
Marriage, 304–315
  divorce, 311–312
  expectations of, 306–308
  factors in a good marriage, 308–309
  factors in marital discord, 309–311
  myths about love, 304–305
  readiness for, 305–306
  selecting a mate, 305
  self-management procedures, 312–313
  self-management projects, 313–314
Martial, 134
Martin, G. L., 59, 88, 113, 152, 170, 182, 190, 232, 260, 283, 284
Mathews, V. D., 310, 311
Mayer, G. R., 10, 11, 12, 19, 23, 26, 37, 45, 55, 56
McGinnis, J. M., 137
McGoldrick, M., 311
McKay, M., 76, 232
McNamara, J. R., 249, 250
Meditation, 65–68
Meichenbaum, D., 71
Meltzer, E. O., 178, 180
Mencken, H. L., 356
Mihanovich, C. S., 310, 311
Millinson, J. R., 87
Mind reading, 76–77
Minerals, sources and functions of, table, 164
Mischel, W., 2–3, 61
Modeling, 70
  imagined, 70
Models of decision making and problem solving, 28–34
  application of solutions, 31–32
  decision making, 32–33
  exploration of additional solutions, 34
  generation of solutions, 31–32
  problem definition, 30–31
  problem solving, 28–34
  table, 30
  verification of success or failure, 34
Moffatt, B., 205
Multiple baseline design, 39–41, 42

Myths about love, 304–305

National Institute of Aging, 329
National Task Force on the Prevention and Treatment of Obesity, 173, 358
Negative reinforcement, 56–58
  avoidance learning, 56
  escape learning, 56
Negotiation, rules for, table, 320
Nezu, A. M., 30, 33
Nezu, C. M., 30, 33
NIH Technology and Assessment Conference Panel, 357, 358
Nin, Anais, 237
Norcross, J. C., 181, 192, 195
Northwestern National Life Insurance Company, 289
Nutrition basics, 161–164

Operant conditioning, 53–58
  generalization, 57–58
  negative reinforcement, 56–57
  positive reinforcement, 54–56
  punishment, 57
Osborne, J. G., 59, 88, 113, 152, 170, 182, 190, 232, 260, 283, 284
Overgeneralization, 76

Parlee, M. B., 238
Parrish, S., 205
Patterson, G. R., 321
Pavlov, I., 58
Peake, P. K., 61
Pear, R., 139
Personalization, 77
Persson, L., 344
Peters, T. J. et al., 302
Petrocelli, W., 220, 222, 223
Petrovich, H., 358
Physical changes that occur with age, table, 326
Physiological basis of emotions, 88–90
Pi-Sunyer, F. X., 357, 358
Polarized thinking, 76
Positive reinforcement, 54–56
  chaining, 55
  conditioned reinforcers, 56
  extinction, 54–55
  generalized reinforcers, 56
  Premack Principle, 55–56
  shaping, 55
  stimulus control, 55
Premack, D., 55, 56
Problem solving, models of, 28–34
  table, 30
Prochaska, J. O., 181, 192, 195
Proper diet, self-management procedures for establishing, 168–169
Punishment, 57
  response cost, 57
  time-out, 57

Rational-emotive restructuring, 84–86
Rehearsal, 68–70
  fantasy, 70
  imagined plus relaxation, 69–70
  imagined plus self-statements, 70
Relapse prevention and management, 348–355

  decision-making strategies, 352–354
  strategies, 348–352
Relapse process, 344–345
Relaxation, 65
Renwick, P. A., 264
Repa, B. K., 220, 222, 223
Resume preparation, 259–263
Reynolds, R. V. C., 30, 66
Robinson, F. P., 125
Rodin, J., 172, 358
Roiphe, K., 210, 211, 214
Rotter, J. B., 60, 105
Rudestam, K. E., 65, 70, 76
Rush, J., 83

Schachter, S., 28
Schachter-Singer theory, 91
Schefft, B., 3, 4, 12
Schrier, R. W., 178
SCIENCE, 28, 29
Scientific inquiry, seven stages, 29
Seldon, John, 189
Selecting a problem: decision making and problem solving, 28–35
  models, 28–54
Seligman, M. E. P., 192, 358
Self-efficacy, 61–74, 332–336
  developing, 334–335
  influence of, 332–334
  social cognitive theory, 61–62
  social learning techniques, 62–74
Self-instruction, 24–25
Self-management
  additional components, 18–27
  of alcohol use, 192–195
  components of, 9–17
  examples of projects, 5
  importance of, 3–5
  limitations of, 5–8
  model, 10
  of nutritional needs, 165–168
  procedures for avoiding rape, 217
  procedures for controlling shyness and increasing assertiveness, 232–233
  projects, 141–144, 195–196, 205–208, 217–218, 225, 234–236, 255–256, 269
  of sexual harassment, 224–225
  smoking cessation projects, 184–188
  strategies, 98–99
  of tobacco use, 183–184
  weight loss programs, 174–176
Self-management failure, elements of, 341–346
  attention in self-management, 345–346
  relapse process, 344–345
  successful vs. unsuccessful self-management, 343–344
Self-management failure, three models of, 338–341
  closed loop, 338–339
  cognitive-behavioral relapse, 340–341
  self-efficacy, 339–340
Self-management redux, 356–362
  components of self-management, 359–361
  individual self-management, 356–358

Self-management redux (cont.)
  parting comment, 361
Self-management skills, table, 2
Self-monitoring, 63–65
  reperception of situation, 64
  self-statements, 63–64
  self-statements plus distraction, 64
  thought stopping, 64
  thought substitution, 64–65
Self-reaction, 26–27
Self-statements, 24–25, 63–64
  effective use of, table, 24
  and incompatible behavior, 72–74
  plus distraction, 64
Seneca, 9
Sexual behavior, 198–209
  overcoming sexual problems, 198–201
  safe-sex practices, 205, 207
  self-management project, 205–208
  sexually transmitted diseases, 201–205
Sexual harassment, 220–226
  self-management of, 224–225
  self-management project, 225
  ways to end, 223–224
Sexual violence, 210–219
  self-management procedures for avoiding rape, 217
  self-management projects, 217–218
  strategies for men, 216
  strategies for women, 211–216
Selye, H., 102, 103
Sharp, D. S., 358
Shaw, B., 83
Shoda, V., 61
Shoulds, 77
Shyness and assertiveness, 227–236
  becoming assertive, 230–232
  reasons for lack of assertiveness, 228
  self-management and assertiveness, 232–233
  self-management procedures for controlling shyness and increasing assertiveness, 233–234
  self-management projects, 234–236
  shyness, 228–230
Sichel, J. L., 76
Simon, H. B., 147, 179
Sjoberg, L., 344
Sjostrom, L. V., 357
Skinner, B. F., 52, 53
Social cognitive theory, 61–62
  language ability, 61
  observational learning, 61
  purposeful behavior, 61
  self-analysis, 62
Social learning and cognitive procedures, 60–74
  imagery, 68
  meditation, 65–68
  modeling, 70–71
  rehearsal, 68–70

relaxation, 65
self-monitoring, 63–65
self-statements and incompatible behavior, 72–72
social cognitive theory, 61–62
stress inoculation, 71–72
Social learning techniques, 62–74
Sockrider, M. M., 179
SOFTEN, 242–243
Sontag, S., 139
Spiegel, J., 205
SQ3R method, 125
Staddon, J., 57
Stanley, Edward, 145
Stein, B. S., 29, 30, 31
Stern, L., 292
Stevenson, Robert Louis, 249
Stolz, V., 321
Stoppard, M., 198, 199, 200
Stress, conception of, 102–103
  alarm, 102–103
  exhaustion, 103
  resistance, 103
Stress, coping with, 101–112
  conception of stress, 102–103
  general strategies, 103–109
  specific strategies, 109–111
Stress, general strategies for coping, 103–109
  accept yourself, 108–109
  acknowledge that you will experience, 104
  appraise situation, 104–105
  call for personal health, 108
  consider possible strategies, 106–107
  develop friendships, 108
  help others, 108
  manage time and resources, 107
Stress inoculation, 71–72
Study habits, developing effective, 124–127
  active listening, 125–126
  improving memory, 126–127
  schedule, 124–125
  setting, 124
Studying, strategies for, 129–133
Stunkard, A. J., 358
Successful behavior modification plans, 47–49
  Model 1, 48
  Model 2, 48–49
  Model 3, 49
Successful students, characteristics of, 122–123
Suinn, R. M., 80, 82, 85
Sulzer-Azaroff, B., 10, 11, 12, 19, 23, 26, 37, 45, 55, 56
Syphilis, 202

Tannen, D., 251
Test-taking, 127–129
Tharp, R. G., 20, 22, 23, 29–30, 68, 69, 70
Thompson, J. K., 170
Thought control, 80–82
Thought stopping, 64, 80
Thygerson, A. L., 134, 147, 152, 161, 205
Tice, D. M., 239, 339, 341

Time management, 113–121
  self-management and, 117–121
  tips, 114–116
Tobacco cessation program, components of, 180–183
Tobacco use, 178–188
  components of tobacco cessation program, 180–183
  self-management of, 183–184
  self-management smoking cessation projects, 184–188
Tomarken, A. J., 337, 338, 341, 342, 346
Townsend, R., 34, 295, 296, 297

Ullman, S., 127, 317, 319
Unhealthy people, characteristics of, 136–137

Verderber, K. S., 283
Verderber, R. F., 283
Virgil, 332
Vitamins, sources and functions of, table, 163
Voltaire, 270

Wadden, T. A., 358
Wassmer, A., 242
Waterman, R. H. Jr., 302
Watson, D. L., 20, 22, 23, 29–30, 68, 69, 70
Wechsler, H. et al., 190, 214
Weight control, principles of, 169–173
Weiner, E., 139
Weitan, W., 125, 128, 304
Wellness, characteristics of, 138–139
Wheeler, D. D., 29, 31, 32, 33
Whitman, Walt, 227
Why self-management fails, 337–347
  avoiding failure, 346
  elements of, 341–346
  three models of failure, 338–341
Wigal, J. K., 23, 348, 350
Williams, R. L., 48, 49, 182, 193, 273, 275, 279, 280, 281, 284, 285
Wing, R. R., 173, 358
Winstead, B. A., 170
Wolpe, J., 58, 80
Workplace, the, 278–286
  dealing with difficult coworkers, 281–283
  self-management and job performance, 279–281
  self-management procedures, 285–285
  self-management skills, 283–285
  starting a new job, 278–279

Yeager, R. J., 76
Yo-yo dieting, 173

Zhang, Y. et al., 172
Zimbardo, P. G., 228, 230, 243
Zimmerman, B. J., 122